T0260708

ADVANCED COMPUTER
ARITHMETIC DESIGN

ADVANCED COMPUTER ARITHMETIC DESIGN

Michael J. Flynn

Stuart F. Oberman

Computer Architecture and Arithmetic Group
Stanford University

A WILEY-INTERSCIENCE PUBLICATION

JOHN WILEY & SONS, INC.

New York / Chichester / Weinheim / Brisbane / Singapore / Toronto

Library of Congress Cataloging in Publication Data:

Flynn, M. J. (Michael J.), 1934-
Advanced computer arithmetic design / Michael J. Flynn, Stuart F. Oberman.
p. cm.
ISBN 978-0-471-41209-0
1. Computer arithmetic and logic units. I. Oberman, Stuart F., 1971-
II. Title.
TK7895.A65 F59 2001
004'.01'513--dc21   2001017653

CONTENTS

PREFACE

Computer arithmetic is a fundamental discipline that drives many modern digital technologies. High performance VLSI implementations of 3D graphics, encryption, streaming digital audio and video, and signal processing all require fast and efficient computer arithmetic algorithms. The demand for these fast implementations has motivated us to explore innovative techniques and algorithms.

This book brings together a slice of the current "state of the art" in the design of computer arithmetic units. The work described is the result of ten years of effort—largely here at Stanford—under the SNAP (Sub-Nanosecond Arithmetic Processor) Project sponsored primarily by the National Science Foundation. The book is not written as a textbook, but rather, it is written with computer designers and researchers in mind. Therefore its focus is on *design*, not on other aspects of computer arithmetic, such as, number systems, representation, or precision.

The chapters span the basic arithmetic operations and the floating-point variants. Each chapter starts with a review of conventional/textbook design approaches, analyzes the possibilities for improvement, and presents new research that advances the state-of-the-art.

Chapter 1 begins with the first arithmetic operation, addition, and describes practical implementations of the fastest known adder, the Ling adder. Chapter 2 investigates floating point addition, and introduces two significant improvements to the design of floating point addition. First is a technique that reduces execution time for all data operands. Second is a new class of algorithms whose execution time varies with the relative data operand sizes. Chapter 3 through 5 investigates multiplication. Chapter 3 presents a new encoding scheme which reduces the execution time for multiplication. Chapter 4 and 5 investigate the effects of technology scaling on multiplication, demonstrating that the optimal choice of multiplier is highly dependent upon process technology.

Chapters 6 through 8 advance the state-of-the-art in division and its impact on system performance. The focus is on new techniques for digit-by-digit division. Chapter 9 presents a novel approximation technique for higher-level functions, including square root, logarithms, and trigonometric functions. This technique exploits the use of an existing multiplier and has the result that the delay is similar to that of a multiplier.

Chapter 10 describes a new way to assess the cost-performance of an arithmetic unit, illustrating this by reviewing recent microprocessor implementations and evaluating them in the context of this new metric. Chapter 11 describes a new approach to clocking which increases the frequency of the operation of computers.

The final chapter presents a novel implementation of a well-know mathematical approach, continued fractions, to the approximation of functions.

MICHAEL J. FLYNN
STUART F. OBERMAN

November 2000

ACKNOWLEDGEMENT

We are indebted to the National Science Foundation for support through the Directorate of Computer and Information Science and Engineering under grants MIP 88-22961 and 93-13701, the NSF Graduate Fellowship Program, and a seed grant from Stanford's Center for Integrated Systems.

We acknowledge with thanks the primary contributors to individual chapters, citing sources at the beginning of each chapter.

Chapter 1 is based on work described in G. Bewick, P. Song, G. De Micheli, and M. Flynn, "Approaching a nanosecond: A 32-bit adder," in *Proceedings of the International Conference on Computer Design*, Dec. 1988, and in N. T. Quach and M. J. Flynn, "High-speed addition in CMOS," *IEEE Transactions on Computers*, Dec. 1992. It was assembled with additional contributions from Grant McFarland.

Chapter 2 is based on work described in N. T. Quach and M. J. Flynn, "An improved algorithm for high-speed floating-point addition," Tech. Rep. CSL-TR-90-442, Computer Systems Lab., Stanford University, Aug. 1990 and in S. F. Oberman and M. J. Flynn, "Reducing the mean latency of floating point addition," *Theoretical Computer Science*, 1998.

Chapter 3 is based on work described in G. Bewick, *Fast Multiplication: Algorithms and Implementations*, PhD thesis, Stanford University, Feb. 1994.

Chapter 4 is based on work described in Hesham Al-Twaijry, *Area and Performance Optimized CMOS Multipliers*, PhD thesis, Stanford University Department of Electrical Engineering, Aug. 1997.

Chapter 5 is based on work described in Hesham Al-Twaijry, *Area and Performance Optimized CMOS Multipliers*, PhD thesis, Stanford University Department of Electrical Engineering, Aug. 1997.

Chapter 6 is based on work described in S. F. Oberman and M. J. Flynn, "Design issues in division and other floating-point operations," *IEEE Transactions on Computers*, Feb. 1997.

Chapter 7 is based on work described in S. F. Oberman and M. J. Flynn, "Minimizing the complexity of SRT tables," *IEEE Transactions on VLSI Systems*, Mar. 1998.

Chapter 8 is based on work described in D. Wong and M. Flynn, "Fast division using accurate quotient approximations to reduce the number of iterations," *IEEE Transactions on Computers*, Aug. 1992, and in Patrick Hung, Hossam Fahmy, Oskar Mencer, and Michael J. Flynn, "Fast Division Algorithm with a Small Lookup Table," *Asilomar Conference on Signals, Systems, and Computers*, Nov. 1999.

Chapter 9 was assembled and edited by Patrick Hung, based on Eric M. Schwarz, *High-Radix Algorithms for High-Order Arithmetic Operations*, PhD thesis, Stanford University Department of Electrical Engineering, Apr. 1993.

Chapter 10 is based on work described in Steve Fu, *Cost Performance Optimizations of Microprocessors*, PhD thesis, Stanford University Department of Electrical Engineering, 2000.

Chapter 11 is based on work described in Kevin Nowka, *High Performance CMOS VLSI System Design Using Wave Pipelining*, PhD thesis, Stanford University Department of Electrical Engineering, Sep. 1995.

Chapter 12 is based on work described in Oskar Mencer, *Rational Arithmetic Units in Computer Systems*, PhD thesis, Stanford University Department of Electrical Engineering, Jan. 2000.

We would like to thank Hossam Fahmy for his valuable reviews, and Susan Gere for her editing and manuscript preparation. Special thanks are due to Ranganathan Sudhakar for his combination of review and overall editing support.

M. J. F.
S. F. O.

NOTATION

The notation for frequently used signals is as follows:

a_i, b_i	ith addend and augend bits
c_i	ith carry-in bit
c_{i+1}	$(i + 1)$th carry-in bit; ith carry-out bit
$C_i = c_j$	Carry-out of group i; corresponds to bit j
$g_i = a_i b_i$	ith bit generate
$p_i = a_i + b_i$	ith bit propagate
$G_i = G_{j:k}$	The ith group generate spanning bits j through k
$P_i = P_{j:k}$	The ith group propagate spanning bits j through k
$G'_i = G'_{j:k}$	The ith generate from a group of groups spanning bits j through k
$P'_i = P'_{j:k}$	The ith propagate from a group of groups spanning bits j through k
h_i	Bit pseudocarry
$H_i = H_{j:k}$	As above, for pseudocarry group
$H'_i = H'_{j:k}$	As above for pseudocarry group of groups

The notation for numerical bit-strings is as follows:

$a_{n-1} a_{n-2} \ldots a_0$	The integer number whose value is $a_{n-1} 2^{n-1} + a_{n-2} 2^{n-2} + \cdots + a_0$
$a_0 . a_{(1)} a_{(2)} \ldots$	The floating-point number line whose value is $a_0 + a_{(1)} 2^{-1} + a_{(2)} 2^{-2} + \ldots$

ADVANCED COMPUTER ARITHMETIC DESIGN

1

INTEGER ADDITION

Although integer addition typically has the smallest delay of all the arithmetic functions, it has the largest effect on overall computer performance. In addition to the integer arithmetic–logic unit (ALU), all the floating-point operations use integer addition in their calculations. Memory accesses require integer addition for address generation, and branches use addition for forming instruction addresses and making greater-than or less-than comparisons. All of these different uses suggest that modern microprocessors typically contain several integer adders, many of which may appear on frequency-limiting paths. Therefore, optimizing integer-adder delay has been an area of active research for many years. The SNAP group has studied in detail one of the fastest possible integer adder implementations originally proposed by Ling [94].

1.1 BACKGROUND

This section gives an overview of many of the most commonly used integer addition algorithms. The sum for bit i with input operands a_i, b_i and c_i (carry-in) is

$$s_i = a_i \oplus b_i \oplus c_i.$$

The carry-out of bit i is

$$c_{i+1} = a_i\, b_i + b_i c_i + a_i c_i.$$

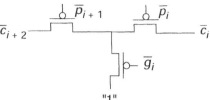

Figure 1.1   Manchester carry chain for $C_{out} = 1$.

We define a carry propagate p_i as

$$p_i = a_i + b_i$$

and define a carry generate g_i as

$$g_i = a_i b_i,$$

so c_{i+1} can also be written as

$$c_{i+1} = g_i + p_i c_i.$$

1.1.1   Ripple Adders; Manchester Carry Chain

In adding together two n-bit numbers, the simplest approach is to serially connect the carry bits together, giving a *carry ripple adder*. This requires about $2n$ gate delays to complete the determination of the result. The *Manchester carry chain* is a circuit-optimized implementation of a ripple adder. The bit propagate signals (p_i) are serially arranged using high-speed pass transistor logic. Figure 1.1 illustrates a signal path for a simplified version—the transistors are activated by inverting the p_i, g_i. The result is a circuit which propagates the carry signal rapidly across a small chain of n transistors (for n small, say less than 8).

1.1.2   Carry Skip Adders; Multilevel Carry Skip

In n-bit adders, we can group together bits and create carry bypass logic for each group (Figure 1.2). Here, the adder is divided into $[n/r - 1]$ groups of $(r - 1)$ bits each. A group propagate signal, P, is defined as

$$P_i = p_{[i(r-1)+r-2]} \cdots p_{[i(r-1)+2]} p_{[i(r-1)+1]} p_{[i(r-1)]}$$
$$= p_{(i+1)(r-1)-1} \cdots p_{i(r-1)},$$

where C_i is the carry into the ith group.

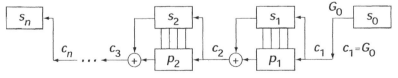

Figure 1.2   Carry skip logic.

The value of r is determined either by a fan-in limit for a single gate delay or by other delay considerations within the block. Since the internally generated carries ripple across the block, these rippled carries determine the worst-case adder delay rather than the carry-out from the highest-order bit. In the simplest implementation, the block size is fixed across the adder at $r - 1$ bits (defined by the limit of r inputs to P_i: $r - 1$ p signals and one C_i signal). There is no skip logic for either the lowest group (no carry-in) or the highest group. So we have $\lceil n/(r - 1) \rceil - 2$ blocks with carry skip. Each block passes a carry in 2 gate delays. Assuming 2 gate delays to ripple a carry, it takes $2(r - 1)$ gate delays to ripple the carry in each of the first and last blocks. For a single-level carry skip with fixed block size of $r - 1$,

$$\text{carry skip delay} = 4(r - 1) + 2\left(\left\lceil \frac{n}{r - 1} \right\rceil - 2\right)$$

$$= 4(r - 2) + 2\left\lceil \frac{n}{r - 1} \right\rceil.$$

Of course, the first and last blocks need not be $r - 1$ in size—they can be larger or smaller. Optimizations are obviously possible. Using the Manchester carry chain with a block reduces the $4r$ term in the delay equation to $2r$ transistor delays. We could use multiple levels of carry skips. Here we collect $r - 1$ groups together and carry skip the $(r + 1)$ blocks in 2 gate delays rather than $2(r - 1)$ gate delays. This reduces the long carry propagation. For further reduction, the groups can be optimally sized to minimize the internally generated and propagated carries within the groups.

1.1.3 Carry-Select and Conditional-Sum Adders

The concept behind these adders is that addition across a group of bits can be completed twice, in parallel assuming $c_{in} = 1$ and $c_{in} = 0$. When the true c_{in} is known, the correct result is selected. Simple structures as shown in Figure 1.3 are commonly called *carry-select adders*. This approach is commonly used with other approaches for implementing the adder blocks. Of course, it is possible to extend the carry select down to block sizes of r bits

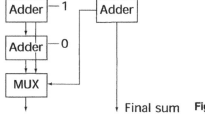

Final sum   **Figure 1.3** Carry select addition.

(r again defined as a fan-in or delay limitation on a gate). Now we have $2\lceil n/r \rceil - 1$ adder groups, each of r bits—each group assuming $c_n = 1$ or 0, except the least significant group, which is assumed to have the true carry input. We use a binary selection tree to finally select the complete sum. This selection tree process is called *conditional-sum addition*. It has a delay, (see [192]) given by

$$\text{delay} = K + 2\left\lceil \log_2\left(\left\lceil \frac{n}{r} \right\rceil - 1\right) \right\rceil,$$

where K is a constant. The process can be improved by selecting correct sums across more than two groups. For (fan-in) $r \geq 4$, we can improve the delay to

$$\text{delay} = K + 2\left\lceil \log_{r-1}\left(\left\lceil \frac{n}{r} \right\rceil - 1\right) \right\rceil,$$

where $K \approx 5$ for common implementations.

1.1.4   Carry Lookahead Adders; Canonic Adders

The *carry lookahead* (CLA) adder is probably the best-known textbook adder implementation. As before,

$$s_i = a_i \oplus b_i \oplus c_i,$$

$$c_{i+1} = a_i b_i + c_i(a_i + b_i),$$

since

$$g_i = a_i b_i,$$

and

$$p_i = a_i + b_i,$$

$$c_{i+1} = g_i + c_i(p_i).$$

We can express c_i as a function of lower-order bit terms to provide a carry lookahead function, for example, starting at c_0:

$$c_1 = g_0 + p_0\, c_0,$$

$$c_2 = g_1 + p_1 c_1 = g_1 + p_1 g_0 + p_1 p_0 c_0,$$

$$c_3 = g_2 + p_2 g_1 + p_2 p_1 g_0 + p_2 p_1 p_0 c_0,$$

and continuing up to some fan-in or delay limit r. At this point, we can define a group generate G_0, and a group propagate signal P_0:

$$G_0 = G_{2:0} = g_2 + p_2 g_1 + p_2 p_1 g_0,$$

$$P_0 = P_{2:0} = p_2 p_1 p_0$$

and the carry-out of the 0th group, C_0, is

$$C_0 = C_{2:0} = G_0 + P_0 c_0.$$

Notice that a group consists of r bits, so our adder consists of $\lceil n/r \rceil$ groups, each of which provides a P and a G signal.

Now we take r groups at a time to form a second-level group with its own generate G_0' and propagate P_0':

$$G_0' = G_{8:0}' = G_2 + P_2\, G_1 + P_2 P_1 G_0,$$

$$P_0' = P_{8:0}' = P_2 P_1 P_0.$$

We can create third- and higher-level groups in a similar way until we have spanned all n bits. This requires $\lceil \log_r n \rceil$ levels. Since each level takes two gate delays, it requires $2\lceil \log_r n \rceil + 1$ (for p and g) gate delays to form the output carry. This is not the worst delay; however, the most significant sum bit (s_{n-1}) becomes the worst case delay. In $\lceil \log_r n \rceil$ levels, we generate the carry-out of the most significant bit (msb) but not the carry into that bit. For example, to determine c_{64} for $r = 4$ and $n = 64$, three levels of lookahead are required ($\lceil \log_4 64 \rceil$) or 6 gate delays plus 1 to generate the p_i and g_i signals. As we form c_{64}, we also form c_{48} and c_{32} with the same number of gate delays.

Now the problem is to take c_{48} and have it determine s_{63}. With $r = 4$, c_{48} affects the four 4-bit groups 48:51, 52:55, 56:59, 60:63. The carry into the last group, c_{60}, is determined by

$$c_{60} = P_{56:59} P_{52:55} P_{48:51} c_{48} + P_{56:59} P_{52:55} G_{48:51} + P_{56:59} G_{52:55}.$$

Then c_{60} in turn determines $c_{63} = p_{62} p_{61} p_{60} c_{60} + \cdots$. If we simply distribute the carries in levels as we have propagated them, we span $\lceil \log_r n \rceil - 1$ levels. Including the final s_{n-1} exclusive-OR delay, we have

$$\text{CLA delay} = 2\lceil \log_r n \rceil + 1 + 2\lceil \log_r n - 1 \rceil + 1$$

$$= 4\lceil \log_r n \rceil.$$

Conceptually, we can improve this by building a special carry lookahead tree for each bit, not simply for c_n. We would thus build a lookahead tree for $s_{n-1}, s_{n-2}, s_{n-3}, \ldots$, and avoid the carry distribution delay. This is not quite as impractical as it sounds, since many terms in the trees can be shared. Such adders, called *canonic adders*, have

$$\text{canonic delay} = 2\lceil \log_r n \rceil + 2.$$

1.2 LING ADDERS

Ling adders are a variation upon the commonly used CLA adders [118]. In Ling and CLA adders logic functions are implemented which calculate whether groups of bits will generate or propagate a carry. These group generate and propagate signals can be hierarchically combined to calculate the carry into any bit. Ling adders use a simplified version of the group generate signal which takes less time to compute. Both Ling and CLA adders use the following terms:

$$g_i \equiv a_i b_i, \tag{1.1}$$

$$p_i \equiv a_i + b_i, \tag{1.2}$$

$$t_i \equiv a_i \oplus b_i. \tag{1.3}$$

How Ling adders reduce delay is seen by comparing the two schemes for calculating the s_6 bit of the sum, assuming both adders divide their carry logic into three-bit groups. Assume a fan-in limit of $r = 3$ for both Ling and traditional adders. A traditional CLA adder would calculate s_6 as follows [assuming $c_0 = 0$, no carry-in to the least significant bit (lsb)]:

$$s_6 = t_6 \oplus c_6, \tag{1.4}$$

$$c_6 = G_1 + P_1 G_0, \tag{1.5}$$

$$G_1 = G_{5:3} = g_5 + p_5 g_4 + p_5 p_4 g_3, \tag{1.6}$$

$$G_0 = G_{2:0} = g_2 + p_2 g_1 + p_2 p_1 g_0, \tag{1.7}$$

$$P_1 = P_{5:3} = p_5 p_4 p_3. \tag{1.8}$$

The delay of s_6 is completely determined by the delay of c_6. If the delay of the carry term is reduced by increasing the delay of some other term, the overall delay will be reduced as long as the carry term is still the critical path. Ling observed that every term in c_6 contains p_5 except for the very first term, which is simply g_5. However, c_6 can still be simplified by noting the following:

$$g_i \equiv p_i g_i. \tag{1.9}$$

Therefore, p_5 can be factored out of c_6 to create the pseudocarry h_6. The signal p_2 is also moved from G_0 and into P_1. This gives the following:

$$s_6 = t_6 \oplus (p_5 h_6), \tag{1.10}$$

$$h_6 = H_1 + P_{4:2} H_0, \tag{1.11}$$

$$H_1 = g_5 + g_4 + p_4 g_3, \tag{1.12}$$

$$H_0 = g_2 + g_1 + p_1 g_0, \tag{1.13}$$

$$P_{4:2} = p_4 p_3 \, p_2 \tag{1.14}$$

Both equations for s_6 are factored so that the proper result may be chosen by a mux controlled by the carry or pseudocarry:

$$s_6 = t_6 \oplus c_6 = \overline{c_6} t_6 + c_6 \overline{t_6}, \tag{1.15}$$

$$s_6 = t_6 \oplus (p_5 h_6) = \overline{h_6} t_6 + h_6 (t_6 \oplus p_5). \tag{1.16}$$

In both these expressions the carry term forms the critical path, but h_6 can be generated in less time than c_6. The overall delay to form s_i is reduced by moving p_{i-1} out of the critical path. To reduce the total delay, the group generate signals of a CLA or Ling adder may be generated directly from the input bits using a single complex gate instead of first generating the local generate and propagate signals (g_i and p_i). In this case the equations for the CLA and Ling first group generate signals become:

$$G_0 = a_2 b_2 + a_2 a_1 b_1 + b_2 a_1 b_1$$
$$\quad + a_2 a_1 a_0 b_0 + a_2 b_1 a_0 b_0 + b_2 a_1 a_0 b_0 + b_2 b_1 a_0 b_0, \tag{1.17}$$
$$H_0 = a_2 b_2 + a_1 b_1 + a_1 a_0 b_0 + b_1 a_0 b_0. \tag{1.18}$$

In this form the CLA group generate has seven terms with a maximum fan-in of 4, while the Ling generate has only four terms with a maximum fan-in of 3.

1.3 ADDER IMPLEMENTATIONS

We summarize the adder algorithms in Table 1.1. The following two sections present details of two hybrid adders using Ling, CLA and carry select designs. The first is an ECL implementation, and the second is a CMOS adder. Both these designs make use of Ling's pseudocarry to reduce delay.

TABLE 1.1 The adder parade

Type	Variation	Basic Idea	Speed[1]	Reference
Basic	Ripple	Serial carry propagate	$2n$ (assumes 2 gate delays per adder bit)	—
Carry skip	Manchester carry chain	Ripple adder using fast pass transistors to implement carry	r pass delays for r bits	Kilburn et al. [77]
	Carry skip	Detect when an r-bit group will pass a low-order C_{in}	$\sim (2n/r + k)$	Babbage [11]
	Babbage's "carriage anticipating"	Detect "all 9's" in a group to pass a carry	—	Babbage [11]
Carry select	Conditional sum	Perform bit add with and without C_{in}; select correct sum based on neighboring carry in	$2\log_2(m/r - 1) + k$	Slansky [165]
	Carry select	As above with r-sized select groups	$2\log_{r-1}(n/r) + k$	Bedrij [15]

	Apply carry skip to r skip groups		Chan et al. [32]
Carry look ahead	Multilevel carry skip	Apply carry skip to r skip groups		Chan et al. [32]
	Carry lookahead (CLA)	Define propagate (p) and generate (g) functions at bit level, then r-bit group level, then form the hierarchy. Use similar p, g to distribute carries.	$4\lceil \log_r n \rceil$	Weinberger and Smith [194]
	Canonic	As with CLA, but define CLA signal for each higher-level bit.	$2\lceil \log_r n \rceil + 2$	Waser and Flynn [192]
	Prefix	Similar to canonic with $r = 2$	$2\lceil \log_2 n \rceil + 1$	Ladner and Fischer [90]
Other	CSA-carry save adders	In adding m operands ($m > 2$), add bit columns first, then propagate carry only for final addition (CPA).	$2\log_{3/2} n/2 + \mathrm{CPA}(n)$	MacSorley [99]
	Ling adders	Recode basic bit adder to eliminate delay in forming p, g functions	Reduces adder delay by one gate	Ling [94]
	Hybrid	Almost all modern adders are hybrid, using a combination of Ling, CLA and carry select	Varies	—

[1]Speed measured in gate delays.

1.4   AN ECL LING ADDER

Based upon work by Gary Bewick

This section presents the design of a 32-bit ECL Ling adder with a worst-case delay of three complex gates [18]. This adder creates group generate and propagate signals across 4-bit groups, and makes extensive use of the wired-OR capability of ECL circuits to minimize delay. A lookahead network is implemented in a single gate delay to produce the carry into each group, and then another single gate delay produces the sum bits from each group. The overall structure of the adder is shown in Figure 1.4.

1.4.1   Group Generates

By making use of the simpler Ling pseudocarry and the wired OR of ECL, the group generate signals are formed across 4 bits in a single gate:

$$H_0 = g_3 + g_2 + p_2 g_1 + p_2 p_1 g_0, \tag{1.19}$$

$$H_0 = a_3 b_3 + a_2 b_2 + a_2 a_1 b_1 + b_2 a_1 b_1$$
$$+ a_2 a_1 a_0 b_0 + a_2 b_1 a_0 b_0 + b_2 a_1 a_0 b_0 + b_2 b_1 a_0 b_0 \tag{1.20}$$

By using the complements of a and b this equation is implemented using eight standard NOR gates with a maximum of four inputs. The gate outputs are combined by a wired OR. By comparison, the traditional CLA group generate across 4 bits would require 15 NOR gates with a maximum of five inputs. Each 4-bit slice also produces the single-bit generate and propagate signals in complemented form and sends to the lookahead network two copies of the complemented group propagate signal

$$\overline{P_0} = \overline{P_{3:0}} = \overline{p_3} + \overline{p_2} + \overline{p_1} + \overline{p_0}. \tag{1.21}$$

One of the group propagate signals is combined with that of another group by a wired OR to create the propagate signals across two groups. These are the signals $\overline{P'_{6,5}}$, $\overline{P'_{4,3}}$, and $\overline{P'_{2,1}}$ in Figure 1.4. The 4-bit groups also send the complement of the single-bit propagate signal from the most significant bit of the group to be combined with the pseudocarry in the lookahead in order to create the true carry, i.e.,

$$\overline{P'_{6,5}} = \overline{P_6} + \overline{P_5} = \overline{P'_{27:20}}.$$

1.4.2   Lookahead Network

A single level of lookahead is used to compute the carries into each 4-bit group. From each group i, the lookahead network inputs the pseudogenerate (H_i), the complement of the group propagate ($\overline{P_i}$), and the complement of the local propagate of the most significant bit. The carry on the critical path is

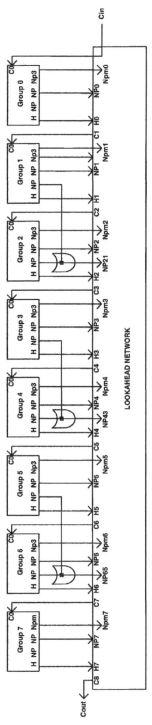

Figure 1.4 ECL ling adder.

the carry into the most significant group (C_{28}). In CLA form this signal would be written

$$C_7 = c_{28} = C_{27:0}$$
$$= G_6 + P_6 G_5 + P_6 P_5 G_4 + P_6 P_5 P_4 G_3 + P_6 P_5 P_4 P_3 G_2$$
$$+ P_6 P_5 P_4 P_3 P_2 G_1 + P_6 P_5 P_4 P_3 P_2 P_1 G_0 + P_6 P_5 P_4 P_3 P_2 P_1 P_0 c_{in}. \quad (1.22)$$

Substituting $P_i\ H_{i:i-r}$ for each $G_{i:i-r}$ and making use of the two group propagate signals allows C_7 to be written as follows (ignoring complement forms):

$$C_7 = c_{28} = C_{27:0} = p_{27} H_{27:24} + p_{27} P_{26:23} H_{23:20}$$
$$+ p_{27} H_{27:24} + p_{27} P_{26:23} H_{23:20} + p_{27} P'_{26:19} H_{19:16}$$
$$+ p_{27} P'_{26:19} P_{18:15} H_{15:12} + p_{27} P'_{26:19} P'_{18:11} H_{11:8}$$
$$+ p_{27} P'_{26:19} P'_{18:11} P_{10:7} H_{7:4} + p_{27} P'_{26:19} P'_{18:11} P'_{10:3} H_{3:0}$$
$$+ p_{27} P'_{26:19} P'_{18:11} P'_{10:3} P_{2:0} c_0. \quad (1.23)$$

Because all the propagate signals are provided in complement form, a special inverting AND gate is used with up to four inverting inputs and one noninverting input. The five-input form of this gate is shown in Figure 1.5. Eight of these gates with a maximum of five inputs and their outputs combined by a wired OR are used to implement C_7. The other group carries are produced in a similar manner but are not on the critical path.

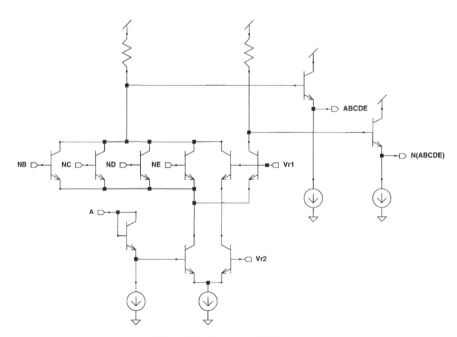

Figure 1.5 Inverting AND gate.

1.4.3 Final Sum

Each group produces the complements of four sum bits in a single gate delay after the carry into the group arrives. The slowest sum bit is the most significant bit of the group (s_3):

$$s_3 = a_3 \oplus b_3 \oplus c_3 = t_3 \oplus c_3. \qquad (1.24)$$

This carry into the third bit (c_3) is related to the carry into the group (C_0) by the following:

$$c_3 = g_2 + p_2 g_1 + p_2 p_1 g_0 + p_2 p_1 p_0 c_0,$$
$$c_3 = G_{2:0} + P_{2:0} c_0, \qquad (1.25)$$

where

$$G_{2:0} = g_2 + p_2 g_1 + p_2 p_1 g_0, \qquad (1.26)$$
$$P_{2:0} = p_2 p_1 p_0. \qquad (1.27)$$

The terms $G_{2:0}$ and $P_{2:0}$ can be formed in parallel with the formation of the group carries. Therefore, the output $\overline{s_3}$ is written to remove this delay for the critical path:

$$\overline{s_3} = \overline{t_3 \oplus (G_{2:0} + P_{2:0} c_0)},$$
$$\overline{s_3} = t_3 \overline{G_{2:0}}\,\overline{P_{2:0}} + t_3 \overline{G_{2:0}}\,\overline{c_0} + \overline{t_3} G_{2:0} + \overline{t_3} P_{2:0} c_0. \qquad (1.28)$$

This equation is implemented using four of the inverting AND gates shown in Figure 1.5 with a maximum of three inputs and their outputs combined by a wired OR. The circuit used to generate all the sum bits of a group is shown in Figure 1.6.

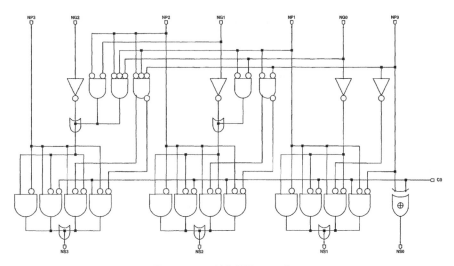

Figure 1.6 4-bit ECL sum slice.

TABLE 1.2   ECL Ling critical path

Operation	Signal	Gate	Wired OR
Group generate	G_i	4-in NOR	8-way
Group carry	C_7	5-in AND	8-way
Final sum	s_{31}	3-in AND	4-way

1.4.4   Critical Path

The critical path of this adder contains only three gates: the initial group generate, the lookahead stage, and the final sum generation. The worst-case delay of the initial group generate is a four-input NOR driving an eight-way wired-OR. For the lookahead stage the worst case is a five-input inverting AND driving an eight-way wired OR, and the final stage is a three-input inverting AND driving a four-way wired OR. This path is summarized in Table 1.2. Each of the inverting AND gates used in this path use a stack of only two transistors.

1.4.5   Implementation

This adder design was fabricated in 1987 using the HS3.5 bipolar technology from Signetics. An automatic channel router was used to make connections with each 4-bit group and between the groups and the lookahead network. This gave a total area for the adder of approximately 25 mm². The adder uses 0.5-V logic swings and a 4.5-V power supply. All the gates use tail currents of 500 μA, as do most of the emitter followers. Some heavily loaded wires on the critical path, such as those connecting the 4-bit groups to the lookahead network, are driven by emitter followers with currents of 2000 μA to reduce delay. The total power dissipation is 0.9 W, not including the output driver current. The total delay is 2.1 ns, excluding output driver and package delay.

1.5   A CMOS LING ADDER

Based upon work by N. Quach

Although the original design proposed by Ling was for an ECL adder, the Ling pseudocarry can also be used to improve the performance of CMOS adders. This section presents the design of a 32-bit CMOS Ling adder with a worst-case delay of four complex gates [138]. This adder uses 3-bit groups, which are then combined into 9-bit blocks. The total delay is reduced to a single mux delay after the formation of the carry into each block by methods similar to carry select adders. The overall structure of the adder is shown in Figure 1.7.

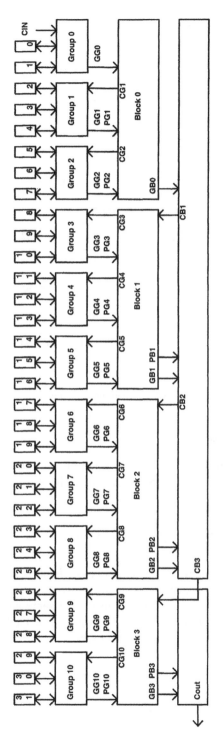

Figure 1.7 CMOS Ling Adder.

15

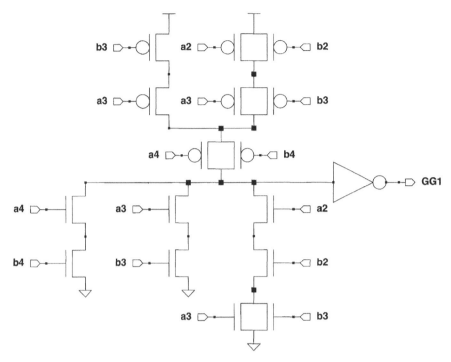

Figure 1.8   Ling group generate.

1.5.1   Group Generates

Making use of the Ling pseudogenerate signal allows each of the 3-bit group generates (H_i) to be formed in a single gate. The equation for group 1 is shown below:

$$H_1 = H_{4:2} = a_4 b_4 + a_3 b_3 + (a_3 + b_3) a_2 b_2. \qquad (1.29)$$

The gate used to implement the group generate signal is shown in Figure 1.8 and has one less series transistor than an equivalent CLA gate. The Ling group propagate signals (P_i) are formed using the same gates as in the CLA design, but they are shifted one bit to the right. The CLA and Ling group propagate signals for group 1 are shown below.

$$P_{4:2} = p_4 p_3 p_2 \qquad \text{for CLA,} \qquad (1.30)$$

$$P_{3:1} = p_3 p_2 p_1 \qquad \text{for Ling.} \qquad (1.31)$$

The group propagate signals are formed with a simple three-input AND gate.

1.5.2 Lookahead Network

The generate and propagate signals from each gate are then used to form generate and propagate signals for each block (GB_i, HB_i, and PB_i). For block 1 in Figure 1.7, these are as follows:

$$HB_1 = H_1^2 = H'_{16:8} = H_5 + P_5(H_4 + P_4\,H_3)$$

$$= H_{16:14} + P_{15:13}\,(H_{13:11} + P_{12:10}\,H_{10:8}), \qquad (1.32)$$

$$PB_1 = P_1^2 = P'_{15:7} = P_5\,P_4\,P_3 = P_{15:13}\,P_{12:10}\,P_{9:7}. \qquad (1.33)$$

The block generates are formed using the gate shown in Figure 1.9, while the block propagate is formed with a three-input AND. In the final stage of lookahead, the pseudocarries into each block are formed from the block

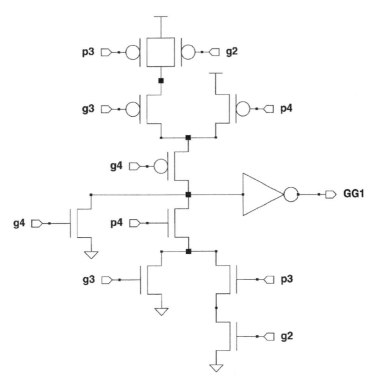

Figure 1.9 Fan-in-3 generate gate.

generate and propagate signals (again referring to Figure 1.7):

$$CB_1 = H'_0 = H'_{7:0}, \tag{1.34}$$

$$CB_2 = H'_1 + P'_1 \, H'_0 \tag{1.35}$$

$$= H'_{16:8} + P'_{15:7} \, H'_{7:0}, \tag{1.36}$$

$$CB_3 = H'_2 + P'_2([H'_1 + P'_1 \, H'_0]) \tag{1.37}$$

$$= H'_{24:17} + P'_{23:16} \, (H'_{16:8} + P'_{15:7} + H'_{7:1}), \tag{1.38}$$

$$H_{\text{out}} = H'_3 + P'_3 \left[H'_2 + P'_2 \, (H'_1 + P'_1 \, H'_0) \right] \tag{1.39}$$

$$= H'_{32:25} + P'_{31:24} \left[H'_{24:17} + P'_{23:16} \, (H'_{16:8} + P'_{15:7} + H'_{7:0}) \right]. \tag{1.40}$$

The true C_{out} is simply $p_{31} H_{\text{out}}$, which could be formed with a simple AND gate, but this would make it the critical path. Instead, the final group generate signal ($G_{10} = G_{31:28}$) is formed using the CLA expression rather than the Ling group generate. Also the final group propagate ($P_{10} = P_{31:28}$) is formed with a four-input AND instead of a three-input AND, to include p_{31}. These changes allow the true C_{out} to be formed from the block generate and propagate signals, as shown above, without making it the critical path. With this change, the critical path is CB_3, which is formed using the same gate as shown in Figure 1.9.

1.5.3 Final Sum

In a simple implementation the block carries would go through two more stages of logic to be converted into the carry into each group and then the carry into each bit. However, these operations can be moved off the critical path by computing two sets of sum bits in parallel with the block carry formation. One set assumes the carry into each block will be 0, and the other set assumes it will be 1. The block carries are then used to control a mux which selects the proper set of sum bits. This is the same method used in carry select adders.

The sum for bit 23 is written as a function of the block carry as follows:

$$s_{23} = t_{23} \oplus c_{23}, \tag{1.41}$$

$$s_{23} = t_{23} \oplus \{ p_{22}[H'_7 + P'_7(G'_6 + P_6 \, CB_2)] \} \tag{1.42}$$

$$= t_{23} \oplus \{ P_{22}[H_{22:20} + P_{21:19} \, (H_{19:17} + P_{18:16} \, H'_{16:0})] \}. \tag{1.43}$$

This expression is converted to a mux controlled by CB_2 by defining the signals CGF_8 and CGT_8:

$$CGF_8 = p_{22}(H'_7 + P'_7 G'_6), \tag{1.44}$$

$$CGT_8 = p_{22}[H'_7 + P'_7(G'_6 + P'_6)] \tag{1.45}$$

$$= p_{22}[H_{22:20} + P_{21:19}(H_{19:17} + P_{18:16})]. \tag{1.46}$$

The signal CGF_8 is the carry into group 8 assuming the block carry is zero, and CGT_8 assumes the block carry is one. The final sum bit is then written as

$$s_{23} = \overline{CB_2}[CGF_8 \oplus t_{23}] + CB_2[CGT_8 \oplus t_{23}] \tag{1.47}$$

Using these signals, the other sum bits of the group are written as

$$s_{24} = \overline{CB_2}[(g_{23} + p_{23}CGF_8) \oplus t_{24}]$$
$$+ CB_2[(g_{23} + p_{23}CGT_8) \oplus t_{24}], \tag{1.48}$$
$$s_{25} = \overline{CB_2}[(g_{24} + p_{24}(g_{23} + p_{23}CGF_8)) \oplus t_{24}]$$
$$+ CB_2[(g_{24} + p_{24}(g_{23} + p_{23}CGT_8)) \oplus t_{24}]. \tag{1.49}$$

Because the signals CGF_8 and CGT_8 will appear after the local generate and propagate signals, the critical path delay can be further reduced by applying the same principle to make the inputs to the sum select mux the output of muxes controlled by CGF_8 and CGT_8. This also allows the simplification of $g_i + p_i = p_i$ to be applied:

$$s_{23} = \overline{CB_2}(\overline{CGF_8}t_{23} + CGF_8\overline{t_{23}})$$
$$+ CB_2(\overline{CGT_8}t_{23} + CGT_8\overline{t_{23}}), \tag{1.50}$$
$$s_{24} = \overline{CB_2}[\overline{CGF_8}(g_{23} \oplus t_{24})CGF_8(p_{23} \oplus t_{24})]$$
$$+ CB_2[\overline{CGT_8}(g_{23} \oplus t_{24}) + CGT_8(p_{23} \oplus t_{24})], \tag{1.51}$$
$$s_{25} = \overline{CB_2}\{\overline{CGF_8}[(g_{24} + p_{24}g_{23}) \oplus t_{25}] + CGF_8[(g_{24} + p_{24}p_{23}) \oplus t_{25}]\}$$
$$+ CB_2\{\overline{CGT_8}[(g_{24} + p_{24}g_{23}) \oplus t_{25}] + CGT_8[g_{24} + p_{24}p_{23} \oplus t_{25}]\}. \tag{1.52}$$

The 3-bit slice which implements these functions is shown for group 8 in Figure 1.10.

1.5.4 Critical Path

For an n-bit Ling adder combining r groups at each level of lookahead, the critical path must pass up $\lceil \log_r n \rceil - 1$ levels of logic, each using $r + 1$ series transistors. The carry select mux eliminates the need to travel back up the levels of the adder to form the local carries. The mux delay from the arrival of the control signal is counted as one series transistor to form the complement of the control signal and one transistor to pass the input to the output.

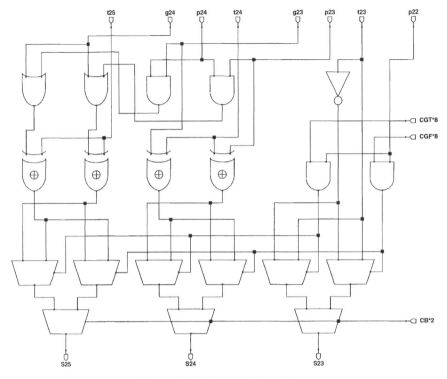

Figure 1.10 3-bit CMOS sum slice.

The number of series transistors in the critical path is therefore

$$T_d = (\lceil \log_r n \rceil - 1)(r + 1) + 2. \tag{1.53}$$

For the 32-bit adder shown here with $r = 3$ this gives a total of 14 series transistors along the critical path. This path is summarized in Table 1.3.

1.5.5 Implementation

An 11 bit version of this adder design was manufactured in a 1.0-μm-drawn-length CMOS process. Using a standard cell layout, the total area was approximately 0.39 mm^2. SPICE simulations indicate that a full 32-bit implementation would have a delay of 4.0 ns at 5 V driving a 0.3-pF load.

TABLE 1.3   CMOS Ling critical path

Operation	Signal	Series Tran.	Total Tran.
Group generate	GG_i	4	4
Block generate	GB_2	4	8
Block carry	CB_3	4	12
Sum select mux	s_{31}	2	14

1.6 CONCLUSION

Ling's pseudocarry scheme, together with more conventional approaches, realizes a hybrid adder. This enables a 32-bit ECL adder to be designed with a critical path of only 3 gate delays, and a 32-bit CMOS adder to be designed with a delay of only 4 gates. As microprocessors move toward larger-bit-width registers and addresses as well as fabrication technologies which are more limited by wire delays, the need for fast adder designs only increases. To satisfy these performance demands considering algorithms, circuit, or layout styles separately is not sufficient. Increasingly, designers must consider all these aspects simultaneously in order to make continued improvements in performance.

2

FLOATING-POINT ADDITION

Based upon work by N. Quach

Floating-point (FP) addition and subtraction are very frequent FP operations. Together, they account for over half of the total FP operations in typical scientific applications [173]. Despite its conceptual simplicity, FP addition in many modern high-speed arithmetic units has roughly the same latency as FP multiplication. This is largely because the standard FP addition algorithms require two addition steps, as well as one or two operand-length shifts. In order to achieve higher overall system performance on FP applications, it is necessary to minimize the latency of the fundamental FP operations. The SNAP group has therefore studied several techniques for reducing the latency of FP addition.

In the first study, an algorithm is proposed which exploits hardware parallelism to reduce the number of addition and shift operations required in FP addition computations. The second study presents several observations regarding the characteristics of operands. Careful exploitation of these characteristics allows for a further reduction in addition latency.

2.1 IMPROVED ALGORITHMS FOR HIGH-SPEED FP ADDITION

In this section, an FP addition algorithm is described that has only one significand addition step in the worst-case path, offering a considerable speed advantage over earlier algorithms [139]. We briefly review existing FP addition algorithms in Section 2.1.1 and present an improved algorithm in Section 2.1.2.

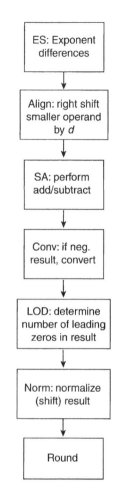

Figure 2.1   Floating-point addition: Algorithm A1.

2.1.1   A Brief Review of FP Addition Algorithms (A1 and A2)

An FP addition operation, as illustrated in Figure 2.1, consists of the following steps [192]:

Algorithm A1   (the standard FP adder)

1. *Exponent Subtraction* (ES): Subtract the exponents, and denote the difference by $|E_a - E_b| = d$.
2. *Alignment* (Align): Right shift the significand of the smaller operand by d bits. Denote the larger exponent by E_f.
3. *Significand Addition* (SA): Perform addition or subtraction according to the effective operation, E_o, which is the arithmetic operation actually carried out by the adder in the FP unit.

4. *Conversion* (Conv): Convert the result to sign–magnitude representation if the result is negative. The conversion is done with an addition step. Denote the result by S_f.

5. *Leading-one Detection* (LOD): Compute the amount of left or right shift needed, and denote it by E_n. E_n is positive for a right shift and negative otherwise.

6. *Normalization* (Norm): Normalize the significand by shifting E_n bits, and add E_n to E_f.

7. *Rounding* (Round): Perform IEEE rounding [72] by adding 1 when necessary to the least significant bit lsb of S_f. This step may cause an overflow, requiring a right shift. The exponent, E_f, in this case has to be incremented by 1.

Algorithm A2   (the two-path FP adder)

The above algorithm (Algorithm A1) is slow because the composing steps are essentially performed serially. We can improve the algorithm in the following ways:

1. We create a two-path adder structure (Figure 2.2): one path (CLOSE) for where the exponent difference $|d|$ is 0 or 1, the other path (FAR) for the other cases, $|d| > 1$. This has the primary advantage of eliminating one of the long shifts (either the align or the normalization step) in A1. In the CLOSE path, we do not need a long align shift (at most a right shift of one is required), but a long normalization (left) shift can be required in subtraction when A and B are very close. In the FAR path, we generally need a long right shift to align, but the long normalization step cannot occur, since A and B cannot be close.

2. Additionally, in Algorithm A1, the Conv step is only needed when the result is negative and can be avoided by swapping the significands. By examining the sign of the result of the ES step, we can swap the significands accordingly so that the smaller significand is subtracted from the larger one. In the case of equal exponents, the result may still be negative and requires a conversion. But, as will be explained later, no rounding is needed in this case. Hence, rounding and conversion are made mutually exclusive by the swapping step, allowing us to combine them. Note that an associated advantage of swapping is that only a shifter is now needed.

3. In a final improvement, the LOD step can be performed in parallel with the SA step, removing it from the critical path. This optimization is important when a massive left shift is required as a result of significand cancellation in the case of an effective subtraction.

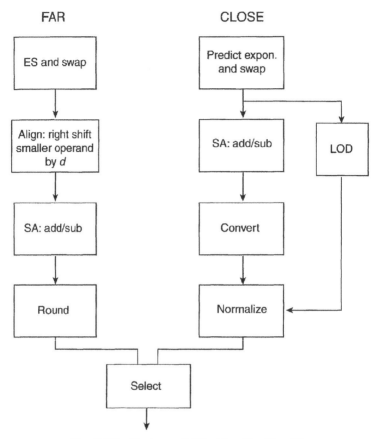

Figure 2.2 The two-path FP adder: Algorithm A2.

So far, we have been able to reduce the number of steps down to ES, Swap, Align, SA‖LOD, Conv‖Round, and Norm (the symbol "‖" indicates that the steps can be executed in parallel; see Figure 2.2).

The steps in Algorithm A1 and the two-path algorithm (Algorithm A2) are summarized in Table 2.1. In Algorithm A2, the Pred step in the $d \leq 1$ path predicts whether a one-bit right shift is needed to align the significands. Note that Algorithm A2 increases the speed by executing more steps in parallel, requiring therefore more hardware.

Algorithm A2 is commonly used, in one form or another, in today's high-performance FP arithmetic units [16, 96, 28]. From the above discussion, we see that Algorithm A2 requires two addition steps involving the significands in the critical paths in both the $d \leq 1$ and the $d > 1$ paths (SA, Convert, and Round).

TABLE 2.1   Steps in conventional FP addition algorithms

	Algorithm A2	
Algorithm A1	CLOSE	FAR
ES	Pred + Swap	ES + Swap
Align		Align
SA	SA‖LOD	SA
Conv	Conv‖Round	Round
LOD		
Norm	Norm	
Round	Select	Select

2.1.2 A New Algorithm: A3 (Two-Path with Integrated Rounding)

General Ideas

The key ideas behind our approach can be summarized as follows:

The two-path adder can be improved by eliminating the delay in each path of the rounding (addition) step (Table 2.2). We can do this by using a compound adder (Figure 2.3) for the significand add step. The compound adder simultaneously produces the sum (S) and the sum plus 1 $(S + 1)$. We then shift and select the correct result at a final step. Since the sum and the sum plus 1 are generated before the final normalization (shift), we must ensure that these two results suffice. Indeed, for simple round to nearest, as explained later, they do suffice, but an $S + 2$ can be required for RTPI and RTNI, the round-to-larger IEEE FP rounding modes.

Figure 2.4 outlines the rounding operational configuration. The smaller operand, b, is shifted by d, the exponent difference, with respect to the larger operand, a. In Algorithm A1 or A2, the result of the significand addition (before normalization) has low-order bits $N' L' G' R' s'$, where N' is the second bit (next to the lsb), L' is the lsb, G' is the guard bit, R' is a round bit, and s' is the sticky bit (the OR of all lower order bits). As shown in Figure 2.5, when this result is normalized, we are left with LGs. (In most cases, the bits s' and R' determine s).

TABLE 2.2   Steps in the current FP addition algorithm

Algorithm A3	
CLOSE	FAR
Pred + Swap	ES + Swap
SA‖Conv‖Round‖LOD	Align
Norm	SA‖Round
Select	Select

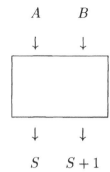

Figure 2.3 Compound adders.

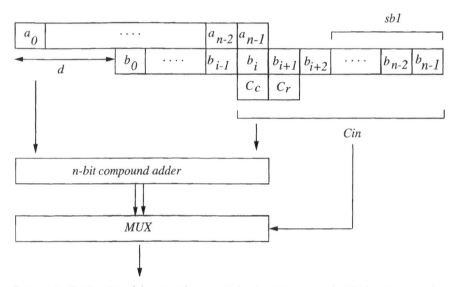

Figure 2.4 Explanation of the general approach for the RTN mode. The bit C_r is the rounding carry, and the bit C_c is the complementation carry.

Because the significand is 53-bit and because a right shift of up to 52 bits may be needed during alignment, a 105-bit adder is potentially needed. Since we are only concerned with the higher-order 53 bits, we use a 53-bit adder in the interest of hardware efficiency. In the case of complementation, a 1 needs to be added at the bit position 105. How far left into the higher-order bits this complementing 1 bit propagates and whether it reaches the adder clearly depend on the lower-order bits of the shifted significand. When the carry does reach the adder, it is added to the L bit position. The rounding bit C_r, on the other hand, is always added to the rounding bit position R. Table 2.2 lists the steps in the new algorithm.

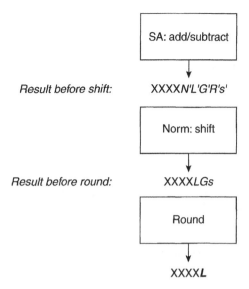

Figure 2.5 Resulting low-order bit configurations during FP addition.

The rounding actions are specified in Table 2.3 (round to nearest). If we did a rounding add, we would determine C_r from Table 2.3 to be used in the rounding addition. If we use a compound adder (Figure 2.3), we select either $A + B = S$ or $A + B + 1 = S + 1$ (i.e., either $C_{in} = 0$ or 1). The selection is specified in Table 2.3; see also Figure 2.4. The difficulty arises when we form S and $S + 1$ based on the *unnormalized* adder result, and then must shift and select the correct final result. As mentioned above, this is possible in round to nearest (RTN) mode, but additional hardware is needed to implement other modes.

Let us analyze the various cases in RTN.

TABLE 2.3 Truth table for the round-to-nearest mode: C_r is added to G in a conventional round step; C_{in} selects S or $S + 1$ from a compound adder.

L	G	S	C_r	C_{in}^1
0	0	0	x	0
0	0	1	x	0
0	1	0	0	0
0	1	1	1	1
1	0	0	x	0
1	0	1	x	0
1	1	0	1	1
1	1	1	1	1

[1]Select $S + 1$ when $C_{in} = 1$.

The Case of Subtraction

1. $|e_B - e_A| \leq 1$ (CLOSE path)
   (a) No shift; positive result
   (b) No shift; negative result
   (c) Left-shift by ≤ 1
2. $|e_B - e_A| > 1$ (FAR path)
   (a) No shift required
   (b) One leftshift required

In the CLOSE path, case 1(b) is the case of recomplementation of a result. This can only happen when $|E_B - E_A| = 0$, so all G, R and s bits are zero and no rounding is required.

Even if $|E_A - E_B| = 1$, then $R = 0$ and $s = 0$, so if a left shift is required, then no rounding is required (G will be forced to zero, and $s = 0$).

Only in the case of $d = 1$ with a positive result and no shift required can rounding be required. Thus, rounding can occur only if no shifting or recomplementation is required.

In the FAR path there are two possible results: no shift, or one left shift. The case of no shift, Table 2.3 applies straightforwardly. In the case of one left shift, some complications arise, since we have added 1 to the L' bit rather than the G' bit in forming $S + 1$. This is not a problem, since it is only in the case where $G = 1$ that a rounding can occur, and in this case the carry out of G into L adds 1 to the L bit.

Note that in the case of one left shift, the rounding selection (S or $S + 1$) *depends* on knowledge that the left shift is to occur. For example, if we had

$$L'G'R's' = 0011$$

and then $LGs = 001$ and no shift, we would select S ($C_{in} = 0$), while if a left shift were to be required,

$$L'G'R's' = 0011$$

becomes

$$LGs = 011$$

and we would select $S + 1$.

The Case of Addition

Addition can occur in either the FAR or CLOSE path; the analysis is similar. Since the sum can be only $1.XX$ or $1X.XX$, there are only two possible postshifts—either 0 or a right shift of 1; a long postshift cannot occur. Following the (normalizing) postshift, the sum appears as

$$1.XXXX \ldots LGs.$$

TABLE 2.4 RTN action: Addition with one right shift; circled actions (C_{in}) indicate critical paths for correct selection

Before one right shift				Action[1]	After			Correct action (C_{in})	
N'	L'	G'	$R' + s'$		L	G	s		
0	0	0	0	0	0	0	0	0	
0	0	0	1	0	0	0	1	0	
0	0	1	0	0	0	0	1	0	
0	0	1	1	1	0	0	1	0	Late select
0	1	0	0	0	0	1	0	0	
0	1	0	1	0	0	1	1	1	Late select
0	1	1	0	1	0	1	1	1	
0	1	1	1	1	0	1	1	1	
1	0	0	0	0	1	0	0	0	
1	0	0	1	0	1	0	1	0	
1	0	1	0	0	1	0	1	0	
1	0	1	1	1	1	0	1	0	Late select
1	1	0	0	0	1	1	0	1	Late select
1	1	0	1	0	1	1	1	1	Late select
1	1	1	0	1	1	1	1	1	
1	1	1	1	1	1	1	1	1	

[1]Action based on unnormalized result.

The LGs combination now defines a rounding action (e.g., see Table 2.3): a carry C_r to be added to the G bit.

If no shift is required, we can apply the actions of Table 2.3 immediately and select either the sum, S, or $S + 1$.

If a right shift is required (see Table 2.4), then $N'L'G'R's'$ becomes

$$N' \to L, \qquad L' \to G, \qquad G' + R' + s' \to s.$$

Now we have formed $S + 1$ based on addition to L'. This is not a problem for RTN, since in the $S + 1$, the 1 is added to the G bit and carries into L only when $G = 1$. The compound adder recognizes this and forms S and $S + 1$ by adding $+1$ into L' (which becomes G on a right shift).

Table 2.4 illustrates the type of analysis required for each case where a postaddition shift is required (normalize). For most cases, the action based on the unshifted results correspond to the correct final action. In the circled instances, the correct action differs from that predicted by the unshifted sum. These cases must be identified, and the detection logic for these cases will form the worst-case delay path for the final mux result selection.

There is a problem in the *round-positive* and *round-negative* modes. Suppose we have RTPI:

N'	L'	G'	s'
1	0	1	1

Now the compound adder forms S and $S + 1$ based on the unshifted L. But after one right shift,

$$N'L'G'R's' = 101X1$$

becomes $LGs = 101$. In the *round-to-nearest* (RTN) mode, we would select S ($C_{in} = 0$), but now under RTPI node, we want to select $S + 1$ based on the N or L bit. This L could carry into higher-order bits, so we need (for this case) $S + 2$. Given $S + 1$ and a carry-in, we can realize $S + 2$ with an additional row of half adders.

In the IEEE RTN mode, computing $A + B = S$ and $A + B + 1 = S + 1$ is sufficient to account for all the normalization possibilities to be discussed below. By selecting the results using C_{in} computed based on the lower-order bits of the significands, complementation and rounding can be done simultaneously, saving one addition step.

Hence, the challenge is in deriving the equation for C_{in}. Since in FP addition, normalization of the result may require a one-bit right shift, no shift, or a left shift which may be of as many bits as the length of the significand, C_{in} needs to allow for all these normalization possibilities, so that the final selected result will appear to be rounded properly.

Implementing the *round-to-zero* mode is easy because a simple truncation suffices in this case and no rounding is needed. The logic equation for C_{in} for the RTN mode, which is the default IEEE rounding mode, can be derived by extending Table 2.4 to each shifted case—applying Table 2.3 to each instance and combining the results.

The discussion presented thus far is a straightforward description of the algorithm's implementation. Many optimizations are possible to improve minor details. For example, if we define the $S + 1$ to be such that the 1 is added to the G' position (i.e., in the location of C_r), then all the late-select cases could be eliminated for the RTN mode. Looking back at Table 2.3, it is clear that C_r must be 0 for only one case ($LGS = 010$); otherwise C_r could be set to 1. In Table 2.4 we see that after the shift only one case has $LGS = 010$, namely $N'L'G'S' = 0100$. So in general, C_{in} can be always 1, except that for $LGS = 010$ it will be set to 0. This case of $LGS = 010$ occurs if there is no shift and $L'G'S' = 010$ or if there is one right shift and $N'L'G'S' = 0100$. If the logic for the *action* is such that it is 0 only if $N'L'G'S' = 0100$ or $L'G'S' = 010$, the late-select cases are eliminated and the action based on the prenormalized bits is always equal to that of the true result.

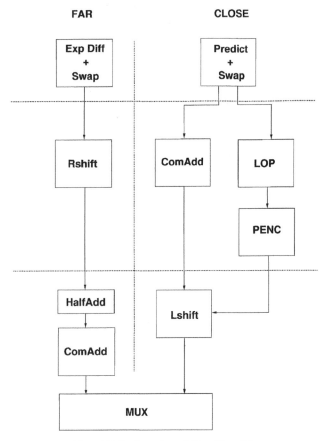

Figure 2.6   A version of Algorithm A3.

2.1.3 Summary

Algorithm A3 has only one addition step involving the significand in the critical path while performing full IEEE rounding (Figure 2.6). In FP addition, 2's complementation of one of the significands is needed in the case of an effective subtraction. The key ideas included in Algorithm A3 are: First, complementation and rounding are mutually exclusive and can be combined. Second, for the RTN mode, precomputing $A + B$ and $A + B + 1$ is enough to account for all the normalization possibilities. Round-to-infinity modes are more difficult to speed up than the RTN mode; they require an extra row of half adders to perform rounding correctly.

2.2 VARIABLE-LATENCY FP ADDITION

To further reduce the latency beyond previously reported techniques, it is necessary to remove one or more of the remaining serial components in the dataflow. This section outlines an algorithm which reduces the number of serial components depending upon the input operands, reducing the average addition latency. This section is abstracted from [128], which may be consulted for further details.

To take advantage of the reduced average latency, it is necessary that the processor be able to exploit a variable-latency functional unit. Thus, the processor must use some form of dynamic instruction scheduling with out-of-order completion in order to use the reduced latency and achieve maximum system performance.

2.2.1   Variable-Latency Algorithm

From Figure 2.6, it can be seen that the long latency operation in the first cycle occurs in the FAR path. It contains hardware to compute the absolute difference of two exponents and to conditionally swap the exponents. Depending upon the FP representation used within the floating-point unit (FPU), the exponents are either 11 bits for IEEE double precision or 15 bits for extended precision. The minimum latency in the FAR path comprises the delay of an 11-bit adder and two multiplexers. The CLOSE path, in contrast, has relatively little computation. A few gates are required to inspect the low-order two bits of the exponents to determine whether or not to swap the operands, and a mux is required to perform the swap. Thus, the CLOSE path is faster than the FAR path by a minimum of

$$\Delta t_{\mathrm{d}} \geq t_{\mathrm{mux}} + \left(t_{\mathrm{add11}} - t_{\mathrm{2bit}} \right).$$

2.2.2   Two-Cycle Algorithm

Rather than letting the CLOSE-path hardware sit idle during the first cycle, it is possible to take advantage of the duplicated hardware and initiate CLOSE-path computation one cycle earlier. This is accomplished by moving both the second- and the third-stage CLOSE-path hardware up to their preceding stages. As it has been shown that the first stage in the CLOSE path completes very early relative to the FAR path, the addition of the second-stage hardware need not result in an increase in cycle time.

The operation of the proposed algorithm is as follows. Both paths begin speculative execution in the first cycle. At the end of the first cycle, the true exponent difference is known from the FAR path. If the exponent difference dictates that the FAR path is the correct path, then computation continues in that path for two more cycles, for a total latency of three cycles. However, if the CLOSE path is chosen, then computation continues for one more cycle, with the result available after a total of two cycles. While the maximum latency of the adder remains three cycles, the average latency is reduced due to the faster CLOSE path. If the CLOSE path is a frequent path, then a considerable reduction in the average latency can be achieved. A block diagram of the two-cycle algorithm is shown in Figure 2.7.

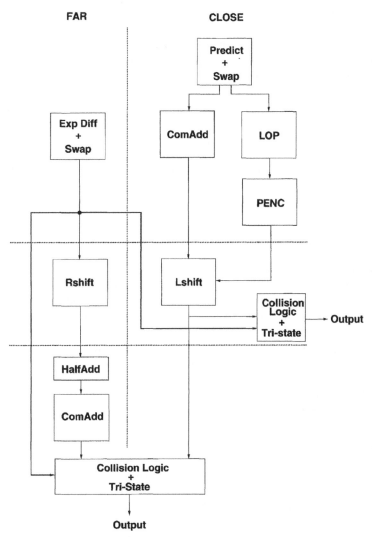

Figure 2.7 Two- or three-cycle variable-latency adder.

It can be seen that a result can be driven onto the result bus in either stage 2 or stage 3. Therefore, some logic is required to control the tristate buffer in the second stage to ensure that it only drives a result when there is no result to be driven in stage 3. In the case of a collision with a pending result in stage 3, the stage-2 result is simply piped into stage 3. While this has the effect of increasing the CLOSE-path latency to three cycles in these instances, it does not affect the throughput. As only a single operation is initiated every cycle, it is possible to retire a result every cycle.

The frequency of collisions depends upon the actual processor microarchitecture as well as the program. Worst-case collisions would result from a stream of consecutive addition operations which alternate in their use of the CLOSE and FAR paths. The distance between consecutive operations depends upon the issue width of the processor and the number of functional units.

Scheduling the use of the results of an adder implementing the two-cycle algorithm is not complicated. At the end of the first cycle, the FAR-path hardware will have determined the true exponent difference, and thus the correct path will be known. Therefore, a signal can be generated at that time to inform the scheduler whether the result will be available at the end of one more cycle or two more cycles. Typically, one cycle is sufficient to allow for the proper scheduling of a result in a dynamically scheduled processor.

2.2.3   One-Cycle Algorithm

Further reductions in the latency of the CLOSE path can be made after certain observations. First, it can be seen that the normalizing left shift in the second cycle is not required for all operations. A normalizing left shift can only be required if the effective operation is subtraction. Since additions never need a left shift, addition operations in the CLOSE path can complete in the first cycle. Second, in the case of effective subtractions, small normalizing shifts, such as $d \leq 2$, can be separated from longer shifts. While longer shifts still require the second cycle to pass through the full-length shifter, short shifts can be completed in the first cycle through the addition of a separate small mux. Both of these cases have a latency of only one cycle, with little or no effect on cycle time. If these cases occur frequently, the average latency is reduced. A block diagram of this adder is shown in Figure 2.8.

The one-cycle algorithm allows a result to be driven onto the result bus in any of the three stages. As in the two-cycle algorithm, additional control for the tristate buffers is required to ensure that only one result is driven onto the bus in any cycle. In the case of a collision with a pending result in any of the other two stages, the earlier results are simply piped into their subsequent stages. This guarantees the correct FIFO ordering on the results. While the average latency may increase due to collisions, throughput is not affected.

Scheduling the use of the results from a one-cycle adder is somewhat more complicated than for a two-cycle. In general, the instruction scheduling hardware needs some advance notice to schedule the use of a result for another functional unit. It may not be sufficient for this notice to arrive at the same time as the data. Thus, an additional mechanism may be required to determine as soon as possible before the end of the first cycle whether the result will complete either (1) in the first cycle or (2) in the second or in the third cycle. A proposed method is as follows. First, it is necessary to determine quickly whether the correct path is the CLOSE or the FAR path.

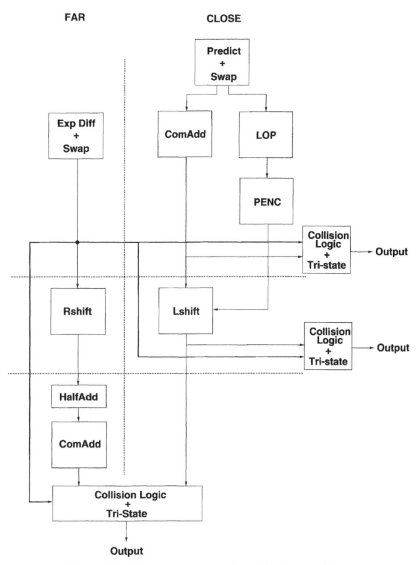

Figure 2.8 One-, two- or three-cycle variable latency adder.

This can be determined from the absolute difference of the exponents. If all bits of the difference except for the lsb are 0, then the absolute difference is either 0 or 1 depending upon the lsb, and the correct path is the CLOSE path. To detect this situation fast, an additional small leading-one predictor is used in parallel with the exponent adder in the FAR path to generate a CLOSE–FAR signal. This signal is very fast, as it does not depend on exactly where the leading one is, so long as it is past the lsb.

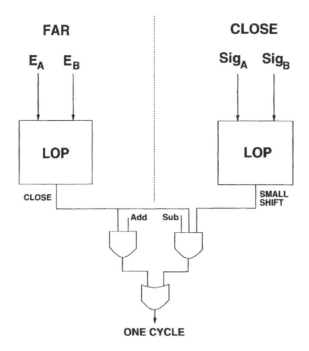

Figure 2.9 Additional hardware for one-cycle operation prediction

Predicting early in the first cycle whether or not a CLOSE-path operation can complete in one or two cycles may require additional hardware. Effective additions require no other information than the CLOSE–FAR signal, as all CLOSE path effective additions can complete in the first cycle. In the case of effective subtractions, an additional specialized leading-one predictor can be included in the significand portion of the CLOSE path to predict quickly whether the leading one will be in any of the high-order three bits. If it will be in these bits, then it generates a one-cycle signal; otherwise, it generates a two-cycle signal.

A block diagram of the additional hardware required for early prediction of one-cycle operations is shown in Figure 2.9. An implementation of this early-prediction hardware should produce a one-cycle signal in less than 8 gate delays, or about half a cycle.

2.3 PERFORMANCE RESULTS

To demonstrate the effectiveness of these two algorithms in reducing the average latency, the algorithms were simulated using operands from actual applications. The data for the study was acquired using the ATOM instrumentation system [170]. ATOM was used to instrument 10 applications from

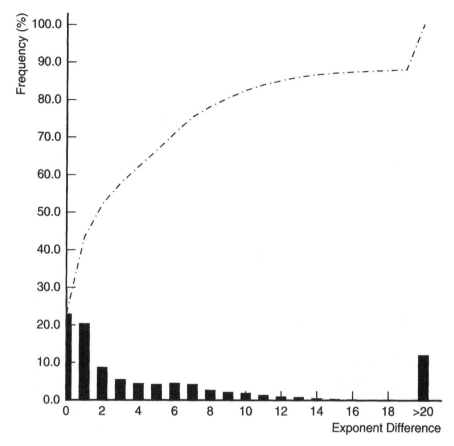

Figure 2.10 Histogram of exponent difference.

the SPECfp92 [169] benchmark suite. These applications were then executed on a DEC Alpha 3000/500 workstation. The benchmarks used the standard input data sets, and each executed approximately 3 billion instructions. All double precision FP addition and subtraction operations were instrumented. The operands from each operation were used as input to a custom FP adder simulator. The simulator recorded the effective operation, exponent difference, and normalizing distance for each set of operands.

Figure 2.10 shows a histogram of the exponent differences for the observed operands, and also a graph of the cumulative frequency of operations for each exponent difference. This figure shows the distribution of the lengths of the initial aligning shifts. It should be noted that 57% of the operations are in the FAR path with $E_d > 1$, while 43% are in the CLOSE path. An implementation of the two-cycle algorithm therefore utilizes the two cycle-path 43% of the time with a performance of

$$\text{average latency} = 3 \times 0.57 + 2 \times 0.43 = 2.57 \text{ cycles},$$
$$\text{speedup} = 3/2.57 = 1.17.$$

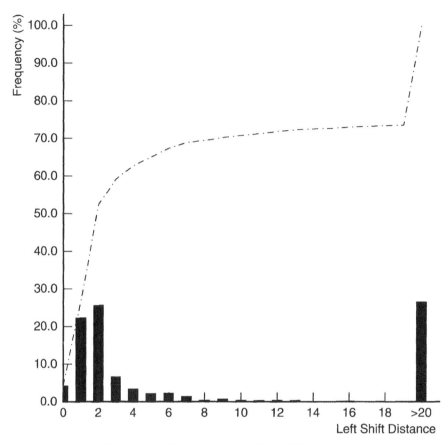

Figure 2.11 Histogram of normalizing-shift distance.

Thus, an implementation of the two-cycle algorithm has a speedup in average addition latency of 1.17, with little or no effect on the cycle time.

Implementations of the one-cycle algorithm reduce the average latency even further. An analysis of the effective operations in the CLOSE path shows that the total of 43% can be broken down into 20% effective addition and 23% effective subtraction. As effective additions do not require any normalization in the CLOSE path, they complete in the first cycle. An implementation allowing effective addition to complete in the first cycle is referred to as *adds*, and has the following performance:

average latency = $3 \times 0.57 + 2 \times 0.23 + 1 \times 0.20 = 2.37$ cycles,

speedup = $3/2.37 = 1.27$.

Thus, adds reduces the average latency to 2.37 cycles, for a speedup of 1.27.

Figure 2.11 is a histogram of the normalizing-left-shift distances for effective subtractions in the CLOSE path. From Figure 2.11, it can be seen that the majority of the normalizing shifts occur for distances of less than 3 bits. Only 4.4% of the effective subtractions in the CLOSE path require no normalizing shift. However, 22.4% of the subtractions require a 1-bit normalizing left shift, and 25.7% of the subtractions require a 2 bit normalizing left shift. In total, 52.5% of the CLOSE-path subtractions require a left shift less than or equal to 2 bits. The inclusion of separate hardware to handle these frequent short shifts provides a performance gain.

Three implementations of the one-cycle algorithm could be used to exploit this behavior. Denoted by subs0, subs1 and subs2, they allow completion in the first cycle for effective subtractions with maximum normalizing-shift distances of 0, 1, and 2 bits respectively. The most aggressive implementation, subs2, has the following performance:

$$\text{average latency} = 3 \times 0.57 + 2 \times 0.11 + 1 \times 0.32 = 2.25 \text{ cycles},$$

$$\text{speedup} = 3/2.25 = 1.33.$$

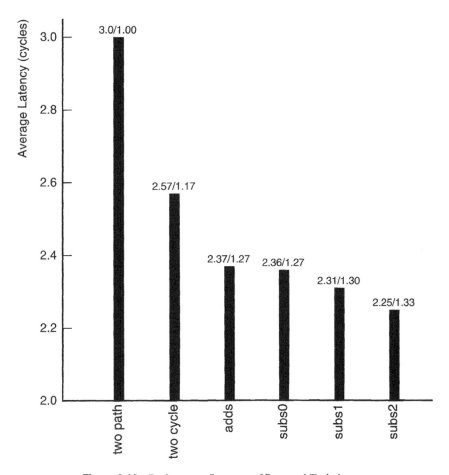

Figure 2.12 Performance Summary of Proposed Techniques.

Allowing all effective additions and those effective subtractions with normalizing-shift distances of 0, 1, and 2 bits to complete in the first cycle reduces the average latency to 2.25 cycles, for a speedup of 1.33.

The performance of the proposed techniques is summarized in Figure 2.12. For each technique, the average latency is shown, along with the speedup provided over the base two-path FP adder with a fixed latency of three cycles.

2.4 CONCLUSION

This study has presented two techniques for reducing the average latency of FP addition. Previous research has shown techniques to guarantee a maximum latency of three cycles in high clock-rate processors. This study shows that additional performance can be achieved in dynamic instruction scheduling processors by exploiting the distribution of operands that use the CLOSE path. It has been shown that 43% of the operands in the SPECfp92 applications use the CLOSE path, resulting in a speedup of 1.17 for the two-cycle algorithm. By allowing effective additions in the CLOSE path to complete in the first cycle, a speedup of 1.27 is achieved. For even higher performance, an implementation of the one-cycle algorithm achieves a speedup of 1.33 by allowing effective subtractions requiring very small normalizing shifts to complete in the first cycle. These techniques do not add significant hardware, nor do they affect the cycle time. They provide a reduction in average latency while maintaining single-cycle throughput.

3

MULTIPLICATION · WITH PARTIALLY REDUNDANT MULTIPLES

Based upon work by Gary Bewick

3.1 INTRODUCTION

Multiplication is an important basic arithmetic operation. VLSI designers have recognized this by dedicating significant area to integer and FP multipliers. Where possible, we must reduce the cost of these multipliers by using efficient algorithms that do not compromise performance. The SNAP group has explored several aspects of multiplier design, including encoding, reduction-tree organizations, final propagate adder design, circuit design, and the effects of processing technology.

This chapter describes an extension to Booth's algorithm for binary multiplication that, in many implementations, reduces its area or cost. To explain this scheme, background material on existing algorithms is presented. These algorithms are then extended to produce the new method. Since the method is somewhat complex, we avoid implementation details.

To simplify discussion, only unsigned multiplication is considered, but the algorithms are easily generalized to deal with signed numbers.

3.2 BACKGROUND

3.2.1 Add and Shift

The first and simplest method of multiplication is the *add-and-shift* multiplication algorithm. This algorithm conditionally adds together copies of the multiplicand (partial products) to produce the final product, and is illustrated in Figure 3.1 for a 16 × 16 bit multiply. Each dot is a placeholder for a single

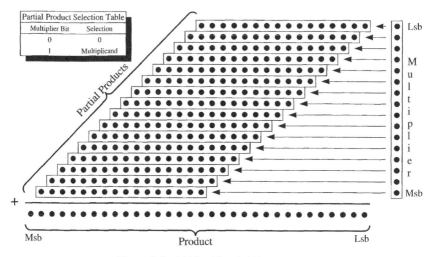

Figure 3.1 16-bit add and shift multiply.

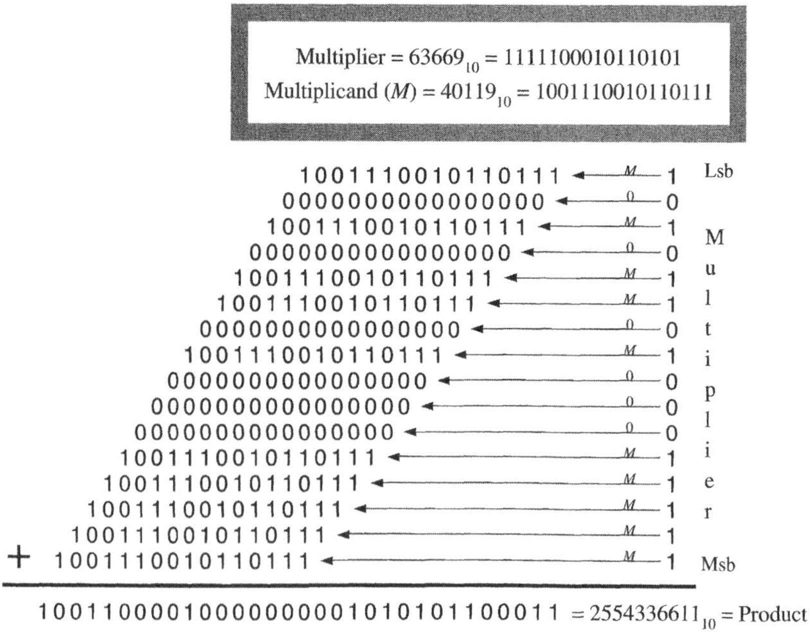

Multiplier = 63669_{10} = 1111100010110101
Multiplicand (M) = 40119_{10} = 1001110010110111

1001110010110111 ← M — 1	Lsb
0000000000000000 ← 0 — 0	
1001110010110111 ← M — 1	M
0000000000000000 ← 0 — 0	
1001110010110111 ← M — 1	u
1001110010110111 ← M — 1	l
0000000000000000 ← 0 — 0	t
1001110010110111 ← M — 1	i
0000000000000000 ← 0 — 0	
0000000000000000 ← 0 — 0	p
0000000000000000 ← 0 — 0	l
1001110010110111 ← M — 1	i
1001110010110111 ← M — 1	e
1001110010110111 ← M — 1	r
1001110010110111 ← M — 1	
+ 1001110010110111 ← M — 1	Msb

1001100001000000000101010101100011 = 2554336611_{10} = Product

Figure 3.2 16-bit add and shift example.

bit, which can be a zero or one. Each horizontal row of dots represents a single copy of the multiplicand *M* (i.e. one partial product), which is conditioned upon a particular bit of the multiplier. The conditioning algorithm is shown in the selection table in the upper left-hand corner of the figure. The multiplier itself is represented on the right edge of the figure, with the least significant bit at the top. The final product is represented by the row of 32 horizontal dots at the bottom of the figure.

An example of the add-and-shift algorithm using binary numbers is shown in Figure 3.2.

3.2.2 Dot Diagrams

The *dot diagram*, as Figure 3.1 is called, can provide information which can be used as a guide for examining various multiplication algorithms. Roughly speaking, the number of dots (256 for Figure 3.1) in the partial product section of the dot diagram is proportional to the amount of hardware required (though time multiplexing can reduce the hardware requirement, at the cost of slower operation [149]) to sum the partial products and form the final product.

The latency of an implementation of a particular algorithm is also related to the height of the partial-product section (i.e., the maximum number of dots in any vertical column) of the dot diagram. This relationship can vary from logarithmic (for a tree implementation where interconnect delays are insignificant) to linear (for an array implementation where interconnect delays are constant) to something in between (for a tree implementation where interconnect delays are significant). Implementation issues are discussed in Sections 4.3.2 and 4.4. For this discussion, we assume that a smaller height will be faster.

Finally, the logic which selects the partial products can be deduced from the partial product selection table. For the add-and-shift algorithm, the logic is particularly simple and is shown in Figure 3.3. This figure shows the selection logic for a single partial product (a single row of dots). Frequently this logic can be merged directly into whatever hardware is being used to sum the partial products. This can reduce the delay of the logic elements to the

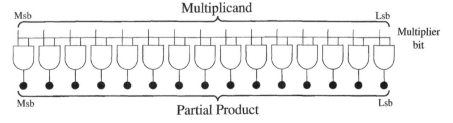

Figure 3.3 Partial product selection logic for add-and-shift.

point where the extra time due to the selection elements can be ignored. However, any implementation has interconnect delay due to the physical separation of the common inputs of each AND gate and to the distribution of the multiplicand to the selection elements.

3.2.3 Booth's Algorithm

Since fewer dots can be faster and require less hardware, how can the number (and height) of dots be reduced? A common method is to use *Booth's algorithm* [21]). Hardware implementations commonly use a slightly modified version of Booth's algorithm, referred to appropriately as the *Modified Booth's algorithm* [99]. Figure 3.4 shows the dot diagram for a 16×16 multiply using the 2-bit version of this algorithm (Booth 2). The multiplier is partitioned into overlapping groups of three bits, and each group is decoded to select a single partial product as per the selection table. Each partial product is shifted 2 bit positions with respect to its neighbor. The number of partial products has been reduced from 16 to 9. In general, there are $\lfloor (n + 2)/2 \rfloor$ partial products, where n is the operand length. The various required multiples can be obtained by a simple shift of the multiplicand (these are *easy* multiples). Negative multiples, in 2's-complement form, can be obtained using a bit-by-bit complement of the corresponding positive multiple, with a 1 added in at the least significant position of the partial product (the S bits along the right side of the partial products). An example

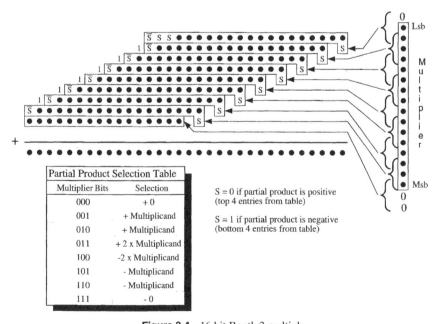

Partial Product Selection Table	
Multiplier Bits	Selection
000	+ 0
001	+ Multiplicand
010	+ Multiplicand
011	+ 2 x Multiplicand
100	-2 x Multiplicand
101	- Multiplicand
110	- Multiplicand
111	- 0

$S = 0$ if partial product is positive
(top 4 entries from table)

$S = 1$ if partial product is negative
(bottom 4 entries from table)

Figure 3.4 16-bit Booth 2 multiply.

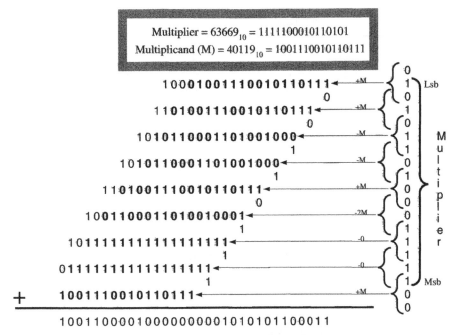

Figure 3.5 16-bit Booth 2 example.

is shown in Figure 3.5. In addition, the number of dots has decreased from 256 to 177 (this includes sign extension and constants). This reduction in dot count is not a complete saving—the partial-product selection logic is more complex (Figure 3.6). In fact, depending on actual implementation details, the extra cost and delay due to the more complex partial-product selection logic may overwhelm the savings due to the reduction in the number of dots [148].

3.2.4 Booth 3

Shift amounts greater than 2 between adjacent partial products are also possible [99], with a corresponding reduction in the height and number of dots in the dot diagram. A 3-bit Booth dot diagram is shown in Figure 3.7, and an example is shown in Figure 3.8. Each partial product could be from the set $\{\pm 0, \pm M, \pm 2M, \pm 3M, \pm 4M\}$. All multiples with the exception of $3M$ are easily obtained by simple shifting and complementing of the multiplicand. The number of dots, constants, and sign bits to be added is now 126 (for the 16×16 example), and the height of the partial product section is now 6.

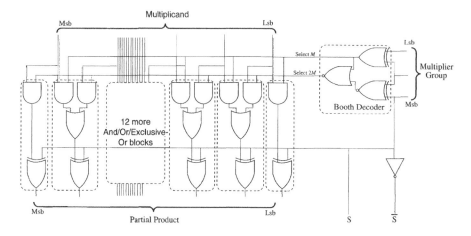

Figure 3.6 16-bit Booth 2 partial-product selector logic.

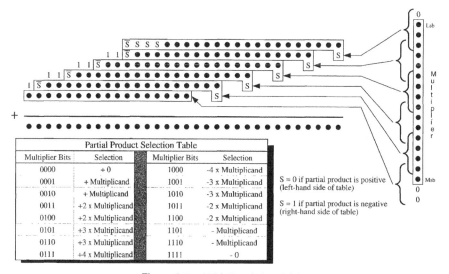

Partial Product Selection Table			
Multiplier Bits	Selection	Multiplier Bits	Selection
0000	+ 0	1000	-4 x Multiplicand
0001	+ Multiplicand	1001	-3 x Multiplicand
0010	+ Multiplicand	1010	-3 x Multiplicand
0011	+2 x Multiplicand	1011	-2 x Multiplicand
0100	+2 x Multiplicand	1100	-2 x Multiplicand
0101	+3 x Multiplicand	1101	- Multiplicand
0110	+3 x Multiplicand	1110	- Multiplicand
0111	+4 x Multiplicand	1111	- 0

S = 0 if partial product is positive (left-hand side of table)

S = 1 if partial product is negative (right-hand side of table)

Figure 3.7 16-bit Booth 3 multiply.

Generation of the multiple $3M$ (referred to as a *hard* multiple since it cannot be obtained via simple shifting and/or complementing of the multiplicand) generally requires some kind of carry-propagate adder. This adder may increase the latency, mainly due to the long wires that are required for propagating carries from less significant to more significant bits. Sometimes the generation of this multiple can be overlapped with an operation which sets up the multiply (e.g., the fetching of the multiplier).

Another drawback to this algorithm is the complexity of the partial product selection logic, an example of which is shown in Figure 3.9, along with the extra wiring needed for routing the $3M$ multiple.

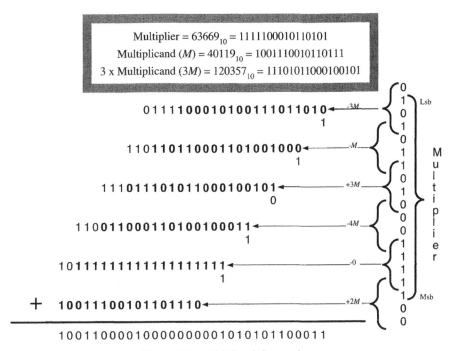

Figure 3.8   16-bit Booth 3 example.

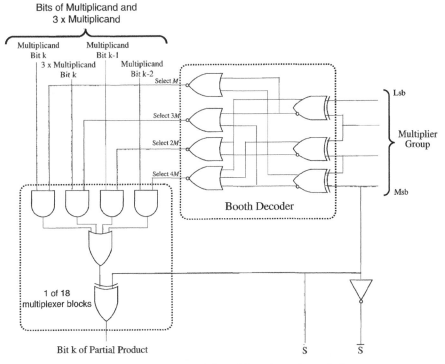

Figure 3.9   16-bit Booth 3 partial-product selector logic.

Partial Product Selection Table							
Multiplier Bits	Selection	Multiplier Bits	Selection	Multiplier Bits	Selection	Multiplier Bits	Selection
00000	+ 0	01000	+4 x Multiplicand	10000	-8 x Multiplicand	11000	-4 x Multiplicand
00001	+ Multiplicand	01001	+5 x Multiplicand	10001	-7 x Multiplicand	11001	-3 x Multiplicand
00010	+ Multiplicand	01010	+5 x Multiplicand	10010	-7 x Multiplicand	11010	-3 x Multiplicand
00011	+2 x Multiplicand	01011	+6 x Multiplicand	10011	-6 x Multiplicand	11011	-2 x Multiplicand
00100	+2 x Multiplicand	01100	+6 x Multiplicand	10100	-6 x Multiplicand	11100	-2 x Multiplicand
00101	+3 x Multiplicand	01101	+7 x Multiplicand	10101	-5 x Multiplicand	11101	- Multiplicand
00110	+3 x Multiplicand	01110	+7 x Multiplicand	10110	-5 x Multiplicand	11110	- Multiplicand
00111	+4 x Multiplicand	01111	+8 x Multiplicand	10111	-4 x Multiplicand	11111	- 0

Figure 3.10   Booth 4 partial-product selection table.

3.2.5   Booth 4 and Higher

A further reduction in the number and height in the dot diagram can be made, but the number of hard multiples required goes up exponentially with the amount of reduction. For example the Booth 4 algorithm (Figure 3.10) requires the generation of the multiples $\{\pm 0, \pm M, \pm 2M, \pm 3M, \pm 4M, \pm 5M, \pm 6M, \pm 7M, \pm 8M\}$. The hard multiples are $3M$ ($6M$ can be obtained by shifting $3M$), $5M$ and $7M$. The formation of the multiples can take place in parallel, so the extra cost mainly involves the adders for producing the multiples, and the additional wires that are needed to route the various multiples around.

3.3   REDUNDANT BOOTH

The following sections present a new variation on the Booth 3 algorithm, which eliminates much of the delay and part of the hardware associated with the multiple generation, yet produces a dot diagram which can be made to approach that of the conventional Booth 3 algorithm. Before introducing this variation, a simple and similar method (which is not particularly hardware-efficient) is explained. This method is then extended to produce the new variation. Methods of further generalizing to a Booth 4 algorithm are then discussed.

3.4   BOOTH 3 WITH FULLY REDUNDANT PARTIAL PRODUCTS

The time-consuming carry-propagate addition that is required for the higher Booth algorithms can be eliminated by representing the partial products in a fully redundant form. This method is illustrated by examining the Booth 3 algorithm, since it requires the fewest multiples. A fully redundant form represents an n-bit number using two $(n - 1)$-bit numbers whose sum equals the number it is desired to represent (there are other possible redundant forms [180]). For example the decimal number 14568 can be represented in redundant form as the pair $(14568, 0)$, or $(14567, 1)$, or the like. Using this representation, it is trivial to generate the $3M$ multiple required by the Booth 3 algorithm, since $3M = 2M + 1M$, and $2M$ and $1M$ are easy multiples. The dot diagram for a 16-bit Booth 3 multiply using this redundant form for the

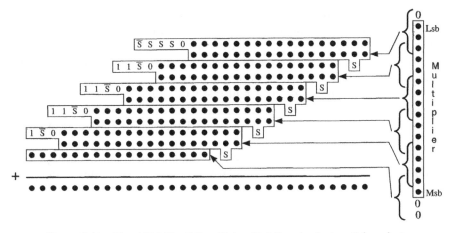

Figure 3.11 16 × 16-bit Booth 3 multiply with fully redundant partial products.

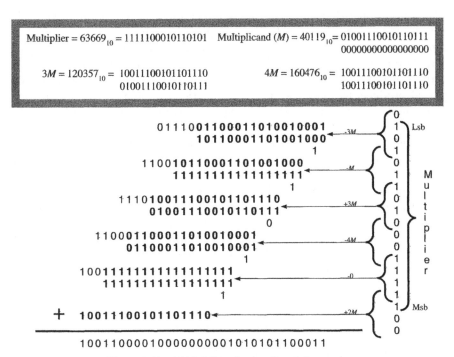

Figure 3.12 16-bit fully redundant Booth 3 example.

partial products is shown in Figure 3.11 (an example appears in Figure 3.12). The dot diagram is the same as that of the conventional Booth 3 dot diagram, but each of the partial products is twice as high, giving roughly twice the number of dots and twice the height. Negative multiples are obtained by the same method as in the previous Booth algorithms—bit-by-bit complementation of the corresponding positive multiple with a 1 added at the lsb. Since every partial product now consists of two numbers, there are two 1's added at the lsb, which can be combined into a single 1 that is shifted one position to the left.

Although (due to the doubling of the number of dots in each partial product) this algorithm is not particularly attractive, it provides a stepping stone to a related, efficient algorithm.

3.5 BOOTH 3 WITH PARTIALLY REDUNDANT PARTIAL PRODUCTS

The conventional Booth 3 algorithm assumes that the $3M$ multiple is available in non-redundant form. Before the partial products can be summed, a time-consuming carry-propagate addition is needed to produce this multiple. The Booth 3 algorithm with fully redundant partial products avoids the carry-propagate addition, but has the equivalent of twice the number of partial products to sum. The new scheme tries to combine the smaller dot diagram of the conventional Booth 3 algorithm with the ease of hard-multiple generation of the fully redundant Booth 3 algorithm.

The idea is to form the $3M$ multiple in a *partially redundant* form by using a series of small-length adders, with no carry propagation between the adders (Figure 3.13). If the adders are of sufficient length, the number of dots per partial product can approach the number in the nonredundant representation. This reduces the number of dots needing summation. If the adders are small enough, then carries are not propagated across large distances, and are faster than in a full-carry propagate adder. Also, less hardware is required due to the elimination of the logic which propagates carries between the small adders. There is, however, a design tradeoff which must be resolved.

3.5.1 Dealing with Negative Partial Products

There is a difficulty with the partially redundant representation described by Figure 3.13. Recall that Booth's algorithm requires the negative of all multiples. The negative (2's complement) can normally be produced by a bit-by-bit complementation, with a 1 added in at the lsb of the partial product. If this procedure is done to a multiple in partially redundant form, then the large gaps of zeros in the positive multiple become large gaps of

Fully redundant form

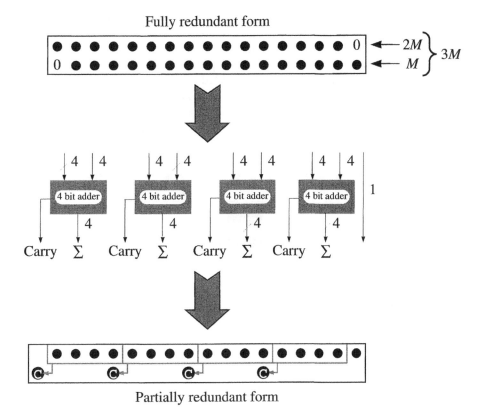

Partially redundant form

Figure 3.13 Computing the $3M$ multiple in a partially redundant form.

ones in the negative multiple (see Figure 3.14). In the worst case (all partial products negative), summing the partially redundant partial products requires as much hardware as representing them in the fully redundant form. The problem then is to find a partially redundant representation which has the same form for both positive and negative multiples, and allows easy generation of the negative multiple from the positive multiple (or vice versa). The simple form used in Figure 3.13 cannot meet both of these conditions simultaneously.

3.6 BOOTH WITH BIAS

In order to produce multiples in the proper form, Booth's algorithm needs to be modified slightly. This modification is shown in Figure 3.15. Each partial product has a bias constant added to it before being summed to form the final product. The bias constant K is the same for both positive and negative multiples, but it may be different for each partial product. The only restriction is that K, for a given partial product, cannot depend on which particular multiple is selected for use in producing the partial product. With this assumption, the constants for each partial product can be added (at design time!), and the negative of this sum added to the partial products (the *compensation constant*). The net result is that zero has been added to the partial products, so the final product is unchanged.

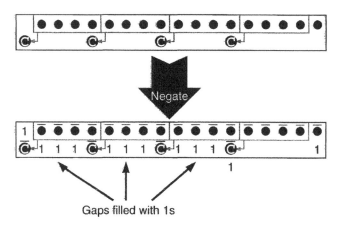

Figure 3.14   Negating a number in partially redundant form.

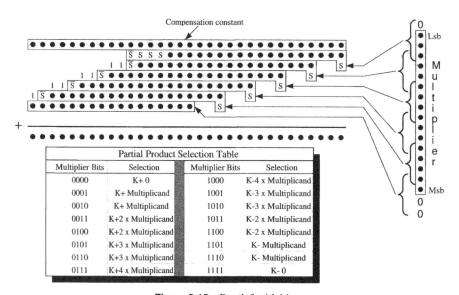

Figure 3.15   Booth 3 with bias.

3.6.1 Choosing the Right Constant

Now consider a multiple in the partially redundant form of Figure 3.13, and choose a value for K such that there is a 1 in the positions where a C dot appears and zero elsewhere, as shown in the top part of Figure 3.16. Notice the topmost circled section enclosing three vertical items (two dots and the constant 1). These items can be summed as per the middle part of the figure, producing the dots X and Y. The three items so summed can be replaced by the two equivalent dots shown in the bottom part of the figure to produce a redundant form for the sum of K and the multiple. This is very similar to the simple redundant form described earlier, in that there are large gaps of zeros in the multiple. The key advantage of this form is that the value for K − Multiple can be obtained very simply from the value of K + Multiple.

Figure 3.17 shows the sum of K + Multiple with a value Z which is formed by the bit-by-bit complement of the nonblank portions of K + Multiple and the constant 1 in the lsb. When these two values are summed together, the result is $2K$ (this assumes proper sign extension to however many bits are desired). That is,

$$K + \text{multiple} + Z = 2K,$$

$$Z = K - \text{multiple}.$$

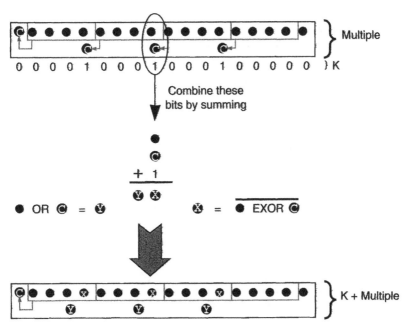

Figure 3.16 Transforming the simple redundant form.

In short, $K -$ multiple can be obtained from $K +$ multiple by complementing all of the nonblank bits of $K +$ multiple and adding 1. This is exactly the same procedure used to obtain the negative of a number when it is represented in its nonredundant form.

This partially redundant form satisfies the two conditions presented earlier, that is, it has the same representation for both positive and negative multiples, and also it is easy to generate the negative given the positive form (the entries from the right side of the table in Figure 3.15 will continue to be considered as negative multiples).

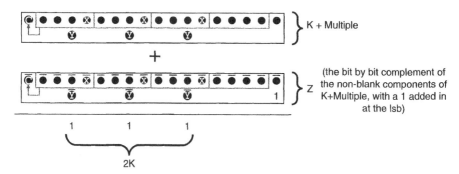

Figure 3.17 Summing $K -$ multiple and Z.

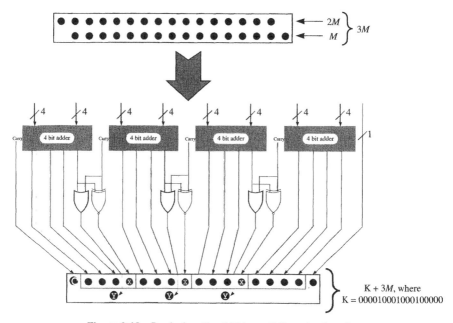

Figure 3.18 Producing $K + 3M$ in partially redundant form.

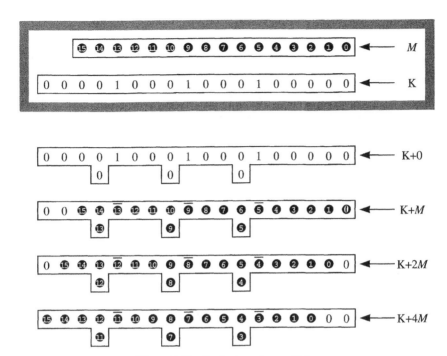

Figure 3.19   Producing other multiples.

3.6.2   Producing the Multiples

Figure 3.18 shows in detail how the biased multiple $K + 3M$ is produced from M and $2M$ using 4-bit adders and some simple logic gates. The simple logic gates will not increase the time needed to produce the biased multiple if the carry-out and the lsb from the small adder are available early. This is usually easy to assure. The other required biased multiples are produced by simple shifting and inverting of the multiplicand as shown in Figure 3.19. In this figure the bits of the multiplicand (M) are numbered (lsb = 0) so that the source of each bit in each multiple can be easily seen.

3.6.3   Redundant Booth 3

Combining the partially redundant representation for the multiples with the biased Booth 3 algorithm provides a workable redundant Booth 3 algorithm. The dot diagram for the complete redundant Booth 3 algorithm is shown in Figure 3.20 for a 16×16 multiply. The compensation constant has been computed given the size of the adders used to compute the $K + 3M$ multiple (4 bits in this case). There are places where more than a single constant is to be added (on the left-hand diagonal). These constants could be merged into a single constant to save hardware. Ignoring this merging, the number of dots,

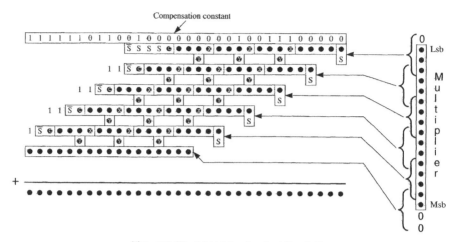

Figure 3.20 16×16 redundant Booth 3.

constants, and sign bits in the dot diagram is 155, which is slightly more than that for the nonredundant Booth 3 algorithm (previously given as 126). The height[1] is 7, which is one more than that for the Booth 3 algorithm. Each of these measures are less than that for the Booth 2 algorithm (although the cost of the small adders is not reflected in this count).

A detailed example for the redundant Booth 3 algorithm is shown in Figure 3.21. This example uses 4-bit adders as per Figure 3.18 to produce the multiple $K + 3M$. All of the multiples are shown in detail at the top of the figure.

The partial-product selectors can be built out of a single mux block, as shown in Figure 3.22. This figure shows how a single partial product is built out of the multiplicand and $K + 3M$ generated by logic in Figure 3.18.

3.6.4   Redundant Booth 4

At this point, a possible question is "Can this scheme be adapted to the Booth 4 algorithm?" The answer is yes, but it is not particularly efficient and probably is not useful. The difficulty is concerned with the biased multiples $3M$ and $6M$. The problem arises when the biased multiple $K + 6M$ is required. The normal (unbiased) Booth algorithms obtain $6M$ by a single left shift of $3M$. If this is tried using the partially redundant biased representation, then the result is not $K + 6M$, but $2K + 6M$. This violates one of the original premises, that the bias constant for each partial product is independent of the multiple being selected. In addition to this problem, the actual positions of the Y bits are shifted.

---

[1] The diagram indicates a single column (20) with height 8, but this can be reduced to 7 by manipulation of the S bits and the compensation constant.

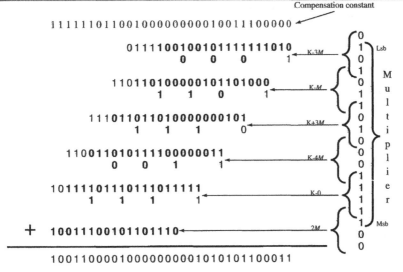

Multiplier = 63669_{10} = 1111100010110101   Multiplicand (M) = 40119_{10}= 01001110010110111

K = 000010001000100000

Multiples (in redundant form)

K+0 =   000010001000100000
     0   0   0

K+M = 001011111010010111   K+2M = 010001101101001110
   0   0   1   1   0   1

K+3M = 011011010000000101   K+4M = 100101000011111100
    1   1   1   1   1   0

Compensation constant

1 1 1 1 1 1 0 1 1 0 0 1 0 0 0 0 0 0 0 0 0 1 0 0 1 1 1 0 0 0 0 0 ◄——

  0 1 1 1 1 0 0 1 0 0 1 0 1 1 1 1 1 1 1 0 1 0   K-3M
    0   0   0   1 ◄——

   1 1 0 1 1 0 1 0 0 0 0 0 1 0 1 1 0 1 0 0 0   K-M
     1   1   0   1 ◄——

   1 1 1 0 1 1 0 1 1 0 1 0 0 0 0 0 0 0 0 1 0 1   K+3M
     1   1   1   0 ◄——

  1 1 0 0 1 1 0 1 0 1 1 1 1 0 0 0 0 0 0 1 1   K-4M
    0   0   1   1 ◄——

 1 0 1 1 1 1 0 1 1 1 0 1 1 1 0 1 1 1 1 1   K-0
   1   1   1   1 ◄——

+   1 0 0 1 1 1 0 0 1 0 1 1 0 1 1 1 0 ◄——   2M

1 0 0 1 1 0 0 0 0 1 0 0 0 0 0 0 0 0 0 1 0 1 0 1 0 1 1 0 0 0 1 1

Figure 3.21 16-bit partially redundant Booth 3 multiply.

These problems can be overcome by choosing a different bias constant, as illustrated in Figure 3.23. The bias constant is selected to be non-zero only in bit positions corresponding to carries *after* shifting to create the $6M$ multiple. The three bits in the area of the non-zero part of K (circled in the figure) can be summed, but the summation is not the same for $3M$ (left side of the figure) as for $6M$ (right side of the figure). Extra signals must be routed to the Booth muxes to simplify them as much as possible (there may be many of them if the multiply is fairly large). For example, to fully form the three dots labeled X, Y, and Z requires the routing of five signal wires. Creative use of hardware-dependent circuit design (e.g., creating OR gates at the inputs of the muxes) can reduce this to four, but this still means that there are more routing wires for a multiple than there are dots in the multiple. Of course since there are now three multiples that must be routed ($3M$, $5M$ and $7M$), these few extra wires may not be significant.

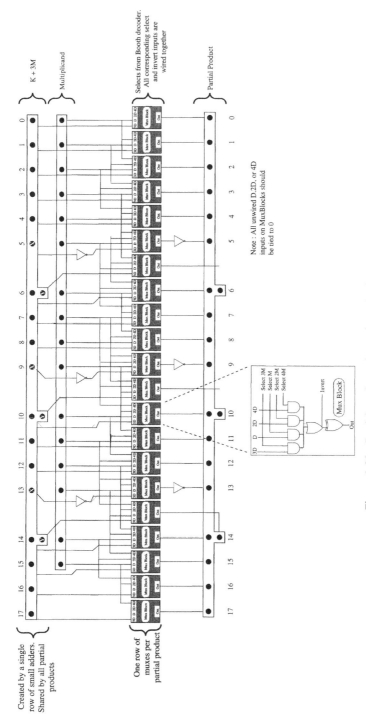

Figure 3.22 Partial-product selector for redundant Booth 3.

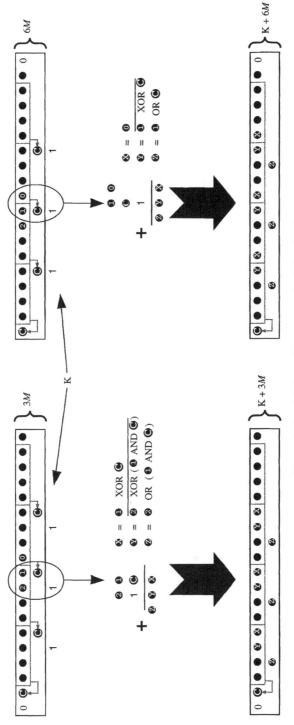

Figure 3.23 A different bias constant for $6M$ and $3M$.

61

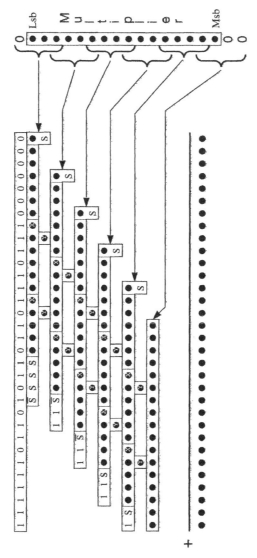

Figure 3.24 Redundant Booth 3 with 6-bit adders.

There are many other problems, which are inherited from the nonredundant Booth 4 algorithm. Larger muxes—each mux must choose from eight possibilities, twice as many as for the Booth 3 algorithm—are required. There is also a smaller hardware reduction in going from Booth 3 to Booth 4 then there was in going from Booth 2 to Booth 3.

Optimizations are also possible for generation of the $3M$ multiple. These optimizations are not possible for the $5M$ and $7M$ multiples, so the small adders that generate these multiples must be of a smaller length (for a given delay). This means more dots in the partial product section to be summed.

Thus a redundant Booth 4 algorithm is possible to construct, but probably has little speed or implementation advantage over the redundant Booth 3 algorithm. The hardware saving due to the reduced number of partial products is exceeded by the cost of the adders needed to produce the three hard multiples, and of the increased complexity of the multiplexers required to select the partial products.

3.6.5 Choosing the Adder Length

By and large, the rule for choosing the length of the small adders is straightforward—the largest possible adder should be chosen. This minimizes the amount of hardware needed for summing the partial products. Since the multiple generation occurs in parallel with the Booth decoding, there is little point in reducing the adder lengths to the point where they are faster than the Booth decoder. The exact length is dependent on the actual technology used in the implementation, and must be determined empirically.

Certain lengths should be avoided, as illustrated in Figure 3.24. This figure assumes a redundant Booth 3 algorithm, with a carry interval of 6 bits. Note the accumulation of dots at certain positions in the dot diagram. In particular, the column forming bit 15 of the product is now 8 high (vs 7 for a 4-bit carry interval). This accumulation can be avoided by choosing adder lengths which are relatively prime to the shift amount between neighboring partial products (in this case, 3). This spreads the Y bits out so that accumulation won't occur in any particular column.

3.7 CONCLUSION

This chapter has described a new variation on conventional Booth multiplication algorithms. By representing partial products in a partially redundant form, hard multiples can be computed without a slow, full-length carry-propagate addition. With such hard multiples available, a reduction in the amount of hardware needed for summing partial products is then possible using the Booth 3 multiplication method.

4

MULTIPLIER TOPOLOGIES

Based upon work by Hesham Al-Twaijry

The previous chapter presented the most common methods for generating the partial products. After the N partial products are generated, they must be accumulated to obtain the final product. Using carry-propagate adders, the time-consuming carry-propagate addition is repeated $N - 1$ times. Several techniques have been proposed and implemented in order to reduce the latency required, including signed digit addition [9]. However, the method most commonly used is carry-save addition [10]. In carry-save addition, the carry propagation is done in the last step, while in all other intermediate steps a sum and carry are generated for each bit position. When two bits are added together, the carry propagates only to the next bit position and no ripple carry propagation occurs. The concept of carry-save addition has been known since the 1950s [143]. However, the term carry-save addition (CSA) was not used until later.

The summation of the partial products is done using some variation of a carry-save adder, referred to generally as *counters*. These counters can be connected by several different methods. As used here, *topology* refers to implementation differences in (1) the way the counters are interconnected, (2) the allowable number of wires per wiring channel, and (3) the length of the wires required to connect the counters.

The topologies can be broadly classified into regular and irregular topologies. In a *regular topology*, the counters are connected in a regular pattern that is replicated. The regular connections make the design of the partial-product array a hierarchical design. In contrast, in an *irregular topology*, the counters are connected in order to minimize the delay, disregarding the ease of laying out the multiplier.

4.1 REVIEW OF ISSUES IN PARTIAL-PRODUCT SUMMATION

The previous chapter developed techniques to generate partial products through Booth encoding of the multiplier. When the partial products (PPs) have been determined, they must be summed. The obvious accumulation of PPs by shift + add would be too slow. The alternative is to simultaneously add all PP bit columns, producing two results: sum and carry. These can then be added together using a carry-propagate adder (CPA) to produce the final product. This chapter is concerned with reducing the PPs to a pair of sum-and-carry operands which can be input to a CPA.

The basic element used in reducing a PP column is a CSA. This is nothing more than a binary full adder that takes 3 bits of the same significance as inputs and produces a sum bit and a carry bit (of one-bit-higher-significance).

The CSA is also referred to as a $(3, 2)$ counter—using the terminology of Dadda [37] and Stenzel et al. [172], counters are referred to as $(C_i, C_{i-1}, \ldots, d)$, where C_i refers to the column height of bit i which the counter is to sum, and d is the number of bits in the output. Some common counter forms are shown in Figure 4.1. While higher-level counters [i.e., more complex than $(3, 2)$] can be specially designed, they are usually implemented from $(3, 2)$ counters. Figure 4.2 shows a $(7, 3)$ realized from $(3, 2)$ counters. Efficient designs can use the delay difference between the sum and carry signals to some advantage.

Compressors are a special form of counters. These are counter configurations designed to support regular tree topology implementations. Thus, the counter interconnection (and resulting number of counters) and the wires per channel are determinable from the number of partial products without further design optimization. Compressors generally have two outputs (powers of 2 are also possible), ignoring intercolumn carries. The most common compressor is the [4:2]. Note here that compressor notation differs from counter notation in ignoring intercolumn carries. Except for figures where the terms are written out, we use $[x{:}y]$ to indicate a compressor and (x, y) to indicate a counter. So a [4:2] compressor is a particular form of $(5, 3)$ counter (Figure 4.3) with one carry entering and one leaving the compressor column. The potential advantage of compressors will be seen later in their regularity and wirability.

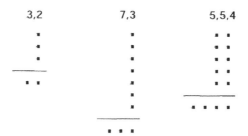

Figure 4.1 Some counters.

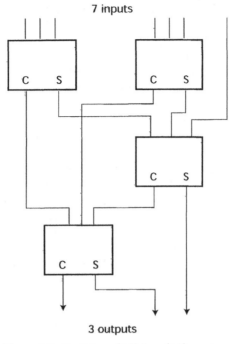

Figure 4.2   Realizing a $(7, 3)$ from $(3, 2)$ counters.

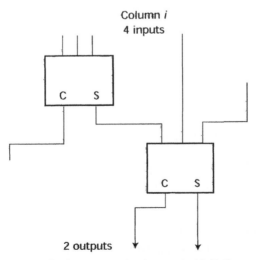

Figure 4.3   A [4:2] compressor implemented with $(3, 2)$ counters.

Once a counter or compressor has been selected, it must be interconnected to produce the two-input operand to the CPA. In a multiplier topology there are two basic approaches: a linear (2D) array interconnection, or a tree (3D) interconnection.

In the linear arrays a typical implementation has a $(3, 2)$ counter for each bit in the PP. This counter simply produces the sum and carry of its own PP bit plus the sum and carry bits from the previous corresponding bits in the preceding row. If we summed n PPs, we would need $n - 2$ $(3, 2)$ delays (the first row sums three PPs, as it has no previous sum and carry inputs).

The tree implementations are a more aggressive approach to PP summation. Here, all bits in a PP bit column are summed concurrently using counters. The best-known tree implementation is the Wallace tree using $(3, 2)$ counters. Implementation proceeds generally as we saw in Figure 4.2, which reduced seven inputs to three outputs. These could be reduced to two by using a final level of $(3, 2)$ counters.

A final issue of review is wirability. The PP reduction is implemented by columns of counters. A column implementation is repeated across all significant column bits. The physical width of the implemented column defines a *channel*. This channel can accommodate a number of wires (usually implemented on top of the channel logic). This is referred to as the maximum number of *wiring tracks* per channel. If an implementation requires more wires than allowed, then that implementation must either increase the channel size or use multiple channels. Clearly, neither alternative is desirable —spreading out the design causes additional wire delay and requires additional area for the implementation.

This chapter introduces the most common multiplier topologies used in PP reduction, and compares them in terms of the number of tracks per channel and the summing time. Then an algorithm for counter placement in PP reduction using an irregular tree is compared with the best regular topology.

4.2 REGULAR TOPOLOGIES

The regular topologies are the topologies most commonly used in custom design, since they provide a compromise between optimization and design effort. The regularity allows designers to build a small group of building blocks that contain connected counters and compressors and then connect these blocks to form the topology.

For the regular topologies the maximum number of counters and compressors in series defines the delay of the topology. Regular topologies can be classified as either *array topologies* or *tree topologies*.

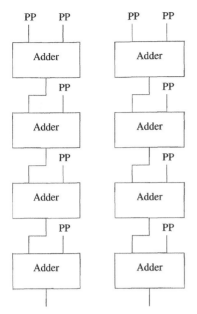

Figure 4.4 Array topology.

4.2.1 Array Topologies

In an array, the counters and compressors are connected in an identical manner for all bit slices of the PP parallelogram. The counters and compressors are connected mostly serially. In arrays, the number of tracks per channel is usually small and is independent of the number of PPs. As can be seen from Figure 4.4, the array topology is a two-dimensional structure that fits nicely on the VLSI planar process. There are several possible array topologies, including simple, double, and higher-order arrays.

Simple Array

A simple array multiplier consists of rows of $(3, 2)$ counters [23]. Figure 4.5 shows a portion of a linear array and the associated routing. The output of each row of counters is the input to the next row of counters. In the figure, each box represents a $(3, 2)$ counter, while the small diamonds each represent bits of the PPs. In the simple array, each row of $(3, 2)$ counters adds a partial product to the partial sum, generating a new partial sum and a sequence of carries. The delay of the array to produce the final partial sum and carry depends on the depth of the simple array. Therefore, the summing time for the simple array is $N - 2$ $(3, 2)$ counter delays, where N is the number of partial products. The term -2 occurs because the first $(3, 2)$ counter reduces three PPs.

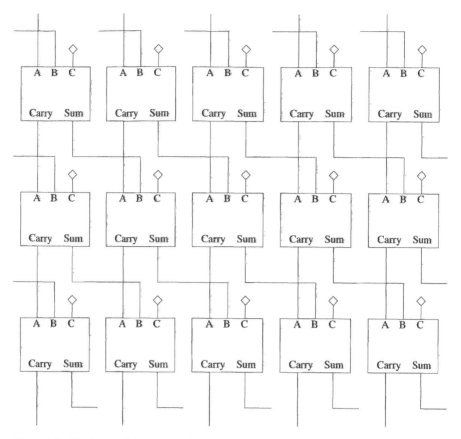

Figure 4.5 The layout of three rows of a simple array. Notice that a particular bit, i, of the sum is shifted by each row.

The simple array is a very regular design, consisting of replicated rows of $(3, 2)$ counters. Simple arrays using single-rail[1] circuits need three tracks per channel.

A problem with this design is that the hardware is underutilized. Each row of PPs is used only once in the calculation of the result. The counters are not used in the remaining time. This low efficiency can be remedied by pipelining the array so that several multiplications can occur simultaneously. Although the pipelining of the array can greatly increase the throughput of the multipliers, it is not without cost, since both the latency and the area of the multiplier are increased due to additional latches. Fully pipelining the array is seldom done, since the clock rate would be much faster than that used by processor. Therefore, latches are usually inserted between groups of counters in the array.

[1]Single-rail circuits use one wire to connect an output to another circuit's input. The alternative is a dual-rail (two-wire) circuit system. Dual-rail circuits are potentially faster than single-rail.

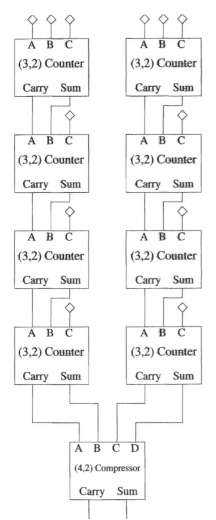

Figure 4.6 Reduction of a bit slice of partial products using a double array.

Double Array

The delay required to generate the result for the simple array can be halved by having two adds proceed in parallel [67]. The idea of this design is to add the odd-numbered PP rows separately from the even-numbered ones. When all the PPs are accumulated, the two partial sums are combined using a [4:2] compressor. Figure 4.6 illustrates a bit-slice reduction using this method. Since the carry output of the $(3, 2)$ counter has weight $i + 1$ (as opposed to the inputs and sum, which have weight i), it is connected to the adjacent bit slice. Therefore, the carry connections shown are actually from the adjacent bit slice, although the carries are drawn as direct connections to lower rows for clarity.

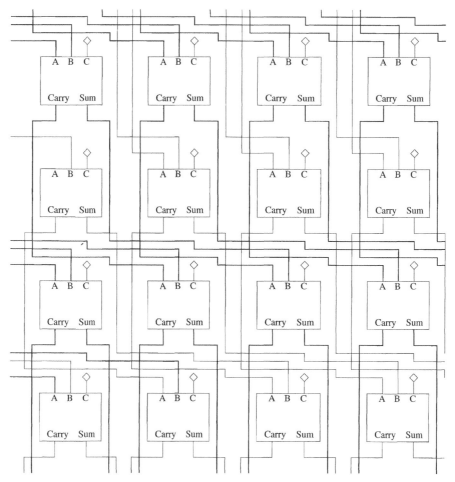

Figure 4.7   The layout of four rows of a double array.

The double array also consists of rows of $(3, 2)$ counters. However, the output of the counter is the input to the row after the next row. Figure 4.7 presents four rows of the PP reduction array, showing the two arrays interleaved. The reduction in the delay compared to the simple array is not without expense: the number of tracks per channel for the double array increases to five.

The delay required to reduce the partial products is

$$\left\lceil \frac{N}{2} - 2 \right\rceil (3, 2) \text{ counters} + 1 \, [4{:}2] \text{ compressor.}$$

It should be noted that both the simple array and the double array reduce the partial products in linear time, $O(n)$.

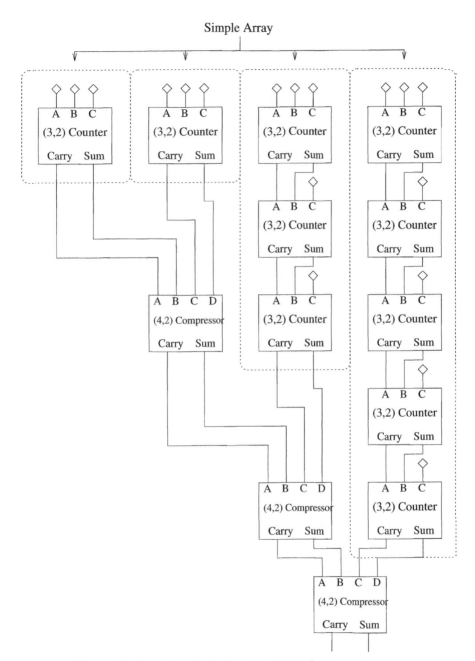

Figure 4.8 Reduction of a bit slice using a (3-3-5-7) higher-order array.

Higher-Order Array

The delay required to produce the final result can be reduced even further by noticing that it is possible to perform even more adds concurrently. The idea is to partition the array into more subarrays and use [4:2] compressors to combine the subarrays [2]. This is accomplished by connecting progressively longer simple arrays together. The [4:2] compressor is connected between a simple array and the other arrays when the delay of the simple array is equal to the total delay of the combined arrays. The connections are made using this scheme so that the number of tracks per channel is constant. The number of tracks per channel is 5, the same as the number used by the double array. Figure 4.8 illustrates a bit slice of PP bits reduced using higher-order arrays. Figure 4.9 presents the layout of a high order array and shows how the subarrays are combined.

Higher-order arrays can be classified according to the number of PPs in each subarray before combining occurs. For example, the (6-6-8-10) high-order array combines two simple arrays that each reduce six PPs using a [4:2] compressor. The resulting structure is combined with a simple array that reduces eight PPs. Finally, the resulting structure is combined with a simple array that sums ten PPs. The difference between the lengths of the subarrays that are combined with the existing structure is two (3, 2) counters, approximately the delay of the [4:2] compressor.

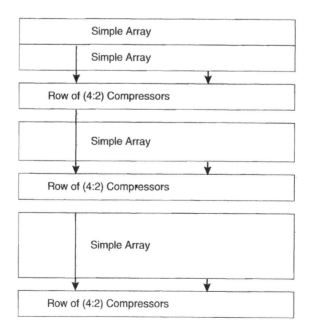

Figure 4.9   General structure of higher-order array.

As an example, consider the (6-6-8) high-order array. The delay for each of the simple arrays that reduce six PPs is four $(3, 2)$ counter delays. When these two simple arrays are combined, the resulting delay is

$$4_{(3, 2) \text{ counters}} + 1_{[4:2] \text{ compressor}} \approx 6_{(3, 2) \text{ counters}}$$

This is connected to the simple array that sums eight PPs and has a delay of six $(3, 2)$ counters. Therefore, the delay of the larger subarray is approximately equal to the delay of the combined subarrays. The delay required to reduce the PPs using higher-order arrays is equal to $\lfloor \sqrt{4N - 9} \rfloor$ (i.e., proportional to $2\sqrt{N}$).

4.2.2 Tree Topologies

Trees are very fast structures for summing PPs. In a tree, counters and compressors are connected differently for each bit slice in the PP parallelogram. The counters and compressors are connected mostly in parallel as shown in Figure 4.10. Although trees are faster than arrays, they both use the same number of counters and compressors to reduce the PPs. The difference is in the interconnections between the counters. Trees create a 3D structure, as can be seen in Figure 4.10. However, integrated circuits are planar; these trees must be flattened to fit in the 2D plane. The flattening is achieved by placing the counters and compressors linearly. The width of each tree is the width of a counter. When the counters and compressors are laid out using this method, the outputs of some counters may be inputs to nonadjacent counters. The outputs of these counters therefore have to pass on top of the

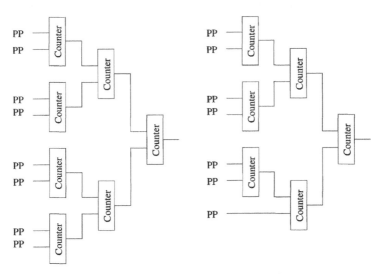

Figure 4.10   Parallel connection of counters in trees.

intermediate counters that lie between the input and the output counters and compressors. The bypassing is achieved by routing the wires that interconnect the counters using the available tracks.

The first trees were the irregular Wallace [190] trees. Wallace showed that PPs could be reduced by connecting $(3, 2)$ counters in parallel in a tree topology.

The Wallace tree topologies have irregular interconnections. Regularity is an important issue in VLSI design. Regular topologies allow a multiplier to be structured from building blocks where the interconnections between the counters are achieved by tiling the building blocks in a consistent pattern. Regular trees have a predictable (or known) number of tracks per channel that is a function of the number of PPs (tree depth). The irregular topology of the Wallace tree makes it difficult to design and lay out.

The complexity of the Wallace tree has caused designers to turn to regular topologies that simplify the design with a slight increase in the number of counter levels over those used by Wallace trees. These regular trees include binary, balanced-delay, and overturned-staircase trees, and [9:2] compressors.

Binary Tree

The first departure from the Wallace tree occurred when Shen and Weinberger [162] introduced the [4:2] compressor in 1978. The [4:2] compressor is the basis for binary-tree multipliers (Weinberger [193]). Using the redundant representation (carry-save) and [4:2] compressors led to a fast, symmetric and regular design.

This binary tree is not to be confused with the binary tree that was built by Takagi et al. [180]. That tree uses the signed-digit number representation to remove the carry propagation from the intermediate steps. The binary trees

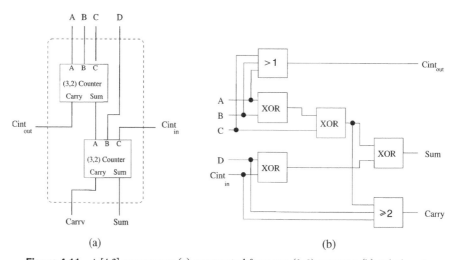

(a)   (b)

Figure 4.11   A [4:2] compressor: (a) constructed from two $(3, 2)$ counters; (b) redesigned.

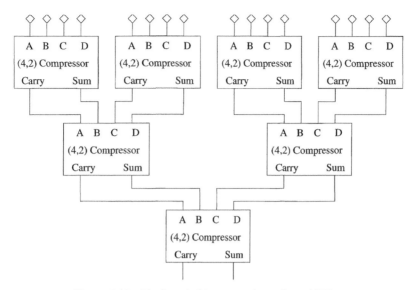

Figure 4.12   Bit slice of a binary tree that reduces 16 PPs.

referred to here are only of the type that was built by Weinberger [193] and by Santoro [148].

While the [4:2] compressor can be built by connecting two $(3, 2)$ counters in series as shown in Figure 4.11(a), that design can be improved on. Toshiba [129] redesigned the [4:2] compressor as a single unit, as shown in Figure 4.11(b). The new design has three XORs in its critical path, rather than the four that result when serially connecting the two $(3, 2)$ counters. This reduces the [4:2] compressor delay by approximately 25%.

Figure 4.12 is a 2D view of a bit slice of the 16-bit binary tree. In this figure the interconnections Cint_{in} and Cint_{out} are not shown. This example of a binary tree is shown in Figure 4.13. Seven rows of [4:2] compressors are used to form the binary tree. In the binary tree, for each four inputs that are reduced, two outputs are produced, which are reduced in the next level.

To construct the physical layout the tree must be flattened. This is accomplished by placing the [4:2] compressors for the tree one adjacent to the other and routing the connections between the compressors across the cells using the available tracks per channel, as shown in Figure 4.14. The tracks used are shown to the side of the bit slice for clarity.

The [4:2] compressor reduces the PPs in logarithmic time, because of its 2-to-1 reduction ratio. A binary tree reduces N PPs using $\lceil \log_2 (N/2) \rceil$ [4:2] compressor stages.

The number of tracks per channel that the binary tree needs to reduce the partial products is a function of the number of PPs N:

$$\text{tracks per channel} = 2\{\lceil \log_2(N) \rceil - 2\} + 4.$$

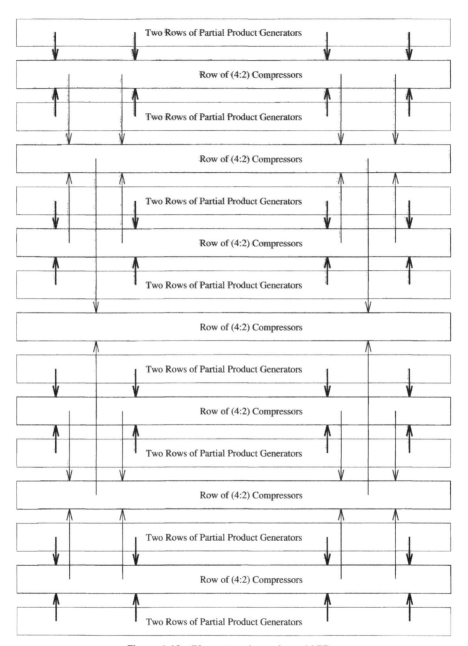

Figure 4.13 Binary tree that reduces 16 PPs.

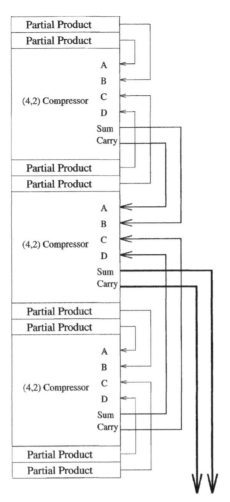

Figure 4.14   8-bit binary-tree bit slice.

Balanced-Delay Tree

The balanced-delay tree was proposed by Zuras and McAllister (ZM) [205]. The ZM tree is a regular tree topology, in which any tree is constructed from a few building blocks.

An example of a ZM tree that reduces 18 PP bits is shown in Figure 4.15. This tree is a balanced-delay tree of type 1 (ZM_1). It is constructed by connecting progressively longer serial chains of $(3, 2)$ counters in a tree. When the delay of the longest chain is equal to the delay of the remainder of the tree a new chain is started.

To reduce the number of $(3, 2)$ counter levels needed to reduce the PPs, higher-order balanced-delay trees can be built by recursively replacing the

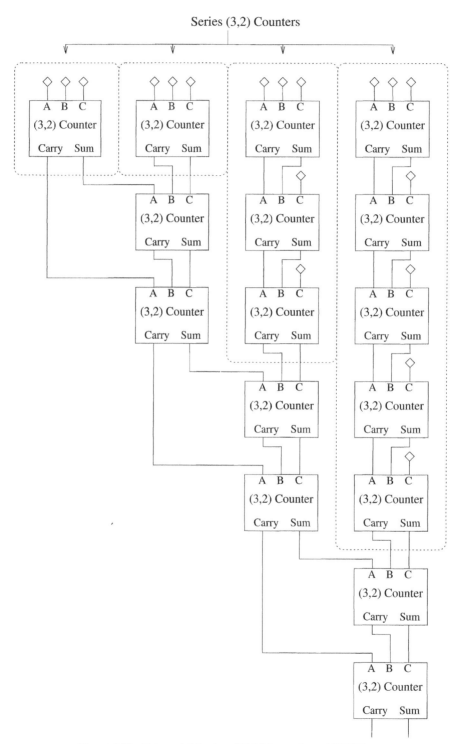

Figure 4.15   Balanced-delay tree (ZM_1) that reduces 18 PP Bits.

serial chains of $(3, 2)$ counters with a balanced-delay tree of type 1. For example, a ZM_2 tree is built by replacing every series chain of counters with ZM_1 trees that have the same delay. The higher the order of the balanced tree, the less regular it is.

The 2D representation of the ZM tree in Figure 4.15 is flattened similarly to the binary tree. This is illustrated in Figure 4.16(a) for a balanced-delay tree that reduces 11 bits. However, an optimization is possible by noticing that the highlighted $(3, 2)$ counters are connected similarly to the [4:2] compressor in Figure 4.11(a) and can be replaced by a [4:2] compressor. This is shown in Figure 4.16(b).

The balanced-delay tree of type 1 reduces the partial products in $O(2\sqrt{N})$ counter stages. The higher-order ZM trees reduce the partial products in $O(kN^{1/(p+1)})$ $(3, 2)$ counter stages, where p is the order of the tree and k is a constant.

The reduction in the number of counter levels by using higher-order ZM trees is achieved by increasing the number of tracks per channel. The number of tracks per channel needed by a balanced-delay tree is a function of the order of the tree. To reduce N PP bits using an order-p ZM tree requires $2p + 3$ tracks per channel.

Overturned-Staircase Tree

The overturned-staircase (OS) tree [133] achieves the same number of $(3, 2)$ counter levels as Wallace for many values of the PPs, but is designed recursively and is thus regular. This tree receives its name because the resulting topology resembles an overturned staircase. The "steps" are obtained from the recursive definition of the tree.

An example of an OS tree that reduces 18 partial products is shown in Figure 4.17. This tree is constructed from a root and the body. The root is the last $(3, 2)$ counter. The body is defined recursively as shown in Figure 4.17. A body of height k, where k is the maximum number of $(3, 2)$ counters in series, is constructed from a body of height $k - 1$ and a branch of serially connected $(3, 2)$ counters. The smaller body and the branch are connected using a *connector*. The connector is made of two $(3, 2)$ counters, each of which takes five inputs and produces three outputs[2].

This recursive method builds an OS tree of type 1. The number of counter levels needed to reduce the partial products can be reduced even further, by increasing the number of tracks per channel used by building a higher-order OS tree. An OS_2 tree is built by replacing each branch in the tree with an OS_1 tree that has the same delay. This method can be further extended to build even higher-order OS trees by replacing the branches in the OS_2 tree with OS_1 trees.

---

[2] The connector is not a counter, because its outputs are not the binary encoding of the inputs. It is not a compressor, either, because it has more than two outputs.

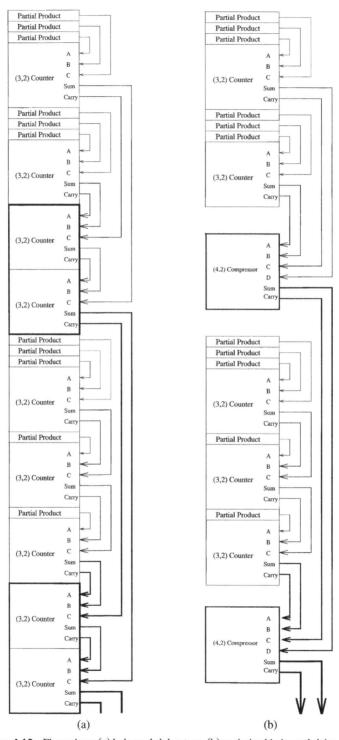

Figure 4.16   Floor plans: (a) balanced-delay tree; (b) optimized balanced-delay tree.

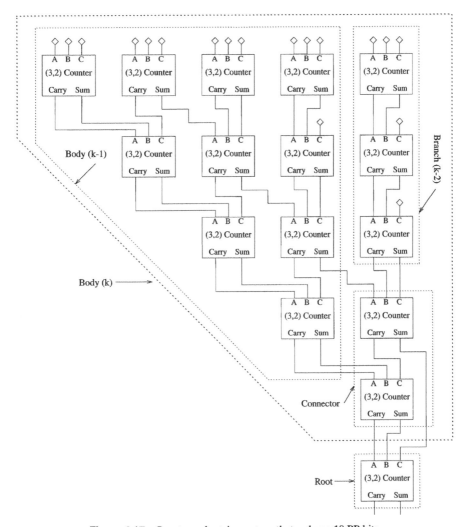

Figure 4.17 Overturned–staircase tree that reduces 18 PP bits.

The 2D representation of the OS tree in Figure 4.17 is flattened using the same method as the other tree topologies, as illustrated in Figure 4.18 for an 11-bit OS tree. The number of tracks per channel required by the OS tree is larger than what is required by a balanced-delay tree. The number of tracks per channel is a function of the order of the tree and is $3p + 3$ for a pth order OS tree.

The OS tree of order 1 reduces N PP bits in

$$\left\lceil \sqrt{2N - 5.75} + \tfrac{1}{2} \right\rceil (3, 2) \text{ counter stages}$$

Generally an OS tree of order p reduces in $O(kN^{1/p+1})$ stages, where p is the order of the tree and k is a constant that is smaller than the constant for an equivalent-order balanced delay tree.

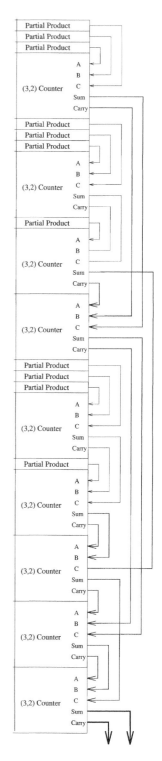

Figure 4.18 Floor plan for an OS tree that reduces 11 PP bits.

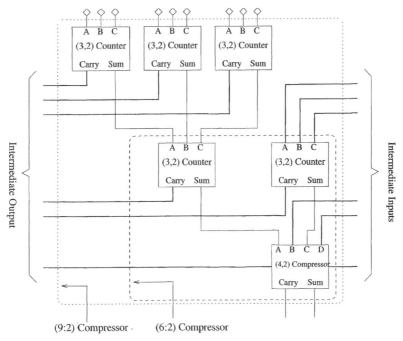

Figure 4.19   [9:2] compressor family.

[9:2] Compressor Family

The [9:2] compressor is a larger compressor that can be constructed from a [4:2] compressor and several (3:2) counters [167]. Figure 4.19 illustrates one possible configuration for connecting the compressor and the counters to build a [9:2] compressor. The figure also shows how a [6:2] compressor is designed. The use of the larger compressors makes the design of the PP reduction tree of the multiplier a modular process in which the larger compressors are designed and then used to reduce the PPs. For example, 27 PPs are first reduced using three [9:2] compressors. These compressors produce six outputs, which are then reduced using a [6:2] compressor.

4.2.3   Effects of the Number of Tracks per Channel

A measure required for all the regular topologies is the maximum number of counters and compressors in the critical path. This does not take into account the number of tracks per channel that each topology uses. The regular topologies reduce the number of counter and compressor stages required in summing the partial products by increasing the number of tracks per channel. The limitation of the number of tracks per channel is related to the availability of the single-rail and dual-rail logic families. The dual-rail logic requires twice as many tracks per channel as the single-rail logic, but is faster

TABLE 4.1 **Number of counter stages for double-precision Booth 2 encoding**

Topology	Stages of Counters
Double linear array	14 (3, 2) counters
Higher-order array	9 (3, 2) counters
Binary tree	4 [4:2] compressors
Balanced-delay tree	9 (3, 2) counters
Overturned-staircase tree	8 (3, 2) counters

than single-rail. Therefore, it is possible for some simple topologies to use dual-rail logic, while other topologies have to use single-rail logic.

The simulations presented were obtained using HSPICE. The results are for the MOSIS 0.8-μm process. The results are for typical process parameters at 25°C. The simulations include the capacitance and resistance of the wires used to connect the counters and compressors. The single-rail logic family used is the pass-transistor logic family. The dual-rail logic family is domino. The results presented here are for an IEEE double-precision Booth 2 encoded multiplier. The significand for double precision is 53 bits summing 27 PPs. The number of counter and compressor stages required is summarized in Table 4.1.

The tree topologies use the fewest counter stages. In fact the OS tree achieves the same number of stages as the irregular Wallace tree [theoretical minimum number of (3, 2) counter stages]. The array topologies use a larger

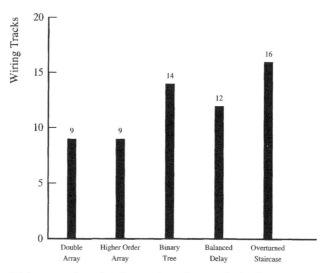

Figure 4.20 Minimum number of tracks per channel to use dual-rail circuits: double-precision Booth 2 encoding.

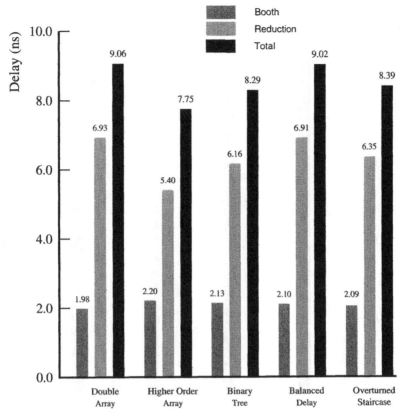

Figure 4.21 Delay and delay compensation for various topologies: 10 tracks per channel, double precision, Booth 2 encoding.

number of counter levels, but use a smaller number of tracks per channel, enabling the use of dual-rail logic circuits. Figure 4.20 shows that the array topologies require only 9 tracks per channel, enabling the use of dual-rail logic. Of the tree topologies, the balanced delay tree required the fewest tracks, followed by the binary tree. The number of tracks required is small because the number of partial products is 27 and the number of tracks that a binary tree needs is related logarithmically to the number of PPs. Finally, the OS tree that achieves the theoretical minimum number of counter stages requires the most tracks per channel.

If the bit pitch is limited to 10 tracks per channel for routing between the counters (Figure 4.21), the higher order array has the smaller latency, since it uses the faster (dual rail) domino logic circuits.[3] Surprisingly, the double

[3]There is a difference between the overall delay and the sum of the Booth encoding and PP reduction delays. This difference is the clock delay used to initiate the evaluation phase in the domino circuits. It can be minimized by careful design.

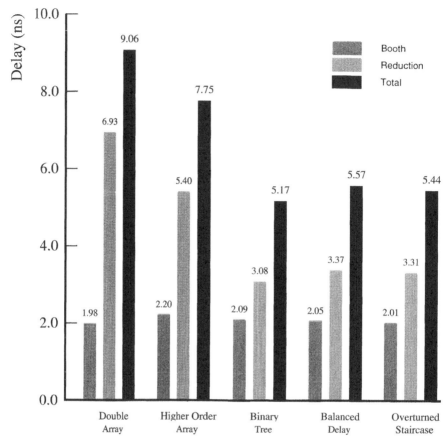

Figure 4.22 Delay for various topologies: 20 tracks per channel, double precision, Booth 2 encoding.

array, which uses double the number of stages that the OS requires, has almost the same delay as the OS. This is because of the difference in circuit latency between the dual-rail and single-rail circuits.

When enough tracks per channel are available for routing for all the topologies, the tree topologies, using dual-rail logic, provide the smallest latency. Among the tree topologies, the binary tree is the fastest (Figure 4.22), since it uses the optimized [4:2] compressor. The total delay for the binary tree is 12 XORs, while the number of XORs in the critical path for the OS tree is $2 \times 7 = 14$ XORs.

The number of counter stages in the critical path is about as important as the number of tracks per channel in determining the latency of the multiplier partial PP reduction. For a small number of tracks per channel, the use of the higher-order arrays and dual-rail circuits provides the smallest latency.

When there is a sufficient number of tracks per channel, the tree topologies and especially the binary tree provide the reduction schemes with the smallest latency.

The number of tracks per channel that tree topologies require increases with the number of PPs. In addition, the increase in the maximum number of counter stages that are required to reduce the PPs for tree topologies and higher-order arrays are similar. Therefore, the effect of the number of tracks per channel is larger when the number of PPs increases.

4.3 IRREGULAR TOPOLOGIES

Irregular topologies connect the counters and compressors in order to minimize the total delay. They do not have a regular pattern for connecting the counters.

4.3.1 Wallace Tree

An example for an 18-bit Wallace tree is given in Figure 4.23(a). Figure 4.23(b) illustrates how the tree is laid out. Wallace trees are irregular in that the informal description does not specify a systematic method for the counter connections. The number of counter stages required by the Wallace tree is proportional to $\log_{3/2} N$. The Wallace tree is irregular and therefore can require a large number of tracks per channel. The number of tracks per channel used is greater than $\log N$.

4.3.2 Algorithmic Generation

The previous topologies use a simple delay model for the counters. In this model the delays from each input to each output of the counter are equal and the delay due to interconnection is ignored. Unfortunately, such simple models do not accurately reflect the performance of actual implementations where not all inputs have the same delay and where the added delay due to interconnect is significant, especially for minimum feature sizes below $0.5~\mu$m.

However, counters and compressors do have different input-to-output delays, which are data-dependent. The delay from an input depends on the values of the other inputs and on the transition it will take ($0 \to 1$, $1 \to 0$).

Designing an optimized PP reduction tree using $(3, 2)$ counters requires taking into account all delay components. Further, organizing the counters in order to minimize worst-case delay is not trivial. Therefore, an algorithmic approach to the design, using a sophisticated delay model that takes into account the interconnect delay due to counter placement and the different path delays, is required.

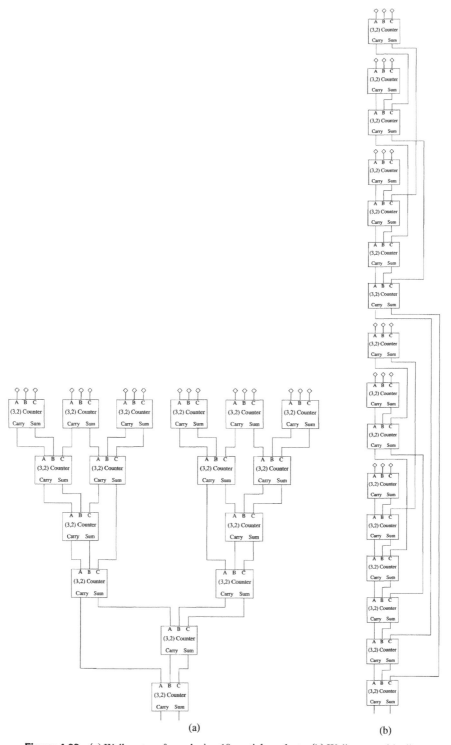

Figure 4.23   (a) Wallace tree for reducing 18 partial products; (b) Wallace-tree bit slice.

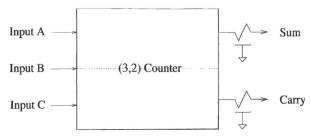

Figure 4.24   A better delay model.

A Better Model

The algorithmic approach uses a delay model, illustrated in Figure 4.24, based upon logic elements in which each input has a different arrival time at the counter. In addition, there is an output delay that is proportional to the length of the wire being driven.

The values for each input–output pair are determined by running HSPICE and characterizing the counter, as is the proportionality constant for the wire delays.

Previous Work

Several algorithms have been developed to aid designers in building the PP reduction tree. Bewick [17] developed a tool that lays out a multiplier in ECL. It compensates for the extra delays caused by the wires by increasing the current to selected gates. This fine tuning is not feasible for CMOS designs, because the current drive in CMOS is related to the transistor widths, and varying the transistor widths affects the previous stages, unlike ECL. Fadavi-Ardekani [47] developed an algorithm that connects the counters in a Wallace tree, and compensates for the different path delays by bypassing stages. This method does not have a separate input–output delay for each pair; rather it uses the simple delay model. Half adders are used extensively in this design. This model also ignores the incremental delays due to wires. Another algorithm was developed by Oklobdzija et al. [130] where the design is based upon the (3, 2) counter. This algorithm takes into account the different delays for the paths, in addition to the different input–output delays. However, it ignores the incremental wiring delay that is caused by the placement of the counters.

A problem with these tools is that they assume routing channels with a virtually unlimited number of tracks per channel for connecting the counters. Therefore, these tools might connect the counters by building trees that require more tracks than are available, and the designs thus obtained cannot be implemented.

Placing a (3, 2) Counter

The goal of the algorithm is to place and connect the counters in a column given a PP generation scheme. Using the available tracks per channel the counters are connected in order to minimize the total delay, producing two rows, sum and carry. These two rows are added together to produce the final result.

At any point during the placement of the $(3, 2)$ counters, there are a number of counter outputs and PP bits that have not been connected. The next counter to be placed is connected to three of the unwired counter outputs or PP bits according to the following heuristic:

- Connect the *fastest* three counter outputs or PP bits to the inputs of the $(3, 2)$ counter. The fastest signal is connected to the counter input with the largest delay. The slowest signal is connected to the counter input with the smallest delay.

- The new counter is placed directly after its last input. Calculate the number of tracks used, by first setting the number of tracks per channel used equal to zero and starting from the PP bit generator that is the farthest from the final CPA in the bit slice. Then, for each PP bit generator or carry wire that is encountered, increment the number of tracks per channel used by one. Whenever a counter is encountered, decrement the number of tracks per channel used by two. After processing each element in the bit slice, the calculated number of tracks per channel is stored in the element.

- If the number of tracks per channel has been exceeded in the element that is directly before the new counter (this element is the counter input that is closest to the final CPA), then:
  - Create a list L of the unconnected counter outputs that occur before the new counter, and then remove this counter.
  - If the list contains at most two elements, connect them and the PP bits. This will create a simple array.
  - Otherwise, connect the fastest three elements in L if their delays are comparable. However, if the latency difference in the delays of the fastest three elements in L is larger than a specified threshold, then the fastest two are connected with a PP bit.
  - Place the new counter after its last input.

In effect this is a greedy algorithm, which repeatedly chooses to add a $(3, 2)$ counter to the fastest path available, thereby equalizing the delays of the different paths. This makes the selection of where to place the next counter simpler.

To reduce the number of tracks per channel used, the algorithm chooses to add the counter to the path that is farthest from the final CPA when given two paths of equal delay.

Placing Half Adders

The algorithm connects a single half adder to the first two PP bits for each bit slice that has an even number of bits [PP bits and carries of the $(3, 2)$ counters from the previous bit slice.] The use of a half adder is necessary because each $(3, 2)$ counter reduces three inputs of weight i and produces a single output sum of the same weight.[4] Therefore, to produce a single output sum s_i for column i, the number of bits in the bit slice has to be odd. The half adder is connected for bit slices with an even number of elements because it removes an element from the bit slice.

The Counter Placement Algorithm

The algorithm starts by reading the high level parameters, such as the length of the multiplier and the encoding scheme used. Separately input to the algorithm is the technology specific information, such as the input–output delays for the $(3, 2)$ counter and the half adder, the number of tracks per channel, and the proportionality constant for the wires.

The algorithm then creates two lists D_i and P_i for each column of the generated PPs. Each element in the delay list D_i consists of two components. The first is the PP bit's name, p_{ij}, which uniquely identifies the element as a PP bit with its column and PP numbers. The second component of each element in D_i is the element's delay. Initially all the PPs are assumed to be available at the same time, and thus this time is set to zero. Each element in the placement list P_i has four components. The first component is the same PP bit's name that is in the delay list D_i. The second is the number of tracks that are in use after the element. The third signals whether the element has been connected to the input of a counter. The final component in P_i comprises the names of its inputs if the element is a counter or half adder. Initially the delay and placement lists are sorted so that for each bit slice the first PP is the first element in the list.

Starting with the bit slice that has the least arithmetic significance, each bit slice i in the PP parallelogram is reduced as follows:

1. If the number of elements in D_i is even and greater than two, then connect a half adder as specified in the previous sub-sub section.
2. The half adder is connected to the first two elements in D_i, and the two new nodes h_{i1} and c_{i1} are created. The delays for the two new nodes are

$$h_{i1} = \max(d_{a-h}, d_{b-h}),$$

$$c_{i1} = \max(d_{a-c}, d_{b-c}),$$

[4]The carry output of the counters has been ignored in this discussion, because the carries are reduced by the column of weight $i + 1$.

where D_i represents the delay for input i, and d_{i-j} represents the delay from input i to output j. The values for d_{i-j} are implementation-specific. They are obtained from running HSPICE, and they depend on the circuit chosen and the available technology.

3. In the placement list mark the inputs of the half adder as connected. Place the inputs names in the interconnection component of h_{i1}.

4. h_{i1} is inserted in D_i and P_i, and c_{i1} is inserted in D_{i+1} and P_{i+1}. Remove the two inputs to the half adder from D_i.

5. If the number of elements in D_i is greater than three, then:

   (a) Sort the elements in D_i in ascending order by the values of the delays and then by the names contained in the elements of the list.

   (b) Connect a counter using the specified heuristic.

   (c) Create two new nodes s_{ij} and c_{ij}. Calculate the delays for the two new nodes, using

   $$s_{ij} = \max(D_a + d_{a-s}, D_b + d_{b-s}, D_c + d_{c-s}),$$
   $$c_{ij} = \max(D_a + d_{a-c}, D_b + d_{b-c}, D_c + d_{c-c}).$$

   (d) In the placement list P_i mark the inputs as connected and place the connection information in s_{ij}.

   (e) Update the delays for the unconnected nodes that occur above the node in the placement list. The nodes are updated to have their delay increased either by the incremental delay that is caused by a counter or by the delay of a counter and the number of PPs the counter has as its inputs.

   (f) Insert the sum node s_{ij} in D_i and P_i; also insert the carry node c_{ij} into D_{i+1} and P_{i+1} at the correct locations. Remove the three nodes that have been connected only from the delay list.

The above steps are repeated until there are only three unconnected nodes.

6. Connect the three remaining nodes using a $(3, 2)$ counter. The outputs of the counter are the inputs for the final CPA. Create two new nodes s_{ij} and c_{ij}. Calculate the delays for the two new nodes, using

   $$s_{ij} = \max(D_a + d_{a-s}, D_b + d_{b-s}, D_c + d_{c-s}),$$
   $$c_{ij} = \max(D_a + d_{a-c}, D_b + d_{b-c}, D_c + d_{c-c}).$$

7. In the placement list P_i, mark the inputs as connected, and place the connection information in s_{ij}. Insert s_{ij} and c_{ij} in a new list that has the final counter delays.

The above process is then repeated for the next column, until all columns have been processed.

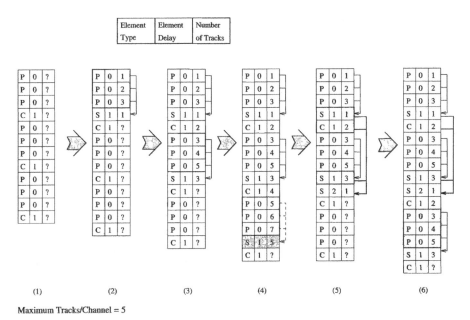

Figure 4.25   The first few steps in reducing a column of PP bits.

Example

An example of how part of a column in a multiplier is reduced is given in Figure 4.25. In this example the delays from each input to each output are equal. Initially the placement list for the column is as shown in step 1, and the number of tracks per channel used is unknown for each element in the placement list. In addition there are some carries in this list. These carries are outputs of $(3, 2)$ counters from the reduction of the previous column. The algorithm always connects the fastest three elements in the delay list.

Whenever there are more than three elements with the same delay, the algorithm connects the elements that occur first in the placement list, as shown in step 2. The number of tracks used is then calculated. Since the number of tracks per channel has not been exceeded, this counter is finalized and its connection is made permanent as shown in step 2. The carry for this counter is inserted in the placement and delay lists for the next column. The exact same process as in step 2 is repeated for step 3.

In step 4, the fastest three elements are connected. Then the number of tracks per channel used is calculated. For this counter, the number of tracks per channel used to connect its inputs has been exceeded. Therefore, this counter is removed. Then the fastest three outputs of previously inserted counters are connected, as shown in step 5. This step causes the number of tracks per channel used to decrease by absorbing the outputs of the previous counters and replacing them with the counter's output. Finally, step 6 is able to connect the elements that were impossible in step 4.

TABLE 4.2   Element input-output delays in XORs

Input		Output	
Technique	Gate	Sum (XOR)	Carry (XOR)
HA	A	1	0.5
	B	1	0.5
CSA	A	2	1
	B	2	1
	C_{in}	1	1

XOR Delay

This sub-sub section uses the number of XOR gates in the critical path as the basis for comparison. The delays from each input to each output are given in Table 4.2. There are no wiring delays associated with these circuits. This delay model is more refined than the simple delay model that is used to design the regular layout. This delay model gives a better approximation for the actual delay of a (3, 2) counter.

The arrival profiles at the inputs of the final adder for two multipliers that are designed using different delay models are shown in Figure 4.26. The

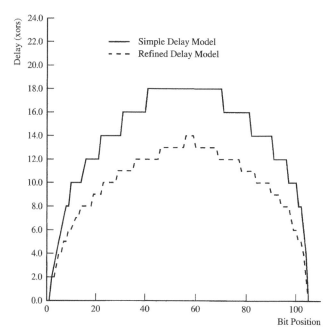

Figure 4.26 Delay using a more refined delay model: 20 tracks per channel, non-Booth, double precision.t

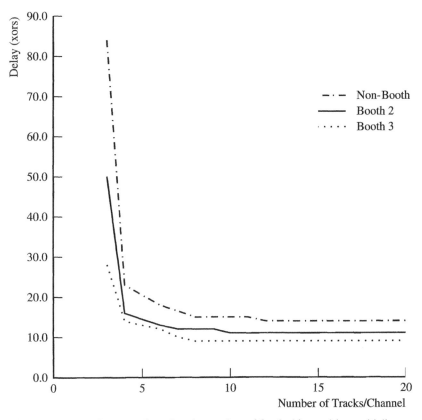

Figure 4.27   Delay vs number of tracks per channel for double-precision multiplier.

figure illustrates the improvement in delay that is achieved by using a more refined delay model. The extra information about the different input–output pair delays is used to hide the extra delay of the long paths. This reduces the total delay of the multiplier from 18 XOR gates to 14 for the same number of tracks.

Figure 4.27 illustrates the tradeoff between the maximum delay of the multiplier and the number of tracks per channel. The figure shows that the tradeoffs between dual-rail and single-rail logic families are still valid. The number of tracks per channel used is of minimal use after a certain number of tracks. The extra tracks may be better used if dual-rail logic is used and half the number of available tracks per channel are used to interconnect the $(3, 2)$ counters. In addition there is minimal gain in increasing the number of tracks per channel used beyond 10.

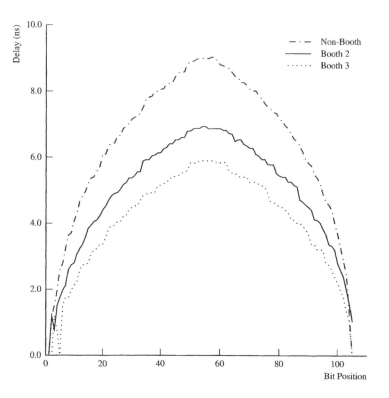

Figure 4.28   Delay vs encoding scheme for double-precision multiplier.

Actual Circuit

To test the algorithm's ability to design a multiplier using actual circuits, the algorithm was given the technology-specific information from the characterization of a double-pass-transistor logic (3, 2) counter [174] that was implemented using MOSIS 0.8 μm.

Figure 4.28 illustrates the arrival profiles for the three most common encoding schemes. The profiles given do not include the encoding delay. The first thing that one notices from the arrival profiles at the inputs is that they are smooth and that there are no steps, in contrast to the previous delay model (XOR delays). The profiles are smooth because of the incremental delay due to the wires. However, the same general shape occurs for both delay models (inputs of the final adder arrive earlier at the ends of the multiplier).

4.4 CONCLUSION

This chapter has presented different methods for connecting the counters and compressors to reduce the PPs. The topologies were classified as either regular or irregular. The regular topologies were compared, and it was proven that the number of counters in series in the critical path is not the determining factor in deciding the latency of the PP reduction. The number of tracks per channel is just as important in determining the latency. The use of topologies (high-order arrays) that allow the use of dual-rail circuits at the expense of more counter stages provides the best performance for a small number of tracks per channel. On the other hand, regular tree topologies provide the smallest latency for regular topologies when sufficient tracks per channel are present.

Then an algorithm for connecting the PPs was presented. The algorithm uses a more advanced delay model for the counter. This model allowed the delay of the multiplier to be reduced compared to the simple model that was used by the regular topologies.

5

TECHNOLOGY SCALING
EFFECTS ON MULTIPLIERS

Based upon work by Hesham Al-Twaijry

Since integrated circuits were invented, fabrication engineers have been able to steadily decrease the dimensions of the devices (transistors). The reduction in minimum feature sizes has contributed to improved performance.

The previous chapter presented the design of the multiplier for a fixed feature size. However, actual device dimensions are decreasing. In addition, the dimensions of the interconnect used to connect the active transistors have also scaled. The decreasing dimensions of the physical devices causes the capacitances and resistances of the different parts of the multiplier to change. Therefore, the relative delay due to each part of the multiplier changes. In addition the encoding schemes used to generate the partial products and the different topologies used in the reduction of the partial products affect the total latency of the multiplier.

This chapter examines the effects of smaller device dimensions on multipliers. As the interconnect becomes more important, generating the partial products (PPs) using an algorithm provides the minimum latency for small feature sizes.

5.1 EFFECTS OF SMALLER FEATURE SIZES

As the feature size decreases to submicron values, supply voltages also decrease. For extremely short submicron channel lengths, the supply voltage can be in the 1–2-V range. Therefore, at these small channel lengths, logic designers cannot use NMOS pass-transistor logic, because of the threshold voltage drops. At these small feature sizes, the logic families that use transmission gates with both NMOS and PMOS transistors operate correctly, given the threshhold voltage drops.

When scaling the dimensions of physical devices from one technology to another, the devices (transistors) are reduced in size, reducing the lengths of the local interconnect (wires) required to connect the transistors. Therefore one would expect that the relative delay due to the devices and interconnect should remain constant. However, wires scale at a slower rate than transistors. In *ideal* scaling, all physical dimensions are scaled equally. The transistor delay goes down by the scaling factor. In contrast, the delay due to ideally scaled wires remains constant, since the wire resistance per unit length grows quadratically as the cross section of the wire is decreased. Therefore, the resistance of each wire increases by the scaling factor. The capacitance per length for wires remains constant. The lengths of the wires decrease by the scaling factor, and therefore the wire capacitance decreases by the scaling factor. Thus, the interconnection RC is constant, so that the wire delay is constant.

However, wires are not scaled ideally, but use quasiideal scaling. If wires scaled ideally, the width, spacing, and wire thickness (and field oxide) would all scale directly as the feature scale factor $s = 1/$(feature size). Quasiideal interconnections scale the wire thickness by $1/\sqrt{s}$, not $1/s$, creating a relatively taller wire with a larger cross section. The net effect of quasiideal scaling of wires is that the wire delay decreases at a rate slower than the scaling factor. Thus, at small feature sizes, wires contribute a larger part of the total delay.

The changes in the relative delays of the devices and the interconnects causes the latencies of the different encoding schemes and topologies to vary with the changing of the feature size.

5.2 WIRE EFFECTS

This section examines the effects of decreasing the dimensions of transistors and wires using the same scaling factor. The wires are scaled using the quasiideal scaling in which the wire height is reduced at a lower rate than the wire length.

The simulations are based upon the scalable SPICE transistor models developed by McFarland and Flynn [107]. The delays are for a 25°C operating temperature. The latencies are calculated from the 50% V_{dd} points. The counters used in the multiplier are all double-pass-transistor logic (DPL) circuits [174].

In the remainder of this chapter, we present relative data to compare various approaches.

Figure 5.1 illustrates the effects of wires on the latency of a Booth 2 encoded binary-tree double-precision multiplier. The figure illustrates the

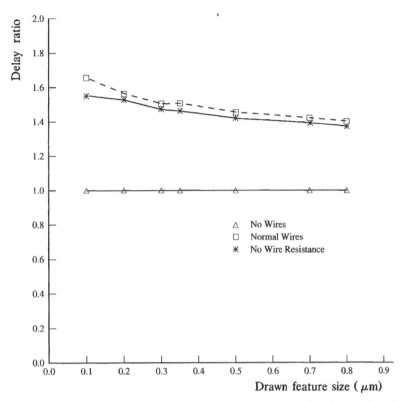

Figure 5.1   Delay of a binary tree relative to its no-wire implementation for Booth 2, double precision.

delay due to wires compared to the same topology without wires (no interconnect delay). The delay due to wires increases at smaller feature sizes. At the 0.1-μm feature size, wires contribute approximately 75% of the overall delay in this IEEE double-precision Booth 2 multiplier.

Even at these deep submicron device sizes, wire capacitance is the significant contributor to the delay of the multiplier. Wire resistance is not a significant portion of the total delay, for two reasons:

1. The wires in multipliers are short and hence the resistance of each wire is small.
2. The wires in multipliers are driven by transistors that have narrow widths. Therefore, the effective resistance of the transistors is large.

These two factors cause the ratio of transistor resistance to wire resistance to be large, and hence insensitive to increases in the wire resistance.

The wire effects on the different encoding schemes are shown in Figure 5.2. In this figure each point is a ratio of the encoding scheme's delay

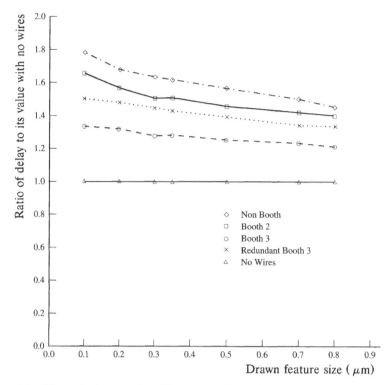

Figure 5.2 Effect of wires on the different encoding schemes for double precision and binary-tree encoding.

to that of the same scheme with no wires. The relative positions of the different curves do *not* reflect the relative delays of the different encoding schemes.

The Booth 3 encoding scheme is the least affected by the incremental wire delay. This is due to two factors:

1. Booth 3 generates the smallest number of partial products, and consequently has the shortest wires.
2. Booth 3 has the largest amount of logic in its critical path, due to the adder that is used to generate the three-times multiple. This extra logic means that there are more transistors in the critical path of the multiplier. Thus, the wire capacitance and resistance are a smaller fraction of the total capacitance and resistance.

Both Booth 2 and non-Booth encoding have approximately the same number of transistors on the critical path. However, wire effects for non-Booth-encoded partial products are larger, because non-Booth encoding has more partial products and therefore longer wires. These longer wires cause the wire capacitance and resistance to be a more significant part of the total capacitance and resistance than for Booth 2.

The effects of wires for redundant Booth 3 encoding closely match those for Booth 3. The only differences are that redundant Booth 3 has longer wires and a slightly smaller number of logic levels. Therefore, redundant Booth 3 is affected by wires to a slightly larger degree than Booth 3.

The wire effects for the procedurally (algorithmically) generated PP reduction tree and the binary tree are shown in Figure 5.3 for a double-precision, Booth 2 encoded multiplier. In this figure each point is a ratio of a topology's delay with wires to that of the same topology without wires. The relative positions of the different curves do *not* reflect the relative delays of the different topologies. The procedural generation was accomplished by the algorithm described in Section 4.3.2 on irregular topologies.

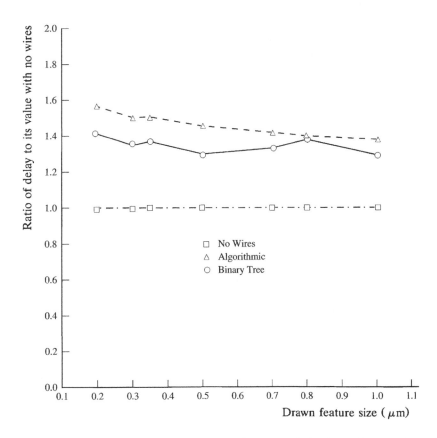

Figure 5.3 Effect of wires on the different PP reduction topologies for double precision and Booth 2 encoding.

TABLE 5.1 Delay of procedural reduction relative to binary tree for 0.3 μm for three encoding schemes

Significand	Relative Delay		
Length (bits)	Non-Booth	Booth 2	Booth 3
Single (24)	0.85	0.85	0.85
Double (53)	0.88	0.85	0.85
Extended (64)	0.96	0.82	0.88
Extended + 4 (68)	0.79	0.77	0.88
Quad (113)	0.95	0.90	0.86

The curve for the procedurally designed PP reduction tree is nonmonotonic. This is because each point for the tree is a different design that is obtained using the delays for the counters and the wires at the corresponding feature size.

The procedurally generated PP reduction tree is affected by wires to the same extent as the binary tree for large feature sizes. However, at the smaller feature sizes, wire delay is a larger part of the total delay. The ability of the procedurally generated trees to hide the extra delay of the long wires using the *fast* input to the output path of the $(3, 2)$ counter causes them to be less affected by wires.

5.3 BINARY TREES VS PROCEDURAL LAYOUTS

The previous section showed that procedurally generated PP reduction trees are less affected by wire delay. In order to determine the performance tradeoffs for the use of regular topologies as opposed to such trees, the regular topology with the minimum latency (i.e., the binary tree) and the irregular procedurally designed trees were simulated for several PP generation schemes, precisions and minimum feature sizes. Some results are shown in Table 5.1.

The absolute performance of the procedurally generated PP reduction tree and that of the binary tree for double-precision non-Booth encoded multipliers are shown in Figure 5.4(a). The relative performance is shown in Figure 5.4(b). The relative performance graph gives a clear comparison between the two reduction schemes. The latency of the binary tree and that of the procedurally generated PP reduction tree are comparable for large feature sizes, where interconnect does not significantly affect the total delay of the binary tree. However, at smaller feature sizes the procedural layouts outperform the binary tree. In addition, the procedural approach is better able to hide the interconnect delay.

The same reasoning applies to multipliers built using Booth 2 encoding for quad precision (113 bits), because the number of partial products is approximately the same in both cases.

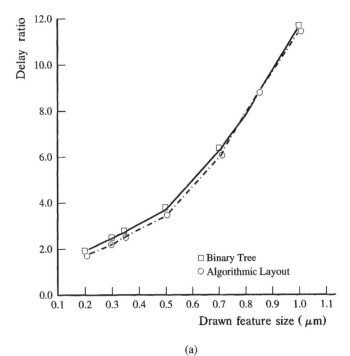

(a)

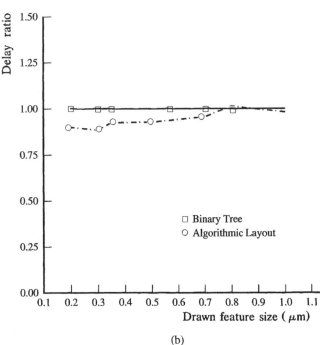

(b)

Figure 5.4 Delay of procedural layout and of binary tree for non-Booth double precision:
(a) absolute; (b) relative.

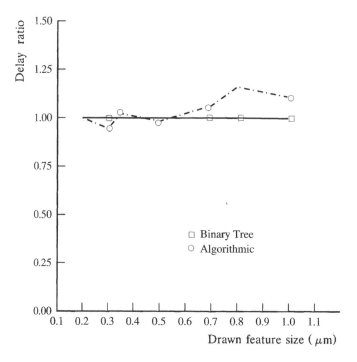

Figure 5.5   Delay of procedural layout relative to binary tree for non-Booth quad precision.

The performance of the procedurally generated PP reduction tree relative to that of binary trees for quad precision non-Booth-encoded multipliers is shown in Figure 5.5. The latency of the binary tree is smaller than that of the procedurally generated arrays for large feature sizes. The quad format has a large number of PPs and therefore requires a larger number of counters in the critical path. However, at smaller feature sizes, interconnect has a significant effect on the total delay. The procedural approach is able to provide comparable latency to the binary tree because of its ability to hide interconnect delay by connecting the slow inputs on the longer wires with the fast inputs for the counters.

Table 5.2 summarizes the performance results from Figures 5.4 and 5.5 along with several other common significand precisions and possible encoding schemes. A tie is declared whenever the relative delays of the encoding schemes are within 3%. The table clearly shows that the procedural approach to the design of the PP reduction tree outperforms the best regular topology.

It is also true that the current form of the procedural approach can be improved. One would expect that the procedural advantage would be monotonically greater at smaller feature sizes. This is not the case in Figure 5.5 when going from 0.3 to 0.2 μm.

TABLE 5.2   Reduction topology choice which minimizes latency across feature sizes for three encoding schemes

Significand	Topology		
Length (bits)	Non-Booth	Booth 2	Booth 3
Single (24)	Procedural	Procedural	Procedural
Double (53)	*Tie* ⇒ procedural	Procedural	Procedural
Extended (64)	*Tie*	Procedural	Procedural
Extended + 4 (68)	Procedural	Procedural	Procedural
Quad (113)	Binary tree ⇒ *Tie*	*Tie* ⇒ Procedural	Procedural

5.4   SCALING EFFECTS ON ENCODING SCHEMES

The previous sections showed that the procedurally generated PP reduction tree provides smaller latency than the best regular topology (binary tree). However, nothing was said about which of the encoding schemes gives the minimum latency as the feature sizes decrease.

This section compares the encoding schemes used to generate the partial products in terms of latency and latency × area. The comparisons are made for several significand sizes and topologies. Some results are shown in Table 5.3.

Figure 5.6 compares the encoding schemes for a double-precision binary-tree multiplier and shows that the Booth 2 encoding provides the minimum latency for the multiplier for all feature sizes. However, at deep submicron feature sizes, Booth 3 is approximately 5% slower while being significantly smaller.

Figure 5.7 compares the encoding schemes for a single-precision procedurally generated PP reduction-tree multiplier. Both non-Booth and Booth 2 encoding schemes provide the minimum latency for the multiplier for all feature sizes. The latency reduction in reducing the number of PP in Booth 2 is offset by the extra latency required for generating the PP.

TABLE 5.3   Latency of encoding schemes relative to Booth 2 for 0.3 μm and two PP reduction methods

Significand	PP Relative Latency			
	Algorithmic		Binary Tree	
Length (bits)	Non-Booth	Booth 3	Non-Booth	Booth 3
Single (24)	1	1.15	0.98	1.12
Double (53)	1.18	1.14	1.14	1.15
Extended (64)	1.25	1.12	1.07	1.04
Extended + 4 (68)	1.22	1.16	1.19	1.02
Quad (113)	1.23	1.13	1.18	1.19

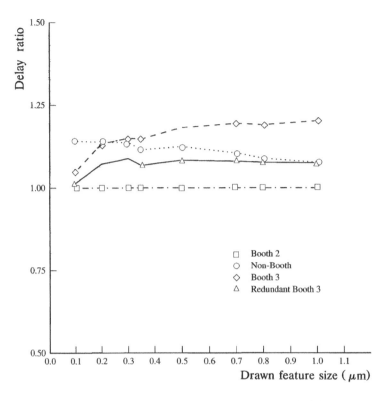

Figure 5.6   Relative delay: encoding schemes for binary tree, double precision.

Table 5.4 summarizes the choice of encoding scheme which results in the minimum latency from Table 5.3 and Figures 5.6, 5.7, along with several other significand sizes. The results are shown for the two choices of reduction topology and for different feature sizes. From this table, as the length of the significand increases, Booth 2 is the choice that minimizes latency. In most cases, the reduction in the number of summands achieved when moving from Booth 2 to Booth 3 encoding is not large enough to offset the extra delay needed to generate the hard (three-times) multiple required for Booth 3. Note that in Table 5.3 the entries are *relative* to Booth 2 entries with the same design parameters. It shows the advantage of Booth 2, but it cannot be used to compare algorithmic and binary tree designs.

5.4.1   Topology

The encoding schemes that minimize latency for all the topologies for double precision multipliers are shown in Table 5.5. As with earlier tables, a tie is recorded whenever the values for the latencies are within 3% of each other.

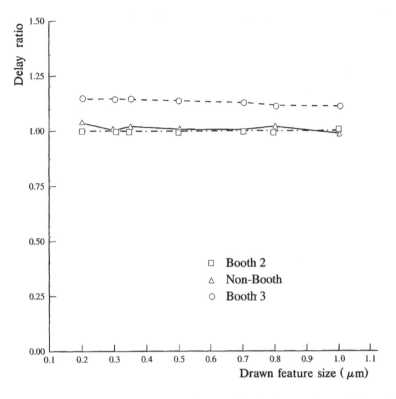

Figure 5.7 Relative delay: encoding schemes for procedurally generated tree, single precision.

TABLE 5.4   Encoding scheme which minimizes latency across feature sizes for two PP reduction methods

Significand Length	Encoding Scheme	
	Procedural	Binary Tree
Single (24)	Non-Booth, Booth 2 (*tie*)	Non-Booth, Booth 2 (*tie*)
Double (53)	Booth 2	Booth 2
Extended (64)	Booth 2	Non-Booth, Booth 2 (*tie*)
Extended + 4 (68)	Booth 2	Booth 2, Booth 3 (*tie*)
Quad (113)	Booth 2	Booth 2

The double linear array, whose latency is directly proportional to the number of PPs, has both Booth 3 and redundant Booth 3 providing the minimum latency. The extra latency for redundant Booth 3 due to the larger number of PPs is offset by the reduction in latency due to not requiring the generation of the three-times multiple.

Redundant Booth 3 provides the minimum latency for the higher-order array, because the latency is related quadratically to the number of partial

TABLE 5.5 Encoding scheme which minimizes latency for double precision and all feature sizes

Topology	Encoding Scheme
Double linear array	Booth 3, redundant Booth 3 (*tie*)
Higher-order array	Redundant booth 3
Binary tree	Booth 2
Balanced-delay tree	Booth 2, redundant Booth 3 (*tie*)
Overturned-staircase tree	Booth 2
Procedurally generated tree	Booth 2

products. Therefore, the reduction in the number of summands for Booth 3 is not as significant as in the linear double array.

For the remaining tree topologies, Booth 2 provides the minimum latency. The only aberration occurs for the balanced-delay tree, which has redundant Booth 3 as well. The balanced-delay tree requires different numbers of counter levels for Booth 2 and for redundant Booth 3. The extra latency due to the difference in the number of counter levels offsets the extra latency in generating the partial products for the redundant Booth 3 encoding scheme.

5.4.2 Area × Time Product

Not all multiplier implementations require minimum latency. For these cases, the areas of the multipliers are also important. The relative areas of the designs are given in Figure 5.8 For single precision, all the encoding schemes have approximately the same area. The reduction in area due to the smaller number of partial products for the Booth encoding schemes is offset by the larger area for the PP generators and, in the case for Booth 3, the three-times adder.

As the significand's size increases, the reduction in area due to Booth encoding is larger. The reduction in area for Booth 2 is 25% compared to non-Booth for quad precision. Area is affected by three factors:

1. Booth 2 reduced the number of PPs compared to non-Booth by about one-half.
2. The PP generators for Booth 2 are larger than those for non-Booth.
3. Extra logic is needed to select the possible values for the PPs (Booth encoders).

Thus, Booth 3 does not reduce the area to a third of what is required by non-Booth. Additionally, Booth 3 requires a dedicated (three-times) adder.

In cases where the minimum latency is not the only criterion for designing the multipliers, Table 5.6 summarizes the choice of encoding scheme that minimizes the latency × area product.

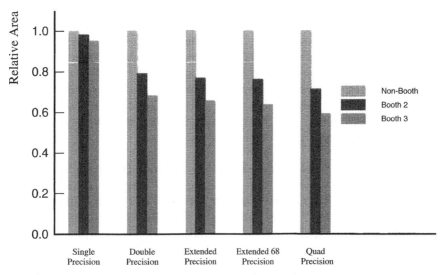

Figure 5.8   Relative areas: procedural tree.

TABLE 5.6   Encoding schemes that minimize latency × area product for all feature sizes and two PP reduction methods

Significand Length	Encoding Scheme	
	Procedural	Binary Tree
Single (24)	Non-Booth, Booth 2 (*tie*)	Non-Booth, Booth 2 (*tie*)
Double (53)	Booth 2, Booth 3 (*tie*)	Booth 2, Booth 3 (*tie*)
Extended (64)	Booth 3	Booth 3
Extended + 4 (68)	Booth 3	Booth 3
Quad (113)	Booth 3	Booth 2

For single precision, both the latency and the area of non-Booth and Booth 2 encoding are approximately the same. As a result, the latency × area product is the same for both. Non-Booth encoding is recommended in this case for its simplicity of implementation. For other precisions, Booth 3 encoded multipliers are 10–15% smaller and 5–20% slower than Booth 2 encoded multipliers.

5.4.3   Pipelining

Pipelined multipliers pose the added problem of partitioning the multiplier into stages, each stage suited to the processor cycle. Processors have diverse cycle-time constraints. Some processors are designed to have fewer long cycles for instruction execution; others use a larger number of fast cycles. In general, if we measure cycle time by the equivalent delay of a serial chain of fanout-4 (FO4) CMOS gates, cycle times vary between 15 and 35 FO4 delays. A double-precision floating-point multiplier requires multiple cycles for execution, with more than 60 FO4 delay units. With pipeline latches as additional overhead, one should expect between 2- and 5-processor-cycle execution latency for such a multiplier, depending on the processor cycle.

Partitioning makes the design decisions significantly more complex, and further research in this area is required. However, we offer the following observations for large, fast multipliers:

1. *Encoding.* Generating the Booth partial products, including the ± 3 multiples, takes about as long as the final carry-propagate addition. This makes Booth 3 (or redundant Booth 3) attractive if PP reduction can be made to fit into a single cycle (i.e., 3-cycle multiples).

2. PP *Reduction.* If the tree must be partitioned, the binary tree has the advantage of predictable, partitioning latch points. These points lie at [4, 2] compressor outputs. On the other hand, as one can think of compressors as consisting of two (3, 2) counters, there are fewer compressors than serial (3, 2) counters. Thus, (3, 2) based Wallace trees offer the most flexibility in latch-point placement.

3. *Overall.* It is usually desirable to keep the final carry propagate as a single stage. If a Booth 3 PP generation cannot be fitted into a single stage (as suggested above), then try Booth 2.

An algorithmically designed Wallace tree offers the most flexibility in tree partitioning, but also is the most complex in design effort. See [2] for some additional comments on tree partitioning.

5.5 POWER

The third component in determining the performance of a multiplier is the amount of power that the multiplier consumes. The power consumption of CMOS circuits can be separated into three parts:

- *Dynamic Charging and Discharging:* This is the power that is used to charge and discharge the circuit capacitances. It can be calculated from

$$P \propto CV^2 f,$$

where C is the capacitance of the circuit (the sum of the transistor capacitances and the interconnect "wire" capacitances), V is the voltage difference in switching from one logic value to the other, and f is the frequency at which the circuit operates.

- *Short Circuit:* This is the short-circuit power that is consumed when the NMOS and PMOS transistors are both in the linear region during switching.
- *Static Leakage:* This is the leakage power due either to not having full voltage swings internally in the circuit, or to the small leakage currents in the off transistors.

Multipliers can be classified by the encoding scheme used to generate the PPs and by the topology used to reduce them.

5.5.1 Encoding Schemes

For a given topology and significand length, each encoding scheme generates a different number of PPs. Therefore, each encoding scheme requires a different number of counters to reduce the PPs. Consequently, the number of transistors used and the lengths of the wires used to connect the counters are different for each encoding scheme.

The first component of the power is the capacitive charging and discharging. The total capacitance of the multiplier is a function of the number of transistors used and the lengths of the wires that are used to interconnect the counters.

Booth 3 encoding has the smallest number of counters, and consequently the smallest number of transistors with the shortest total wire length. Therefore, Booth 3 has the least capacitance and uses the least amount of power for capacitive charging and discharging. Booth 2, which has a larger number of PPs, requires more power, while non-Booth encoding requires the most power. The encoding power usage of redundant Booth 3 for capacitive charging and discharging lies between those of Booth 2 and Booth 3.

For the other two types of power consumption (signal switching and static leakage), the different encoding schemes use approximately the same amount of power. This is because on average all the encoding schemes generate the same number of ones in the PPs. These ones cause approximately the same number of counter outputs to change (causing signal-switching power loss), and the same number of gates to be at the voltage source (causing static leakage).

Therefore, for a given frequency the effect of the encoding scheme used to generate the PPs is that Booth 3 encoding uses the least amount of power.

5.5.2 Topology

For a given encoding scheme and significand size the number of PPs generated is a constant. These PPs require the same number of counters to reduce them for all the topologies. The topologies differ in the interconnections used to connect the counters and therefore in the total wire length used. Since the number of counters is independent of the topology, the number of transistors used and consequently the transistor capacitance are the same for all the topologies. However, tree topologies with their more complex interconnections have longer wires on average and larger wire capacitances. Therefore, tree topologies have more capacitance than arrays. The dynamic charging–discharging power for trees is larger than that for arrays, because of the increase in the capacitance due to the wire length.

The number of ones in the PPs is the same for all the topologies. However, array topologies reduce the PPs serially and on average have more switching power than tree topologies.

The reduction of the power used by the array topologies by virtue of the shorter wires is offset by the extra switching that occurs in the arrays, so that the end result is that the power used by both the topologies is roughly the same. In addition, the static power, which is relatively small, is independent of the topology.

5.6   CONCLUSION

As feature sizes shrink to submicron lengths, wires will contribute a larger portion of the total delay of the multiplier. Wire capacitance will continue to be a significant contributor to the total delay of the multiplier.

The procedurally generated PP reduction tree is less affected by wire delay than is the binary tree. Therefore, the use of an algorithm in the design of the PP reduction tree gives the smallest latency of all the topologies.

Booth 2 encoding provides the minimum latency for almost all the significant sizes and topologies. However, Booth 3 provides the best latency $\times$ area. At the smaller feature sizes, non-Booth is less attractive in terms of delay because of its longer wires.

6

DESIGN ISSUES
IN DIVISION

The theory underlying the implementations of the core arithmetic operations is well documented in the literature. The higher-level effects of different arithmetic implementations has not received the same attention. The SNAP group has investigated several system-level issues in the design of floating-point units.

6.1 INTRODUCTION

Modern applications are often comprised of the FP operations, among them addition, multiplication, division, and square root. In recent FPUs emphasis has been placed on designing ever-faster adders and multipliers, with division and square root receiving less attention. The typical range for addition latency is 2 to 4 cycles, and the range for multiplication is 2 to 8 cycles. In contrast, the latency for double-precision division ranges from 6 to 61 cycles, and square root is often far worse [111]. More emphasis has been placed on improving the performance of addition and multiplication. As the performance gap widens between these two operations and division, FP algorithms and applications have been slowly rewritten to avoid the use of division. Thus, current applications and benchmarks are usually written assuming that division is an inherently slow operation and should be used sparingly.

While the methodology for designing efficient high-performance adders and multipliers is well understood, the design of dividers still remains a serious design challenge, often viewed as a "black art" among system designers. Extensive theory exists, however, for division. Subtractive methods

117

—such as nonrestoring SRT division, which was independently proposed by and subsequently named for Sweeney, Robertson, and Tocher—are described in detail in [8], [29], [42], [123], [181], and [182]. Multiplication-based algorithms such as functional iteration are presented in [5], [56], [61], and [192]. Various division and square-root implementations have been reported in [5], [6], [38], and [196]. However, little emphasis has been placed on studying the effects of FP division on overall system performance.

This study investigates in detail the relationship between FP functional-unit latencies and system performance. The application suites considered for this study included the NAS Parallel Benchmarks [116], the Perfect Benchmarks [36], and the SPECfp92 [169] benchmark suite. An initial analysis of the instruction distribution determined that the SPEC benchmarks had the highest frequency of FP operations, and they were therefore chosen as the target workload of the study to best reflect the behavior of FP-intensive applications.

These applications are used to investigate several questions regarding the implementation of FPUs:

- Does a high-latency division–square-root operation cause enough system performance degradation to justify dedicated hardware support?
- How well can a compiler schedule code in order to maximize the distance between FP result production and consumption?
- What are the effects of increasing the width of instruction issue on effective division latency?
- If hardware support for division and square root is warranted and a multiplication-based algorithm is utilized, should the FP multiplier hardware be shared, or should a dedicated functional unit be designed?
- Should square root share the division hardware?
- What operations most frequently consume division results?
- Is on-the-fly rounding and conversion necessary?

The organization of this chapter is as follows: Section 6.2 describes the method of obtaining data from the applications. Section 6.3 presents and analyzes the results of the study. Section 6.4 is the conclusion.

6.2 SYSTEM-LEVEL STUDY

6.2.1 Instrumentation

System performance was evaluated using 11 applications from the SPECfp92 benchmark suite. The applications were each compiled on a DECstation 5000 using the MIPS C and Fortran compilers at each of three levels of optimization: no optimization (O0), O2 optimization, and O3 optimization. O2 performs common subexpression elimination, code motion, strength reduction, code scheduling, and inlining of arithmetic statement functions. O3 performs all of O2's optimizations, but it also implements loop unrolling and other code-size increasing optimizations [132]. Among other things, varying the level of compiler optimization varies the total number of executed instructions and the distance between a division operation and the use of its result. The compilers utilized the MIPS R3000 machine model for all schedules assuming double-precision FP latencies of 2 cycles for addition, 5 cycles for multiplication, and 19 cycles for division.

In most traditional computer architectures, a close match exists between high-level-language semantics and machine-level instructions for FP operations [69]. Thus, the results obtained on a given architecture are applicable to a wide range of architectures. The results presented were obtained on the MIPS architecture, primarily due to the availability of the flexible program analysis tools *pixie* and *pixstats* [166]. *pixie* reads an executable file and partitions the program into its basic blocks. It then writes a new version of the executable containing extra instructions to dynamically count the number of times each basic block is executed. The benchmarks use the standard input data sets, and each executes approximately 3 billion instructions. *pixstats* is then used to extract performance statistics from the instrumented applications.

6.2.2 Method of Analysis

To determine the effects of a FP operation on overall system performance, the performance degradation due to the operation needs to be determined. This degradation can be expressed in terms of *excess cycles per instruction* (CPI), the CPI due to the result interlock. Excess CPI is a function of the dynamic frequency of the operation, the urgency of its results, and the functional unit latency. The *dynamic frequency* of an operation is the number of times that a particular operation is executed in the application. The *urgency* of a result is measured by how soon a subsequent instruction needs to consume the result. To quantify the urgency of results, interlock distances were measured for division results. The *interlock distance* is the distance between the production of a division result and its consumption by a subsequent instruction. It is clear that the dynamic frequency is solely a function of the application, urgency is a function of the application and the compiler, and functional unit latency depends upon the hardware implementation. The system designer has the most control over the functional unit latency. Through careful design of the processor architecture, though, the designer has some limited influence on the urgency. Adding extra registers and providing for out-of-order instruction execution are two means by which the system designer can influence urgency.

6.3 RESULTS

6.3.1 Instruction Mix

Figure 6.1 shows the average frequency of division and square-root operations in the benchmark suite relative to the total number of FP operations,
where the applications have been compiled using O3 optimization. This
figure shows that simply in terms of dynamic frequency, division and square
root seem to be relatively unimportant instructions, with about 3% of the
dynamic FP instruction count due to division and only 0.33% due to square
root. The most common instructions are FP multiply and add. It should be
noted that add, subtract, move, and convert operations typically utilize the
FP adder hardware. Thus, FP multiply accounts for 37% of the instructions,
and the FP adder is used for 55% of the instructions. However, in terms of
latency, division can play a much larger role. By assuming a machine model
of a scalar processor, where every division operation has a latency of
20 cycles and the adder and multiplier each have a 3-cycle latency, a distribution of the stall time due to the FP hardware was formed, also shown in
Figure 6.1. Here, FP division accounts for 40% of the latency, FP add
accounts for 42% and multiply accounts for the remaining 18%. It is
apparent that the performance of division is significant to the overall system
performance.

6.3.2 Compiler Effects

In order to analyze the effect that the compiler can have on improving system
performance, the urgency of division results was measured as a function of
compiler optimization level. Figure 6.2 shows a histogram of the interlock
distances for division instructions at O0, as well as a graph of the cumulative

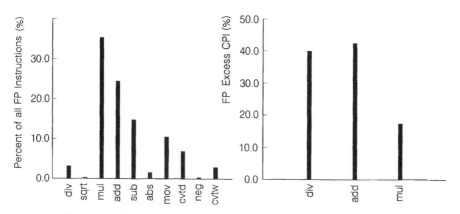

Figure 6.1   Instruction-count and functional-unit stall time distributions.

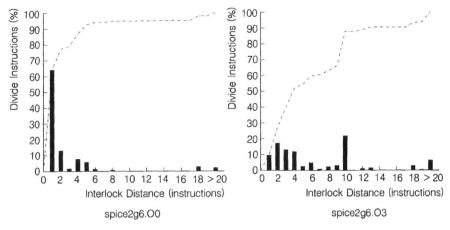

Figure 6.2 SPICE with optimizations O0 and O3.

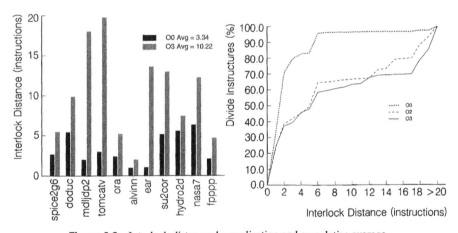

Figure 6.3 Interlock distances by application and cumulative average.

interlock distance for the SPICE benchmark. Figure 6.2 also shows the same data when compiled at O3. Figure 6.3 shows the average interlock distances for all of the SPEC applications at both O0 and O3 levels of optimization. It is clear that by intelligent scheduling and loop unrolling, the compiler is able to expose instruction-level parallelism in the applications, decreasing the urgency of division results. Figure 6.3 shows that the average interlock distance can be increased by a factor of three by compiler optimization. An average of the division interlock distances from all of the benchmarks was formed, weighted by division frequency in each benchmark.

The distribution result is also shown in Figure 6.3 for the three levels of compiler optimization. In this graph, the curves represent the cumulative

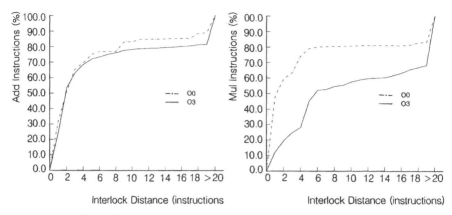

Figure 6.4   Cumulative average add and mul interlock distances.

percentage of division instructions at each distance. The results from Figure 6.3 show that the average interlock distance can be increased to approximately 10 instructions only. Even if the compiler assumed a larger latency, there is little parallelism left to exploit that could further increase the interlock distance and thereby reduce excess CPI. If the compiler scheduled instructions assuming a low latency, the excess CPI could only increase for dividers with higher latencies than that for which the compiler scheduled. This is because the data shows the maximum parallelism available when scheduling for a latency of 19 cycles. If the compiler scheduled for a latency much less than 19 cycles, then it would not be as aggressive in its scheduling, and the interlock distances would be smaller, increasing urgency and therefore excess CPI.

The results for division can be compared with those of addition and multiplication, shown in Figure 6.4.

6.3.3 Performance and Area Tradeoffs

The excess CPI due to division is determined by summing all of the stalls due to division interlocks, which is the total penalty, and dividing this quantity by the total number of instructions executed. The performance degradation due to division latency is displayed in Figure 6.5. This graph shows how the excess CPI due to the division interlocks varies with division-unit latency between 1 and 20 cycles for O3 optimization. Varying the optimization level also changed the total number of instructions executed, but left the number of division instructions executed constant. As a result, the fraction of division instructions is also a function of optimization level. While the CPI due to division actually increases from O0 to O2, the overall performance at O2 and O3 increases because the total instruction count decreases. This effect is summarized in Table 6.1, where the division latency is taken to be 20 cycles.

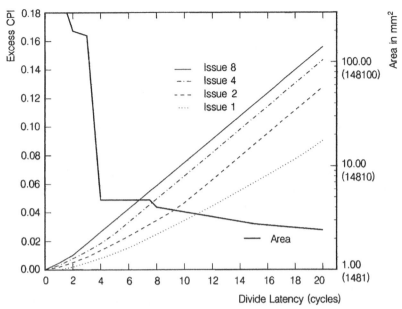

Figure 6.5 CPI and area vs division latency—low latency.

TABLE 6.1 **Effects of compiler optimization**

Opt. Level	Div. Freq.	Excess CPI
O0	0.33	0.057
O2	0.76	0.093
O3	0.79	0.091

Figure 6.5 also shows the effect of increasing the number of instructions issued per cycle on excess CPI due to division. To determine the effect of varying instruction issue rate on excess CPI due to division, a model of an underlying architecture must be assumed. In this study, an optimal super-scalar processor is assumed, such that the maximum issue rate is sustainable. This model simplifies the analysis while providing an upper bound on the performance degradation due to division. The issue rate is used to appropriately reduce the interlock distances. As the width of instruction issue increases, the urgency-of-division data increases proportionally. In the worst case, every division-result consumer could cause a stall equal to the functional-unit latency. The excess CPI for the multiple-issue processors is then calculated using the new interlock distances.

Figure 6.5 also shows how the area increases as the functional-unit latency decreases. The estimation of area is based on reported layouts [125, 196, 202], all of which have been normalized to 1.0-μm scalable CMOS layout rules. As division latencies decrease below 4 cycles, a large tradeoff must be made. Either a very large area penalty must be incurred to achieve this latency by utilizing a very large lookup table, or large cycle times may result if an SRT method is utilized.

In order to make the comparison of chip areas technology independent, the register bit equivalent (rbe) model of Mulder et al. [114] was used. In this model, one rbe equals the area of a one-bit storage cell. For the purposes of this study, an rbe unit is referenced to a six-transistor static cell, with an area of $675f^2$, where f is the minimum feature size. The area required for one static RAM bit, as would be used in an on-chip cache, is about 0.6 rbe. Since all areas are normalized to an $f = 1.0$-μm process, 1 mm^2 = 1481 rbe.

Figure 6.6 shows excess CPI versus division latency over a larger range of latencies. This graph can roughly be divided into five regions. Table 6.2 shows that inexpensive 1-bit SRT schemes use little area but can contribute in the worst case up to 0.50 CPI in wide-issue machines. Increasing the radix of SRT implementations involves an increase in area, but with a decrease in excess CPI. The region corresponding to 4-bit SRT schemes also represents the performance of typical multiplication-based division implementations, such as Newton–Raphson or series expansion [38]. The additional area required in such implementations is difficult to quantify, as implementations

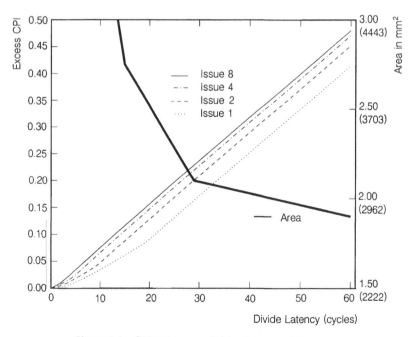

Figure 6.6 CPI and area vs division latency—full range.

TABLE 6.2   Five regions of division latency

Divider Type	Latency (cycles)	Excess CPI	Area (rbe)
1-Bit SRT	> 40	< 0.5	< 3000
2-Bit SRT	[20, 40]	[0.10, 0.32]	3110
4-Bit SRT	[10, 20]	[0.04, 0.10]	4070
8-Bit SRT and Self-timed	[4, 10]	[0.01, 0.07]	6665
Very-high radix	< 4	< 0.01	> 100,000

to date have shared existing multipliers, adding control hardware to allow for the shared functionality. At a minimum, such implementations require a starting approximation table that provides at least an 8-bit initial approximation. Such a table occupies a minimum of 2 Kbit, or 1230 rbe. The final region consists of very high radix dividers of the form presented in [45] and [202]. To achieve this performance with CPI < 0.01, large area is required for very large lookup tables, often over 500,000 rbe.

To better understand the effects of division latency on the system performance of multiple-issue processors, the excess CPI due to division can be expressed as a percentage of the base-processor CPI. Figure 6.7 shows this relationship quantitatively. As the instruction width increases, the degradation of system performance increases markedly. Not only does increasing the width of instruction issue reduce the average interlock distance, but the penalty for a division interlock relative to the processor issue rate dramatically increases. A slow divider in a wide-issue processor can easily reduce system performance by half.

6.3.4   Shared-Multiplier Effects

If a multiplication-based division algorithm is chosen, such as Newton–Raphson or series expansion, one must decide whether to use a dedicated multiplier or to share the existing multiplier hardware. The area of a well-designed 3-cycle FP multiplier is around 11 mm^2, again using the 1.0-μm process. Adding this much area may not be always desirable. If an existing multiplier is shared, this will have two effects. First, the latency through the multiplier will likely increase due to the modifications necessary to support the division operation. Second, multiply operations may be stalled due to conflicts with division operations sharing the multiplier.

The effect of this structural hazard on excess CPI is shown in Figure 6.8. The results are based on an average of all of the applications when scheduled

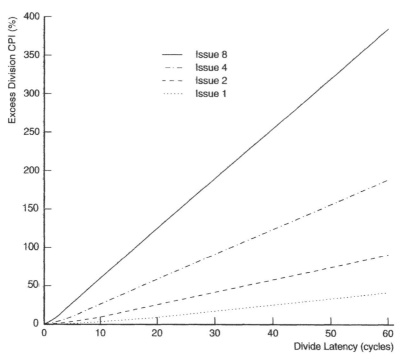

Figure 6.7   Excess CPI as a percentage of base CPI for multiple-issue processors.

with O3. In all cases for a division latency less than 20 cycles, the excess CPI is less than 0.07. For reasonable implementations of multiplication-based division, with a latency of approximately 13 cycles, the actual penalty is $0.02 < CPI < 0.04$. For these applications, due to the relatively low frequency of division operations, the penalty incurred for sharing an existing multiplier is not large. For special classes of applications, such as certain graphics applications, division and multiplication frequencies could be higher, requiring a separate division unit to achieve high performance.

6.3.5   Shared Square Root

The recurrence equation for square root is very close in form to that of division for both subtractive and multiplicative algorithms. Accordingly, division hardware can be implemented with additional functionality to perform square-root computation. The design tradeoff then becomes whether a possi-

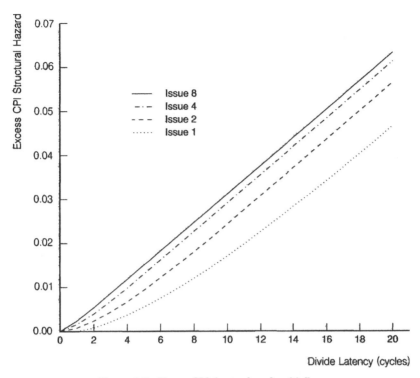

Figure 6.8   Excess CPI due to shared multiplier.

ble increase in hardware complexity and/or cycle time can be justified by an increase in overall performance.

The results of this study show that FP square root on the average accounts for 0.087% of all executed instructions. This is a factor of 9.1 less than division. To avoid significant performance degradation due to square root, the latency of square root should be no worse than a factor 9.1 greater than division. However, any hardware implementation of square root will more than likely meet the requirement of this bound. Even a simple 1-bit-per-itera-tion square root would contribute only 0.05 CPI for a scalar processor. Accordingly, these results suggest that the square-root implementation does not need to have the same radix as the divider, and the sharing of division hardware is not crucial to achieving high system performance. Only if the additional area is small and the cycle-time effect is negligible should division and square root share the same hardware.

6.3.6   On-the-Fly Rounding and Conversion

In a nonrestoring division implementations such as SRT, an extra cycle is often required after the division operation completes. In SRT, the quotient is

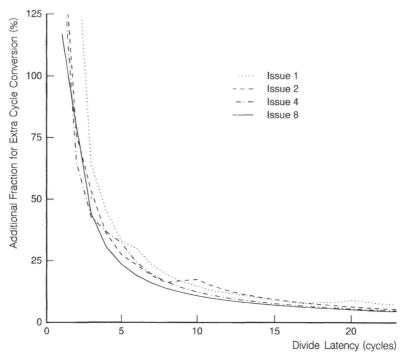

Figure 6.9 Effects of on-the-fly rounding and conversion.

typically collected in a representation where the digits can take on both positive and negative values. Thus, at some point, all of the values must be combined and converted into a standard representation. This requires a full-width addition, which can be a slow operation. To conform to the IEEE standard, it is necessary to round the result. This, too, can require a slow addition.

Techniques exist for performing this rounding and conversion on-the-fly, and the extra cycle may not be needed [42]. Because of the complexity of this scheme, the designer may not wish to add the additional required hardware. Figure 6.9 shows the consequence for performance of requiring an additional cycle after the division operation completes. For division latencies greater than 10 cycles, less than 20% of the total division penalty in CPI is due to the extra cycle. At very low division latencies (less than or equal to 4 cycles), the penalty for requiring the additional cycle is obviously much larger, often greater than 50% of the total penalty.

6.3.7 Consumers of Division Results

In order to reduce the effective penalty due to division, it is useful to look at which operations actually use division results. Figure 6.10 is a histogram of

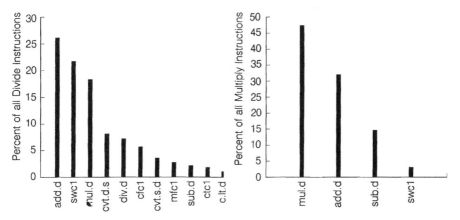

Figure 6.10   Consumers of division and multiply results.

instructions that consume division results. This can be compared with the histogram for multiply results, also in Figure 6.10. For multiply results, the biggest users are multiply and add instructions. It should be noted that both add.d and sub.d use the FP adder. Thus, the FP adder is the consumer for nearly 50% of the multiply results. Accordingly, fused operations such as multiply–accumulate are reasonable. Because the multiply–add pattern occurs frequently in such applications and it does not require much more hardware than the separate functional units, fused multiply–adders are often used in modern processors.

Looking at the consumers of division results, the FP adder is the largest consumer, with 27% of the results. The second biggest consumer is the store operation, with 23% of the results. It is possible to overcome the penalties due to a division–store interlock, though, with other architectural implementations. A typical reason why a store would require a division result and cause an interlock is register pressure due to a limited number of registers. By either adding or renaming registers, it may be possible to reduce the urgency due to store.

While the percentage of division results that the adder consumes is not as high as that of multiply results, the former are still large in number. A designer could consider the implementation of a fused divide–add to increase performance. In division implementations where on-the-fly conversion and rounding is not used, an extra addition cycle exists for this purpose. It may be possible to make this a three-way addition, with the third operand coming from a subsequent add instruction. Because this operand is known soon after the instruction is decoded, it can be sent to the three-way adder immediately. Thus, a fused divide–add unit could provide additional performance.

6.4 CONCLUSION

This study has investigated the issues of designing an FP divider in the context of an entire system. The frequency and interlock distance of division instructions in SPECfp92 benchmarks have been determined, along with other useful measurements, in order to answer several questions regarding the implementation of an FP divider.

The data shows that for the slowest hardware divider, with a latency greater than 60 cycles, the CPI penalty can reach 0.50. This indicates that to achieve reasonable system performance, some form of accelerated hardware division is required. However, at very low divider latencies, two problems arise: the area required increases exponentially or the cycle time becomes impractical. This study shows a knee in the area–performance curve near 10 cycles. Dividers with lower latencies do not provide significant system performance benefits, and their areas are too large to be justified.

The results show the compiler's ability to decrease the urgency of division results. Most of the performance gain is in performing basic compiler optimizations, at the level of O2. Only marginal improvement is gained by further optimization. The average interlock distance increases by a factor of three by using compiler optimization. Accordingly, for scalar processors, this study shows that a division latency of 10 cycles or less can be tolerated.

It is clear that increasing the number of instructions issued per cycle also increases the urgency of division results. On the average, increasing the number of instructions issued per cycle to 2 causes a 38% increase in excess CPI, increasing it to 4 causes a 94% increase in excess CPI, and increasing it to 8 causes a 120% increase in excess CPI. Further, as the width of instruction issue increases, the excess CPI due to division expressed as a percentage of base CPI increases even faster. Wide-issue machines utilize the instruction-level parallelism in applications by issuing multiple instructions every cycle. While this has the effect of decreasing the base CPI of the processor, it exposes the functional-unit latencies to a greater degree and accentuates the effects of slow functional units.

In most situations, an existing FP multiplier can be shared when using a multiplication-based division algorithm. The results show that for a division latency of around 13 cycles, the CPI penalty is between 0.025 and 0.040. Thus, due to the low frequency of division operations combined with the low frequency of multiply instructions that occur in between the division result's production and its consumption, the structural hazard is also very infrequent. While the CPI penalty is low when the multiplier is shared and modified to also perform division, the designer must also consider latency effects through the multiplier, which could have an effect on the cycle time.

On-the-fly rounding and conversion is not essential for all division implementations. For division latencies greater than 10 cycles, the lack of on-the-fly rounding and conversion does not account for a significant fraction of the excess CPI, and thus is not necessarily required. However, for very high-radix implementations where the area and complexity are already large, this method is a practical means of further reducing division latency.

Addition and store operations are the most common consumers of division results. Accordingly, the design of a fused divide–add unit is one means of achieving additional system performance.

While division is typically an infrequent operation even in FP-intensive applications, ignoring its implementation can result in system performance degradation. By studying several design issues related to FP division, this chapter has attempted to clarify the important tradeoffs in implementing an FP divider in hardware.

7

MINIMIZING THE COMPLEXITY OF SRT TABLES

An important component of the floating-point unit is the divider. There are many methods for designing division hardware, including quadratically converging algorithms, such as Newton–Raphson, and linearly converging algorithms, the most common of which is SRT [124]. SRT division computes a quotient one digit at a time, with an iteration time independent of the operand length. Newton–Raphson division converges to the quotient quadratically, doubling the number of retired bits after every iteration. The SNAP group has investigated several techniques to increase the performance of linearly converging division implementations.

There are many performance and area tradeoffs when designing an SRT divider. One metric for comparison of different designs is the minimum required truncations of the divisor and partial remainder for quotient-digit selection. Atkins [8] and Robertson [144] provide such analyses of the divisor and partial-remainder precisions required for quotient-digit selection. Burgess and Williams [29] present in more detail allowable truncations for divisors and both carry-save and borrow-save partial remainders. However, a more detailed comparison of quotient-digit selection complexity between different designs requires more information than the input precision. This chapter analyzes in detail the effects of algorithm radix, redundancy, divisor and partial-remainder precision, and truncation error on the complexity of the resulting table. Complexity is measured by the number of product terms in the final logic equations, and the delay and area of standard-cell implementations of the tables. These metrics are obtained by an automated design flow using the specifications for the quotient-digit selection table as input, a Gray-coded programmed logic array (PLA) as an intermediate representation, and an LSI Logic 500K standard-cell implementation as the output.

This chapter also examines the effects of additional techniques such as table folding and longer external carry-assimilating adders on table complexity. Using the methodology presented, it is possible to automatically generate optimized high-radix quotient-digit selection tables.

7.1   THEORY OF SRT DIVISION

SRT division belongs to the digit-recurrence class of division algorithms. Digit-recurrence algorithms use subtractive methods to calculate quotients, one digit per iteration. Such algorithms can be divided into *restoring* and *nonrestoring* division. Restoring division is similar to the familiar paper-and-pencil algorithm. When dividing two n-digit numbers, the division can require up to $2n$ additions or subtractions. Nonrestoring division algorithms eliminate the restoration cycles, and thus only require up to n additions. This can be accomplished by allowing negative values of the quotient as well as positive values. In this way, small errors in one iteration can be corrected in subsequent iterations.

7.1.1   Recurrence

In SRT division, the quotient can be computed as follows:

$$q = \frac{\text{dividend}}{\text{divisor}}.$$

This expression can be rewritten as

$$\text{dividend} = q \times \text{divisor} + \text{remainder}$$

such that

$$|\text{remainder}| < |\text{divisor}| \times \text{ulp} \quad \text{and} \quad \text{sign}(\text{remainder}) = \text{sign}(\text{dividend}),$$

where the input operands are given by the dividend and divisor, and the results are q and the remainder. The precision of the quotient is defined by the unit in the last position (ulp), where for an integer quotient ulp $= 1$, and for a fractional quotient using a binary representation ulp $= 2^{-n}$, assuming an n-digit quotient. The *radix r* of the algorithm, typically chosen to be a power of 2, determines how many quotient bits b are retired in each iteration, such that $r = 2^b$. Accordingly, a radix-r algorithm requires $\lfloor n/b \rfloor$ iterations to compute an n-digit quotient.

The following recurrence is used at every iteration:

$$rP_0 = \text{dividend}, \tag{7.1}$$

$$P_{j+1} = rP_j - q_{j+1}\text{divisor}, \tag{7.2}$$

where P_j is the partial remainder, or residual, at iteration j.

In each iteration, one digit of the quotient is determined by the quotient-digit selection function:

$$q_{j+1} = \text{SEL}(rP_j, \text{divisor}). \qquad (7.3)$$

In order for the next partial remainder P_{j+1} to be bounded, the value of the quotient digit is chosen such that

$$|P_{j+1}| < \text{divisor}. \qquad (7.4)$$

The final quotient is the weighted sum of all of the quotient digits selected throughout the iterations:

$$Q_{\text{final}} = \sum_{j=1}^{n/b} q_j r^{-j}. \qquad (7.5)$$

As can be noted from equations (7.1) and (7.2), each iteration of the recurrence comprises the following steps:

- Determine the next quotient digit q_{j+1} by the quotient-digit selection function.
- Generate the product $q_{j+1} \times$ divisor.
- Subtract q_{j+1} divisor from rP_j to form the next partial remainder.

Each of these components can contribute to the overall cost and performance of the algorithm. To reduce the time for partial-remainder computation, intermediate partial-remainders are often stored in a redundant representation, either carry-save or signed-digit form. Then, the partial remainder computation requires only a full adder delay, rather than a full-width carry-propagate addition. The rest of this chapter is concerned with the quotient-digit selection component.

7.1.2 Choice of Radix

The fundamental method of decreasing the overall latency (in machine cycles) of the SRT algorithm is to increase the radix r of the algorithm. On choosing the radix to be a power of 2, the product of the radix and the partial remainder can be formed by shifting. Accordingly, throughout this study, only power-of-2 radices are considered. Assuming the same quotient precision, the number of iterations of the algorithm required to compute the quotient is reduced by a factor of k when the radix is increased from r to r^k. For example, a radix-4 algorithm retires 2 bits of quotient in every iteration. Moving to a radix-16 algorithm will allow for retiring 4 bits in every iteration, for a $2 \times$ reduction in latency.

This reduction does not come free. As the radix increases, the quotient-digit selection becomes more complex. Since the quotient-digit selection is typically on the critical path of the algorithm, even though the number of cycles may have been reduced due to the increased radix, the time per cycle may have increased. As a result, the total time required to compute an n-bit quotient may not be reduced by the factor k. Accordingly, the radix r is a fundamental parameter in determining the complexity of the quotient-digit selection table.

7.1.3 Choice of Quotient-Digit Set

A range of digits is decided upon for the allowed values of the quotient in each iteration. The simplest case is where, for radix r, there are exactly r allowed values of the quotient. However, it is often desirable to utilize a *redundant digit set* which simplifies the quotient-digit selection table, thereby increasing the performance of the divider. Such a digit set can be composed of symmetric signed-digit consecutive integers, where the maximum digit is a. Namely,

$$q_j \in \mathscr{D}_a = \{-a, -a+1, \ldots, -1, 0, 1, \ldots, a-1, a\}.$$

The redundancy of a digit set is determined by the value of the redundancy factor ρ, which is defined as

$$\rho = \frac{a}{r-1}, \qquad \rho > \frac{1}{2}. \tag{7.6}$$

For all partial remainders to be bounded when a redundant quotient digit set is used, the value of the quotient digit must be chosen so that

$$|P_{j+1}| < \rho \times \text{divisor}. \tag{7.7}$$

The calculation of the final quotient using a redundant quotient-digit set involves either a full carry-propagate addition to subtract the negative quotient digits from the positive quotient digits at the completion of the iterations, or the use of on-the-fly quotient conversion techniques [42].

After the redundancy factor ρ is chosen, it is possible to derive the quotient-digit selection function. To guarantee that the shifted partial remainder remains bounded for all valid quotient digits and divisors, expressions for the quotient-digit selection intervals must be computed. A *selection interval* is the region in which a particular quotient-digit can be safely chosen so that the shifted partial remainder will remain bounded. The expressions for the selection intervals are given by

$$U_k = (\rho + k)d, \qquad L_k = (-\rho + k)d,$$

where U_k (L_k) is the largest (smallest) value of rP_j such that it is possible to choose $q_{j+1} = k$ and still keep the next shifted partial remainder bounded. The *continuity condition* requires that for all valid values of rP_j, it must be possible to select at least one quotient digit [42]. This is expressed mathematically as

$$U_{k-1} \geq L_k - r^{-n}. \tag{7.8}$$

Because rP_j is represented by a maximum of n bits, the term r^{-n} is the resolution of the partial remainder.

The *P–D diagram* is a useful visual tool when designing a quotient-digit selection function. It has as axes the shifted partial remainder and the divisor. The selection-interval bounds U_k and L_k are drawn as lines starting at the origin with slope $\rho + k$ and $-\rho + k$, respectively. A P–D diagram is shown in Figure 7.1 with $r = 4$ and $a = 2$. The shaded regions are the overlap regions where more than one quotient-digit may be selected.

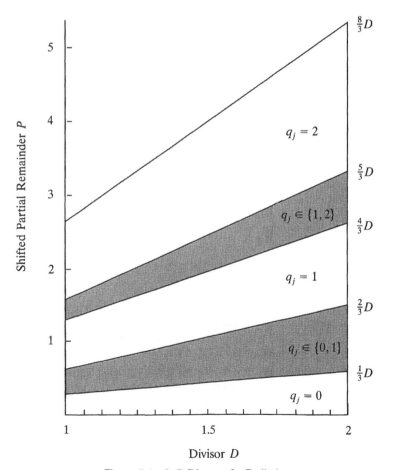

Figure 7.1   *P–D* Diagram for Radix 4.

7.2   IMPLEMENTING SRT TABLES

7.2.1   Divisor and Partial-Remainder Estimates

To reduce the size and complexity of the quotient-digit selection table for a given choice of r and a, it is desirable to use as input to the table estimates of the divisor and shifted partial remainder which have fewer bits than the true values. Assuming IEEE FP compliance, the input operands are in the range $1 \leq D < 2$. Therefore, n-bit operands normalized to this range have an ulp $= 2^{-n+1}$. Further, a leading integer one can be assumed for all divisors, and the table only requires fractional divisor bits to make a quotient-digit selection. The shifted partial remainder, though, requires both integer and fractional bits as inputs to the table. The shifted partial remainder rP_j and divisor d can be approximated by estimates $r\hat{P}_j$ and $\hat{d}$ using the c most significant bits of rP_j and the δ most significant bits of d. The c bits in the truncated estimate $r\hat{P}_j$ can be divided into i integer bits and f fractional bits, such that $c = i + f$. The table can take as input the partial-remainder estimate directly in redundant form, or it can use the output of a short carry-assimilating adder that converts the redundant-partial remainder estimate to a nonredundant representation. The use of an external short adder reduces the complexity of the table implementation, as the number of partial-remainder input bits is halved. However, the delay of the quotient-digit selection function increases by the delay of the adder.

It is not possible to determine the optimal choices of δ and f analytically, as several factors are involved in making these choices. However, it is possible to determine a lower bound on δ using the continuity condition and the fact that the next partial remainder must remain bounded:

$$2^{-\delta} \leq \frac{2\rho - 1}{2(a - \rho)}, \tag{7.9}$$

$$\delta \geq \left\lceil -\log_2 \frac{2\rho - 1}{2(a - \rho)} \right\rceil. \tag{7.10}$$

Because the divisor is IEEE-normalized with a leading one, only the leading $b = \delta - 1$ fractional bits are required as input to the table. The next quotient digit can then be selected by using these estimates to index into a 2^{b+c} entry lookup table, implemented either as a PLA or with random logic.

Assuming a nonredundant 2's-complement partial remainder, the estimates have nonnegative truncation errors ϵ_d and ϵ_p for the divisor and shifted partial-remainder estimates, respectively, where

$$\epsilon_d \leq 2^{-b} - 2^{-n+1} \approx 2^{-b}, \tag{7.11}$$

$$\epsilon_p \leq 2^{-f} - 2^{-n+1} \approx 2^{-f}. \tag{7.12}$$

Thus, the maximum truncation error for both the divisor and the nonredundant shifted partial-remainder estimates is strictly less than 1 ulp.

For a redundant 2's-complement partial remainder, the truncation error depends upon the representation. For a carry-save representation, the sum and carry estimates both have nonnegative truncation error ϵ_p, assuming that both the sum and carry estimates are represented by the c most significant bits of their true values. The resulting estimate $r\hat{P}_{j(cs)}$ has truncation error

$$\epsilon_{p(cs)} \leq 2 \times (2^{-f} - 2^{-n+1}) \approx 2^{1-f}. \tag{7.13}$$

Thus, the maximum truncation error for an estimate of a carry-save shifted partial remainder is strictly less than 2 ulps.

From this discussion, the number i of integer bits in $r\hat{P}_j$ can be determined analytically. Using the general recurrence for SRT division, the maximum shifted partial remainder is given by

$$rP_{j(max)} = r\rho d_{max} \tag{7.14}$$

For IEEE operands,

$$d_{max} = 2 - 2^{-n+1} \tag{7.15}$$

As previously stated, for a carry-save 2's-complement representation of the partial remainder, the truncation error is always nonnegative, and therefore the maximum estimate of the partial remainder is

$$r\hat{P}_{j(max)} = \frac{\lfloor r \times \rho \times (2 - 2^{-n+1}) \times 2^f \rfloor}{2^f}. \tag{7.16}$$

The minimum estimate of the partial remainder is

$$r\hat{P}_{j(min)} = \frac{\lceil -r \times \rho \times (2 - 2^{-n+1}) \times 2^f \rceil}{2^f} - \epsilon_{\{p(cs)}. \tag{7.17}$$

Accordingly, i can be determined from

$$r\hat{P}_{j(max)} - r\hat{P}_{j(min)} \leq 2^i, \tag{7.18}$$

$$i \geq \left\lceil \log_2\left(r\hat{P}_{j(max)} - r\hat{P}_{j(min)}\right) \right\rceil. \tag{7.19}$$

7.2.2 Uncertainty Regions

By using a redundant quotient-digit set, it is possible to correctly choose the next quotient digit even when using the truncated estimates $r\hat{P}_j$ and $\hat{d}$. Due to the truncation error in the estimates, each entry in the quotient-digit selection table has an uncertainty region associated with it. For each entry, it is necessary for all combinations of all possible values represented by the estimates $r\hat{P}_j$ and $\hat{d}$ to lie in the same selection interval. For a carry-save representation of the shifted partial remainder, this involves calculating the maximum and minimum ratios of the shifted partial remainder and divisor, and ensuring that these ratios both lie in the same selection interval:

$$\text{ratio}_{\text{max}} = \begin{cases} \dfrac{r\hat{P}_j + \epsilon_{\text{p(cs)}}}{\hat{d}} & \text{if } P_j \geq 0, \\[2ex] \dfrac{r\hat{P}_j}{\hat{d}} & \text{if } P_j < 0, \end{cases} \tag{7.20}$$

$$\text{ratio}_{\text{min}} = \begin{cases} \dfrac{r\hat{P}_j}{\hat{d} + \epsilon_{\text{d}}} & \text{if } P_j \geq 0, \\[2ex] \dfrac{r\hat{P}_j + \epsilon_{\text{p(cs)}}}{\hat{d} + \epsilon_{\text{d}}} & \text{if } P_j < 0. \end{cases} \tag{7.21}$$

If an uncertainty region is too large, the maximum and minimum ratios may span more than one selection interval, requiring one table entry to return more than one quotient digit. This would signify that the estimate of the divisor and/or the shifted partial remainder has too much truncation error.

Figure 7.2 shows several uncertainty regions in a radix-4 P–D plot. Each uncertainty region is represented by a rectangle whose height and width is a function of the divisor and partial-remainder truncation errors. The value of $\text{ratio}_{\text{max}}$ corresponds to the upper left corner of the rectangle, while $\text{ratio}_{\text{min}}$ corresponds to the lower right corner. In this figure, the four valid uncertainty regions include a portion of an overlap region. Further, the lower right uncertainty region is fully contained within an overlap region, allowing the entry corresponding to that uncertainty region to take on a quotient digits of either 0 or 1. The other three valid uncertainty regions may take on only a single quotient digit. The upper left uncertainty region spans more than an entire overlap region, signifying that the corresponding table entry, and as a result the entire table, is not valid.

To determine the valid values of b and f for a given r and a, it is necessary to calculate the uncertainty regions for all 2^{b+i+f} entries in the table. If all uncertainty regions are valid for given choices of b, i, and f, then they are valid choices.

7.2.3 Reducing Table Complexity

The size of the table implementation can be reduced nearly in half by *folding* the table entries as suggested in Fandrianto [49]. Folding involves the conversion of the 2's-complement representation of $r\hat{P}_j$ to signed magnitude,

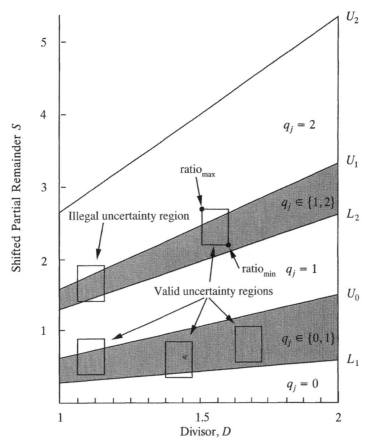

Figure 7.2   Uncertainty regions due to divisor and partial-remainder estimates.

allowing the same table entries to be used for both positive and negative values of $r\hat{P}_j$. This reduction does not come free. First, it requires additional logic outside the table, such as a row of XOR gates, to perform the representation conversion, adding external delay to the quotient-digit selection process. Second, it may place further restrictions on the table design process. When a carry-save representation is used for rP_j and a truncated estimate $r\hat{P}_j$ is used to consult the table, the truncation error is always nonnegative, resulting in an asymmetrical table. To guarantee the symmetry required for folding, additional terms must be added to the table, resulting in a less than optimal implementation.

A complexity-reducing technique proposed in this study is to minimize ϵ_p. As presented previously, when using an external carry-assimilating adder for a truncated 2's-complement carry-save partial-remainder estimate, the maximum error $\epsilon_{p(cs)}$ is approximately 2^{1-f}. This error can be further reduced by using g fractional bits of redundant partial remainder as input to the external adder, where $g > f$, but only using the most significant f fractional output bits of the adder as input to the table. The maximum error in the output of the adder is

$$\epsilon_{\text{p(adder)}} = 2^{-g} + 2^{-g} - 2^{1+n}. \tag{7.22}$$

Then, by using f bits of the adder output, the maximum error for the input

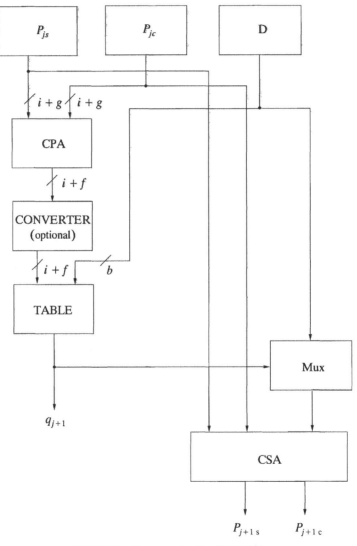

Figure 7.3 Components of an SRT divider.

to the table is

$$\epsilon_{p(cs)} = 2^{-f} - 2^{-g} + \epsilon_{p(adder)}$$
$$= 2^{-f} + 2^{-g} - 2^{-n+1} \approx 2^{-f} + 2^{-g}. \qquad (7.23)$$

For the case $g = f$, the error remains approximately 2^{1-f}. However, by increasing g, the error $\epsilon_{p(cs)}$ is reduced, converging towards the error for a nonredundant partial remainder which is approximately 2^{-f}. Reducing the truncation error $\epsilon_{p(cs)}$ decreases the height of the uncertainty region in the P–D diagram. This has the effect of allowing more of the entries' uncertainty regions to fit fully within overlap regions, increasing the flexibility in the logic minimization process, and ultimately reducing the complexity of the final table. A block diagram illustrating the various components of an SRT divider is shown in Figure 7.3.

7.3 EXPERIMENTAL METHODOLOGY

The focus of this chapter is to quantitatively measure the tradeoffs between the parameters r, a, b, i, f, g, and the complexity of the logic equations, measured by the number of product terms, as well as the complexity of the resulting random logic implementations of the tables, as measured by implementation delay and area. The design flow in Figure 7.4 was used to automatically generate quotient-digit selection tables in random logic:

In this study, a carry-save 2's-complement representation is used for the partial remainder in all tables.

7.3.1 *TableGen*

The program *TableGen* performs the analytical aspects of the quotient-digit selection-table design. This program takes the table parameters as input, and it produces the unminimized PLA entries necessary to implement the table. First, all of the uncertainty regions for all entries in the table are computed. *TableGen* determines whether or not the choice of input parameters results in a valid table design. If the table is valid, it then computes the allowable quotient digits for each entry in the table, based upon the size of the uncertainty region. The allowable quotient digits are then written in PLA form for all 2^{i+b+f} possible (shifted partial remainder, divisor) pairs.

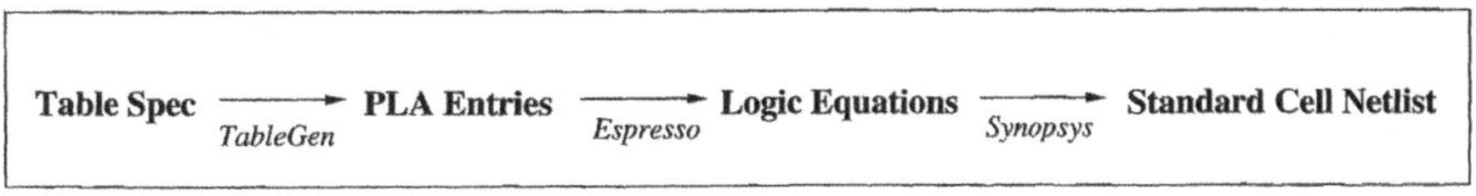

Table Spec $\xrightarrow[\text{\textit{TableGen}}]{}$ PLA Entries $\xrightarrow[\text{\textit{Espresso}}]{}$ Logic Equations $\xrightarrow[\text{\textit{Synopsys}}]{}$ Standard Cell Netlist

Figure 7.4 Design flow.

TABLE 7.1 Gray encoding for maximally redundant radix 4

Allowable Digits	Encoding
0	00
1	01
0 or 1	0x
2	11
1 or 2	x1
3	10
2 or 3	1x

To allow for the greatest reduction in the complexity of the table implementations, it is proposed in this study to use a Gray code to encode an entry's allowable quotient digits. In a Gray encoding, neighboring values only differ in one bit position [14]. This allows for the efficient representation of multiple allowable quotient digits in the PLA output, while still only requiring $\lceil \log_2 r \rceil$ bits. The Gray coding of the digits is recommended to ensure that given a choice between two allowable quotient digits in an overlap region, the optimal choice can be automatically determined that will result in the least complex logic equations.

Accordingly, there are $\lceil \log_2 r \rceil$ outputs of the table, which are the bits of the encoded quotient digit. Table entries where $ratio_{min}$ and $ratio_{max}$ are both greater than ρr are unreachable entries. Thus, their outputs are set to *don't care*. An example of Gray coding for $r = 4$ and $a = 3$ is shown in Table 7.1. In this example, a value of x implies a *don't care*. Because the table stores digits in encoded form, all tables in this study require an explicit decoder to recover the true quotient-digit and select the appropriate divisor multiple. This results in the addition of a decoder delay into the critical path. However, since all tables in this study use the same encoding, this is a constant delay that only grows as the log of the radix.

Alternatively, the quotient digits could be stored in an unencoded form, removing the need for the decoder. Optimal logic minimization becomes a much more difficult problem for unencoded digits.

Espresso is used to perform logic minimization on the output PLA. This produces a minimized PLA and logic equations representing the PLA in sum-of-products form. The number of product terms in these expressions is one metric for the complexity of the tables. To verify the correctness of the tables, an SRT divider was simulated using a DEC Alpha 3000/500 with the minimized logic equations as the quotient-digit selection function. After each table was generated, the equations were incorporated into the simulator. Several thousand random and directed IEEE double-precision vectors were used as input to the simulator, and the computed quotients for each table were compared with the computed results from the Alpha's internal FPU.

7.3.2 Table Synthesis

To quantify the performance and area of random logic implementations of the tables, each table was synthesized using a standard-cell library. The *Synopsys Design Compiler* [177] was used to map the logic equations describing each table to an LSI Logic 500K 0.5-μm standard-cell library [98]. In the mapping stage, low flattening and medium mapping effort options were used. However, area was always sacrificed to reduce the latency. In order to minimize the true critical path of the tables, the input constraints included the late arrival time of all partial-remainder inputs due to an external carry-assimilating adder.

Area and delay estimates were obtained from a Design-Compiler pre-layout report. Each delay includes the intrinsic gate delay, the estimated interconnect wire delay, and the input load of subsequent gates. All delays were measured using nominal conditions. Each area measurement includes both cell and estimated routing area. The delay and area are reported relative to those for a base radix-4 table, which is Gray-coded with $i = 4$, $f = 3$, $g = 3$, and $b = 3$. The base table requires 43 cells and has a delay of 1.47 ns.

The data are presented in Tables 7.2 through 7.6. The complexity of the tables is measured by the number of product terms, the relative delay, and the relative area for each configuration. The terms result contains both the number of product terms for each output of the table, and the total number of terms in the table. For a given radix r, there are exactly $n_{\text{out}} = \log_2 r$ outputs of the table. Accordingly, this column first lists the number of terms in each of the n_{out} outputs. Because there is usually some internal sharing of product terms, the last number, which is the total number of unique terms required to implement the table, is typically less than the sum of the terms for the individual outputs. The reported delay is the worst-case delay of any of the n_{out} outputs, typically corresponding to the output which has the largest number of product terms.

7.4 RESULTS

7.4.1 Same-Radix Tradeoffs

Table 7.2 shows the results for various radix 4 configurations. The parameters varied in this table are: (1) the number of g bits vs f bits, (2) folding, (3) the method of choosing values in the overlap regions, and (4) the amount of redundancy. The first entries examine the effects of using g bits of the redundant partial remainder in the short CPA outside of the table, while only using f bits of the adder output as input to the table. Simply extending the CPA by one bit reduces the delay by 12% and area by 7%. Extending the CPA by two bits reduces the delay by 16% and the area by 9%. In the limit, where $g = n$ and a full-mantissa carry-propagate addition is required, the delay and area are both reduced by 23%. This demonstrates that increasing

TABLE 7.2 Radix-4 tradeoffs

Description	a	b	i	f	g	Terms	Relative Delay	Relative Area
Baseline	2	3	4	3	3	19,8,25	1.00	1.00
	2	3	4	3	4	17,8,23	0.88	0.93
	2	3	4	3	5	17,8,23	0.84	0.91
	2	3	4	3	52	14,6,18	0.77	0.77
Folded	2	3	4	3	4	13,5,17	0.79	0.65
Folded +								
t-bit conv.	2	3	4	3	4	12,4,16	0.71	0.57
Line Encode	2	3	4	3	4	17,7,23	0.84	0.86
Choose highest	2	3	4	3	4	22,13,33	1.05	1.23
Max red	3	2	5	1	1	6,9,14	0.80	0.54
	3	2	5	1	52	3,6,9	0.63	0.30

the width of the CPA by as little as one or two bits can reduce the complexity of the table.

The next two entries demonstrate the effects of using folded tables. For both tables, it is assumed that $f = 3$ and $g = 4$, which matches the format of the table suggested in Fandrianto [49]. The use of only a 2-complement-to-sign-magnitude converter yields the first folded table, which achieves an additional delay reduction of 10% and an additional area reduction of 30% in comparison with the $f = 3$ and $g = 4$ table without folding. This introduces a serial delay of an XOR gate external to the delay of the table. When the sign-magnitude converter is combined with a *t-bit converter*, which further constrains the range of input values to the table, the delay is reduced relative to the simple folded table by an additional 10% and the area is reduced by an additional 12%. This converter introduces the serial delay of an OR gate external to the table. These results show that folding can reduce the size and delay of the table. However, the delay of the required external gates must be considered for the overall design. If the sum of the XOR- and OR-gate delays is less than 29% of the base-table delay, table folding can result in a net decrease in delay.

Different encodings of the quotient digits can change the complexity of the tables. The lower bound for delay and area of the table is achieved when each boundary between two consecutive quotient digits is individually encoded. The recovery of the unencoded quotient digit may require a large external decoder. When using such a *line* encoding scheme, again with $f = 3$ and $g = 4$, the delay and area are reduced by 5% and 8%, respectively, relative to the base Gray-coded table, also with $f = 3$ and $g = 4$. However, the external decoder delay grows linearly with increasing a for line encoding, while only growing as the log of a for Gray coding.

Another common encoding scheme always uses the highest digit whenever a choice is available between two consecutive quotient digits. This is represented in the table as *choose highest* encoding. While simplifying the table generating process, this method increases the resulting table delay by 19% and area by 32% over the base $f = 3$ and $g = 4$ table. Thus, this study shows that Gray coding of the quotient digits achieves delays and areas approaching the lower bound of line encoding, while requiring less complex external decoders.

The redundancy of the digit set has an influence on table complexity. The final entries in the table are for maximally redundant radix-4 tables, with $a = 3$. For an implementation with $f = g = 1$, the delay and area are reduced by 20% and 46% respectively. When g increases to $n = 52$, requiring a full mantissa-width CPA, the delay is further reduced by 21% and the area by 44%. These results show that if the hardware is available to generate the $3 \times$ divisor multiple, the iteration time can be reduced by over 20%, due to the restriction in table complexity and length of the external short CPA.

Table 7.3 shows the complexity of a basic radix-2 table. This table can be implemented by a single three-input gate, as it only has 3 PLA terms, which can be contrasted with the 25 terms in the baseline radix-4 table. The resulting delay is 65% less than for the base radix-4 table, while 93% less area is required. Accordingly, the radix-2 table is 2.86 times faster than the base radix 4 table, and 2.40 times faster than a $g = 5$ radix-4 table.

7.4.2 Higher Radices

Tables 7.4, 7.5, and 7.6 show the complexity for tables that directly implement radix 8, 16, and 32 respectively. The allowable choices of i, b, and f determined in this study correspond with the results presented in [29] for radix 8 and 16. In our study, we extend the allowed operand truncations to radix 32. For radix 16 and radix 32, the minimally redundant configurations required 20 or more inputs to the table. Due to computational constraints, table optimization was limited to configurations containing fewer than 20 inputs. Those configurations where optimization was infeasible are denoted with a dagger in the tables.

For a given choice of radix and redundancy, there exists more than one possible table design. As discussed previously, a minimum number of divisor estimate bits is required as input for a given configuration. This corresponds to a maximum number of partial remainder bits that need to be used. However, it is possible to trade an increase in divisor bits for a reduction in

TABLE 7.3   Radix 2

a	b	i	f	g	Terms	Relative Delay	Relative Area
1	0	3	1	1	3	0.35	0.07

TABLE 7.4   Radix 8

a	b	i	f	g	Terms	Relative Delay	Relative Area
4	7	5	4	4	137, 59, 114, 292	1.85	10.2
	7	5	4	5	111, 48, 94, 240	1.76	8.80
	6	5	5	5	110, 50, 94, 240	1.70	8.85
	5	5	6	6	104, 50, 85, 221	1.67	8.21
5	5	5	3	3	42, 19, 69, 122	1.45	5.21
	4	5	4	4	35, 14, 57, 103	1.47	4.05
6	5	5	2	2	26, 35, 39, 92	1.46	4.82
	4	5	3	3	24, 33, 38, 88	1.46	4.46
	3	5	5	5	27, 29, 33, 78	1.36	4.03
7	6	6	1	1	16, 23, 43, 76	1.46	3.90
	3	6	2	2	15, 21, 35, 64	1.41	3.53

TABLE 7.5   Radix 16

a	b	i	f	g	Terms	Relative Delay	Relative Area
8	11	6	5	5	†	†	†
	8	6	6	6	†	†	†
	7	6	8	8	†	†	†
9	7	6	4	4	198, 98, 176, 481, 871	2.56	32.9
	6	6	5	5	170, 81, 154, 410, 745	2.50	29.0
10	7	6	3	3	120, 58, 231, 280, 616	2.37	24.8
	6	6	4	4	105, 57, 191, 240, 530	2.32	21.4
	5	6	5	5	96, 49, 183, 227, 497	2.24	21.1
11	6	6	3	3	80, 44, 159, 258, 484	2.21	21.1
	5	6	4	4	68, 39, 142, 208, 418	2.10	18.9
12	7	6	2	2	79, 138, 144, 228, 481	2.17	25.0
	6	6	3	3	66, 112, 119, 172, 373	2.09	19.1
13	6	6	2	2	60, 105, 105, 207, 393	2.14	20.4
	5	6	3	3	62, 104, 99, 186, 344	2.07	18.5
14	5	6	2	2	48, 101, 136, 169, 383	2.14	20.2
	4	6	6	6	54, 92, 110, 139, 310	2.06	16.5
15	9	7	1	1	47, 76, 135, 193, 383	2.16	19.2
	5	7	2	2	39, 69, 99, 136, 281	2.03	15.4
	4	7	3	3	42, 61, 93, 125, 261	1.94	14.8

TABLE 7.6 Radix 32

a	b	i	f	g	Terms	Relative Delay	Relative Area
17	9	7	5	5	†	†	†
	8	7	6	6	†	†	†
18	9	7	4	4	†	†	†
	8	7	5	5	†	†	†
	7	7	7	7	†	†	†
19	8	7	4	4	351, 208, 352, 945, 1633, 3119	4.56	141
	7	7	5	5	309, 191, 308, 860, 1445, 2767	4.18	79.1
20	9	7	3	3	312, 164, 660, 891, 1527, 3218	4.69	144
	7	7	4	4	257, 156, 531, 727, 1215, 2592	4.24	106
21	8	7	3	3	237, 128, 507, 649, 1274, 2499	4.13	73.2
	7	7	4	4	206, 118, 424, 541, 1060, 2099	4.06	94.8
	6	7	6	6	180, 108, 366, 466, 912, 1826	3.91	80.5
22	7	7	3	3	192, 119, 450, 733, 1032, 2127	4.31	101
	6	7	5	5	178, 90, 356, 596, 794, 1696	4.07	80.9
23	7	7	3	3	158, 85, 365, 607, 946, 1865	4.11	92.5
	6	7	4	4	140, 84, 316, 527, 814, 1621	3.86	78.6
24	9	7	2	2	207, 408, 421, 678, 1073, 2243	4.62	92.5
	7	7	3	3	147, 327, 314, 491, 780, 1678	3.63	86.8
	6	7	4	4	142, 286, 277, 458, 699, 1497	3.61	73.3
25	8	7	2	2	185, 330, 318, 543, 985, 1978	4.36	99.6
	6	7	3	3	144, 252, 258, 425, 747, 1534	3.70	76.3
26	8	7	2	2	154, 291, 299, 607, 838, 1783	3.95	91.6
	6	7	3	3	123, 249, 235, 505, 687, 1475	3.73	75.1
27	7	7	2	2	141, 263, 266, 535, 798, 1620	3.73	86.4
	6	7	3	3	126, 221, 227, 439, 661, 1377	3.63	73.7
28	7	7	2	2	146, 233, 359, 494, 717, 1578	3.86	82.0
	6	7	3	3	134, 218, 322, 413, 599, 1327	3.76	74.4
29	7	7	2	2	226, 233, 342, 431, 697, 1480	3.75	82.1
	6	7	3	3	116, 188, 259, 349, 573, 1241	3.73	69.8
30	6	7	2	2	145, 220, 318, 461, 656, 1433	4.14	76.0
	5	7	7	7	165, 184, 252, 351, 505, 1143	3.78	61.0
31	11	8	1	1	†	†	†
	6	8	2	2	89, 170, 241, 399, 555, 1158	4.05	61.3
	5	8	4	4	86, 152, 219, 333, 486, 1021	3.52	57.2

the number of partial-remainder bits. This might initially seem desirable, as the partial-remainder bits must first be assimilated in an external adder, adding to the overall iteration time. By using fewer partial-remainder bits in the table, the external adder can be smaller, reducing the external delay. However, for carry-save partial remainders, the maximum partial-remainder truncation error $\epsilon_{p(cs)}$ is greater than the maximum divisor truncation error ϵ_d. By trading off fewer partial remainder bits for more divisor bits, the height of the uncertainty region increases at approximately twice the rate at which the width of the region decreases. As a result, the overall uncertainty-region area increases as fewer partial-remainder bits are used. This result can be seen quantitatively in Tables 7.4, 7.5, and 7.6. For any given choice of radix and redundancy, the use of the maximum number of divisor bits and minimum number of partial-remainder bits results in the largest total number of product terms, and typically the largest delay and area. As the number of divisor bits is reduced and the number of partial-remainder bits increased, the number of product terms, the delay, and the area are all typically reduced.

This study confirms that as the radix increases, the complexity of the tables also increases. Fitting the average area at a given radix to a curve across the various radices determines that the area increases geometrically with increasing radix R:

$$\text{area} = 0.1\ R^2 \tag{7.24}$$

gives the table area relative to that of the base radix-4 divider. Similar analysis of the average delay demonstrates that it increases only linearly with increasing radix. For radix 8, the delay is on the average about 1.5 times that of the base radix-4 table. However, it can require up to 10 times as much area. While radix-16 tables have about 2 times the base delay, they can require up to 32 times the area. In the case of radix 32, it was not even possible to achieve a delay of 2.5 times the base delay, the maximum desired delay; the actual delays were between 3.5 and 4.7 times the base delay. The area required for radix 32 ranges from 57 to 141 times the base area. These results show that radices 16 and 32 are clearly impractical design choices, even ignoring practical implementation limitations such as generating all divisor multiples. This study shows that it is possible to design radix-8 tables with reasonable delay and area; a minimally redundant radix-8 table is demonstrated to be a practical design choice.

7.5 CONCLUSION

This study has demonstrated a methodology for generating quotient-digit selection tables from a table specification through an automated design flow. Using this process, performance and area tradeoffs of quotient selection tables in SRT dividers have been presented for several table configurations. The use of Gray coding is shown to be a simple yet effective method that allows automatic determination of optimal choices of quotient digits which reduce table complexity.

Short external carry-assimilating adders are necessary to convert redundant partial remainders to a nonredundant form. By extending the length of these adders by as little as one or two bits, it is shown that table complexity can be further reduced. The conventional wisdom for SRT table specification has been that whenever possible, the length of the partial-remainder estimate should be reduced at the expense of increasing the length of the divisor estimate in order to reduce the width, and thus the delay, of the external adder. However, this study quantitatively demonstrates that such a choice also increases the size and delay of the table, canceling the performance gain provided by the narrower adder. Accordingly, the overall iteration time is not reduced through such a tradeoff.

As the radix increases, it is shown that the table delay increases linearly. However, the area increases quadratically with increasing radix. This fact, combined with the difficulty in generating all of the required divisor multiples for radix 8 and higher, limits practical table implementations to radix 2 and radix 4.

8

VERY HIGH
RADIX DIVISION

Based upon work by Derek Wong

This chapter describes a number of division algorithms that are designed to operate with a very high-radix. These high-radix division algorithms use lookup tables and multipliers for very fast division of two numbers. Unlike traditional SRT algorithms, which produce one, two, or three quotient digits in each iteration, the very high-radix division algorithms produce a large number of quotient digits in each iteration. Some other related division algorithms are described and discussed in Section 8.5.

8.1 TAYLOR SERIES EXPANSION

Three very high-radix division algorithms are presented in Sections 8.2, 8.3, and 8.4. These algorithms can be derived and analyzed using the well-known Taylor series. The Taylor series for $f(Y)$ about $Y = b$ is defined by

$$f(Y) = f(b) + f'(b)(Y - b) + \frac{f''(b)(Y - b)^2}{2!} + \frac{f^{(3)}(b)(Y - b)^3}{3!} + \cdots .$$

$$(8.1)$$

It converges if

$$\lim_{n \to \infty} \frac{f^{(n)}(Y_0)(Y - b)^n}{n!} = 0,$$

$$(8.2)$$

where Y_0 is a number between Y and b.

153

In our case, the function $f(Y)$ is equal to the quotient $1/Y$, and the series converges if $Y - b$ is less than one. Suppose Y contains q significant bits. If we use a single table to look up q significant bits of $1/Y$, the table size is equal to $2^q \cdot q$ bits. In general, the table size can be very large, resulting in a huge physical table and very long access time. For example, the table sizes are 2.4 Mbyte for $q = 23$ and 3×10^{16} bytes for $q = 52$.

To reduce the table size, we use only the most significant m bits of Y to look up $1/Y$. In the first two high-radix algorithms (Algorithms A and B), we set b to Y_h, which contains the leading m bits of Y extended with 1's to get a q-bit number. As a result, Y_h is greater than or equal to Y. Let $\Delta Y = Y_h - Y$, and substitute ΔY in Equation (8.1) to get.

$$\frac{1}{Y} = \frac{1}{Y_h} - \frac{\Delta Y}{Y_h^2} + \frac{(\Delta Y)^2}{Y_h^3} - \frac{(\Delta Y)^3}{Y_h^4} + \frac{(\Delta Y)^4}{Y_h^5} + \cdots . \qquad (8.3)$$

Only the first two terms in the Taylor series are used in Algorithm A, but more terms are used in Algorithm B.

In Algorithm C, we set b to Y_H instead of Y_h, where Y_H also contains the leading bits of Y but extended with all 0's instead of all 1's. Y is represented by $Y_H + Y_L$, where both Y_H and Y_L are positive. Combining the first two terms in the Taylor series, we get

$$\frac{1}{Y} \approx \frac{Y_H - Y_L}{Y_H^2} . \qquad (8.4)$$

Similarly, if we combine the first four terms in the Taylor series, we get

$$\frac{1}{Y} \approx \frac{Y_H - Y_L}{Y_H^2} \left(1 + \frac{Y_L^2}{Y_H^2} \right) . \qquad (8.5)$$

In both equations, only one lookup table $(1/Y_H)$ is needed for the very high-radix division.

8.2 ALGORITHM A

As RAM and ROM density and speed increases, the use of larger lookup tables becomes practical and advantageous. This algorithm estimates the reciprocal of the divisor using large lookup tables, and produces many quotient bits in each iteration.

Denote the dividend register by X, the divisor register by Y, and the quotient register by Q. Denote a bit of a register using an index (e.g. $X_{(j)}$,)[1] with higher negative indices indicating less significant bits. All numbers are assumed to have the same width q, but the algorithm can easily be modified for numbers of different width:

$$X = 0.X_{(1)}X_{(2)} \cdots X_{(q)}, \tag{8.6}$$

$$Y = 0.Y_{(1)}Y_{(2)} \cdots Y_{(q)}. \tag{8.7}$$

Without loss of generality, we consider the binary representations of X and Y to be fixed-point fractional numbers ($\frac{1}{2}$ is a special case) between $\frac{1}{2}$ and 1. The most significant bits ($X_{(1)}$ and $Y_{(1)}$) are assumed to be one. X and Y are positive numbers, but it is straightforward to handle negative numbers using a sign–magnitude representation.

This algorithm calculates successive adjustments to a quotient approximation which becomes increasingly more accurate. Each estimate is always less than or equal to the true quotient, so each new adjustment is always nonnegative. The quotient is successively refined. For example by forming 14 bits each iteration after the Nth iteration, the quotient is accurate to approximately within one part in 2^{14N}. For instance, the quotient would be accurate to 56 bits after four iterations. Since the algorithm can supply the remainder, correct rounding of the result is straightforward.

Given the first p bits of X, the value of X is known within an error of $1/2^p - 1/2^q$. The minimal value of X is $0.X_{(1)} \cdots X_{(p)}$ and the maximal value is $0.X_{(1)} \cdots X_{(p)} + 1/2^p - 1/2^q$. The range of uncertainty is slightly smaller than $1/2^p$. Similarly, given the first m bits of Y, we know Y to within $1/2^m - 1/2^q$.

Define X_h as the leading p bits of X extended with 0's to get a q-bit number, and define Y_h as the leading m bits of Y extended with 1's to get a q-bit number:

$$X_h = 0.X_{(1)} \cdots X_{(p)}, \tag{8.8}$$

$$Y_h = 0.Y_{(1)} \cdots Y_{(m)} + 2^{-m} - 2^{-q}. \tag{8.9}$$

Let $\Delta X = X - X_h$ and $\Delta Y = Y - Y_h$. The deltas ΔX and ΔY are the adjustments needed to get the true X and Y from X_h and Y_h. From the definitions, ΔX is always nonnegative, and ΔY is always nonpositive. The value $1/Y_h$ is clearly less than or equal to the true reciprocal $1/Y$, and X_h/Y_h is always less than or equal to X/Y. A division algorithm that uses a reduced number of iterations can be conceptually summarized as follows:

1. Set the estimated quotient Q to 0 initially.
2. Let j and k denote the numbers of bits that X and Y have been left-shifted. Initially, both are set to the amounts of preshifting required to normalize X and Y.

[1]Recall that in our number notation $X_1X_0.X_{-1}X_{-2}\ldots$ is represented as $X_1X_0.X_{(1)}X_{(2)}\ldots$.

3. Get an approximation of $1/Y_h$ from a lookup table called G_1. The index to the lookup table is the leading m bits of Y. Each table word is b_1 bits wide, where $b_1 = m$, as discussed later in this chapter.

4. Compute the new dividend[2] using $X' = X - X_h(1/Y_h)Y$. By ordering the multiplies correctly, this formula only requires the latency of one multiplication and one subtraction per iteration. By doing the multiplication of X_hY while the lookup of $1/Y_h$ is being performed, only one subsequent multiply is needed in the first iteration. Similarly, $(1/Y_h)Y$ need only be computed once, since it is invariant across the iterations. If this is performed in the first iteration: then the second and later iterations only require one multiply plus one subtract to complete. At full speed, this requires two multiplies in parallel during the first iteration;

5. Compute the new quotient using $Q' = Q + (X_h/Y_h)(1/2^{j-k}) = Q + X_h(1/Y_h)(1/2^{j-k})$. In the above formulas for Q' and X', X_h can be composed of $p = m + 1$ leading digits of X followed by 0's.

6. Left shift X' by $m - 2$ bits to get rid of the guaranteed leading 0's that occur (as discussed in the next subsection). Shift 0's into the lsb of X' during this process. Calculate a revised $j' = j + m - 2$.

7. Set $j = j'$, $Q = Q'$, and $X = X'$.

8. Repeat steps 4 through 7 until $j \geq q$.

9. The final Q is the quotient. Note that there are more bits in the quotient register than q. Let $Q_h = Q_{(1)} \cdots Q_{(q)}$, and let $Q_l = Q_{(q+1)} \cdots Q_{(q+e)}$ where e is the number of excess bits. Q (including both Q_h and Q_l) is within one ulp of the true infinite-precision quotient, where an ulp is the unit of the jth digit of Q (i.e., $Q_{(j)}$). Here j is always greater than or equal to q. Some of the Q_l bits are not necessarily correct, since another iteration of the algorithm would add into those bits.

10. The residual dividend X should be right-shifted by $j - q$ bits to get the remainder, assuming the entire Q is the quotient. If Q is truncated to q bits, the true remainder can be computed by then adding Q_lY to X.

Since the algorithm reduces X' by $m - 2$ bits per iteration, the algorithm terminates after $\lceil q/(m-2) \rceil$ iterations. Next, we analyze this method to show why $m - 2$ bits per iteration are guaranteed in the worst case.

---

[2]Although it might appear possible to simplify this to $X' = X - X_h(Y_h + \Delta Y)/Y_h = X_h + \Delta X - X_h(1 + \Delta Y/Y_h) = \Delta X - X_h\Delta Y/Y_h$, this does not actually work, because the calculation of X' and Q' would be uncoordinated. Different roundoff errors would occur in X' and Q' in each iteration.

8.2.1 Number of Accurate Bits per Iteration

Theorem 1: Number of Bits per Iteration Using Algorithm A   *X' is reduced by at least m − 2 bits per iteration if m ≥ 5, the number p of significant bits in X_h is equal to m + 1, and the word width b_1 of the table G_1 is m.*

The number of bits that are reduced per iteration depends on the accuracy of the quotient estimates in each iteration. If the first quotient estimate is accurate beyond the required number of bits of the division, then the algorithm will terminate after a single iteration. In practice, the lookup-table size and the width of the variables used is limited to control the size of the divide hardware. This places a limit on the accuracy of the quotient estimates. In this section, we carefully analyze this accuracy to prove that a certain minimum number of bits is reduced from X in each iteration. Although the widths of the variables and the size of the lookup table can be varied arbitrarily, this analysis also shows that the default size and width specifications given above have been chosen intelligently, so that the different contributions to the accuracy limit are reasonably related to each other.

The initial value of X is between $\frac{1}{2}$ and 1, since the leading bit is 1 ($X_{(1)} = 1$). By determining the largest possible value of X', we can determine the worst-case minimum number of bits eliminated per iteration. If we can guarantee that $X' < 1/2^r$, then the most significant bit that could be nonzero has significance $1/2^{r+1}$. In this case, there are r guaranteed leading zeros that can be eliminated per iteration. Let us examine the formula for X':

$$X' = X - X_h(1/Y_h)Y \tag{8.10}$$

In this case, two sources of inaccuracy affect the approximation $1/Y_h \approx 1/Y$. Let the error sources be defined by

$$1/Y_h = 1/Y - E_B - E_C, \tag{8.11}$$

where E_B represents an error term due to using $1/Y_h$ instead of $1/Y$, and E_C represents the error in storing $1/Y_h$ to only a finite number of bits in the table G_1. The error E_B is always nonnegative, since $Y_h \geq Y$ implies $1/Y_h \leq 1/Y$. The error E_C is also always nonnegative, since $1/Y_h$ is stored into G_1 by always rounding down to the finite width b_1. Then

$$X' = X - X_h(1/Y_h)Y$$
$$= X_h + \Delta X - X_h(1/Y - E_B - E_C)Y$$
$$= \Delta X + X_h(E_B + E_C)Y. \tag{8.12}$$

If E_B and E_C can be accurately bounded, then this will give the maximal value of X'.

To compute the worst-case E_B, we examine a Taylor series expansion of $1/Y$ about the point $Y = Y_h$:

$$B = 1/Y$$

$$= \frac{1}{Y_h} - \frac{\Delta Y}{Y_h^2} + \frac{(\Delta Y)^2}{Y_h^3} - \frac{(\Delta Y)^3}{Y_h^4} + \frac{(\Delta Y)^4}{Y_h^5} + \cdots. \qquad (8.13)$$

The $(w+1)$th term is denoted by $B_{w+1} = (-\Delta Y)^w / Y_h^{(w+1)}$. All terms of B are nonnegative, since ΔY is nonpositive. The worst case occurs when $-\Delta Y = 1/2^m - 1/2^q$. In this case, the following bound holds:

$$B_{w+1} < (1/2^{mw})(1/Y_h^{w+1}). \qquad (8.14)$$

In this case, the approximation $1/Y_h \approx 1/Y$ is equivalent to truncating the Taylor series after the first term. A bound on the sum of the remaining terms can serve as a bound on E_B:

$$E_B = \sum_{g=1}^{\infty} B_{g+1} < \sum_{g=1}^{\infty} \frac{1}{2^{mg}} \times \frac{1}{Y_h^{g+1}} = \frac{(1/2^m)(1/Y_h)^2}{1 - 1/(2^m Y_h)}. \qquad (8.15)$$

For $m \gg 1$, this is just slightly greater than $(1/2^m)(1/Y_h)^2$. For $m \geq 5$, a nonstringent bound on E_B is

$$E_B < \frac{1.1}{2^m Y_h^2}. \qquad (8.16)$$

E_C comes from not using the exact value of $1/Y_h$ but instead using a finite-precision table G_1. Denote the output of the table by $\{(1/Y_h)\}_a$. Let the error between the table lookup and the true value be ϵ_1:

$$(1/Y_h)_a = \epsilon_1 + 1/Y_h, \qquad (8.17)$$

$$E_C = \epsilon_1. \qquad (8.18)$$

Suppose the table G_1 is b_1 bits wide. Since $\frac{1}{2} < Y_h < 1$, the maximal value of $1/Y_h$ is slightly less than 2. If words in the table G_1 can represent values up to but not including 2, the unit of the most significant binary digit in the table G_1 should have value 1. The unit of the least significant binary digit for table G_1 is then $1/2^{b_1-1}$. The error ϵ_1 is less than the unit of the least significant digit:

$$E_C = \epsilon_1 < 1/2^{b_1-1}. \qquad (8.19)$$

Using this, we can determine the proper word width b_1. Suppose we wish the error E_C to be bounded by

$$E_C < 1/2^{m-1}. \tag{8.20}$$

Then we should set b_1 to

$$b_1 = m. \tag{8.21}$$

Now we can substitute the bounds for E_B and E_C into Equation (8.12) for X'. Since $X_h < 1$ and $\Delta X \leq 1/2^p - 1/2^q$, the worst-case X' is bounded by

$$X' = \Delta X + X_h E_B Y + X_h E_C Y$$
$$< \Delta X + E_B Y + E_C Y, \tag{8.22}$$
$$X' < \frac{1}{2^p} - \frac{1}{2^q} + \frac{1.1Y}{2^m Y_h^2} + \frac{Y}{2^{m-1}}. \tag{8.23}$$

Since $Y_h \geq Y$, we can set $Y_h = Y$ in the worst case and simplify to obtain

$$X' < \frac{1}{2^p} - \frac{1}{2^q} + \frac{1.1}{2^m Y} + \frac{Y}{2^{m-1}}, \tag{8.24}$$
$$X' < X_2, \tag{8.25}$$

where

$$X_2 = \frac{1}{2^p} - \frac{1}{2^q} + \frac{1.1}{2^m Y} + \frac{Y}{2^{m-1}}. \tag{8.26}$$

We now wish to determine the worst-case value of X_2 while Y is allowed to vary over the range $\frac{1}{2} \leq Y < 1$. In order to accomplish this, the first step is to locate all possible maxima and minima by setting the partial derivative $\partial X_2/\partial Y$ equal to zero. The first partial derivative is

$$\frac{\partial X_2}{\partial Y} = -\frac{1.1}{2^m Y^2} + \frac{1}{2^{m-1}}. \tag{8.27}$$

Setting this derivative equal to 0 and solving, we obtain the following:

$$Y = \pm\sqrt{\frac{1.1}{2}}. \tag{8.28}$$

The negative solution is outside of the range $\frac{1}{2} \leq Y < 1$:

$$Y_A = -\sqrt{\frac{1.1}{2}}. \tag{8.29}$$

The positive solution does lie within the allowed range:

$$Y_B = +\sqrt{\frac{1.1}{2}}. \tag{8.30}$$

Next, we use the second derivative $\partial^2 X_2 / \partial Y^2$ to show that Y_B is actually a local minimum. The details are not shown.

Since Y_B is a local minimum and there are no other maxima or minima within the allowed range of Y, we know that the maximum value of X_2 occurs at either $Y = \frac{1}{2}$ or $Y = 1$.

The value of X_2 at $Y = \frac{1}{2}$ is as follows:

$$\text{at} \quad Y = \tfrac{1}{2}, \quad X_2 = \frac{1}{2^p} - \frac{1}{2^q} + \frac{1.1}{2^{m-1}} + \frac{1}{2^m}; \tag{8.31}$$

$$= \frac{1}{2^p} - \frac{1}{2^q} + \frac{1.6}{2^{m-1}}. \tag{8.32}$$

The value of X_2 at $Y = 1$ is as follows:

$$\text{at} \quad .Y = 1, \quad X_2 = \frac{1}{2^p} - \frac{1}{2^q} + \frac{1.1}{2^m} + \frac{1}{2^{m-1}} \tag{8.33}$$

$$= \frac{1}{2^p} - \frac{1}{2^q} + \frac{1.55}{2^{m-1}} \tag{8.34}$$

The highest possible value of X_2 occurs at $Y = \frac{1}{2}$. This is substituted back into equation (8.26) to get

$$X' < \frac{1}{2^p} - \frac{1}{2^q} + \frac{1.6}{2^{m-1}} \tag{8.35}$$

If $p = m + 1$, then this can be converted to:

$$X' < \frac{1}{2^{m+1}} - \frac{1}{2^q} + \frac{1.6}{2^{m-1}}, \tag{8.36}$$

$$X' < \frac{0.25}{2^{m-1}} - \frac{1}{2^q} + \frac{1.6}{2^{m-1}}, \tag{8.37}$$

$$X' < \frac{1}{2^{m-2}}. \tag{8.38}$$

This gives an insight into a good value for p, the number of significant bits in X_h. If $p \geq m + 1$, then the worst-case value of X' is less than $1/2^{m-2}$. In this case, the highest-order bit of X' that could possibly be 1 is the $(m-1)$th bit, $X'_{(m-1)}$. Since p determines the size of the multipliers needed to evaluate X' and Q' and there is very little advantage to having $p > m + 1$, the best value is $p = m + 1$. Thus, at least $m - 2$ bits are skipped per iteration if $p = m + 1$ and $b_1 = m$.

The average number of bits per iteration is a couple of bits more than this worst-case value. However, to take advantage of this requires a leading-0's detect and variable-sized shift in step 6 of the basic algorithm. This slows down the iteration time sufficiently that it is generally not worthwhile for $m \geq 10$ or so. In view of this, we have omitted the analysis for the average number of bits.

8.2.2 Representing X Using Redundancy

In the preceding discussion, we have assumed that X and Q are stored as single binary numbers without redundancy. Each iteration of the algorithm then requires a full carry-propagate addition to generate the revised X and Q. In this section, we describe one way of using redundant representations for X and Q to avoid doing full carry-propagate addition in each iteration (idea initially suggested by [3]).

Suppose X and Q were represented in redundant carry-save form using two parallel rows of bits for each. In other words, X would physically be stored using two registers X_A and X_B of equal width and significance such that $X = X_A + X_B$ (similarly for Q). The formulas in steps 4 and 5 of the basic method are as follows:

$$X' = X - X_h(1/Y_h)Y, \tag{8.39}$$

$$Q' = Q + X_h(1/Y_h)(1/2^{j-k}). \tag{8.40}$$

Using the carry-save representation, the addition and subtraction in the above formulas can be performed using carry-save adders that generate a row of sum bits and a row of carry bits. In fact, the carry-save adder tree for the multiplication in each formula can be fused with the carry-save addition or subtraction.

In the basic method outlined above, only the high bits of X, i.e., the significant bits in X_h, are actually input to multipliers during each iteration. The low-order bits are only input to an adder in step 4. If a carry-save representation for X_h were input to the multipliers, the multiplier would create twice the number of partial products. To avoid this, the high-order bits in the redundant representation of X must be summed using a short carry-propagate addition of width at least p bits before being input to the multipliers. This still saves some time compared to a full addition.

Suppose that the short carry-propagate addition were exactly p bits wide. Since X is represented using two rows of numbers, ΔX would actually be bounded by $\Delta X < 1/2^{p-1} - 1/2^{q-1}$ instead of $\Delta X < 1/2^p - 1/2^q$. The uncertainty would be increased by a factor of 2, because all the low-order bits of each row could range between all 1's and all 0's. To compensate for this, p could be made equal to $m + 2$ instead of $m + 1$, which would cause a one-bit increase in one dimension of the multipliers. If this were done, then X' would be reduced by the same number of bits $(m - 2)$ per iteration.

Alternatively, p could be kept at $m + 1$, but the short carry-propagate addition that generates X_h would include additional bits below bit $X_{(q-p)}$. If the addition had width v, ΔX would be bounded by $\Delta X < 1/2^p + 1/2^v - 1/2^{q-1}$. If the previous analysis for Theorem 1 is reexamined, it can be seen that $v = p + 1$ is sufficient. The last part of the analysis beginning from the constraint (8.35) would be altered as follows:

$$X' = \Delta X + X_h E_B Y + X_h E_C Y$$

$$< \frac{1}{2^p} + \frac{1}{2^v} - \frac{1}{2^{q-1}} + \frac{1.6}{2^{m-1}}, \tag{8.41}$$

$$X' < \frac{1}{2^{m+1}} + \frac{1}{2^{m+2}} - \frac{1}{2^{q-1}} + \frac{1.6}{2^{m-1}}, \tag{8.42}$$

$$X' < \frac{0.25}{2^{m-1}} + \frac{0.125}{2^{m-1}} - \frac{1}{2^{q-1}} + \frac{1.6}{2^{m-1}}, \tag{8.43}$$

$$X' < \frac{1}{2^{m-2}}. \tag{8.44}$$

Therefore, $m - 2$ bits are still reduced per iteration. The Q register is simpler: all the bits of Q can be kept in the redundant form until the final iteration. During the final iteration, full carry-propagate additions must be performed to calculate Q and X in normal binary representation.

8.3 ALGORITHM B

We now describe a faster algorithm based on rapidly calculating a more accurate reciprocal than a simple table lookup. As before, we first define and analyze the algorithm using a nonredundant representation for X and Q before discussing the use of redundancy for greater iteration speed.

Let us examine the Taylor series approximation equation for $1/Y$ about $Y = Y_h$:

$$\frac{1}{Y} = \frac{1}{Y_h} - \frac{\Delta Y}{Y_h^2} + \frac{(\Delta Y)^2}{Y_h^3} - \frac{(\Delta Y)^3}{Y_h^4} + \frac{(\Delta Y)^4}{Y_h^5} + \cdots. \tag{8.45}$$

All these terms are nonnegative, since $\Delta Y \leq 0$.

Our current method is to consider the terms beyond $\Delta Y / Y_h^2$ to be an unavoidable error. Actually, however, it is possible to rapidly calculate one or more adjustment terms to attain additional accuracy in estimating $1/Y$.

The revised method would be as follows:

1. Set the estimated quotient Q to 0 initially.
2. Let j and k denote the numbers of bits that X and Y have been left-shifted. Initially, both are set to the amounts of preshifting required to normalize X and Y.
3. Get an approximation of $1/Y_h$ from lookup table G_1. The index to the lookup table is the leading m bits of Y. Each table word is b_1 bits long. (Note: the table size is optimized later in the chapter.) Simultaneously get approximations of $1/Y_h^2, 1/Y_h^3, \ldots$ using lookup tables G_2, $G_3, \ldots$ with word widths $b_2, b_3, \ldots$, respectively. All tables are indexed using the first m bits of Y. In the next subsection, it will be shown that reasonable table widths b_i are given by

$$b_i = (mt - t) + \lceil \log_2 t \rceil - (mi - m - i). \qquad (8.46)$$

   This equation states that the tables of more significance require more bits of precision. The number of terms in the expansion is t.
4. Compute an approximation B to $1/Y$ using the first t terms from the following series:

$$B = \frac{1}{Y_h} - \frac{\Delta Y}{Y_h^2} + \frac{(\Delta Y)^2}{Y_h^3} - \frac{(\Delta Y)^3}{Y_h^4} + \frac{(\Delta Y)^4}{Y_h^5} + \cdots. \qquad (8.47)$$

   (The number of terms, t, is at least 2; all terms after the second are optional.) This can be done with a generation of partial products followed by a carry-save adder tree. [To accelerate the calculation of B, the least significant partial products in calculating powers of ΔY can be truncated for the higher-order terms, since the higher-order terms are less significant (details in next subsection).]
5. Compute the new dividend using $X' = X - X_h BY$. This formula can be computed in a manner similar to the calculation of $X' = X - X_h(1/Y_h)Y$ in the basic algorithm. By ordering the multiplies correctly, this formula only requires the latency of one multiplication plus subtraction per iteration (see step 4 of basic algorithm).
6. Compute the new quotient using $Q' = Q + X_h B(1/2^{j-k})$. It will be shown later in this chapter that X_h in the formulas for Q' and X' can be composed of the leading $p = mt - t + 2$ bits of X followed by 0's, where t is the number of terms used to calculate B. Also, B can be truncated to the most significant $mt - t + 4$ bits. This limits the size of the multiplies.

7. Left shift X' by $mt - t - 1$ bits to get rid of the guaranteed leading 0's that occur (as discussed in the next subsection). Shift 0's into the lsb of X' during this process. Calculate a revised $j' = j + mt - t - 1$.

8. Set $j = j'$, $Q = Q'$, and $X = X'$.

9. Repeat steps 5 through 8 until $j \geq q$.

10. The final Q is the quotient. Note that there are more bits in the quotient register than q. Let $Q_h = Q_{(1)} \cdots Q_{(q)}$, and let $Q_l = Q_{(q+1)} \cdots Q_{(q+e)}$ where e is the number of excess bits. Q (including both Q_h and Q_l) is within one ulp of the true infinite precision quotient, where an ulp is the unit of digit j of Q (i.e., $Q_{(j)}$). Here $q - j$ is always negative or zero. Some of the Q_l bits are not necessarily correct, since another iteration of the algorithm would add into those bits.

11. The residual dividend X should be right-shifted by $j - q$ bits to get the remainder assuming the entire Q is the quotient. If Q is truncated to q bits, then the true remainder can be computed by then adding $Q_l Y$ to X.

Since the advanced version reduces X' by $mt - t - 1$ bits per iteration, the algorithm terminates after $\lceil q / (mt - t - 1) \rceil$ iterations.

8.3.1 Number of Accurate Bits per Iteration

Theorem 2: Number of Bits Per Iteration Using Algorithm B X' *is reduced by at least* $mt - t - 1$ *bits per iteration if*:

- *The term* Y_h *includes* $m \geq 5$ *leading bits of Y.*
- *The number of Taylor-series terms from equation (8.47) used to construct* B *is* t.
- *The number* p *of significant bits in* X_h *is equal to* $rmt - t + 2$.
- *The word width* b_i *of table* G_i *is* $(mt - t) + \lceil \log_2 t \rceil - (mi - m - i)$ *for* $i = 1, 2, \ldots, t$.
- B *is represented in* $b_b = mt - t + 4$ *bits or more.*
- *The total arithmetic error in calculating* B *is less than* $1/2^{(mt-t+3)}$ (*see below for explanation*).

As in the basic method, m is the most important parameter, since increasing m by 1 requires a doubling of the number of table words. Once m is chosen, the other parameters are set so that the total error from truncating other calculations is less than or equal to the error from including just the leading m bits of Y in Y_h. In this analysis, we show that this is true given the above parameter settings.

As before, we compute the worst-case number of bits that are reduced from X in each iteration. The initial value of X is between $\frac{1}{2}$ and 1, since the leading bit is 1. By determining the largest possible value of X', we can determine the minimum number of bits eliminated per iteration.

Let us examine the formula for X':

$$X' = X - X_h BY, \tag{8.48}$$

where B is the first t terms from $B = 1/Y_h - \Delta Y/Y_h^2 + (\Delta Y)^2/Y_h^3 - (\Delta Y)^3/Y_h^4 + (\Delta Y)^4/Y_h^5 + \cdots$. In this case, three sources of inaccuracy affect the approximation $B \approx 1/Y$. Let the sources be defined by

$$B = 1/Y - E_B - E_C - E_D, \tag{8.49}$$

where:

- E_B represents an error term due to truncating the Taylor series after t terms. The error E_B is always nonnegative, since the truncated terms in the series are all nonnegative.
- E_C represents the error in calculating B using lookup tables with finite-width words. The error E_C is always nonnegative, since B is calculated using tables that are rounded down.
- E_D represents the error in truncating the arithmetic used to calculate B. The error E_D is nonnegative, since all the arithmetic is truncated, thus underestimating B.

Then

$$
\begin{aligned}
X' &= X - X_h BY \\
   &= X_h + \Delta X - X_h(1/Y - E_B - E_C - E_D)Y,
\end{aligned} \tag{8.50}
$$

$$X' = \Delta X + X_h(E_B + E_C + E_D)Y. \tag{8.51}$$

If E_B, E_C, and E_D can be accurately bounded, then this will give the maximal value of X'.

Let us begin by bounding E_B. The $(w + 1)$th term of the Taylor series for B is denoted by $B_{w+1} = (-\Delta Y)^w Y_h^{w+1}$. All terms of B are nonnegative, since ΔY is nonpositive. The worst case occurs when $-\Delta Y = 1/2^m - 1/2^q$. In this case, the following bound holds:

$$B_{w+1} < (1/2^{mw})(1/Y_h^{w+1}). \tag{8.52}$$

If the first t terms are used to construct B, then the remainder E_B is bounded by

$$E_B = \sum_{g=t}^{\infty} B_{g+1} < \sum_{g=t}^{\infty} \frac{1}{2^{mg}} \times \frac{1}{Y_h^{g+1}} = \frac{(1/2^{mt})(1/Y_h)^{t+1}}{1 - 1/(2^m Y_h)}. \tag{8.53}$$

For $m \gg 1$, this is just slightly greater than $(1/2^{mt})(1/Y_h)^{t+1}$. For $m \geq 5$, a nonstringent bound on E_B is

$$E_B < \frac{1.1}{2^{mt} Y_h^{t+1}}. \tag{8.54}$$

E_C comes from using finite-width lookup tables in calculating the value of the first t terms. E_D comes from truncating the arithmetic used to calculate B and truncating the value of B. A cumulative error can be computed where the error in each table lookup is represented by ϵ_i and the truncation error in computing each multiplicative term is δ_i:

$$B = \sum_{i=1}^{t} \left[\delta_i + \left(\epsilon_i + \frac{1}{Y_h^i} \right) (-\Delta Y)^{i-1} \right] \tag{8.55}$$

$$= \sum_{i=1}^{t} \frac{(-\Delta Y)^{i-1}}{Y_h^i} + \sum_{i=1}^{t} \epsilon_i (-\Delta Y)^{i-1} + \sum_{i=1}^{t} \delta_i. \tag{8.56}$$

Then E_C is equal to the sum of the terms involving ϵ_i:

$$E_C = \sum_{i=1}^{t} \epsilon_i (-\Delta Y)^{i-1}. \tag{8.57}$$

Let δ_0 be an additional term that represents truncating B to a certain number of bits after the summation. Then

$$E_D = \sum_{i=0}^{t} \delta_i. \tag{8.58}$$

Let us focus first on E_C. Suppose the table G_i is b_i bits wide. Since $\frac{1}{2} < Y_h < 1$, the maximal value of $1/Y_h^i$ is slightly less than 2^i. If words in G_i can represent values up to but not including 2^i, the unit of the most significant binary digit in G_i should have value 2^{i-1}. The unit of the least significant binary digit for G_i is then $1/2^{b_i - i}$. Each ϵ_i is less than the unit of the least significant digit:

$$\epsilon_i < 1/2^{b_i - i} \tag{8.59}$$

The worst-case value of $-\Delta Y$ is $-\Delta Y = 1/2^m - 1/2^q$. Substituting into equation (8.57) yields

$$E_C < \sum_{i=1}^{t} \frac{1}{2^{b_i - i}} \times \frac{1}{2^{(mi - m)}}, \tag{8.60}$$

$$E_C < \sum_{i=1}^{t} \frac{1}{2^{b_i + m - m - i}}. \tag{8.61}$$

This equation helps to determine the proper word widths b_i. Suppose that the b_i are set to

$$b_i = (mt - t) + \lceil \log_2 t \rceil - (mi - m - i). \tag{8.62}$$

This formula states that each table T_i is $m - 1$ bits wider than the next table T_{i+1}. Since T_i is used in a more significant term of the Taylor series than T_{i+1}, the table T_i must be stored with higher precision.

The total error E_C is then bounded by

$$E_C < \sum_{i=1}^{t} \frac{1}{2^{(mt-t)+\lceil \log_2 t \rceil}}, \tag{8.63}$$

$$E_C < \frac{1}{2^{mt-t}}. \tag{8.64}$$

Now consider E_D. The δ_i represent maximal permissible truncation errors. This concept accelerates the calculation of B by allowing the arithmetic for calculating B to be reduced in size. For instance, suppose $t = 4$, $m = 16$, and $q = 53$. Then the last term of B is $B_4 = (-\Delta Y)^3(1/Y_h^4)$. Since ΔY has $q - m = 53 - 16 = 37$ bits, the full computation of $(-\Delta Y)^3$ would use large multipliers and result in a $37 \times 3 - 2 = 109$-bit result. This is clearly much more than necessary, because the unit of the most significant bit of B_4 will be $1/2^{3m-3} = 1/2^{45}$. The allowable truncation errors δ_i can be used both to prune multiplier trees by discarding least significant PPs and to truncate results to smaller widths. The details are not presented here.

Since $1 \le B < 2$, the msb of B has unit 1. Suppose B is truncated to b_b bits. Since δ_0 is less than the significance of the LSB of B, $\delta_0 < 1/2^{b_b-1}$. In this case, we wish to restrict E_D as follows:

$$E_D < 1/2^{mt-t+2}. \tag{8.65}$$

For the purposes of this chapter, this can be achieved by both restricting δ_0 to

$$\delta_0 < 1/2^{mt-t+3}, \tag{8.66}$$

meaning that B can be truncated to $b_b = mt - t + 4$ bits, and restricting the remaining δ_i to

$$\sum_{i=1}^{t} \delta_i < \frac{1}{2^{mt-t+3}}. \tag{8.67}$$

Now we can substitute the bounds for E_B, E_C, and E_D into the constraint (8.51) to determine the maximum value of X'. Since $X_h < 1$ and $\Delta X \leq 1/2^p - 1/2^q$, the worst-case X' is bounded by

$$X' = \Delta X + X_h E_B Y + X_h E_C Y + X_h E_D Y$$

$$< \Delta X + E_B Y + E_C Y + E_D Y, \tag{8.68}$$

$$X' < \frac{1}{2^p} - \frac{1}{2^q} + \frac{1.1Y}{2^{mt} Y_h^{t+1}} + \frac{Y}{2^{mt-t}} + \frac{Y}{2^{mt-t+2}}. \tag{8.69}$$

Since $Y_h \geq Y$, we can set $Y_h = Y$ in the worst case and simplify to get

$$X' < \frac{1}{2^p} - \frac{1}{2^q} + \frac{1.1}{2^{mt} Y^t} + \frac{Y}{2^{mt-t}} + \frac{Y}{2^{mt-t+2}}, \tag{8.70}$$

$$X' < X_2, \tag{8.71}$$

where

$$X_2 = \frac{1}{2^p} - \frac{1}{2^q} + \frac{1.1}{2^{mt} Y^t} + \frac{Y}{2^{mt-t}} + \frac{Y}{2^{mt-t+2}}. \tag{8.72}$$

We now wish to determine the worst-case value of X_2 while Y is allowed to vary over the range $\frac{1}{2} \leq Y < 1$. In order to accomplish this, the first step is to locate all possible maxima and minima by setting the partial derivative $\partial X_2 / \partial Y$ equal to zero. The first partial derivative is

$$\frac{\partial X_2}{\partial Y} = - \frac{1.1t}{2^{mt} Y^{t+1}} + \frac{1}{2^{mt-t}} + \frac{1}{2^{mt-t+2}}. \tag{8.73}$$

Setting this derivative to 0 and solving, we obtain the following:

$$Y = Y_A = \left(\frac{2^{-t+2} \times 1.1t}{5} \right)^{1/(t+1)}. \tag{8.74}$$

The value Y_A might be in the allowed range $\frac{1}{2} \leq Y < 1$. By testing the value Y_A using $\partial^2 X_2 / \partial Y^2$, we can show that Y_A is a local minimum. The details are not shown.

Since Y_A is a local minimum and there are no other maxima or minima within the allowed range of Y, we know that the maximum value of X_2

occurs at either $Y = \frac{1}{2}$ or $Y = 1$. The value of X_2 at $Y = \frac{1}{2}$ is as follows:

$$\text{at} \quad Y = \frac{1}{2} \quad X_2 = \frac{1}{2^p} - \frac{1}{2^q} + \frac{1.1}{2^{mt-t}} + \frac{1}{2^{mt-t+1}} + \frac{1}{2^{mt-t+3}} \quad (8.75)$$

$$= \frac{1}{2^p} - \frac{1}{2^q} + \frac{1.1}{2^{mt-t}} + \frac{0.5}{2^{mt-t}} + \frac{0.125}{2^{mt-t}} \quad (8.76)$$

$$= \frac{1}{2^p} - \frac{1}{2^q} + \frac{1.725}{2^{mt-t}}. \quad (8.77)$$

The value of X_2 at $Y = 1$ is as follows:

$$\text{at} \quad Y = 1, \quad X_2 = \frac{1}{2^p} - \frac{1}{2^q} + \frac{1.1}{2^{mt}} + \frac{1}{2^{mt-t}} + \frac{1}{2^{mt-t+2}} \quad (8.78)$$

$$= \frac{1}{2^p} - \frac{1}{2^q} + \frac{(1.1)/2^t}{2^{mt-t}} + \frac{1}{2^{mt-t}} + \frac{0.25}{2^{mt-t}} \quad (8.79)$$

Since $t \geq 2$,

$$\text{at} \quad (Y = 1), \quad X_2 \leq \frac{1}{2^p} - \frac{1}{2^q} + \frac{(1.1)/4}{2^{mt-t}} + \frac{1}{2^{mt-t}} + \frac{0.25}{2^{mt-t}} \quad (8.80)$$

$$X_2 \leq \frac{1}{2^p} - \frac{1}{2^q} + \frac{1.525}{2^{mt-t}} \quad (8.81)$$

The highest possible value of X_2 occurs at $Y = \frac{1}{2}$. This is substituted back into constraint (8.72) to get

$$X' < \frac{1}{2^p} - \frac{1}{2^q} + \frac{1.725}{2^{mt-t}} \quad (8.82)$$

If $p = mt - t + 2$, then this can be converted to

$$X' < \frac{1}{2^{mt-t+2}} - \frac{1}{2^q} + \frac{1.725}{2^{mt-t}}, \quad (8.83)$$

$$X' < \frac{0.25}{2^{mt-t}} - \frac{1}{2^q} + \frac{1.725}{2^{mt-t}}, \quad (8.84)$$

$$X' < \frac{1}{2^{(mt-t-1)}}. \quad (8.85)$$

In this case, the highest-order bit of X' that could possibly be 1 is the $(mt - t)$th bit, $X'_{(q-mt+t)}$. For any p such that $p \geq mt - t + 2$, the worst-case value of X' is bounded by the above inequality. In fact, using $p > mt - t + 2$

only improves the convergence by a fraction of a bit, so it is best to use $p = mt - t + 2$ to minimize the size of the multiplies. In summary, at least $mt - t - 1$ bits are skipped per iteration if $p = mt - t + 2$, t is the number of terms used to construct B, and the other conditions in Theorem 2 hold.

8.3.2   Representing X Using Redundancy

As with the basic method, the procedure may be faster if X and Q are kept in a carry-save form. A short carry-propagate addition of width v of the high-order carry-save bits of X is performed to create the bits of X_h in normal binary representation. To reduce the same number of bits per iteration, p can be increased by one to $p = mt - t + 3$. Alternatively, the same number of bits per iteration is guaranteed if all of the following conditions hold:

1. p remains at $p = mt - t + 2$.
2. The error term E_D from the analysis of Theorem 2 is restricted using

$$E_D < 1.5/2^{mt-t+3}. \tag{8.86}$$

For the purposes of this chapter, this can be achieved by both restricting δ_0 to

$$\delta_0 < 1/2^{mt-t+3}, \tag{8.87}$$

meaning that B can be truncated to $b_b = mt - t + 4$ bits, and restricting the remaining δ_i to

$$\sum_{i=1}^{t} \delta_i < \frac{0.5}{2^{(mt-t+3)}}. \tag{8.88}$$

3. The short addition that generates X_h has width $v = p + 3$.

The same procedure used in the previous analysis for Theorem 2 must be repeated using slightly different formulas. It can still be shown that the only possible point of zero derivative within the allowed range $\frac{1}{2} \le Y < 1$ is a local minimum. It can then be shown that $Y = \frac{1}{2}$ is the point of maximum possible value for X_2. The details are omitted.

The resulting guaranteed bound on X' is

$$X' < \frac{1}{2^p} + \frac{1}{2^v} - \frac{1}{2^{(q-1)}} + \frac{1.1}{2^{mt-t}} + \frac{1}{2^{mt-t+1}} + \frac{0.75}{2^{mt-t+3}}, \tag{8.89}$$

$$X' < \frac{1}{2^p} + \frac{1}{2^v} - 1/2^{(q-1)} + \frac{1.69375}{2^{mt-t}}. \tag{8.90}$$

ALGORITHM C   171

If $p = mt - t + 2$ and $v = p + 3$, then this can be converted to

$$X' < \frac{1}{2^{mt-t+2}} + \frac{1}{2^{mt-t+5}} - \frac{1}{2^{q-1}} + \frac{1.69375}{2^{mt-t}}, \qquad (8.91)$$

$$X' < 1/2^{mt-t-1}. \qquad (8.92)$$

Therefore, $mt - t - 1$ bits are still reduced per iteration. During the final iteration, a full carry-propagate addition must be performed to calculate Q and X in normal binary representation. In the advanced method, the number of iterations is smaller and the short addition of v bits to generate X_h is wider than in the basic method. Therefore, the benefits of a redundant representation are not as great.

8.4 ALGORITHM C

The previous algorithms consider each individual term in the Taylor series separately; hence, many lookup tables are needed and the designs are complicated. The third algorithm combines the first two terms of Taylor series together, and only requires a small lookup table to generate accurate results. This algorithm achieves fast division by multiplying the dividend in the first step, which is done in parallel with the table lookup. In the second step, another multiplication operation is executed to generate the quotient.

8.4.1 Theory

Let X and Y be two $2m$-bit fixed-point numbers between one and two defined by equations 8.93 and 8.94 where $x_{(i)}, y_{(i)} \in \{0, 1\}$:

$$X = 1 + 2^{-1}x_{(1)} + 2^{-2}x_{(2)} + \cdots + 2^{-(2m-1)}x_{(2m-1)}, \qquad (8.93)$$

$$Y = 1 + 2^{-1}y_{(1)} + 2^{-2}y_{(2)} + \cdots + 2^{-(2m-1)}y_{(2m-1)}. \qquad (8.94)$$

To calculate X/Y, Y is first decomposed into two groups: the higher-order bits (Y_H) and the lower order bits (Y_L). Y_H contains the $m + 1$ most significant bits, and Y_L contains the remaining $m - 1$ bits:

$$Y_H = 1 + 2^{-1}y_{(1)} + \cdots + 2^{-(m-1)}y_{(m-1)} + 2^{-m}y_{(m)}, \qquad (8.95)$$

$$Y_L = 2^{-(m+1)}y_{(m+1)} + \cdots + 2^{-(2m-1)}y_{(2m-1)}. \qquad (8.96)$$

The range of Y_H is between 1 and Y_{Hmax} $(= 2 - 2^{-m})$, and the range of Y_L is between 0 and Y_{Lmax} $(= 2^{-m} - 2^{-(2m-1)})$. Dividing X by Y, we get

$$\frac{X}{Y} = \frac{X}{Y_H + Y_L} = \frac{X(Y_H - Y_L)}{Y_H^2 - Y_L^2}, \tag{8.97}$$

$$\frac{X}{Y} \approx \frac{X(Y_H - Y_L)}{Y_H^2}. \tag{8.98}$$

Since $Y_H > 2^m Y_L$, the maximum fractional error in equation 8.98 is less than 2^{-2m} (or $\frac{1}{2}$ ulp).

Using the Taylor series, equation (8.97) can be expanded at Y_L/Y_H:

$$\frac{X}{Y_H + Y_L} = \frac{X}{Y_H}\left(1 - \frac{Y_L}{Y_H} + \frac{Y_L^2}{Y_H^2} - \cdots\right) \tag{8.99}$$

The approximation in equation (8.98) is equivalent to combining the first two terms in the Taylor series.

Figure 8.1 shows the block diagram of the algorithm. In the first step, the algorithm retrieves the value of $1/Y_H^2$ from a lookup table and multiplies X with $Y_H - Y_L$ at the same time. In the second step, $1/Y_H^2$ and $X \cdot (Y_H - Y_L)$ are multiplied together to generate the result.

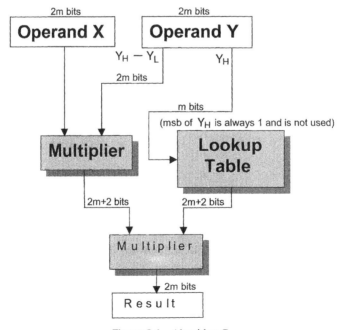

Figure 8.1 Algorithm C.

ALGORITHM C   173

TABLE 8.1   A simple lookup-table example ($m = 3$)

Y_H	$\lfloor 1/Y_H^2 \rfloor$	Table Entry
1.000	1.0000000×1.00	0000000
1.001	1.1001010×0.10	1001010
1.010	1.0100011×0.10	0100011
1.011	1.0000111×0.10	0000111
1.100	1.1100011×0.01	1100011
1.101	1.1000001×0.01	1000001
1.110	1.0100111×0.01	0100111
1.111	$\hat{1}.0010001 \times 0.01$	0010001

8.4.2   Lookup-Table Construction

To minimize the size of the lookup table, the table entries are normalized so that the msb of each entry is one. These msb's are therefore not stored in the table.

A lookup table with $m = 3$ is shown in Table 8.1. $\lfloor 1/Y_H^2 \rfloor$ represents the value of $1/Y_H^2$ truncated to $2m + 2$ significant bits. The exponent part of the $1/Y_H^2$ may be stored in the same table, but can also be determined by some simple logic gates. In this example, the exponent is 1.00 when $y_{(1)} = y_{(2)} = y_{(3)} = 0$, it is 0.10 when $y_{(1)} = 0$ and $y_{(2)} \vee y_{(3)} = 1$, and it is 0.01 when $y_{(1)} = 1$.

8.4.3   Booth Recoding

The Booth recoding algorithm [21] has widely been used to minimize the number of PP terms in a multiplier. In our division algorithm, special Booth recoders are needed to achieve the $X(Y_H - Y_L)$ multiplication without explicitly calculating the value of $Y_H - Y_L$. Lyu and Matula [97] proposed a general redundant binary Booth recoding scheme. In our case, the Y_H and Y_L bits are nonoverlapping, and a cheaper and faster encoding scheme is feasible.

We use Booth 2 recoding to illustrate our encoding algorithm, but the same principle can apply to the other Booth recoding schemes. In Booth 2 recoding, the multiplier is partitioned into overlapping strings of 3 bits, and each string is used to select a single PP.

Unlike conventional Booth 2 recoding, the encoding of $Y_H - Y_L$ consists of four types of encoders. Figure 8.2 shows the locations of these four types: the Y_L group contains all the 3-bit strings that reside entirely within Y_L; the boundary string contains some Y_L bits as well as some Y_H bits; the first Y_H string is located next to the boundary string; the Y_H group contains all the remaining strings within Y_H.

The Y_H bits represent positive numbers, whereas the Y_L bits represent negative numbers. Hence, conventional Booth 2 recoding is used in the Y_H group, but the PPs in the Y_L group are negated. As shown in the diagram,

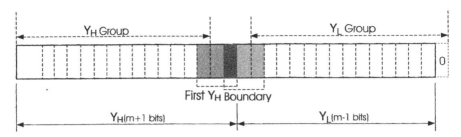

Figure 8.2 Booth recoding.

the boundary region between Y_H and Y_L requires two additional special encoders. Depending on whether m is even or odd, the encoding schemes for these two encoders are different. It is possible that only one such encoder is used in the boundary region, but then that encoder must generate $-3 \times$ multiplicands (for even m). In order to speed up the multiplication and simplify the encoding logic, two special encoders are used to avoid the hard multiples.

Table 8.2 summarizes the four different encoding schemes for both even and odd m. It is important to note that the first Y_H encoder actually needs to examine both the first Y_H string and the boundary string when m is odd. If the boundary string is 101, the lsb of the first Y_H string is set to 0 instead of 1. If the boundary string is not 101, the lsb of the first Y_H string is set to the msb of the boundary string (as usual). This encoding scheme uses all but two normal Booth recoders and is particularly useful if the same multiplier hardware is used for both the first and the second multiplications.

8.4.4 Error Analysis

There are four sources of error: Taylor-series approximation error (E_∞), lookup table rounding error (E_T), the rounding error of the first multiplication (E_{M1}), and the rounding error of the second multiplication (E_{M2}).

TABLE 8.2 Booth recoding of $Y_H - Y_L$

Bits	Y_H Group	Y_L Group	Boundary Even m	Boundary Odd m	First Y_H Even m	First Y_H Odd m
00 0	0	0	0	0	0	0
00 1	+1	-1	-1	-1	0	+1
01 0	+1	-1	-1	+1	+1	+1
01 1	+2	-2	-2	0	+1	+2
10 0	-2	+2	+2	-2	-2	-2
10 1	-1	+1	+1	+1	-2	-1
11 0	-1	+1	+1	-1	-1	-1
11 1	0	0	0	-2	-1	0

ALGORITHM C   **175**

The total error is equal to $E_\infty + E_T + E_{M1} + E_{M2}$. To minimize this error, the divider can be designed such that $E_\infty \leq 0$, $E_T \leq 0$, $E_{M1} \leq 0$, and $E_{M2} \geq 0$. This means that the table entries are truncated to $2m + 2$ bits, the first multiplication is truncated to $2m + 2$ bits, and the second multiplication is rounded up to $2m$ bits.

The Taylor-series approximation error (E_∞) is determined by

$$E_\infty = \frac{X(Y_H - Y_L)}{Y_H^2} - \frac{X}{Y} = -\frac{X \cdot Y_L^2}{Y \cdot Y_H^2}. \qquad (8.100)$$

This error is most significant for large Y_L and small Y_H. The maximum approximation error $|E_\infty|$ is slightly less than $\frac{1}{2}$ ulp when $Y_L = Y_{Lmax}$ and $Y_H = 1$. The lookup table has $2m + 2$ significant bits, so the maximum truncation error $|E_T| < \frac{1}{4}$ ulp. Similarly, the maximum rounding error for the first multiplication $|E_{M1}| < \frac{1}{4}$ ulp, and the maximum rounding error for the second multiplication $|E_{M2}| < 1$ ulp. Thus, the maximum positive error is less than 1 ulp ($|E_{M2}|$), and the maximum negative error is also less than 1 ulp ($|E_\infty + E_T + E_{M1}|$).

8.4.5 Optimization Techniques

This section describes two optimization techniques for the division algorithm. The first technique uses a slightly different lookup table and allows the two multiplications to use the same rounding mode, whereas the second technique uses an error compensation term to further reduce the Taylor-series approximation error.

Alternative Lookup Table

As described in Section 8.4.4, the rounding modes of the first and the second multiplication are different. This may be undesirable if the two multiplications need to share the same multiplier. A simple solution is to use round-to-nearest mode in the two multiplications as well as in constructing the lookup table. Since the error terms can be either positive or negative, the maximum total error becomes the sum of the maxima of all the error terms.

Let $T(Y_H)$ be the table entry at Y_H with infinite precision. The expression for the approximation error E_∞ is

$$E_\infty = X(Y_H - Y_L)T(Y_H) - \frac{X}{Y_H + Y_L}. \qquad (8.101)$$

In order to minimize $|E_\infty|$, $T(Y_H)$ is set to be slightly larger than $1/Y_H^2$. For each Y_H, the optimum table entry is determined by setting the maximum positive error (at $Y_L = 0$) to be the same as the maximum negative error (at $Y_L = Y_{Lmax}$). The following equation shows the expression for the optimum table entry $T(Y_H)_{opt}$:

$$T(Y_H)_{opt} = \frac{2Y_H + Y_{Lmax}}{Y_H(Y_H + Y_{Lmax})(2Y_H - Y_{Lmax})}. \qquad (8.102)$$

The approximation error is at its maximum when $Y_H = 1$ and $Y_L = Y_{Lmax}$. Using equation (8.101), the maximum approximation error can easily be derived as

$$|E_\infty| = \frac{X \cdot Y_{Lmax}^2}{(1 + Y_{Lmax})(2 - Y_{Lmax})}. \qquad (8.103)$$

In this case, $|E_\infty|$ is slightly less than $\frac{1}{4}$ ulp. Using the round-to-nearest rounding mode, we have $|E_{M1}| < \frac{1}{8}$ ulp, $|E_{M2}| < \frac{1}{2}$ ulp, and $|E_T| < \frac{1}{8}$ ulp. As in Section 8.4.4, the total error of the alternative lookup table is also less than 1 ulp. Table 8.3 illustrates the same example shown in Section 8.4.2 with the alternative lookup table, where $RN[T(Y_H)]$ represents the round-to-nearest value of $T(Y_H)$ to $2m + 2$ significant bits.

Error Compensation

The Taylor-series approximation error can be further reduced by adding an error compensation term in the first multiplication. Equation (8.100) shows that the magnitude of the Taylor series approximation error (E_∞) increases when either Y_L gets larger or Y_H gets smaller. By looking at the first few bits of Y_L and Y_H, it is possible to identify large Y_L and small Y_H, and then compensate for the approximation error. However, it is important to ensure that the approximation error does not become overcompensated and become positive; that would increase the total error (Section 8.4.4).

Figure 8.3 depicts a simple error compensation scheme. In this diagram, $C(Y)$ represents the positive error compensation that is used to correct the

TABLE 8.3   Alternative lookup table ($m = 3$)

Y_h	$RN[T(Y_H)]$	Table Entry
1.000	1.0000001×1.00	0000001
1.001	1.1001011×0.10	1001011
1.010	1.0100101×0.10	0100101
1.011	1.0001000×0.10	0001000
1.100	1.1100100×0.01	1100100
1.101	1.1000010×0.01	1000010
1.110	1.0101000×0.01	0101000
1.111	1.0010010×0.01	0010010

ALGORITHM C   177

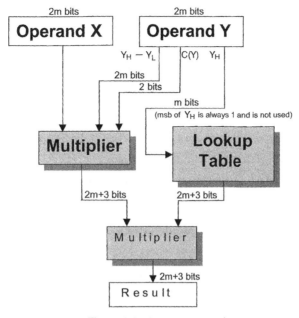

Figure 8.3 Error compensation.

negative Taylor-series approximation error. The new approximation equation becomes

$$\frac{X}{Y} \approx \frac{X\left[Y_{\mathrm{H}} - Y_{\mathrm{L}} + C(Y)\right]}{Y_{\mathrm{H}}^2}. \qquad (8.104)$$

The expression for $C(Y)$ is

$$C(Y) = 2^{-(2m+2)} y_{(m+1)} y_{(m+2)} \left(1 + \overline{y_{(1)}} \cdot \overline{y_{(2)}} \cdot y_{(m+3)}\right). \qquad (8.105)$$

Depending on the first few terms of Y_{H} and Y_{L}, $C(Y)$ is set to 0, $2^{-(2m+2)}$, or $2^{-(2m+1)}$. The error compensation only requires an additional PP in the multiplier and a few simple logic gates [shown in equation (8.105)]. The maximum Taylor-series approximation error is $9/32$ ulp when $Y_{\mathrm{H}} = 1$ and $Y_{\mathrm{L}} = (3Y_{\mathrm{Lmax}} - 1)/4$. Figure 8.4 shows the approximation error with different Y_{L}.

A similar error compensation scheme can also be used for the alternative lookup table shown in Section 8.4.5. The expressions for the new approxima-

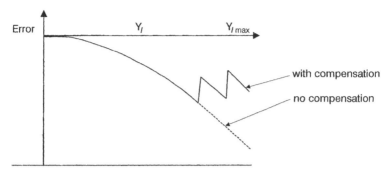

Figure 8.4   Approximation error with error compensation.

tion and the error compensation are determined by

$$\frac{X}{Y} \approx \frac{(2Y_{\mathrm{H}} + Y_{\mathrm{Lmax}})(Y_{\mathrm{H}} - Y_{\mathrm{L}} + C(Y))X}{Y_{\mathrm{H}}(Y_{\mathrm{H}} + Y_{\mathrm{Lmax}})(2Y_{\mathrm{H}} - Y_{\mathrm{Lmax}})}, \qquad (8.106)$$

$$C(Y) = 2^{-2m-2}\left(\overline{y_{(1)} \cdot y_{(m+1)}} \cdot y_{(m+2)} - \overline{y_{(m+1)}}\right), \qquad (8.107)$$

respectively. In this case, $C(Y)$ is set to $-2^{-(2m+2)}$, 0, or $2^{-(2m+2)}$ depending on the first few bits in Y_{H} and Y_{L}.

8.4.6   Discussion

This section presents a simple and fast division algorithm based on Taylor series expansion. Using a multiplier and a lookup table with $2^m(2m + 1)$ bits, this algorithm produces a $2m$-bit result in two steps. For example, a 12.5-Kbyte lookup table is required for single precision (24 bits) FP division.

The same principle can be applied to some elementary functions, such as square root. Using the same definitions of Y, Y_{H}, and Y_{L} as before, we get the following approximation:

$$\sqrt{Y} = \frac{Y}{Y_{\mathrm{H}}^{1/2}}\left(1 - \frac{Y_{\mathrm{L}}}{2Y_{\mathrm{H}}} + \frac{3Y_{\mathrm{L}}^2}{8Y_{\mathrm{H}}^2} - \cdots\right) \approx \frac{Y(Y_{\mathrm{H}} - Y_{\mathrm{L}}/2)}{Y_{\mathrm{H}}^{3/2}}. \qquad (8.108)$$

This is very similar to the approximation used in the division algorithm. The differences are that the Y_{L} term is shifted by one bit in the numerator and the lookup table contains $1/Y_{\mathrm{H}}^{3/2}$ entries instead of $1/Y_{\mathrm{H}}^2$ entries.

We can also combine more than the first two terms in the Taylor series expansion. For example, if we use the first four terms in the expansion, we get the following approximation:

$$\frac{X}{Y} \approx \frac{X(Y_H - Y_L)}{Y_h^2}\left(1 + \frac{Y_L^2}{Y_H^2}\right). \tag{8.109}$$

As before, only a single $1/Y_H^2$ lookup table is needed, but this algorithm also needs to calculate Y_L^2. Our next step is to generalize the existing algorithm and to investigate the optimum Taylor series approximation for different input precisions.

8.5 RELATED ALGORITHMS

The high-radix SRT algorithm is described in Chapter 7. As shown the SRT algorithm is limited by its overhead and complexity. As the radix increases, the table delay increases linearly and the area increases quadratically. Consequently, it is probably inefficient to use a radix higher than 8 or 16 in SRT algorithms.

On the other hand, there are a number of other efficient high-radix algorithms, such as the Cyrix short-reciprocal algorithm, and the division algorithms based on the Newton–Raphson method and MacLaurin series. These algorithms are described later in this section. *Prescaling* is another technique which can be used to reduce the complexity of the high-radix SRT algorithm. By multiplying a scaling factor by both the divisor and the dividend, prescaling transforms the range of the divisor to a number close to one. This allows a simple quotient selection method based on the dividend alone instead of the SRT quotient selection, which is based on both the dividend and the divisor. Detailed description of the prescaling technique can be found in [175, 83, 89].

8.5.1 Cyrix Short-Reciprocal Algorithm

The recently designed Cyrix 83D87 arithmetic coprocessor briefly described in [26, 27, 105, 106] employs a *short-reciprocal* algorithm similar to the basic technique described in this chapter to get 17 bits/iteration. We only discriminate between the two methods here. Each iteration of the Cyrix algorithm uses formulas similar to ours:

$$X' = X - X_h(1/Y_h)Y, \tag{8.110}$$

$$Q' = Q + X_h(1/Y_h)(1/2^{(j-k)}). \tag{8.111}$$

The Cyrix coprocessor does high-radix division using a compact implementation. To conserve hardware, the coprocessor is equipped with only one multiplier, of size 19×69, which is integrated into a fused multiply–add unit. The multiply–add unit is also used in the multiplication and square-root algorithms. Using it, the Cyrix co-processor performs two multiplications in series for each iteration of its division algorithm.

In this case, $X_h(1/Y_h)$ is calculated and then truncated to 19 bits to create a high-radix quotient digit. The lower-order PPs are discarded because they contribute little due to the inherent inaccuracy in using X_h to approximate X and a table lookup of $1/Y_h$ to approximate $1/Y$. The truncated result is then multiplied by Y. This truncation process reduces the size of the second multiply but requires that the two multiplies be performed in series. In contrast, our method requires only one multiply per iteration, because no truncation of $X_h(1/Y_h)$ is performed (details explained earlier).

Unlike our method, the Cyrix method derives its reciprocal approximation using a combination of table lookup and the Newton-Raphson method. Also, the iterative portion of the Cyrix method uses an intentional overestimate of the reciprocal rather than an underestimate. The Cyrix coprocessor can also do square root using a similar iterative scheme [25].

8.5.2 Comparison with the Newton–Raphson Method

In the standard Newton–Raphson technique, an accurate reciprocal B is computed first by an iterative method. This reciprocal is accurate enough so that the quotient can be calculated directly by a final multiplication $Q = XB$. The calculation of the reciprocal approximation in the Newton–Raphson method is necessarily iterative: the improved reciprocal is calculated using $B_{n+1} = B_n \times (2 - Y \times B_n)$ [192, 103]. Each iteration requires two multiplications in $B_n Y B_n$ that cannot be performed simultaneously. Each iteration doubles the number of bits of accuracy in B; to get 56-bit accuracy requires two iterations starting with a 14-bit-accurate reciprocal. A separate calculation is required to produce the remainder, which has been shown to be nonnegative in [192].

In contrast, Algorithms A and B calculate the reciprocal B using one or more terms from a Taylor series that can potentially be implemented in a noniterative manner. Algorithms A and B iterate by calculating a reduced dividend $X' = X - (X_h B)Y$, where $X_h B$ is the approximate quotient based on the approximate reciprocal B. As explained earlier, each iteration requires only one multiplication to reduce the dividend X' by a constant number of bits which depends on the accuracy of B. Since estimates of the quotient are calculated simultaneously in each iteration, no final multiplication is needed to get the quotient Q. In Algorithms A and B, a form of remainder is available directly in the register X, assuming that the entire Q is the quotient. If the quotient is truncated, then the truncated bits multiplied by Y should be added to X. The remainder is never negative.

8.5.3 Comparison with the IBM RISC System/6000

The IBM RISC System/6000 implements FP division using an iterative algorithm employing its multiply-and-add hardware [112, 103].

The algorithm is a modified version of the Newton–Raphson method. One enhancement is used: after a reciprocal is calculated, the method performs one pass of a reduction similar to our method's iteration. Using our notation, it is as follows:

1. $Q = XB$.
2. $X' = X - QY$.
3. $Q' = Q + X'B$.

Markstein [103] describes the algorithm and detailed analyses for guaranteed correct rounding.

In addition to the general differences between the Newton–Raphson and our method, in the former the above reduction is done using a full-precision quotient, that is, $X' = X - QY$ instead of $X' = X - X_h BY$ used in our method.

8.5.4 Comparison with MacLaurin Series

The MacLaurin-series method [192] uses an approximation to the reciprocal:

$$B \approx \frac{1}{Y} = \frac{1}{Z + 1}$$

$$= (1 - Z)(1 + Z^2)(1 + Z^4)(1 + Z^8)(1 + Z^{16}) \cdots . \qquad (8.112)$$

The number of bits of accuracy doubles with each additional factor. In the normal iterative implementation, the first few factors are approximated using a lookup table. Each iteration calculates an additional factor from the previous using one multiplication and an add (or a 2's complement in [192]). An additional multiplication is required to multiply the factor with the current approximation B. This multiplication can overlap the calculation of the next factor, so that each iteration adding one factor takes just one multiplication plus a 2's complement. As discussed in [192], the convergence per iteration is mathematically equivalent to the convergence of the Newton–Raphson method where the initial reciprocal estimate $B_0 = 1$. The quotient and remainder must each be calculated following the generation of B. Unlike our method or the Newton–Raphson, the implementation sizes are somewhat restricted. If one implementation includes the first k multiplicative terms in a lookup table of 2^v words, the next larger implementation includes the first $k + 1$ terms in a table of 2^{2v} words.

Like the Newton–Raphson method, the convergence of the MacLaurin series differs from our method. Also, our method automatically provides a quotient without extra calculations.

8.6 CONCLUSION

By using large, accurate lookup tables for the reciprocal, fast division can be accomplished in just a few iterations using Algorithm A.

In addition, a more accurate reciprocal can be quickly calculated using a Taylor series approximation. Theoretically, the Taylor series can be calculated directly rather than iteratively, unlike the Newton–Raphson. In practice, the higher powers of ΔY may be calculated with staged multiplications, although lookup tables for powers of ΔY remains an unexplored possibility. By using more accurate reciprocals, Algorithm B can divide in two iterations or even one.

Finally, Algorithm C combines several terms in the Taylor series, and the lookup table size is much smaller.

9

USING A MULTIPLIER FOR FUNCTION APPROXIMATION

Based upon work by Eric Schwarz

Many common algorithms for high-order arithmetic operations require an initial approximation. The Newton–Raphson algorithm starts with an approximation and then quadratically converges on the solution. The initial approximation determines the number of iterations of the algorithm and is typically implemented as a lookup table in the form of a ROM or PLA. The SNAP group has investigated a novel method to form an initial approximation using a partial-product array.

9.1 PROPOSED METHOD: IMPLEMENTATION

The proposed method is a nonstandard method of creating an approximation to a high-order arithmetic operation. A partial-product array (PPA) is derived which sums to an approximation of an operation. This PPA is similar to the PPA of a multiplication. It is so similar that the approximation PPA can be summed by a multiplier. Thus, the proposed method consists of determining a PPA that approximates an operation and then summing this array on a multiplier. This section discusses the specifics of the PPAs, related research, and an implementation which adapts an existing design of a multiplier to sum auxiliary PPAs.

9.1.1 Partial-Product Array

The PPA of a binary multiplication is shown in Figure 9.1. The multiplier, Y, is multiplied by the multiplicand, X, to form the product, P. Each operand is

183

			$x_0 \cdot$	$x_{(1)}$	$x_{(2)}$	$x_{(3)}$	$\cdots$	Multiplicand
		X	$y_0 \cdot$	$y_{(1)}$	$y_{(2)}$	$y_{(3)}$	$\cdots$	Multiplier
		$\vdots$	$\vdots$	$\vdots$	$\vdots$			
			$y_{(3)}x_0$	$y_{(3)}x_{(1)}$	$y_{(3)}x_{(2)}$	$y_{(3)}x_{(3)}$	$\cdots$	
		$y_{(2)}x_0$	$y_{(2)}x_{(1)}$	$y_{(2)}x_{(2)}$	$y_{(2)}x_{(3)}$	$\cdots$		
	$y_{(1)}x_0$	$y_{(1)}x_{(1)}$	$y_{(1)}x_{(2)}$	$y_{(1)}x_{(3)}$	$\cdots$			
$y_0 x_0$	$y_0 x_{(1)}$	$y_0 x_{(2)}$	$y_0 x_{(3)}$	$\cdots$				
$p_0 \cdot$	$p_{(1)}$	$p_{(2)}$	$p_{(3)}$	$\cdots$				Product

Figure 9.1 Binary PPA of a multiplication.

expressed in terms of its binary bits. The array formed consists of partial product rows. Each element in the array consists of a multiplication of two Boolean variables. These multiplications can be replaced by logical AND gates. The logical AND of two Boolean elements is itself a Boolean element. Thus, each element of the array is a Boolean element. Each column of the array has an implied weight of a different power of two. The algebraic summation of the Boolean elements yields the product as shown below:

$$P(X,Y) = \sum_{i=0}^{N-1} \sum_{j=0}^{M-1} \left(x_{(i)} \wedge y_{(j)} \right) \times 2^{-(i+j)}.$$

The PPA is a two-dimensional representation[1] of this formula.

A typical multiplication of double-precision IEEE 754 standard [72] numbers involves 53 rows of 53 elements per row. This is a very large array of 2809 elements. A multiplier sums all these Boolean elements to form the product.

If each Boolean element of the multiplication's PPA is replaced by a generalized Boolean element, then a PPA is formed as shown in Figure 9.2. Each element is replaced by a generalized element, which can be any type of Boolean function and must evaluate to zero or one. An example is shown below of a four-way NOR gate:

$$B_{(i,j)}(X) = B_{(i,j)}(x_0, x_{(1)}, x_{(2)}, \ldots, x_{(n)}),$$

that is,

$$B_{(i,j)}(X) = \overline{\left(x_0 \middle| x_{(1)} \middle| x_{(4)} \middle| x_{(5)} \right)},$$

$$B_{(i,j)}(X) \in \{0,1\}.$$

---

[1]The reader should recall our definition of the binary number weights: $a_n a_{n-1} \ldots a_2 a_1 a_0 \ldots$ $a_{-1} a_{-2} a_{-3} \ldots$ is represented as $a_n a_{n-1} \ldots a_1 a_0 \ldots a_{(1)} \, a_{(2)} a_{(3)} \ldots$.

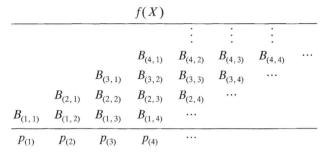

$f(X)$

			$B_{(4,1)}$	$B_{(4,2)}$	$B_{(4,3)}$	$B_{(4,4)}$	$\cdots$
		$B_{(3,1)}$	$B_{(3,2)}$	$B_{(3,3)}$	$B_{(3,4)}$	$\cdots$	
	$B_{(2,1)}$	$B_{(2,2)}$	$B_{(2,3)}$	$B_{(2,4)}$	$\cdots$		
$B_{(1,1)}$	$B_{(1,2)}$	$B_{(1,3)}$	$B_{(1,4)}$	$\cdots$			

$P_{(1)} \qquad P_{(2)} \qquad P_{(3)} \qquad P_{(4)} \qquad \cdots$

Figure 9.2 Generalized binary PPA.

The Boolean elements are chosen such that they sum to an approximation of an operation:

$$f(X) \approx \sum_{i=1}^{M} \sum_{j=1}^{N} B_{(i,j)}(X) \times 2^{-(i+j)+k}.$$

The generalized PPA is a generalization of a multiplication's PPA. Once each Boolean element is evaluated, the elements are summed in the same manner as in the multiplication's PPA. If the array is chosen so that it can be superimposed on the multiplication's PPA, then it can be summed by that multiplier.

There is one other type of PPA that is important. The generalized PPA can be extended by having signed Boolean elements. These are Boolean elements which are multiplied by negative or positive one, and their signs are known *a priori*. An array of signed Boolean elements is shown in Figure 9.3. This array cannot be directly summed by a multiplier. To sum this array requires special adders [136, 155, 157, 158, 156, 102]. It is an intermediate representation that is later transformed into a generalized PPA. Thus, the summation of the signed PPA is expressed as follows:

$$s_{(i,j)} \in \{-1,+1\},$$

$$f(X) \approx \sum_{i=1}^{M} \sum_{j=1}^{N} s_{(i,j)} B_{(i,j)}(X) \times 2^{-(i+j)+k}.$$

The proposed method expresses its equations in the form of a generalized PPA. The shape of this array is chosen so that it can be superimposed on a multiplier's PPA. The Boolean elements are chosen carefully to provide a high-precision approximation. This is analogous to the choosing of coefficients for a polynomial approximation. They are chosen to reduce the maximum error. Thus, a PPA is produced which provides a high-precision approximation and is low-cost because it is summed on existing hardware.

$$f(X)$$

				$\vdots$	$\vdots$	$\vdots$	
			$+B_{(4,1)}$	$+B_{(4,2)}$	$-B_{(4,3)}$	$-B_{(4,4)}$	$\cdots$
		$-B_{(3,1)}$	$-B_{(3,2)}$	$+B_{(3,3)}$	$+B_{(3,4)}$	$\cdots$	
	$-B_{(2,1)}$	$+B_{(2,2)}$	$-B_{(2,3)}$	$+B_{(2,4)}$	$\cdots$		
$+B_{(1,1)}$	$-B_{(1,2)}$	$+B_{(1,3)}$	$-B_{(1,4)}$	$\cdots$			
$P_{(1)}$	$P_{(2)}$	$P_{(3)}$	$P_{(4)}$	$\cdots$			

Figure 9.3 Generalized signed binary PPA.

9.1.2 Related Work

Two other researchers have studied related methods. Renato Stefanelli created formulations for the reciprocal and division operations [171]. He expresses division as the inverse of multiplication ($Q = A/B \Rightarrow QB = A$). A multiplication's PPA is created in which either the multiplier or multiplicand is unknown. A redundant notation is used for the unknown operand. The PPA is restricted to avoid carries between columns, and then each column forms a separate linear equation. These equations are solved for digits of the unknown operand. Stefanelli's formulations for each quotient digit are dependent on all the more significant quotient digits. Thus, the result of calculating each digit is passed on to all the less significant. Stefanelli implements his equations with a dedicated cellular array. The resulting implementation is low-cost but very slow. The latency is linearly dependent on the number of quotient digits back-solved. Stefanelli's approximations have low accuracy in the worst case. Thus, Stefanelli proposes a unique method of deriving approximations which are low-cost but not very accurate (worst case).

David Mandelbaum enhanced Stefanelli's formulations by removing the recursion between digits of the quotient [100, 101, 102]. This is accomplished by back-substitutions. The latency is decreased by this enhancement, since there is a logarithmic dependence resulting from each quotient digit being calculated in parallel. Mandelbaum expresses his equations in the form of a PPA. Mandelbaum's Boolean elements were restricted to be only AND gates of the true input signals. Thus, his arrays are very large. His implementation uses a dedicated counter tree. Due to the high cost of counter trees for large arrays, his studies are limited to 7 bits of accuracy for the reciprocal and 12 bits for the square root. Mandelbaum was the first researcher to propose PPAs for the square root, natural log, and exponential functions. Thus, Mandelbaum's studies provide valuable knowledge of how to enhance Stefanelli's formulations to create PPA approximations with dedicated-counter-tree implementations.

Our work [155,157, 158, 156, 159, 160] enhances these earlier methods by providing a higher-precision approximation at a lower cost. Indeed, by reusing an existing multiplier, we can lower the marginal cost substantially.

9.1.3 Implementation

To create a low-cost high-precision approximation to an operation, a large amount of hardware is reused from an existing design. In this study, a FP multiplier is reused to sum the Boolean elements of the PPA which describes an approximation to an operation. Hardware could be dedicated to the auxiliary operations, but these operations are not executed frequently enough to merit this expense.

FP multiplication is a frequent operation. Thus, it is common to implement a full direct multiplication's PPA in one iteration. The other operations also can benefit from having a large counter tree and adder. Thus, this study suggests reusing a FP multiplier's counter tree and adder to sum the PPAs which approximate auxiliary operations. This section describes two typical multipliers and how to adapt them to sum an auxiliary operation's PPA.

FP multipliers are considered for adaptation because their PPAs are usually bigger than fixed-point multipliers. This study assumes that the FP multiplier to be adapted uses the double-precision IEEE 754 standard [72]. Adapting multipliers that use other standards is possible, and the IEEE standard multiplier is used only as an example.

In general a FP multiplier has a sign, an exponent, and a magnitude unit. The magnitude unit is by far the largest of the three units, and it is the only one discussed in this study.

There are two common types of multipliers: direct and two-bit Booth (sometimes called modified Booth) [21, 99]. Each type is discussed separately. Direct multipliers are simple and have one row in their PPA for each bit in the multiplier operand. Two-bit Booth multipliers recode the multiplier operand bits into digits between -2 and $+2$. The result is approximately half the number of rows in the PPA as in a direct multiplier. The implementations are also slightly different. The Booth multiplier has an extra delay of recoding prior to the elements being summed. This added delay allows a longer delay in the auxiliary operation's path. Thus, there is a tradeoff between the disadvantage of a direct multiplier having more rows, and that of the Booth multiplier having a longer delay prior to the summing of the elements. Typically, the designer of the high-order operations has no choice in the type of multiplier implemented, so both are described for reuse.

Direct Multipliers

In a direct multiplication each bit of one operand, the multiplier, is multiplied by the multiplicand and determines one PP row. The PP is equal to

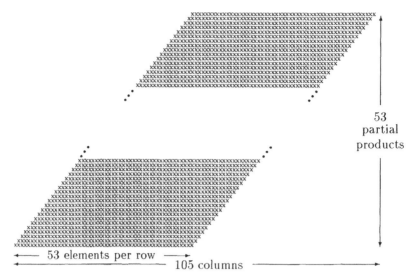

53
partial
products

←—— 53 elements per row ——→
←——————————— 105 columns ——————————→

Figure 9.4   Array for a 53-bit direct multiplier.

zero if the corresponding bit of the multiplier is zero, and is equal to the multiplicand if the bit is a one. For IEEE 754 standard, double-precision operands have 53 bits of significance. Thus, the corresponding PPA consists of 53 PPs of 53 elements as shown in Figure 9.4. Each x represents a Boolean element, which for multiplication is a two-way logical AND. Since this is a very large PPA, it is useful for an implementation of a large auxiliary operation's PPA. An auxiliary PPA is limited to a column height of 53 elements for this type of multiplier.

The dataflow is shown in a 3D representation in Figure 9.5(a). It consists of four parts: (1) Boolean-element creator, (2) counter tree, (3) adder, and (4) normalizer. The Boolean-element creator evaluates each element in the PPA, which for a multiplication is a two-way logical AND. The ones and zeros produced are summed to two rows by the counter tree, which performs carry-free addition. The two rows are then summed to one row by a carry-propagate adder. The result is then shifted appropriately by the normalizer. The counter tree and adder are reused by the auxiliary operation(s). To do this, a mux is placed in front of the counter tree as shown in Figure 9.5(b). The multiplier's PPA or any auxiliary operation's PPA can be selected to be summed on the counter tree and adder. An enlargement of the mux is also shown in Figure 9.5(b). Included in this inset is the Boolean-element creator for one element in the multiplier and the auxiliary operation. The mux can be as simple as a two-way logical OR gate if each element is zero when its operation is not being performed.

In addition to requiring a mux, each auxiliary operation requires a Boolean-element creator. This additional hardware is very small in comparison with the counter tree and adder. A substantial amount of hardware is

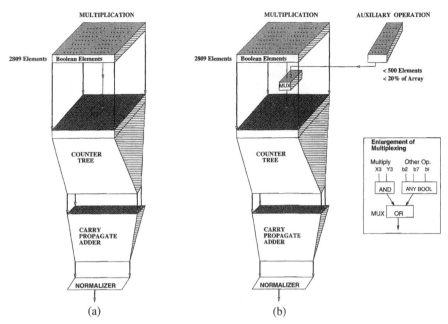

Figure 9.5 Implementation using direct multiplier: (a) multiplier before adaptation; (b) adapted multiplier.

saved vs implementing a separate counter tree and adder. The only disadvantage is that the latency increases slightly, since a mux is added to the path, and there might be a small delay due to differences in the latency of the Boolean-element creators. Thus, the changes to the multiplier are minor in terms of latency and amount of hardware.

The adaptation to a direct multiplier is very simple. A mux is added above the counter tree, and Boolean-element creators are added for each auxiliary operation. Typically, the auxiliary operation's PPA is much smaller than the multiplier's PPA. The mux only needs to be implemented for each bit of the auxiliary operation's PPA, since an operand of the multiplication can be set to zero, causing any unused elements to be zero. For each bit in the auxiliary operation's PPA, one gate is needed to create a Boolean element and one to multiplex it. There is a slight increase in the latency of the multiplier, but there is a substantial savings in hardware vs implementing separate counter trees for each auxiliary operation. The direct multiplier has a very large PPA, which can accommodate large auxiliary function PPAs.

Booth Multipliers

The Booth multiplier has a smaller PPA than a direct multiplier. Several bits of one operand are scanned for each PP row. Typically, two bits are recoded

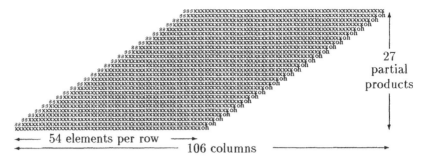

Figure 9.6 Array for a 53-bit Booth multiplier.

into one PP, which decreases the number of rows by half. This is shown in Figure 9.6. There are 27 rows of 54 elements each, neglecting the sign, denoted by s, and the hot-one encoding, denoted by oh. (For more details on this type of multiplier see [99, 71, 192, 185, 186].) To directly use the PPA of this multiplier the auxiliary operation's PPA must have ≤ 27 rows. Thisis much smaller than the direct PPA, and therefore the precision of the approximation is lower than the approximation summed on a direct multiplier.

The dataflow of the Booth multiplier is shown in Figure 9.7. Since each PP is created by scanning several bits, there are extra stages of hardware needed prior to the counter tree. The three stages are: (1) Booth decode, (2) Booth

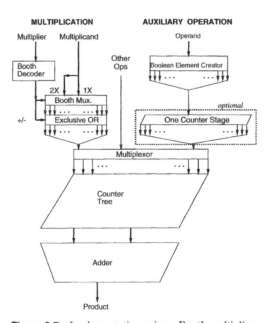

Figure 9.7 Implementation using a Booth multiplier.

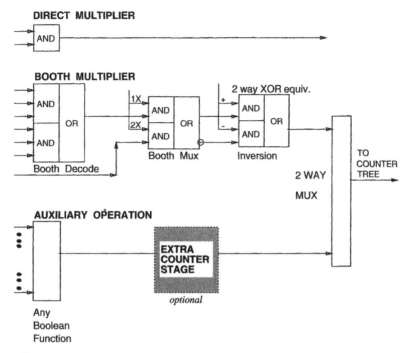

Figure 9.8   Path differences of direct and Booth multiplier vs auxiliary operation.

multiplexing, and (3) inversion. The Booth decoder scans three bits with one bit overlapping per PP. It determines whether to form two times, one times, or zero times the multiplicand, and also whether the row should be negative or positive. This involves in the worst case the latency of a 3-by-2 AND–OR gate (three-way ANDs followed by a two-way OR gate) as shown in Figure 9.8. The second stage multiplexes the different multiples of the multiplicand and requires one 2-by-2 AND–OR gate per bit. The third stage inverts (1's-complementing) the multiple if the PP is negative. This is implemented as an XOR gate for each bit. Thus the latency of the Booth multiplier prior to the counter tree is longer than that of the direct multiplier. This allows the possibility of adding a counter stage into the path of an auxiliary operation. If one $(3, 2)$ counter stage [190, 37] is added, then the auxiliary operation can have a PPA of 40 rows maximum rather than 27. For small arrays with only a few large columns this is a good solution.

A Dadda scheme [37] of counters could be used to reduce the hardware requirements by only placing counters in the columns that exceed the constraints of the multiplier's PPA. For larger arrays the hardware cost may be too great. Thus, two datapaths are possible, depending on whether counter stages are added prior to the counter tree or the Boolean-element creators feed directly into the mux. Note that depending on the path lengths, there also can be premultiplexing of the auxiliary operations. Thus, a Booth multiplier has a longer latency prior to the counter tree, which can aid in the design of the auxiliary operation, but the PPA is smaller than that of a direct multiplier.

9.1.4 Summary of Implementation

The basic method of adapting an auxiliary operation's PPA to that of a multiplier is to limit the PPA's size and shape to the constraints of the multiplier's PPA. The direct multiplier for double-precision IEEE notation has 53 rows, and the Booth multiplier has 27 rows. It might be possible to add more counters to the Booth multiplier without affecting the latency. This would increase the maximum number of rows to 40 for a Booth multiplier. The overall adjustment to either multiplier is to create the elements in each PPA with a separate Boolean-element creator and then multiplex the different elements into the counter tree. The auxiliary operations have the same properties as the multiplier. If the multiplier is pipelined, then the approximations are pipelined. They also have the same latency as the multiplier. Thus, a multiplier easily can be adapted to sum the elements of another operation's PPA.

To summarize the disadvantages, a mux (possibly as simple as a two-way OR gate) is added to the critical path of the multiplier, and there is a hardware cost of approximately 2 logic gates per PPA element. The advantages are: the marginal cost is small, the precision of the approximation is high, many operations can reuse the same multiplier, and the latency is one multiplication. Thus, if a slightly longer latency can be tolerated by the multiplier, then there is a substantial decrease in hardware and an increase in performance of high-order arithmetic operations.

9.2 PROPOSED METHOD: DERIVATION

The proposed method consists of creating a PP array which approximates an operation and summing it on an existing multiplier. We now consider how to derive a PPA which approximates an arithmetic operation. There are two steps or algorithms to the derivation, as shown in Figure 9.9. The first algorithm derives a signed PPA (see Figure 9.3) to approximate an operation, and the second algorithm transforms it into an unsigned PPA (Figure 9.2).

9.2.1 Algorithm 1: Describing an Operation as a Signed PPA

The first step in deriving a PPA is to derive a signed PPA to approximate an operation. First the operation is described as a multiplication (or a series of multiplications and additions). Then, this multiplication (or series) is expanded bit by bit into a PPA. The unknown operand is in a redundant notation and chosen so that the PPA is limited to have no carry propagation

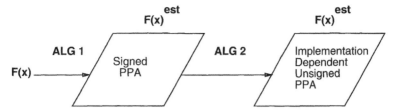

Figure 9.9   Overview of derivation of PPA describing approximation to an operation.

between its columns. Thus, each column forms a separate linear equation which can be back-solved for a digit of the unknown operand. The resulting formulations of several digits are placed into a new PPA and reduced. Sizings of PPAs are used to determine the maximum number of digits to back-solve. Then the error of this PPA is analyzed, and additional Boolean elements are added to compensate for the worst regions of error. The steps are summarized below:

1. Express the operation as a multiplication (or series).
2. Expand the multiplication (or series) into a PPA.
3. Back-solve the PPA for digits of the unknown operand.
4. Form a new PPA and reduce.
5. Choose the number of digits to back-solve.
6 Improve the worst-case error.

The first two and a half steps are based on an algorithm by Renato Stefanelli [171]. Half of the third step and half of the fourth step are based on enhancements by David Mandelbaum [100, 101, 102]. The last two and a half steps of Algorithm 1 and all of Algorithm 2 are enhancements which are key to reducing the cost and increasing the precision of this type of approximation.

As an illustration of this algorithm, these steps are described for a small approximation of the reciprocal operation, which is assumed to be implemented on a 5-bit direct multiplier.

Express the Operation as a Multiplication or Series

This step is similar to the step in the Newton–Raphson algorithm, in which a function is determined which has a root equivalent to the operation. A function is chosen for the proposed method which must be a multiplication or a series of multiplications and additions. The choice of the best function may not be obvious and is discussed elsewhere [157, 158]. However, the choice of a function is simple for the reciprocal, division, and square-root operations. All can be described in terms of one multiplication as shown below:

Division: $\qquad Q = A/B \Rightarrow QB = A.$

Reciprocation: $\quad Q = 1/B \Rightarrow QB = 1 \quad$ or $\quad QB = 0.111\ldots.$

Square root: $\qquad Q = \sqrt{A} \Rightarrow QQ = A.$

For the reciprocal operation either of the two expressions on the right can be used, but it has been determined through simulation that the right most expression gives more accurate results.

Expand the Multiplication or Series into a PPA

The multiplication or series produced in step 1 is expanded into a PPA. This array is the same as a generalized binary PPA (see Figure 9.2) except for two differences. The first is that the operand in the array which is unknown is not the product. For a multiplication's PPA only the product row is unknown and all the internal elements of the array are known. The second difference is that the unknown operand is chosen to be in a redundant, binary-weighted, fractional notation such as described by the following:

$$Q = \sum_{i=0}^{N} q_{(i)} \times 2^{-i}.$$

Each digit of the unknown operand, $q_{(i)}$, can be any real number, but is usually limited to a much smaller range by constraints given in step 3. For the reciprocal operation, the unknown operand's digits, $q_{(i)}$, are limited to the set of integers.

The known operand(s) are chosen in a binary fractional notation:

$$B = -b_0 + \sum_{i=1}^{N} b_{(i)} \times 2^{-i}.$$

Usually the operands are chosen normalized ($0.5 \le B < 1.0$) and unsigned to simplify the formulations:

$$B = -b_0 + \sum_{i=1}^{N} b_{(i)} \times 2^{-i}$$

$$= (0.1)_{(2)} + \sum_{i=2}^{N} b_{(i)} \times 2^{-i}$$

$$= \left(0.1 b_{(2)} b_{(3)} \cdots \right)_{(2)}.$$

Using this notation, a PPA is formed from the multiplication, as shown in Figure 9.10.

				0.	1	$b_{(2)}$	$b_{(3)}$	$b_{(4)}$	$b_{(5)}$	$\cdots$	$= B$
			X	q_0	$q_{(1)}$	$q_{(2)}$	$q_{(3)}$	$q_{(4)}$		$\cdots$	$= Q$
				$\vdots$	$\vdots$	$\vdots$	$\vdots$				
			$q_{(4)}$	$b_{(2)}q_{(4)}$	$b_{(3)}q_{(4)}$	$b_{(4)}q_{(4)}$	$b_{(5)}q_{(4)}$	$\cdots$			
		$q_{(3)}$	$b_{(2)}q_{(3)}$	$b_{(3)}q_{(3)}$	$b_{(4)}q_{(3)}$	$b_{(5)}q_{(3)}$	$\cdots$				
	$q_{(2)}$	$b_{(2)}q_{(2)}$	$b_{(3)}q_{(2)}$	$b_{(4)}q_{(2)}$	$b_{(5)}q_{(2)}$	$\cdots$					
$q_{(1)}$	$b_{(2)}q_{(1)}$	$b_{(3)}q_{(1)}$	$b_{(4)}q_{(1)}$	$b_{(5)}q_{(1)}$	$\cdots$						
q_0	$b_{(2)}q_0$	$b_{(3)}q_0$	$b_{(4)}q_0$	$b_{(5)}q_0$	$\cdots$						
0	1	1	1	1	1	$\cdots$					≈ 1.0

Figure 9.10

The PPA is simple to form for an expression of one multiplication. To transform a series of multiplications and additions into a PPA, each operation is expanded for several bits of significance. Then the terms in the equation are separated by their binary weight. They are placed into columns of the array corresponding to the appropriate weight. Thus, any binary-weighted equation can be expressed as a PPA.

Back-solve the PPA

The third step solves several columns of the PPA for digits of the unknown operand. The unknown operand's digits are chosen such that there are no carries between columns of the array. This results in the columns forming separate equations as delineated in Figure 9.10 by vertical lines. Typically, there is one additional unknown digit introduced for each additional less significant column considered. Thus, there is an equal number of linear equations to unknown digits at any given truncation of the least significant columns of the array. Not all of the columns are back-solved, because the formulations become too complex to implement with a reasonable amount of hardware. In the worst case the complexity of a digit increases exponentially for each less significant digit, but in practice the complexity appears to stay linear for several digits [156].

For this example of the algorithm, five digits of quotient are back-solved. Thus, the first five columns form the following equations:

$$q_0 = 1,$$

$$q_{(1)} + b_{(2)}\,q_0 = 1,$$

$$q_{(2)} + b_{(2)}\,q_{(1)} + b_{(3)}\,q_0 = 1,$$

$$q_{(3)} + b_{(2)}\,q_{(2)} + b_{(3)}\,q_{(1)} + b_{(4)}q_0 = 1,$$

$$q_{(4)} + b_{(2)}\,q_{(3)} + b_{(3)}\,q_{(2)} + b_{(4)}q_{(1)} + b_{(5)}q_0 = 1.$$

These equations are solved to yield the following formulations for five digits of the quotient:

$$q_0 = 1,$$

$$q_{(1)} = 1 - b_{(2)},$$

$$q_{(2)} = 1 - b_{(3)},$$

$$q_{(3)} = 1 - b_{(2)} + 2b_{(2)}\,b_{(3)} - b_{(3)} - b_{(4)},$$

$$q_{(4)} = 1 - b_{(2)}b_{(3)} - b_{(4)} + 2b_{(2)}b_{(4)} - b_{(5)}.$$

Thus, the PPA developed in the previous step is separated into equations for each column. These equations are solved for the unknown operand's digits. Then back-substitutions are performed to directly express the operand's digits in terms of the initial inputs. Thus, any recursion between digits is eliminated.

Form a New PPA and Reduce

The next step is to form a new PPA. Each digit of the unknown operand is weighted by a different power of two, as is each column of a PPA. Thus, in forming a new PPA the equations of each digit are placed in separate columns as is shown below:

q_0	$q_{(1)}$	$q_{(2)}$	$q_{(3)}$	$q_{(4)}$
			$-b_{(4)}$	$-b_{(5)}$
			$-b_{(3)}$	$2b_{(2)}b_{(4)}$
			$2b_{(2)}b_{(3)}$	$-b_{(4)}$
	$-b_{(2)}$	$-b_{(3)}$	$-b_{(2)}$	$-b_{(2)}b_{(3)}$
1	1	1	1	1

Then these equations are reduced.

The PPA is a mixture of two number representations. Each element is a Boolean element, and their summation is performed algebraically. To achieve high speed a tradeoff is made between the two notations. Making the elements more complex reduces the total number of elements and the latency of summing the elements, but increases the latency of creating an element. For the purpose of this study, the elements are limited to one Boolean logic level of at most a nine-way logic gate. In practice, an element on average has a three-way logic gate. This creates a compact array which can be evaluated and summed quickly. The compaction is achieved by applying both algebraic and Boolean equivalences. Thus, equivalences are used to create a good balance of the two notations.

The following are some of the equivalences [151, 156] used to reduce the array:

1. Algebraic Expansion: $Ma \Rightarrow \Sigma k_{(i)} 2^{-i} a$, where M is any real number, a and $k_{(i)}$ are Boolean, and 2^{-i} is implied by the column weight. This step expands all coefficients in the array into their binary components. An example is

$$5a \Rightarrow 4a + a \Rightarrow (a, 0, a) \qquad \text{by columns.}$$

2. Algebraic Reduction: $2a - a \Rightarrow a$.
3. Boolean Reduction: $a + b - ab \Rightarrow a \mid b$ or $a + \bar{a}b \Rightarrow a \mid b$.
4. Boolean Reduction: $a - ab \Rightarrow a(1 - b) \Rightarrow a\bar{b}$.
5. Boolean Reduction: $a + b - 2ab \Rightarrow a \oplus b$.

Here a and b are signed binary variables. The juxtaposition of two or more binary variables means the logical AND of these variables, $\mid$ the logical OR, $\oplus$ the exclusive OR, $+$ addition, $-$ subtraction, and an overbar inversion.

Many orderings can be found for applying these reductions. One algorithm would be to apply the first step to the whole array starting with the least significant columns, then successively apply the other steps until no further reduction is achieved. This is a simple algorithm with no backtracking which produces reasonable results. Other, more complex algorithms might use a smart expansion, such as to expand $a \Rightarrow 2a - a$ only if both new elements, $2a$ and $-a$, can be recombined by other rules.

Applying the simple algorithm to the PPA for five digits back-solved of the reciprocal yields

q_0	$q_{(1)}$	$q_{(2)}$	$q_{(3)}$	$q_{(4)}$
				$\overline{b_{(5)}}$
			$-(b_{(2)} \mid b_{(4)})$	$-b_{(4)}$
1	$\overline{b_{(2)}}$	$(b_{(2)} \mid \overline{b_{(3)}})$	$\overline{b_{(3)}}$	$-b_{(2)}b_{(3)}$

There has been a reduction from 15 total elements and 5 rows maximum to 8 and 3 respectively. The reduction creates a PPA with true and complement positive- and negative-signed Boolean elements.

Choose the Number of Digits to Back-solve

This step improves the average and minimum numbers of correct bits by determining the maximum number of digits to back-solve. PPAs are derived and their size determined for several numbers of digits. A multiplier is chosen for implementation, and its maximum number of rows is noted. Typically, either the 53-row or the 27-row multiplier is chosen. As a small example, it is assumed in this chapter that a 5-bit direct multiplier is used which has a maximum of five rows. This step sizes PPAs for several number of back-solved digits and compares their sizes with the multiplier's PPA. In the reciprocal example, the following is the number of rows per column for several number of back-solved digits:

Column	1	2	3	4	5	6	7	8	9	
5-bit multiplier:	1	2	3	4	5	4	3	2	1	Max 5
5 digits:	1	1	1	2	3					Max 3
6 digits:	1	2	2	3	4	4				Max 4
7 digits:	1	2	2	5	2	4	6			Max 6

Both the 5- and 6-digit PPAs fit in a 5-bit multiplier. The 6-digit PPA is rather tight, since it has two rows of 4. It is assumed that this is too tight, since it will be shown that Algorithm 2 could add one row to the PPA. Thus, the 5-digit PPA is chosen.

Determining the number of digits to back-solve involves deriving several PPAs and comparing their size to the PPA of the multiplier to be reused. The largest PPA that fits comfortably within the constraints of the multiplier is chosen to get the highest-precision approximation possible for this implementation.

Improve the Worst-Case Error

The approximation of the reciprocal operation using the PPA for five digits has a good average number of correct bits but has a large worst-case error. From simulating the most significant 20 bits of the divisor, the approximation was determined to have an average[2] of 5.75 correct bits. Also, the worst-case error is determined to be 3.36 correct bits. Mandelbaum [101] first noticed that there is some significant regions of error in this type of method. Rather than correcting for the error, he chose another method of approximation in these regions, a PLA lookup table.

There is yet another way of reducing the error in these regions. This study suggests adding error-compensating Boolean elements to the array. The correction is in the array, so there is no added latency or special control circuitry, and the added hardware is small. Thus, the worst-case error is decreased by adding error-compensating elements directly to the PPA.

Three steps are used to add compensating elements: (1) plot the error, (2) determine compensating elements, and (3) add them to the PPA and reduce. The first step is to plot the absolute signed error, which is the computed value minus the true value (absolute error is the absolute value of absolute signed error), vs the divisor as shown in Figure 9.11(a).

---

[2] It is assumed that "average" refers to the result of averaging the number of correct bits for a 20-bit simulation, which gives an indication of the true average. Details of the simulation are given in Section 9.2.3.

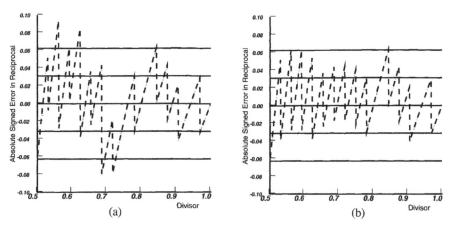

Figure 9.11 Absolute signed error in 5-digit reciprocal approximation: (a) without error compensation; (b) with error compensation.

Several elements can be added to the PPA to compensate for errors. Lines have been added to the plot: the top and bottom lines are $\pm 2^{-4}$, the middle line is 0, and the inner lines are $\pm 2^{-5}$. These lines are useful in determining the effect of a correction term added to the columns of $q_{(4)}$ and $q_{(5)}$ in the PPA. Many terms could be added to reduce the error, but there is a tradeoff between starting with a better approximation and adding more correction terms. Because of this there are many possible PPAs. For this example, two compensating elements are chosen: subtracting 2^{-5} for a divisor between 0.53125 and 0.5625 and between 0.59375 and 0.625 (which can be represented by $\overline{b_{(2)}}\,\overline{b_{(3)}}b_{(5)}$), and adding 2^{-4} between 0.6875 and 0.75 $(\overline{b_{(2)}}b_{(3)}b_{(4)})$. The PPA with compensating elements is shown in Figure 9.12. The added elements are shown in boxes. This array has 10 total elements and a maximum column height of 4. For larger arrays and larger numbers of compensating elements, it is common to have recombination of some of these additional elements. In this example there is no recombination, but the maximum column only increased by one element.

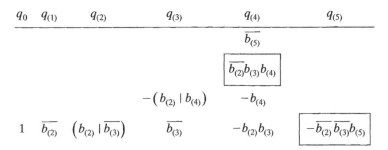

Figure 9.12 Five-digit reciprocal-approximation PPA with error compensation.

$$B = 0.75 = (0.11000\ldots)_2$$

$$b_{(1)} = 1, \quad b_{(2)} = 3, \quad b_{(i)} = 0 \quad \text{for} \quad i > 2$$

q_0	$q_{(1)}$	$q_{(2)}$	$q_{(3)}$	$q_{(4)}$	$q_{(5)}$
				$\overline{b_{(5)}} = 1$	
				$\overline{b_{(2)}}b_{(3)}b_{(4)} = 0$	
			$-(b_{(2)} \mid b_{(4)}) = -1$	$-b_{(4)} = 0$	
1. $\overline{b_{(2)}} = 0$	$\left(b_{(2)} \mid \overline{b_{(3)}}\right) = 1$		$\overline{b_{(3)}} = 1$	$-b_{(2)}b_{(3)} = 0$	$-\overline{b_{(2)}}\,\overline{b_{(3)}}b_{(5)} = 0$
1.	0	1	$-1 + 1$	$1 + 0 + 0 + 0$	0
1.	0	1	0	1	0

Figure 9.13 Example application of the five-digit reciprocal PPA.

The resulting error of the PPA is shown in Figure 9.11(b). Numerically the average number of correct bits has increased to 6.09 and the worst-case error has improved to 3.92 bits, which is an improvement of 0.34 bits on average and 0.56 bits worst case. Thus, a significant improvement has resulted from the addition of two elements. By adding the corrections directly to the array rather than using a PLA, there are savings in hardware, latency, and control.

As an example consider an approximation to the reciprocal of 0.75, shown in Figure 9.13. This PPA provides a good approximation: the actual value is $1.333\ldots = (1.010101\ldots)_2$ and the calculated value is 1.3125. The approximation has an absolute error of $2^{-5.58}$, which corresponds to $5\frac{1}{2}$ bits correct. By evaluating each element and summing the result, a high-precision approximation is possible.

Thus, a method has been described for expressing an approximation to a high-order arithmetic operation as a signed PPA. The algorithm differs from those of other authors in the additional equivalences used and the adding of error-compensating elements. This has resulted in a small signed PPA which describes an approximation to a high-order operation. This technique can be applied to a different number of back-solved digits or a different number of compensating elements. Thus, there are many PPAs that can be derived using this algorithm.

9.2.2 Algorithm 2: Adapting the Signed PPA to the Multiplier's PPA

The next step is to adapt the signed PPA from Algorithm 1 to be unsigned and to fit on a given multiplier's PPA. This step could be skipped if a dedicated counter tree were to be built for each application. The counters would need to be Pezaris-type counters [136] to accept signed Boolean elements. Many previous studies [155, 157, 158, 156, 102] have assumed such an implementation, but due to hardware costs these studies are limited to

q_0	$q_{(1)}$	$q_{(2)}$	$q_{(3)}$	$q_{(4)}$	$q_{(5)}$
Before:				$\overline{b_{(5)}}$	
				$\overline{b_{(2)}}b_{(3)}b_{(4)}$	
			$-(b_{(2)} \mid b_{(4)})$	$-b_{(4)}$	
1	$\overline{b_{(2)}}$	$(b_{(2)} \mid \overline{b_{(3)}})$	$\overline{b_{(3)}}$	$-b_{(2)}b_{(3)}$	$-\overline{b_{(2)}}\,\overline{b_{(3)}}b_{(5)}$
After:				$\overline{b_{(5)}}$	
				$\overline{b_{(2)}}b_{(3)}b_{(4)}$	
			$\overline{b_{(2)}}\,\overline{b_{(4)}}$	$\overline{b_{(4)}}$	
1	$\overline{b_{(2)}}$	$(b_{(2)} \mid \overline{b_{(3)}})$	$\overline{b_{(3)}}$	$(\overline{b_{(2)}} \mid \overline{b_{(3)}})$	$(b_{(2)} \mid b_{(3)} \mid \overline{b_{(5)}})$
			-1	-2	-1

Figure 9.14

lower-precision approximations. To save hardware and allow higher precision, the signed arrays are adapted to be added on a multiplier [159, 160]. Algorithm 2 describes the method for adaptation which consists of three steps:

1. Complement negative variable elements, and subtract one.
2. Sum all constant terms, and add the result to the PPA (2's-complement if negative).
3. Adjust array to match the multiplier.

These steps result in an array that can be mapped onto an array of a multiplier.

Complement Negative Elements and Subtract One

The first step in adapting the signed PPA to be summed on an unsigned PPA is to eliminate any negative variables by complementing them and subtracting one from the appropriate column. The reason this transformation is valid is that: $-a = \bar{a} - 1$, where a is a signed Boolean element. An example is shown in Figure 9.14 using the signed PPA of the five-digit reciprocal approximation with compensation.

Note that De Morgan's law of complementing is applied to the Boolean functions, such as $\overline{b_{(2)}\,\overline{b_{(3)}}b_{(5)}} \Rightarrow (b_{(2)} \mid b_{(3)} \mid \overline{b_{(5)}})$.

Reduce Constants

In this step all the constants are reduced to one row. Then the row is added back to the array. Thus, in the worst case one row is added to adapt a signed array to be unsigned. The constants in the previous example are reduced:

$(1, 0, 0, -1, -2, -1)_2 = (1, 0, -1, 0, 0, -1)_2 = (0, 1, 0, 1, 1, 1)_2$. If the result is negative, then the 2's-complement of it is added back to the array. The following is the result of this step:

q_0	$q_{(1)}$	$q_{(2)}$	$q_{(3)}$	$q_{(4)}$	$q_{(5)}$
				1	
				$\overline{b_{(5)}}$	
			1	$\overline{b_{(2)}} b_{(3)} b_{(4)}$	
	1		$\overline{b_{(2)}}\, \overline{b_{(4)}}$	$\overline{b_{(4)}}$	
	$\overline{b_{(2)}}$	$\left(b_{(2)} \mid \overline{b_{(3)}}\right)$	$\overline{b_{(3)}}$	$\left(\overline{b_{(2)}} \mid \overline{b_{(3)}}\right)$	$\left(b_{(2)} \mid b_{(3)} \mid \overline{b_{(5)}}\right)$

Adjust Array to Match the Multiplier

The last step changes the shape, or aspect ratio, of the application's array to be similar to the multiplier's array, by minor modifications. Two types of modifications that are commonly used are: (1) shifting the application's array to be superimposed on a different set of columns of the multiplier's array, and (2) shifting specific elements in oversized columns of the application's array to lesser significant columns and replicating them.

The first modification is concerned with the positioning of the superimposed array. Column 1 of the application's array can be shifted to be superimposed on any column of the multiplier array.

The second modification is a minor adjustment of one element rather than the whole array. An element can be shifted to a lesser significant column, supposing that it is replicated the appropriate amount. If the element is moved to next less significant column, it must be replicated twice, due to the equivalence $a = a/2 + a/2$, where the fractional constant is implied by the column weight. Thus, there are two methods of adjustment presented that perform a coarse or fine adjustment of the application's array.

An example is shown for the five-digit reciprocal estimate in Figure 9.15. The PPA of the reciprocal estimate is shown in the upper left corner using solid circles, and the multiplier's PPA is shown in the upper right corner using empty boxes. The reciprocal PPA's column heights are $(2, 1, 3, 5, 2)$. Assume that it is to be adapted to a 5-bit direct multiplier which has column heights which increase and decrease linearly $(1, 2, 3, 4, 5, 4, 3, 2, 1)$. Then the first method of modification can be used to sum the reciprocal array on this multiplier. By method 1, the first column with two elements would be matched with the second column of the multiplier which is shown in the bottom left corner of the figure. There is no need to then apply fine adjustments to the array. None of the other columns exceed the multiplier's column heights ($2 \le 2$, $1 \le 3$, $3 \le 4$, $5 \le 5$, and $2 \le 4$). If the column had six elements, including a constant 1 term (shown as a cross-hatched circle), then that term could be moved and replicated twice in the next less significant column. This is shown in the lower right corner of the figure. For this

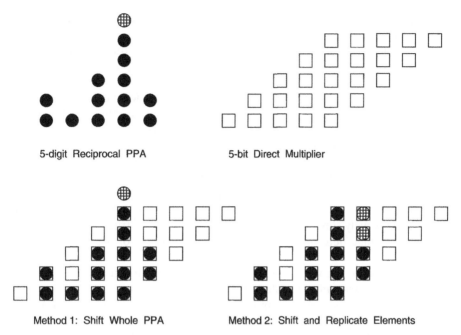

Figure 9.15   Adjusting the array to map onto the multiplier.

example, only a proper shifting of the whole array is needed to adapt the array to a 5-bit direct multiplier.

Thus, the three steps of Algorithm 2 are easy to implement and result in an array that has at most one extra row. By applying Algorithm 1 and Algorithm 2 for different numbers of back-solved digits and different numbers of compensating elements, a variety of PPAs can be derived. The final PPA chosen should fit within the constraints of the given multiplier and produce a reasonable approximation of the high-order operation desired. Thus, a method has been presented for deriving PPAs which describe an approximation to an arithmetic operation and which can be superimposed on a given multiplier's array.

9.2.3   Performance and Comparisons

The proposed method's implementation and derivation has been shown, but two questions need to be answered:

- How is its performance measured?
- How does it compare to other methods?

Performance Measurements

The performance is measured in terms of the number of correct bits. This is equivalent to the number of significant bits. An absolute signed error of less than $\pm 2^{-N}$ implies that all the significant bits are correct up to fractional bit $N - 1$. For the reciprocal approximation the quotient is between 1 and 2, which implies one integer bit of significance. Thus, if the absolute signed error is less than $\pm 2^{-N}$ for the reciprocal operation, then there are N correct bits.

The number of correct bits is not constant, but depends on the input operand. There are two types of measurements that are useful: a pseudoaverage and a minimum (or worst-case) number of correct bits. The actual average is very difficult to calculate, since for a double precision operand 2^{52} test cases would need to be averaged. Instead an average is calculated from simulating 2^{20} test cases. The test cases are an exhaustive simulation of the most significant 20 bits of the input operand which can change. For the reciprocal operation, $0.5 \le B < 1.0$, $b_0 = 0$, and $b_{(1)} = 1$; so bits 2 through 21 are exhaustively simulated. Thus, an indication of the true average is given from this average determined from simulating a subset of the total possible combinations.

The worst-case error is another difficult number to measure. A bound on the error is instead calculated. Interval arithmetic is used, as shown in Figure 9.16. For a reciprocal approximation which uses a 53-row PPA the elements are only dependent on bits 2 through 17. These equations are modeled in a C program. Simulation vectors are input for bits 2 through 21 (denoted $B_{(20)}$) which exhaustively simulates the model but does not exhaustively simulate the bits of a 53-bit operand. B is used to represent a possible input operand (53 bits), and the corresponding simulated value is $B_{(20)}$, a 20-bit truncation of B. The error is determined for the calculated reciprocal, Model($B_{(20)}$), versus the actual value, Act($B_{(20)}$), and is shown by the left

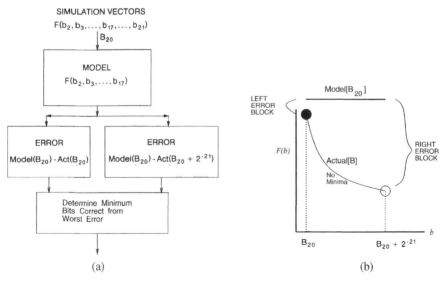

Figure 9.16 Simulation of worst case. (a) control flow of simulation; (b) plot of simulation parameters.

error block of Figure 9.16(a). Also, the error is determined for using the same calculated reciprocal, Model($B_{(20)}$), for the next data point, $B_{(20)} + 2^{-21}$, and is shown in the right error block of Figure 9.16(a). This bounds the worst-case error as shown in Figure 9.16(b). B is greater than or equal to $B_{(20)}$ and less than $B_{(20)} + 2^{-21}$. Since the operations approximated do not have minima within the range considered, the worst case is bounded between these two points. The predicted approximation of the model does not change in this interval. Thus, the worst-case error is bounded by the minimum number of correct bits of the two error calculations.

Thus, the "average" and the minimum number of correct bits are determined for the proposed method using simulation. Most implementations have a fixed number of iterations, which implies that the minimum number of correct bits is the critical measure of performance. For highest performance the minimum number of correct bits is maximized.

Two other measures of an algorithm are its size and latency. The size of an implementation is measured in terms of simple logic gates. The proposed method requires two logic gates for each element in its PPA: one gate to create the element, and one to multiplex it into the array. There are three measures of latency: the latency per iteration, the number of iterations, and the total latency. The total latency is equal to the latency per iteration multiplied by the number of iterations. The number of iterations is inversely proportional to the number of correct bits. The latency per iteration of the proposed method is equal to the delay of one multiplication unless otherwise stated. The total latency is not explicitly determined, but for comparisons the minimum number of correct bits and the latency per iteration are determined.

Thus, the critical measures are the size, latency, and minimum correct bits.

Comparisons

The performance of the proposed method can be measured, but these measures are not useful without a comparison with standard methods. The most common standard method is a lookup table. The lookup table is assumed to be implemented in the form of a ROM. It could be implemented as a PLA, but typically this is only done for small tables. Two comparisons are made in this study. The first assumes a lookup table of equivalent precision to the proposed method's approximation. The latency is assumed to be comparable to or faster than the proposed method, since no arithmetic computation is necessary, though an off-chip delay may be required. The size is calculated from determining the number of bits in the ROM. Each entry in the lookup table has a width equal to the number of correct bits in the proposed method minus the number of bits in the output that do not change. The number of entries is computed from the following formula:

$$|f(x) - f(x - 2^{-n})| \le \epsilon_0,$$

where n is the number of bits of the index into the lookup table, f is the operation considered, and ϵ_0 is the worst-case error (p. 195 of [192]). This equation is solved for n, given the function, its range, and the precision ϵ_0 of the proposed method. For example, if the proposed method had 9 bits of accuracy for the reciprocal operation, then

$$\epsilon_0 = 2^{-9},$$

$$0.5 \leq x < 1.0.$$

For $x = 0.5$,

$$|f(0.5) - f(0.5 - 2^{-n})| \leq 2^{-9},$$

$$\left|2.0 - \frac{1}{0.5 - 2^{-n}}\right| \leq 2^{-9},$$

$$n \geq 11.$$

For $x = 1.0$,

$$n \geq 9.$$

Thus, for 9 bits of accuracy in the reciprocal operation, there needs to be 11 bits of significance for the indexing. Since $b_{(1)}$ is always known, 10 bits of indexing are needed, which results in 2^{10} entries in the lookup table. The ROM is 2^{10} by 8 bits, or 1 Kbyte. To express this in terms of equivalent gate count an approximation of 3.5 gates per byte is assumed (similar types of approximation can be found in [114]). A 1 Kbyte table translates into approximately 3600 logic gates (3.5 × 1024). This conversion method enables a direct size comparison between a lookup-table method and the proposed method.

One other type of comparison is made between the lookup table and the proposed method. The precision is compared for the proposed method vs a common size of lookup table, which is assumed to be 1 Kbyte. This table size provides an 8- to 9-bit approximation. By comparing the look-up table of a commnon size with the proposed method, one gets an indication of how an actual implementation can be improved by the proposed method. The proposed method will be shown to be smaller in size than this typical lookup table and provide a higher-precision approximation.

The other two methods of creating a standard starting approximation are polynomial and rational methods. Though rational methods are used in some computers, no detailed comparisons are made in this study. These methods are too slow for the type of implementations considered here. Their delay consists of at least the latency of a division operation, and for operations such as the reciprocal operation this is much longer than the delay of one iteration.

The polynomial approximations are faster than the rational method and thus are compared with the proposed method. The polynomial method assumed is either a min−max polynomial or a Chebyshev polynomial (which is almost a min−max), unless otherwise stated. A min−max polynomial is the optimal polynomial in the sense of having the minimum maximum error. To compare polynomials with the proposed method an equivalent-latency model is assumed. Since the proposed method has the latency of one multiplication, all comparisons vs polynomials are assumed to be vs a first-order polynomial unless otherwise stated. A first-order polynomial has the delay of one multiplication and an addition. Its size is very small, since only its coefficients need to be stored. Its precision is compared with the proposed method for each high-order operation.

9.2.4 Summary of Derivation

The proposed method is applicable to many operations such as the reciprocal, division, square-root, trigonometric, natural-log, and exponential operations. It consists of two algorithms. Algorithm 1 is performed in six steps:

1. Express operation as a multiplication (or series).
2. Expand the multiplication (or series) into a PPA.
3. Back-solve the PPA for digits of the unknown operand.
4. Form a new PPA and reduce.
5. Choose the number of digits to back-solve.
6. Improve the worst-case error.

The last two steps of the algorithm are unique to this work and result in signed PPAs that are very compact and accurate. The signed PPAs are then transformed into an unsigned multiplier-dependent PPA using three steps (Algorithm 2):

1. Complement negative variable elements, and subtract one.
2. Sum all constant terms, and add the result to the PPA.
3. Adjust the array to match the multiplier.

Thus, a PPA is created which can be superimposed onto a multiplier's PPA and be summed by that multiplier.

Also, performance measures have been defined. In the following, PPAs for several operations are derived and their performance is compared with those of lookup tables and polynomial methods. The proposed method is shown to be much smaller than an equivalent lookup table and to be of much higher precision than an equivalent polynomial method.

9.3 RECIPROCAL, DIVISION, AND SQUARE ROOT

Reciprocal, division, and square root are the most frequently executed high-order arithmetic operations. They are simple compared to natural log, exponential, and trigonometric operations and are commonly implemented in hardware. They also are used for intermediate calculations in other high-order operations. A gain in the performance of these three operations provides a gain in performance for many high-order arithmetic operations.

Now we need to determine the maximum number of digits to back-solve and the number of error-compensating elements. These two steps and Algorithm 2 are the key steps which make the PPA low-cost and high-performance. The previous section separated the derivation by the boundaries of the two algorithms. This is useful from an external point of view, since it provides a separation between the derivation of the signed and unsigned PPAs. This section is concerned with an internal view of the key steps of this method and provides a slightly different separation. The following are the four steps that the derivation is separated into:

1. Derivation of formulas (Algorithm 1: steps 1 through 4)
2. Choice of the number of digits to back-solve (Algorithm 1: step 5)
3. Error compensation (Algorithm 1: step 6)
4. Final array (Algorithm 2)

Step 1 involves deriving the initial formulations of the operation. This step is straightforward for these operations, since all three can be expressed as one multiplication (Algorithm 1, step 1). Step 2 determines the size of several PPAs for different numbers of digits back-solved and decides on the biggest PPA that will fit in a given multiplier. Step 3 adds error-compensating elements to the array. And step 4 presents the final array which can be summed by a given multiplier. The final PPA's shape and size are given along with the performance of this approximation. PPAs are discussed for both a 53- and a 27-row implementation. Finally, this type of approximation is compared with standard methods.

9.3.1 Reciprocal Operation

Deriving an optimal PPA for the reciprocal operation which provides a reasonable approximation and fits on a multiplier requires many PPAs to be derived and simulated. The last two steps of Algorithm 1 and all of Algorithm 2 are the key steps which make the PPA low-cost and high-performance. This section uses four steps for the derivation: derivation of formulas, choosing the number of digits to back-solve, error compensation, and the final array. Step 1 has already been shown for the reciprocal operation.

Choosing the Number of Digits to Back-solve

There are two parameters which can be changed in the PPA design: the number of digits to back-solve, and the number of compensating elements to add. This step performs rough sizings to determine the number of digits to back-solve, and results are reported in Table 9.1.

Given that a direct multiplier with a 53-row PPA is to be reused, the 16-digit approximation easily fits the multiplier's PPA. The 17-digit approximation exceeds the requirements in one column, which is the next to last column. Since Algorithm 2 still can be applied to reshape columns exceeding the constraints to less significant columns, the 17-digit approximation is

TABLE 9.1 Various sizes of PPAs for the reciprocal operation

Digits Back-solved	Rows in PPA
5	3
16	49
17	64
18	78

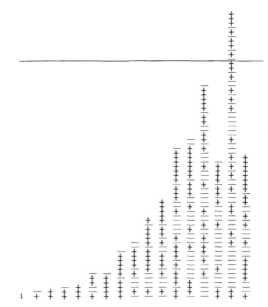

Figure 9.17 Signed PPA of 17-digit reciprocal approximation.

chosen. Its signed PPA is represented in Figure 9.17. Plus signs denote positive Boolean elements, and minus signs denote negative Boolean elements. A line is drawn to show which column exceeds 53 rows. Expansions of the elements in the worst-case column can bring the PPA under 53 rows, and there is also some space to add error-compensating elements.

Error-Compensating Elements

The next step is to add error-compensating elements until the usable elements in the multiplier's PPA are filled. The first step in doing so is to determine the error. The 17-digit PPA has an average of 14.58 correct bits and a worst case of 7.91 correct bits. The absolute signed error is plotted in Figure 9.18(a). Notice that the worst-case error is restricted to a small region between divisors of 0.80 and 0.90. If this region didn't exist, the worst-case error would be better than 10 correct bits. This study adds elements to the PPA to correct for this error. Many elements can be added for this purpose. After this region is improved, the error of the new PPA is plotted and new

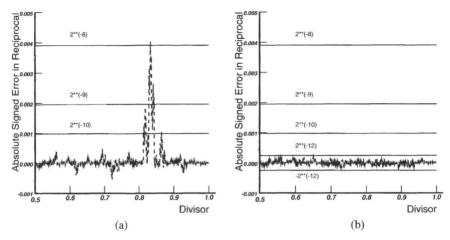

Figure 9.18   Absolute signed error of 17-digit reciprocal approximation: (a) without error compensation; (b) with error compensation.

compensating elements are added. This continues until there is no space in the multiplier's PPA to add new elements. The total number of elements in the PPA without compensating elements is 343, and about 100 compensating elements are added. The array with compensating elements has 15.18 correct bits on average, with a minimum of 12.003 correct bits.

A plot of the error of the PPA with compensating elements is given in Figure 9.18(b). The axis has the same scale as Figure 9.18(a) to give a direct comparison of the error. The minimum number of correct bits has increased by over 4, and the average has improved slightly. A more interesting plot is given in Figure 9.19, which shows the minimum number of correct bits (equal to the negative $\log_2$ of the absolute error, since there is one significant integer bit) vs the divisor. This plot shows several peaks of error near 12 correct bits. Many more compensating elements would need to be added to gain another bit or two correct for the worst case. Thus, 12 correct bits appears to be the limit on the worst-case error for a 53-row PPA implementation.

Final Array

The last step is forming the final array. The shape of the array is shown in Figure 9.20, where x's indicate Boolean elements and 1's indicate the known constant 1. The outline of a direct multiplier's PPA is shown around the reciprocal's PPA. The reciprocal's PPA does not use the whole PPA. Less than 20% of the array is used. The array is restricted by the maximum number of rows. The worst-case error (both relative and absolute) is approximately 2^{-12}, which causes any new compensating elements to be added to columns 13 and 14, which are completely full. Thus, no more significant compensating elements can be added to the array. Thus, a PPA has been

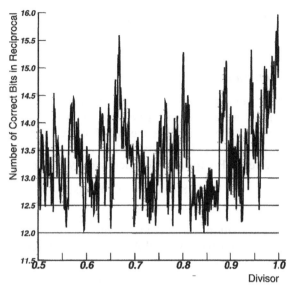

Figure 9.19 Minimum correct bits for 17-digit reciprocal approximation with error compensation.

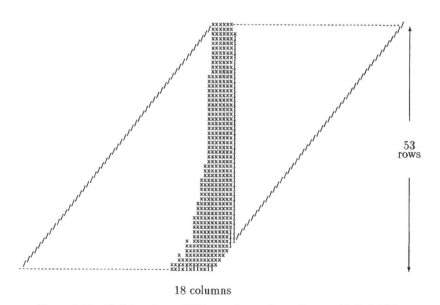

Figure 9.20 17-digit reciprocal PPA superimposed on a direct multiplier's PPA.

created for the reciprocal operation which can fit on a direct multiplier's PPA and has an accuracy of more than 12 correct bits (1 integer bit and 11 fractional bits).

27-Row Implementation

A Booth multiplier implementation also can be derived. For that implementation only 27 rows were used to give a PPA with 175 elements. The approximation produced by this PPA has 12.71 correct bits on average and 9.17 bits in the worst case. This approximation requires the same number of iterations as the direct PPA for a quadratically converging algorithm, since

$$9 \Rightarrow 18 \Rightarrow 36 \Rightarrow 53 + \text{bits},$$
$$12 \Rightarrow 24 \Rightarrow 48 \Rightarrow 53 + \text{bits}.$$

Thus, either approximation can be used with a quadratically converging algorithm for division, but the direct PPA (53 rows) is preferred for a linearly converging algorithm. Note that the Booth PPA is smaller and can be superimposed on either multiplier if only a small-precision approximation is needed.

Comparison

A comparison of the proposed method for the reciprocal operation vs an equivalent-precision lookup table is given in Table 9.2. The reciprocal approximation using a 53-row PPA gives a 12-bit approximation at the cost of approximately 1000 gates. An equivalent-precision lookup table needs to be 11 Kbyte, or approximately 39,000 gates. Thus, the proposed method is $\frac{1}{39}$ the size of an equivalent lookup table for a 12-bit approximation. For the 27-row PPA, a 9.17-bit approximation is achieved at the cost of approximately 400 gates. This is about $\frac{1}{9}$ the size of an equivalent-precision lookup table.

The proposed method also has much higher precision than an equivalent-latency polynomial, as shown in Table 9.3. A first-order polynomial method [4] gives only 4.08 correct bits. Thus, a 53 row PPA has almost three times the number of correct bits, and a 27-row PPA has over twice as many correct bits. Thus, the proposed method for the reciprocal operation produces PPAs which have much greater accuracy than an equivalent-latency polynomial method and are much smaller than an equivalent-precision lookup table.

TABLE 9.2 Size of proposed method vs equivalent lookup table for reciprocal

	Proposed Method			Look-up Table			
Min. Bits	Max. Rows	Total Elements	Equiv. Gates	Shape	Size (Kbyte)	Equiv. Gates	Size Ratio
12.00	53	484	≈ 1000	$2^{13} \times 11$	11	$\approx 39{,}000$	39:1
9.17	27	175	≈ 400	$2^{10} \times 8$	1	≈ 3600	9:1

TABLE 9.3   Accuracy of proposed method vs first-order polynomial for reciprocal

Max. Rows	Proposed Method		Polynomial Min. Bits	Accuracy Ratio
	Total Elements	Min. Bits		
53	484	12.00	4.08	2.94:1
27	175	9.17	4.08	2.25:1

9.3.2 Division Operation

Division is a frequent high-order operation that is commonly computed by using the reciprocal operation and a multiplication. The reciprocal operation is used because it is simpler than division, since it is only dependent on one operand. Approximations for the reciprocal operation are also simpler than those for the division operation. Reciprocal approximations are used by both high-precision algorithms for reciprocation and division, while division approximations are only used for division. Also, algorithms which use the reciprocal approximation can be either quadratically or linearly converging, and the division approximations are only used by linearly converging algorithms. Thus, division approximations have less versatility and typically are used in algorithms which have a slower rate of convergence. So, why create division approximations?

The benefits of using an algorithm which has a division approximation are that rounding is easier, the iteration is typically simpler, and the average error dictates the number of iterations.

Rounding is easier because both the quotient and remainder are typically calculated. This gives all the information necessary for proper rounding without added delays.

The iteration is simpler for linearly converging high-radix algorithms and consists of a subtraction and a small-width multiplication. A quadratically converging algorithm may have less iterations, but not necessarily lower latency, due to its longer delay per iteration. So it is not clear that a method having slower convergence is actually slower overall. Since there are many iterations for a division algorithm, implementations commonly have a variable number of iterations. Having the exact remainder each iteration helps this type of variable-latency implementation, because the number of iterations is decreased if there are leading zeros in the remainder. A variable-latency implementation is more costly than a fixed latency implementation due to the added normalization hardware necessary, but the performance benefits may outweigh the cost.

Since the number of iterations usually varies, the worst-case error does not give the expected latency of the algorithm. The average error gives a better[3]

---

[3]The average in this study is calculated using a uniform distribution, but the actual distribution of operands is better represented by a reciprocal distribution [66]. Thus, the average calculated is only an approximation to the true average.

indication of the expected latency. Thus, the average error is more important than the worst-case error for division. And the average error is always equal to or better than the worst-case error.

Thus, there are advantages in using an algorithm that uses a division approximation.

For either type of implementation—using a division approximation or using a reciprocal approximation—the proposed method results in a smaller number of gates than a lookup table, and higher precision than an equivalent polynomial. Thus, the designer can choose either high-level algorithm and still benefit from using the proposed method for the approximation unit. The previous subsection detailed the reciprocal operation, and this subsection details the division approximation.

The derivation of a PPA for division is separated into the same four steps as was the reciprocal operation: (1) derivation of formulas, (2) choosing the number of digits to back-solve, (3) error compensation, and (4) final array.

Derivation of Formulas

The derivation is similar to the reciprocal operation and proceeds using Algorithm 1.

Express Operation as a Multiplication. The first step is to express the division operation as a function of multiplications and additions. This is shown as follows:

$$Q = A/B \quad \Rightarrow \quad QB = A,$$

where Q is the quotient, A is the dividend, and B is the divisor.

Expand Multiplication into a PPA. The second step is to expand the multiplication into a PPA. Both A and B are assumed binary and unsigned. Thus, the array is the same as the reciprocal array but the product is equal to the dividend, A, rather than equal to one. This is shown by Figure 9.21.

Back-solve the PPA. The quotient digits are in a redundant notation and chosen to not cause any carry propagation in the previous PPA. Thus, the first five columns of the PPA form the following equations:

$$q_0 = 1,$$

$$q_{(1)} + b_{(2)}q_0 = a_{(2)},$$

$$q_{(2)} + b_{(2)}q_{(1)} + b_{(3)}q_0 = a_{(3)},$$

$$q_{(3)} + b_{(2)}q_{(2)} + b_{(3)}q_{(1)} + b_{(4)}q_0 = a_{(4)},$$

$$q_{(4)} + b_{(2)}q_{(3)} + b_{(3)}q_{(2)} + b_{(4)}q_{(1)} + b_{(5)}q_0 = a_{(5)}.$$

	0.	1	$b_{(2)}$	$b_{(3)}$	$b_{(4)}$	$b_{(5)}$	$\cdots$					$= B$
	X	q_0	$q_{(1)}$	$q_{(2)}$	$q_{(3)}$	$q_{(4)}$	$\cdots$					$= Q$
			$\vdots$	$\vdots$	$\vdots$	$\vdots$						
					$q_{(4)}$	$b_{(2)}q_{(4)}$	$b_{(3)}q_{(4)}$	$b_{(4)}q_{(4)}$	$b_{(5)}q_{(4)}$	$\cdots$		
				$q_{(3)}$	$b_{(2)}q_{(3)}$	$b_{(3)}q_{(3)}$	$b_{(4)}q_{(3)}$	$b_{(5)}q_{(3)}$	$\cdots$			
			$q_{(2)}$	$b_{(2)}q_{(2)}$	$b_{(3)}q_{(2)}$	$b_{(4)}q_{(2)}$	$b_{(5)}q_{(2)}$	$\cdots$				
	$q_{(1)}$	$b_{(2)}q_{(1)}$	$b_{(3)}q_{(1)}$	$b_{(4)}q_{(1)}$	$b_{(5)}q_{(1)}$	$\cdots$						
q_0	$b_{(2)}q_0$	$b_{(3)}q_0$	$b_{(4)}q_0$	$b_{(5)}q_0$	$\cdots$							
0.	1	$a_{(2)}$	$a_{(3)}$	$a_{(4)}$	$a_{(5)}$	$\cdots$						$= A$

Figure 9.21

These equations are solved to yield the following formulations for five digits of the quotient:

$$q_0 = 1,$$

$$q_{(1)} = a_{(2)} - b_{(2)},$$

$$q_{(2)} = a_{(3)} - b_{(2)}a_{(2)} + \left(b_{(2)} - b_{(3)}\right),$$

$$q_{(3)} = a_{(4)} - b_{(2)}a_{(3)} + \left(b_{(2)} - b_{(3)}\right)a_{(2)} + \left(-b_{(4)} + 2b_{(2)}\,b_{(3)} - b_{(2)}\right),$$

$$q_{(4)} = a_{(5)} - b_{(2)}\,a_{(4)} + \left(b_{(2)} - b_{(3)}\right)a_{(3)} + \left(-b_{(4)} + 2b_{(2)}\,b_{(3)} - b_{(2)}\right)a_{(2)}$$

$$+ \left(-b_{(5)} + 2b_{(2)}b_{(4)} - 3b_{(2)}b_{(3)} + b_{(3)} + b_{(2)}\right).$$

These equations are slightly more complex than for the reciprocal operation.

Form New PPA and Reduce. The equations of each quotient digit are weighted by a different power of two. They can be placed in a PPA with each digit's equation forming a separate column in the PPA. The PPA is then reduced using Boolean and algebraic equivalencies to yield the PPA in Figure 9.22. The reduced PPA for back-solving five digits has a total of 17 elements and a maximum of 8 rows.

An example of using this PPA is given in Figure 9.23 for 0.875 divided by 0.75. The actual value is $1.1666\ldots$, and the calculated value is $(1.0011)_2 = 1.1875$. The absolute error is $2^{-5.58}$, which implies that there are 5.58 correct bits (1 integer bit and 4.58 fractional bits). This is a very good approximation for a small PPA.

q_0	$q_{(1)}$	$q_{(2)}$	$q_{(3)}$	$q_{(4)}$
				$a_{(5)}$
				$-b_{(2)}a_{(4)}$
				$b_{(3)}\overline{a_{(3)}}$
				$-b_{(2)}a_{(3)}$
			$a_{(4)}$	$-b_{(4)}a_{(2)}$
			$-\overline{b_{(2)}}b_{(3)}a_{(2)}$	$b_{(2)}\overline{a_{(2)}}$
	$a_{(2)}$	$a_{(3)}$	$b_{(2)}\overline{a_{(2)}}$	$-b_{(5)}$
1	$-b_{(2)}$	$-b_{(3)}$	$-\overline{b_{(2)}}b_{(4)}$	$b_{(2)}b_{(3)}$

Figure 9.22   Reduced five-digit PPA for division.

$$A = 0.875 = (0.11100\dots)_2$$

$$a_{(2)} = 1, \qquad a_{(3)} = 1, \qquad a_i = 0 \quad \text{for} \quad i > 3$$

$$B = 0.75 = (0.11000 \cdots)_2$$

$$b_{(2)} = 1, \qquad b_j = 0 \quad \text{for} \quad j > 2$$

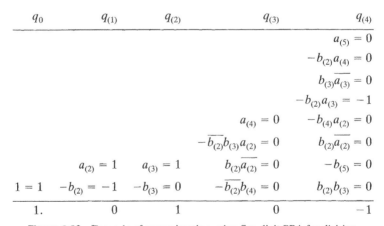

Figure 9.23   Example of approximation using five-digit PPA for division.

Choosing the Number of Digits to Back-solve

The five-digit PPA produces an average of 5.15 correct bits and a minimum of 1.64 correct bits. The average number of correct bits easily can be improved at low cost if a multiplier is reused. The multipliers considered for reuse have 27 or 53 rows available. This step determines the maximum number of digits to back-solve for this type of implementation. Table 9.4

TABLE 9.4   **Various sizes of PPAs for the division operation**

Digits Back-solved	Rows in PPA
5	8
9	$\boxed{25}$
10	29
11	40
12	$\boxed{54}$
13	72

gives the number of rows in the PPAs for several numbers of digits back-solved. The two sizes that are compatible with the multipliers are the 9-digit PPA, which has 25 rows, and the 12-digit PPA, which has 54 rows. The 12-digit PPA exceeds the maximum number of rows by only one. This is easily corrected by moving an element to a less significant column and replicating it the appropriate number of times. Thus, two designs are chosen based on the size of their PPAs.

Error Compensation

Error compensation is more difficult to perform for division than for the other high-order arithmetic functions considered. Division is the only operation presented which has two input operands. To plot the error requires a three-dimensional graph of the divisor, dividend, and absolute signed error as shown in Figure 9.24. Figure 9.24(a) shows a 3D view of the absolute signed error, and Figure 9.24(b) shows a density plot. The solid black squares (error $= -2^{-6}$) and the solid white squares (error $= +2^{-9}$) are the worst

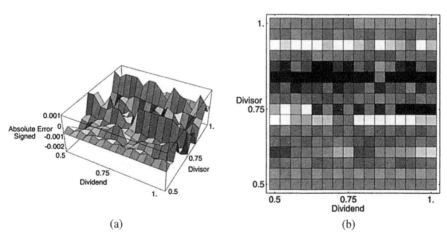

(a)   (b)

Figure 9.24   Absolute signed error in division approximation: (a) three-domensional plot; (b) density plot.

regions of error. It is difficult to determine correction terms from this graph. For the reciprocal operation, 100 correction terms were determined from approximately twenty iterations of graphing and calculating appropriate compensating elements. The added complexity of a third dimension for division makes this step too difficult to perform manually. Since all compensating elements are currently determined manually, this type of correction is suggested for future research.

Final Array

The 9-digit PPA can be superimposed on a Booth multiplier's PPA. It has 25 rows maximum and a total of 97 elements. The PPA gives an average[4] of 7.64 correct bits and a minimum of 3.13 bits. The 12-digit PPA can be used by a direct multiplier. It has a maximum of 53 rows and a total of 269 elements. This PPA gives an average of 9.86 correct bits and a minimum of 3.96 correct bits. Note that no correction terms have been added. Thus, the worst-case error is rather large, but the average number of correct bits of either PPA is very good. Thus, PPAs have been formed for the division operation which provide an approximation of 7.64 and 9.86 bits on average.

Comparison

Since the proposed method for division (unlike the reciprocal operation) is intended for implementations that have a variable number of iterations, the average error is the critical factor determining the overall latency. Thus, the proposed method is compared with a lookup table with the same average number of correct bits. To determine the equivalent-average-precision lookup table an assumption is made: that the numbers of indexing bits of the divisor and dividend are equal. Thus, the lookup table will have a shape of M bits by 2^{2N} entries.

First lookup tables are simulated for M equal to N. A simulation of 20 bits for M and N equal to 7, 8, 9, and 10 bits yields the results shown in Table 9.5. Both M equal to 8 and 10 give results similar to the proposed method. Then a second iteration is performed, letting N be less than M, and a smaller equivalent ROM is determined. To achieve the precision of the 27-row PPA requires an 8×2^{12} ROM, and for the 53-row PPA requires a 10×2^{18} ROM.

The average error of the proposed method is compared with the equivalent lookup table in Table 9.6. The proposed method is much smaller than an equivalent-precision lookup table. It is $\frac{1}{2000}$ to $\frac{1}{70}$ the size of the latter.

The proposed method also compares favorably with a polynomial approximation method. This comparison is not as straightforward as the same comparison for the reciprocal operation. Finding an equal-latency polynomial

---

[4]The average for division is taken from 20-bit simulation. The first 10 bits of the dividend and divisor are simulated exhaustively.

TABLE 9.5   Shape, size, and precision of ROMs for the division operation

Shape	Size (Kbyte)	Ave. Bits	Min. Bits
$2^{14} \times 7$	14	7.04	4.48
$2^{16} \times 8$	64	8.03	5.45
$2^{14} \times 8$	16	7.95	5.08
$2^{12} \times 8$	**4**	**7.63**	**4.57**
$2^{10} \times 8$	1	6.99	3.84
$2^{18} \times 9$	288	9.04	6.44
$2^{20} \times 10$	1280	10.10	7.43
$\mathbf{2^{18} \times 10}$	**320**	**10.00**	**7.03**
$2^{16} \times 10$	80	9.66	6.46

TABLE 9.6   Size of proposed method vs equivalent lookup table for division

Proposed Method				Lookup Table			
Ave. Bits	Max. Rows	Total Elements	Equiv. Gates	Shape	Size (Kbyte)	Equiv. Gates	Size Ratio
9.86	53	269	≈ 550	$2^{18} \times 10$	320	$\approx 1,100,000$	2000:1
7.64	27	97	≈ 200	$2^{12} \times 8$	4	$\approx 14,000$	70::1

is difficult. The division approximation requires the latency of one multiplication. For the polynomial method, a polynomial approximating the reciprocal operation multiplied by the dividend was used. The only way in general to make this a first-order equation is to use a zeroth-order polynomial (a constant). This produces a very large error and would never be implemented, so instead a first-order reciprocal approximation is multiplied by the dividend. The total latency in the general case is two multiplications and an addition, which is over twice the delay of the proposed method.

Another difficulty lies in choosing an appropriate polynomial in which the average error is minimized rather than the worst-case error. Several coefficients were chosen until a minimum was found for 20-bit simulation. The chosen polynomial, $(2.85 - 2.0B)A$, has a shorter latency than the general case, since the first-order coefficient is two, which can be produced by a shift. Thus, the polynomial chosen for comparison has a latency of a shift, an add, and a multiplication. Its results are reported in Table 9.7 along with the results of the proposed method. The polynomial has an average of 5.16 correct bits, compared to 7.64 and 9.86 bits for the proposed method. The proposed method has 50% to 90% more correct bits on average than a similar-latency polynomial method. Thus, the proposed method is much better than an equivalent-precision lookup table and an equivalent-latency polynomial approximation.

TABLE 9.7   Accuracy of proposed method vs first-order polynomial for division

| | Proposed Method | | | Polynomial | | Accuracy |
| Max. | Total | Ave. | Min. | Ave. | Min. | Ratio |
Rows	Elements	Bits	Bits	Bits	Bits	(Ave. Bits)
53	269	9.86	3.96	5.16	1.73	1.91:1
27	97	7.64	3.13	5.16	1.73	1.48:1

9.3.3   Square-Root Operation

Two different square-root approximations are described in this subsection: the square root, and the reciprocal of the square root. Both of these approximations are commonly used in high-precision algorithms for the square-root operation [141]. Approximations are derived for half the range of these functions.

For both the reciprocal and division approximations only the magnitudes were considered. The result's exponent is calculated by a negation for the reciprocal and a subtraction for the division operation. A full range of operands is covered by allowing the magnitude to be in the range $0.5 \leq A < 1.0$. For the square root and its reciprocal, the result's exponent is easy to calculate if the input operand has an even exponent. With that added restriction, the full range of magnitudes must be between $0.25 \leq A < 1.0$. Only half of this range is considered for either the square root or its reciprocal. The other half can be calculated by an additional multiplication by a short constant ($\sqrt{2}$ or $1/\sqrt{2}$). Thus, the latency of the approximations in this section is 1.5 multiplications on average, where the half of a multiplication corresponds to a small-width multiplication.

Approximating the Square Root

The derivation of the formulas for the square root is very similar to the derivation for the reciprocal. The operand is assumed to be normalized in the range $0.25 \leq A < 0.5$, and the exponent is assumed to be even. The new exponent (equal to approximately half the original) is assumed to be calculated elsewhere in hardware. If the exponent is odd, the square root of two must be multiplied by the result's magnitude. The calculation is shown for $\mathscr{A}$, which is A with an exponent, for both the even and odd exponent cases:

$$0.25 \leq A < 0.5,$$
$$\mathscr{A} = A \times 2^e,$$
$$\mathscr{A}^{1/2} = \begin{cases} A^{1/2} \times 2^{e/2}, & \text{even } e, \\ A^{1/2} \times \sqrt{2} \times 2^{(e-1)/2}, & \text{odd } e. \end{cases}$$

This study solves directly for the square root of operands which are normalized within this range and have even exponents, but an additional multiplication by the square root of two is needed for odd exponents. On average 1.5 multiplications are needed using this PPA method. There are two methods that can be used to calculate the full range but both these approaches prove to be more costly and less accurate. Thus, the derivation proceeds assuming only half the range is to be approximated.

Derivation of Formulas

The derivation of the initial formulas proceeds using Algorithm 1:

1. *Express Square Root as a Multiplication.* First the ranges and notation for A, the input operand, and Q, the root, are shown. Then the expression for the square root as a multiplication is given:

$$0.25 \leq A < 0.5,$$

$$a_0 = 0, \qquad a_{(1)} = 0, \qquad a_{(2)} = 1,$$

$$A = 1 \times 2^{-2} + a_{(3)} \times 2^{-3} + a_{(4)} \times 2^{-4} + \cdots;$$

$$0.5 \leq Q < 1/\sqrt{2} = 0.707\ldots,$$

$$q_0 = 0, \qquad q_{(1)} = 1,$$

$$Q = 1 \times 2^{-1} + q_{(2)} \times 2^{-2} + q_{(3)} \times 2^{-3} + \cdots,$$

$$A = Q \times Q.$$

2. *Expand Multiplication into a PPA.* This multiplication is expanded into a PPA using the reduced notation for Q and A (see Figure 9.25).

		0.	1	$q_{(2)}$	$q_{(3)}$	$q_{(4)}$	$q_{(5)}$	$\cdots$		$= Q$
	X	0.	1	$q_{(2)}$	$q_{(3)}$	$q_{(4)}$	$q_{(5)}$	$\cdots$		$= Q$
				$q_{(5)}$	$q_{(2)}q_{(5)}$	$q_{(3)}q_{(5)}$	$q_{(4)}q_{(5)}$	$q_{(5)}q_{(5)}$	$\cdots$	
			$q_{(4)}$	$q_{(2)}q_{(4)}$	$q_{(3)}q_{(4)}$	$q_{(4)}q_{(4)}$	$q_{(4)}q_{(5)}$	$\cdots$		
		$q_{(3)}$	$q_{(2)}q_{(3)}$	$q_{(3)}q_{(3)}$	$q_{(4)}q_{(3)}$	$q_{(5)}q_{(3)}$	$\cdots$			
	$q_{(2)}$	$q_{(2)}q_{(2)}$	$q_{(3)}q_{(2)}$	$q_{(4)}q_{(2)}$	$q_{(5)}q_{(2)}$	$\cdots$				
0.01	$q_{(2)}$	$q_{(3)}$	$q_{(4)}$	$q_{(5)}$	$\cdots$					
0.01	$a_{(3)}$	$a_{(4)}$	$a_{(5)}$	$a_{(6)}$	$\cdots$					$= A$

Figure 9.25

3. *Back-solve the PPA.* The columns form separate equations, which are solved for several digits of Q as shown below:

$$q_0 = 0,$$
$$q_{(1)} = 1,$$
$$q_{(2)} = a_{(3)}/2,$$
$$q_{(3)} = a_{(4)}/2 - a_{(3)}/8,$$
$$q_{(4)} = a_{(5)}/2 + a_{(3)}/16 - a_{(3)}a_{(4)}/4,$$
$$q_{(5)} = a_{(6)}/2 - 5a_{(3)}/128 - a_{(4)}/8 + 3a_{(3)}a_{(4)}/16 - a_{(3)}a_{(5)}/4.$$

4. *Form a New PPA and Reduce.* There are several fractional terms which appear in these equations. All the fractions are powers of two which are easily representable. The PPA formed is wider than for either reciprocation or division, since these terms expand to many less significant columns. An element with a constant divisor of 128 is shifted seven columns to the right (less significant) of the column where its quotient digit appears. Thus, the new array is wide and flat, as shown by the PPA in Figure 9.26 for five digits back-solved. The array has a height of 2 and a width of 12. There are a total of 13 elements in the array. The critical dimension of an operation's PPA is the number of rows. This PPA is smaller for the same number of digits back-solved than division (8 rows) or reciprocation (3 rows). This is an indication that better approximations are possible for the square-root operation. An example is shown in Figure 9.27 for approximating the square root of 0.3125. The actual value is 0.559017, and the calculated value is $(0.100100\overline{1}0100)_2 = 0.55957$, which has an absolute error of $2^{-10.82}$. Thus, the 5-digit PPA for this example has 9.82 correct bits. This is excellent for the size of the PPA.

$q_{(1)}$	$q_{(2)}$	$q_{(3)}$	$q_{(4)}$	$q_{(5)}$	$q_{(6)}$	$q_{(7)}$	$q_{(8)}$	$q_{(9)}$	$q_{(10)}$	$q_{(11)}$	$q_{(12)}$
					$a_{(6)}$	$-a_{(3)}a_{(5)}$			$a_{(4)}$		
1	0	$a_{(3)}$	$a_{(4)}$	$a_{(5)}$	$-a_{(3)}a_{(4)}$	$-a_{(3)}$	$-(a_{(3)} \mid a_{(4)})$	$a_{(3)}a_{(4)}$	$-a_{(3)}$	0	$-a_{(3)}$

Figure 9.26

$$A = 0.3125 = (0.01010000 \cdots)_{(2)}$$

$$a_{(2)} = 1, \quad a_{(3)} = 0, \quad a_{(4)} = 1, \quad a_i = 0 \quad \text{for} \quad i > 4$$

$q_{(1)}$	$q_{(2)}$	$q_{(3)}$	$q_{(4)}$	$q_{(5)}$	$q_{(6)}$	$q_{(7)}$	$q_{(8)}$	$q_{(9)}$	$q_{(10)}$	$q_{(11)}$	$q_{(12)}$
					$a_{(6)}$	$-a_{(3)}a_{(5)}$			$a_{(4)} = 1$		
1	0	$a_{(3)}$	$a_{(4)} = 1$	$a_{(5)}$	$-a_{(3)}a_{(4)}$	$-a_{(3)}$	$-(a_{(3)} \mid a_{(4)}) = -1$	$a_{(3)}a_{(4)}$	$-a_{(3)}$	0	$-a_{(3)}$
1	0	0	1	0	0	0	-1	0	1	0	0

Figure 9.27

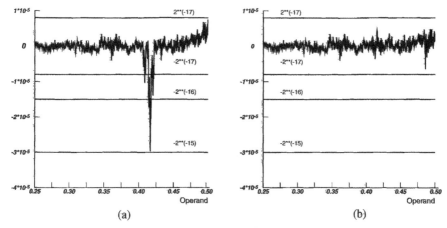

Figure 9.28   Absolute signed error of 19-bit square-root approximation: (a) without error compensation; (b) with error compensation.

Choosing the Number of Digits, Error Compensation, and Final Array

Many digits can be back-solved for direct multiplier implementation. A 19-bit approximation is chosen, because its PPA exceeds 53 rows by a small amount. This approximation provides an average of 19.24 correct bits and a worst case of 14.00 correct bits. This assumes that number of correct bits is equal to negative $\log_2$ of the absolute error minus one. The minus one term is included because there are no significant integer bits. The square root is represented as $Q = 0.1xxx \ldots$. The PPA has 59 rows and 318 total elements, and is truncated to give a 20-bit-wide array. The absolute signed error of this PPA is plotted in Figure 9.28(a).

After 14 error-compensating elements are added, the approximation improves to 19.44 bits on average and 16.08 bits worst case. The absolute signed error is plotted in Figure 9.28(b). There is a significant decrease in the worst-case error. The array is full because it is limited to a maximum of 53 rows. To achieve another bit correct in the worst case requires many more elements. Thus, the point is reached for accepting this final PPA. The signed PPA is then adapted to a direct multiplier by using Algorithm 2. The result is shown in Figure 9.29.

Thus, a PPA describing a square root approximation has been created which has 16 correct bits ($0.1xx\ldots$ with absolute error less than 2^{-17}) in the worst case and an average of 19.44 correct bits. The estimate is 22 bits wide, and the PPA readily maps onto a direct multiplier.

27-Row Implementation

A PPA also can be derived for a 27-row implementation. For this derivation 14 digits are back-solved. The resulting signed PPA has 214 elements with a maximum of 25 rows and on average has 16.00 correct bits and a minimum of

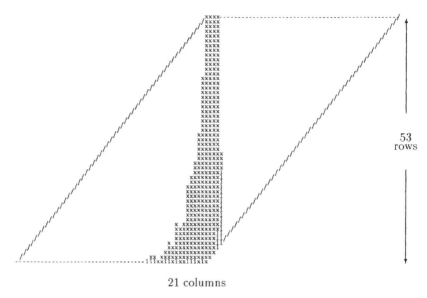

21 columns

Figure 9.29 19-bit square-root PPA superimposed on a direct multiplier's PPA.

11.77 correct bits. Four compensating elements are added to boost the minimum correct bits to 13.07 and the average to 16.10. There are many peaks in the error function, as shown in Figure 9.30. Thus, the final array produces a minimum of 13 fractional correct bits.

The PPAs provide a minimum approximation of 16 bits for a 53-row implementation and 12 bits for a 27-row implementation. These PPAs are much smaller than an equivalent lookup table and have much higher precision than an equivalent polynomial method.

Approximating the Reciprocal of the Square Root

Another useful operation to approximate is the reciprocal of the square root. Division can be eliminated in quadratically converging, high-precision square-root algorithms if an approximation to the reciprocal of the square root is available [141]. Thus, a PPA is derived for this operation which can be applied to a high-level algorithm for the square root.

The four-step process is repeated for the reciprocal of the square root. The derivation and final array are discussed in detail. There are two major differences in this derivation from that of the square-root operation. The normalization is different, and the binary operands are represented as polynomials. The following is the derivation, using Algorithm 1 with some minor modifications for polynomial operands.

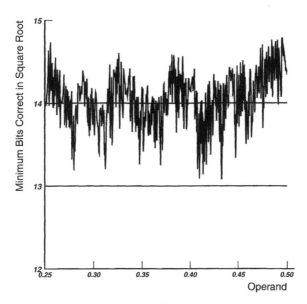

Figure 9.30 Minimum correct bits for 14-digit square-root approximation with error compensation.

Derivation of Formulas

The normalization is assumed to be in the range $0.5 \le A < 1.0$ with A having an even exponent. An additional multiplication by $1/\sqrt{2}$ is necessary if the exponent is odd, as shown below:

$$0.5 \le A < 1.0,$$

$$\mathscr{A} = A \times 2^e,$$

$$\mathscr{A}^{-1/2} = \begin{cases} A^{-1/2} \times 2^{-e/2}, & \text{even } e, \\ A^{-1/2} \times \dfrac{1}{\sqrt{2}} \times 2^{-(e-1)/2}, & \text{odd } e. \end{cases}$$

Also, the root has the range of $1.0 < Q \le \sqrt{2} = 1.414\ldots$.

1. *Express Reciprocal of Square Root as Multiplications.* This step is more complex for the reciprocal of the square root than for any of the previously considered operations. The resulting function that expresses the square root is a product of three operands. Thus, forming a new PPA is more difficult, because it is not obvious what this PPA looks like. To make sorting elements of equal weight easier, the binary variables are transformed into polynomials. On replacing each 2^{-1} by an x it is easier to separate terms by their power of x rather than by

their numerical coefficients. The numerical coefficients include constants that may not be powers of two, as in the term $\frac{3}{2}a$. This term could be placed in a column weighted with 2^{-1} or 2^0. Using polynomials makes it easier to form the new PPA. Also, this notation is used for natural log, exponential, and trigonometric operations. That makes it easier not only to separate the weighted elements, but also to express these operations as series of multiplications and additions. (See [102, 157, 158] for extensive details of using a polynomial notation.) The process is itself rather straightforward. The negative powers of two in the binary variable are replaced by powers of x, as shown below for A and Q:

$$A = a_0 \times 2^0 + a_{(1)} \times 2^{-1} + a_{(2)} \times 2^{-2} + \cdots,$$

$$A(x) = a_0 \times x^0 + a_{(1)} \times x^1 + a_{(2)} \times x^2 + \cdots;$$

$$Q = q_0 \times 2^0 + q_{(1)} \times 2^{-1} + q_{(2)} \times 2^{-2} + \cdots,$$

$$Q(x) = q_0 \times x^0 + q_{(1)} \times x^1 + q_{(2)} \times x^2 + \cdots.$$

For x equal to $\frac{1}{2}$ the polynomials are equal to their corresponding binary variables [$A = A(x = \frac{1}{2})$ and $Q = Q(x = \frac{1}{2})$]. The reciprocal of the square root is expressed as a product, using this notation, by the following equations:

$$Q(x) = 1.0/\sqrt{A(x)},$$

$$A(x)Q(x)^2 = 1.0,$$

$$A(x)Q(x)^2 = 0.111\ldots.$$

Expanding the product for many bits yields the following:

$$Q(x)^2 = q_0^2 x^0 + 2q_0 q_{(1)} x^1 + \left(q_{(1)}^2 + 2q_0 q_{(2)}\right) x^2 + \cdots,$$

$$A(x)Q(x)^2 = a_0 q_0^2 + \left(a_{(1)} q_0^2 + 2a_0 q_0 q_{(1)}\right) x^1$$
$$+ \left(a_{(2)} q_0^2 + 2a_{(1)} q_0 q_{(1)} + a_0 q_{(1)}^2 + 2a_0 q_0 q_{(2)}\right)^2 + \cdots,$$

$$A(x)Q(x)^2 = q_0^2 x^1 + \left(a_{(2)} q_0 + 2q_0 q_{(1)}\right) x^2$$
$$+ \left(a_{(3)} q_0^2 + 2a_{(2)} q_0 q_{(1)} + q_{(1)}^2 + 2q_0 q_{(2)}\right) x^3 + \cdots,$$

$$A(x)Q(x)^2 = 0x^0 + 1x^1 + 1x^2 + \cdots,$$

$$= q_0^2 x^1 + \left(a_{(2)} q_0 + 2q_0 q_{(1)}\right) x^2$$
$$+ \left(a_{(3)} q_0^2 + 2a_{(2)} q_0 q_{(1)} + q_{(1)}^2 + 2q_0 q_{(2)}\right) x^3 + \cdots.$$

This last equation expresses the operation as multiplications. It also can be viewed as two polynomials set equal to each other.

2. *Expand Multiplication into a PPA.* A PPA could be formed, but the result is a very complex PPA. Instead, equivalently, we set corresponding coefficients of the polynomial of x equal to each other. Each power of x represents a separate column in the PPA. On setting the coefficients of the powers in the polynomials equal, in effect the columns of the PPA form these separate equations. The following is the result:

$$1 = q_0^2,$$

$$1 = a_{(2)}q_0^2 + 2q_0 q_{(1)},$$

$$1 = a_{(3)}q_0^2 + 2a_{(2)}q_0 q_{(1)} + q_{(1)}^2 + 2q_0 q_{(2)},$$

$$1 = a_{(4)}q_0^2 + 2a_{(3)}q_0 q_{(1)} + a_{(2)}q_{(1)}^2 + 2a_{(2)}q_0 q_{(2)} + 2q_{(1)}q_{(2)} + 2q_0 q_{(3)}.$$

The 2D representation of the PPA is not very useful, since it is complicated. Instead, for very high-order operations, the 1D representation is used, with each power of the polynomial representing a different column in the PPA. Thus, the linear formulations are considered to be easier to use than the PPA representation for operations such as the reciprocal of the square root.

3. *Back-solve the PPA.* This step back-solves the equations produced in the previous step. The following is the result:

$$q_0 = 1,$$

$$q_{(1)} = \frac{1}{2} - \frac{a_{(2)}}{2},$$

$$q_{(2)} = \frac{3}{8} + \frac{a_{(2)}}{8} - \frac{a_{(3)}}{2},$$

$$q_{(3)} = \frac{5}{16} - \frac{5a_{(2)}}{16} - \frac{a_{(3)}}{4} + \frac{3a_{(2)}a_{(3)}}{4} - \frac{a_{(4)}}{2}.$$

4. *Form a New PPA and Reduce.* Then, these equations are placed in a new PPA. The PPA in this context is a useful representation. The new PPA and its reduced form are shown in Figure 9.31. Thus, back-solving four digits results in a two-row array of seven elements. An example of using this PPA to approximate the reciprocal of the square root of 0.75 is shown by Figure 9.32. The actual value is 1.1547, and the calculated value is 1.125, which has an absolute error of $2^{-5.07}$. Thus, five-bits are correct for this example for the PPA formed from back-solving four digits.

q_0	$q_{(1)}$	$q_{(2)}$	$q_{(3)}$	$q_{(4)}$	$q_{(5)}$	$q_{(6)}$
					$a_{(2)}a_{(3)}$	
					$-a_{(3)}$	
					$-a_{(2)}$	
				$-a_{(4)}$	$a_{(2)}$	
		$-a_{(2)}$		$a_{(2)}a_{(3)}$	1	$-a_{(2)}$
1	0	1	$-a_{(3)}$	1	1	1

Reduces to:

q_0	$q_{(1)}$	$q_{(2)}$	$q_{(3)}$	$q_{(4)}$	$q_{(5)}$	$q_{(6)}$
				$-a_{(4)}$		
1	0	$\overline{a_{(2)}}$	$\overline{a_{(3)}}$	$a_{(2)}a_{(3)}$	$-\overline{a_{(2)}a_{(3)}}$	$\overline{a_{(2)}}$

Figure 9.31

$$A = 0.75 = (0.11000\ldots)_2$$
$$a_{(2)} = 1, \quad a_i = 0 \quad \text{for} \quad i > 2$$

q_0	$q_{(1)}$	$q_{(2)}$	$q_{(3)}$	$q_{(4)}$	$q_{(5)}$	$q_{(6)}$
				$-a_{(4)} = 0$		
$1 = 1$	$0 = 0$	$\overline{a_{(2)}} = 0$	$\overline{a_{(3)}} = 1$	$a_{(2)}a_{(3)} = 0$	$-\overline{a_{(2)}a_{(3)}} = 0$	$\overline{a_{(2)}} = 0$
$1.$	0	0	1	0	0	0

Figure 9.32

Choosing the Number of Digits, Error Compensation, and Final Array

PPAs were sized for many different numbers of digits back-solved, and a 17-digit approximation was chosen. Its PPA has an average of 16.45 correct bits (one integer bit, since $Q = 1.xxx\ldots$) and a worst case of 9.88 correct bits. The PPA has a maximum of 50 rows and a total of 470 elements. Error-compensating elements are then added to this PPA. The final array, after many iterations of adding compensating elements, has an average of 16.97 correct bits and a worst case of 13.52 correct bits. This PPA has a maximum of 53 rows and a total of 534 elements. The PPA can be superimposed on the direct multiplier's PPA. Thus, a PPA can be derived for the reciprocal of the square root which has at least 13.52 correct bits. This array can be summed easily on a direct multiplier.

27-Row Implementation

For a Booth multiplier the implementation is restricted to have 27 rows maximum. 14 digits are back-solved for this implementation. The resulting signed PPA has an average of 14.15 correct bits and a minimum of 8.83

TABLE 9.8   Size of proposed method vs equivalent lookup table for square root

Operation	Min. Bits	Max. Rows	Total Elements	Equiv. Gates	Shape	Size Kbyte	Equiv. Gates	Size Ratio
			Proposed Method			Look-up Table		
Square root	16.08	53	398	≈ 800	$2^{16} \times 14$	112	$\approx 400,000$	500:1
	13.07	26	232	≈ 470	$2^{13} \times 11$	11	$\approx 39,000$	83:1
1/(Square root)	13.52	53	534	≈ 1100	$2^{13} \times 12$	12	$\approx 43,000$	39:1
	11.16	26	304	≈ 610	$2^{11} \times 10$	2.5	$\approx 9,000$	15:1

correct bits. By adding nine correction terms the worst case is improved to 11.16 correct bits and an average of 14.43 bits. The final PPA has 26 rows with a total of 304 elements.

The square-root approximation gives a higher accuracy (16.08 correct bits vs 13.52) than the reciprocal of the square root for the 53-row implementation.

Comparison

The proposed method for the square root and reciprocal of the square root are compared with equivalent-precision lookup tables in Table 9.8. The proposed method for the square root requires 800 and 470 gates for the 53- and 27-row implementations respectively. This is very small, especially for the precision achieved, 16.08 and 13.07 bits. Equivalent-precision lookup tables require 400,000 gates to get 16 bits of precision and 39,000 gates to get 13 bits. The proposed method for a direct multiplier is $\frac{1}{500}$, or 0.2%, the size of an equivalent-precision ROM lookup table. For the Booth multiplier implementation the proposed method is $\frac{1}{83}$ the size of the lookup table.

To approximate the reciprocal of the square root the proposed method requires 1100 gates and 610 gates for the two implementations. An equivalent-precision lookup table requires 43,000 gates and 9000 gates respectively. The proposed method is $\frac{1}{39}$ the size of the lookup table for the 53-row implementation and $\frac{1}{15}$ the size for the 27-row implementation. Thus, the proposed method is much smaller than an equivalent-precision lookup table for both operations, ranging from $\frac{1}{15}$ to $\frac{1}{500}$ the size.

A comparison is also given (Table 9.9) of the proposed method with an equivalent-latency (first-order) polynomial [53]. The polynomial method has a minimum of 7.06 correct bits for the square root and 5.03 correct bits for the reciprocal of the square root. For the square root the proposed method has 1.85 to 2.28 times as many correct bits as the polynomial approximation. For the reciprocal of the square root, the proposed method is 2.22 to 2.69 times the accuracy of the polynomial in terms of number of correct bits. The proposed method is much more accurate than an equivalent-latency polynomial, ranging from 85% to 169% more correct bits. Thus, the proposed

TABLE 9.9 Accuracy of proposed method vs first-order polynomial for square root

Operation	Max. Rows	Proposed Method		Polynomial Min. Bits	Accuracy Ratio
		Total Elements	Min. Bits		
Square root	53	398	16.08	7.06	2.28:1
	26	232	13.07	7.06	1.85:1
1/(Square root)	53	534	13.52	5.03	2.69:1
	26	304	11.16	5.03	2.22:1

method is much smaller than an equivalent-precision lookup table and much more accurate than an equivalent-latency polynomial operation, for the square root and for the reciprocal of the square root.

9.4 CONCLUSION

The proposed method has been applied to the operations of the reciprocal, division, and square root in this chapter. Several PPAs have been derived to approximate these operations. These approximations can be used in the starting approximation step of many high-radix algorithms for these operations. The approximations derived result in low-cost implementations (less than 1100 gates) and high-precision approximations (up to a minimum of 16.08 correct bits). They are much smaller than equivalent-precision lookup tables and equivalent-latency polynomials.

The results of comparing the proposed method with an equivalent-precision lookup table are summarized in Table 9.10. The minimum number of correct bits for the approximations are shown for the reciprocal, square root,

TABLE 9.10 Size of proposed method vs equivalent look-up tables

Operation	Min. Bits	Proposed Method			Lookup Table			Size Ratio
		Max. Rows	Total Elements	Equiv. Gates	Shape	Size (Kbyte)	Equiv. Gates	
Reciprocal	12.00	53	484	≈ 1000	$2^{13} \times 11$	11	$\approx 39{,}000$	39:1
	9.17	27	175	≈ 400	$2^{10} \times 8$	1	$\approx 3{,}600$	9:1
Division	9.86'	53	269	≈ 550	$2^{18} \times 10$	320	$\approx 1{,}100{,}000$	2000:1
	7.64'	27	97	≈ 200	$2^{12} \times 8$	4	$\approx 14{,}000$	70:1
Square root	16.08	53	398	≈ 800	$2^{16} \times 14$	112	$\approx 400{,}000$	500:1
	13.07	26	232	≈ 470	$2^{13} \times 11$	11	$\approx 39{,}000$	83:1
1/(Square root)	13.52	53	534	≈ 1100	$2^{13} \times 12$	12	$\approx 43{,}000$	39:1
	11.16	27	304	≈ 610	$2^{11} \times 10$	2.5	$\approx 9{,}000$	15:1

and reciprocal of the square root. Average numbers are used for the division operation, since they are more critical for this operation (a prime is used to indicate this difference). The proposed method ranges from being $\frac{1}{9}$ to $\frac{1}{2000}$ the size of an equivalent-precision lookup table. This is between 11% and 0.05% of the size of the lookup table. The biggest size advantages are for the division operation and the square root operation. For division, the lookup-table size increases at approximately the rate of $N \times 2^{2N}$ for each added bit of accuracy. One bit of added accuracy requires more than 4 times the lookup-table size. For the square-root operation, the proposed method shows a major advantage in that the approximations are of very high precision (16 bits) and the traditional methods do not perform well here. The proposed method grows exponentially in complexity in the worst case (like the lookup table), but because of reductions the growth appears to be linear for several numbers of digits back-solved. Thus, the proposed method is much better than an equivalent-precision lookup table.

A summary of a comparison with an equivalent-latency polynomial method is given in Table 9.11. The proposed method has between 1.41 and 2.94 times as many correct bits as an equivalent-latency polynomial method. This is a 41% to 194% larger number of correct bits. To achieve a linear increase in the number of correct bits the absolute error must decrease exponentially. For example, the 53-row reciprocal implementation has a minimum of 12 correct bits, which equates to absolute error of 2^{-12}, and the equivalent polynomial has 4 bits, which equates to an error of 2^{-4}. The absolute error of the polynomial is actually 256 times greater than for the proposed method. Thus, the precision of the proposed method, whether it be measured in terms of correct bits or absolute error, is much better than that of an equivalent-latency polynomial method.

A third comparison is given in Figure 9.33. The proposed method for the reciprocal, square root, and reciprocal of the square root is compared with a

TABLE 9.11   Accuracy of proposed method vs first-order polynomial

| Operation | Max. Rows | Proposed Method | | | Polynomial Min. Bits | Accuracy Ratio |
		Total Elements	Min. Bits			
Reciprocal	53	484	12.00		4.08	2.94:1
	27	175	9.17		4.08	2.25:1
Division	53	269	9.86'		5.16'	1.91:1
	27	97	7.64'		5.16'	1.41:1
Square root	53	398	16.08		7.06	2.28:1
	26	232	13.07		7.06	1.85:1
1/(Square root)	53	534	13.52		5.03	2.69:1
	27	304	11.16		5.03	2.22:1

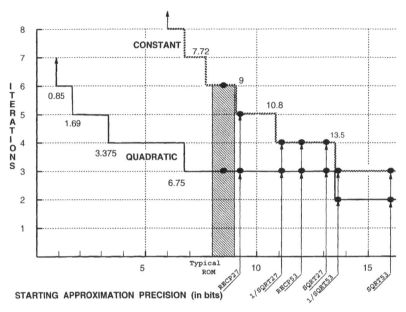

Figure 9.33   Number of iterations for several approximations.

typical implementation of a lookup table. Division is not considered, since this chart is based on worst-case errors. The precision of the starting approximation is graphed vs the number of iterations for a quadratically converging algorithm (solid line) and for a linearly converging algorithm (stippled line). The typical implementation is considered to be a 1-Kbyte ROM, which provides a minimum precision of between 8 and 9 correct bits. The ROM is represented by the shaded region. It requires three iterations for a quadratic algorithm and approximately six iterations for a linearly converging algorithm. Also shown are the proposed method for the reciprocal, square root, and reciprocal of the square root, for implementations of 27 and 53 rows. The 27-row reciprocal has the lowest precision of the proposed approximations. It has 9.17 correct bits in worst case, which requires one less iteration than the typical lookup table for the linearly converging algorithm and the same number of iterations for the quadratic algorithm. Note that it is only $\frac{1}{9}$ the size of the lookup table and has identical or fewer iterations. The 27-row reciprocal of the square root, 53-row reciprocal, and 27-row square root all require two less iterations for the linearly converging algorithm, and the same number for the quadratic algorithm, as compared to the typical lookup table. The 53-row implementations of the reciprocal of the square root and the square root require three less iterations for the linearly converging algorithm and one less iteration for the quadratic algorithm. Thus, this figure shows visually that the proposed method provides a much higher-precision approximation than typical implementations. By replacing the typical lookup table in an implementation with a PPA developed using the proposed method, there is a saving in hardware and possibly a reduction in the number of iterations.

This chapter has shown that the proposed method for the reciprocal, division, and square-root operations results in approximations which are fast, low-cost, and high-precision. All approximations except for the square root have a latency of 1 multiplication, and the square root has a latency of 1.5 multiplications. The additional cost of the PPAs is between 200 and 1100 gates, which is much smaller than the smallest ROM, which is equivalent to 3600 gates. The precision of these approximations is between 7.64 and 16.08 correct bits.

10

FUPA

Based upon work by Steve Fu

10.1 INTRODUCTION

The emergence of metrics that allow floating-point unit (FPU) designers to gauge their designs is long overdue. With the added integration offered by technology scaling, microprocessor designers have gone from software emulation of floating point (FP) operations, to dedicated FP chips (e.g., 80387), to on-chip FPUs, and finally to multiple FPUs on a chip. Meanwhile, the latencies of most FP operations have gone from hundreds of cycles to two or three cycles. The basis of these design efforts is the fundamental need for fast FP performance. Despite these efforts, allocation of die area to FPUs remains an art based on engineering intuition and past experience. We present the *floating-point unit-cost performance analysis metric* (FUPA) to allow quantitative tradeoffs between performance and cost.

FPU design requires the underlying technology to meet the computation and communication complexity of the algorithm. From a cost perspective, the designer floorplans the available die area and divides the area budget by considering the performance benefit of allocating more die area to a specific operation. FUPA uniquely integrates both cost and performance into simple and intuitive formulas for determining the optimality of FPU design; consequently, FUPA enables the first quantitative comparison of microprocessor FPUs.

Without a metric such as FUPA, the task of comparing FP architectures and implementations is a difficult one. Comparisons have been made on

TABLE 10.1 Processor statistics used in FUPA computations

Processor	Announce Date	FPU Area (mm^2)	FPU Latencies (Cycles) add	mul	div	Clock Rate (MHz)	L_{drawn} (μm)	L_{eff} (μm)
Intel P6	Nov. 1995	20.56	3	5	38	150	0.5^1	0.37
MIPS R10000	Oct. 1994	17.9	2	2	19	200	0.5	0.4
Sun UltraSparc	Oct. 1994	50	3	3	22	167	0.47	0.37
DEC21164	Sept. 1994	28.18	4	4	23	300	0.5	0.37
AMD K5	May 1995	19.28	3	7	39	75	0.5	0.4
PA8000	Nov. 1995	32.96^2	3	3	31	200	0.5	0.4

[1]Intel quotes this process at 0.6 μm, but the gate lengths are comparable to those for a 0.5-μm process (*Microprocessor Report*, Apr. 18, 1994.)
[2]This is half the actual FPU size, since there are two independent FPUs on the PA8000.

algorithmic levels by considering number of execution cycles, and on the circuit level by counting the number of transistors and by measuring the critical-path gate delay. However, the absence of any one of five important aspects—latency, die area, power, minimum feature size, and profile of applications—renders most of the comparisons unconvincing. FUPA's strength is its ability to include the above five aspects in an orderly way. Using the data from Table 10.1, we demonstrate the application of FUPA to some recently announced processors.

We summarize the computation of FUPA as follows:

1. *Profile the applications* to obtain dynamic FP operation (add/subtract, multiply, and divide) distribution in the application (Section 10.3.7).
2. *Compute effective latency* (EL) from the clock rate, the FPU latencies (Table 10.1), and the dynamic FP operation distribution obtained in step 1 (Section 10.3.7).
3. *Measure the die area* (Area) of the FPU, not including the register file.

TABLE 10.2 FUPA components and results for commerically announced processors

Processor	Effective Latency (ns)	Normalized Area (mm^2)	Normalized Effective Latency (ns)	FUPA $(cm^2 ns)$
Intel P6	37.67	50.62	75.33	38.13
MIPS R10000	14.25	44.07	28.50	12.56
Sun UltraSparc	23.65	133.43	50.32	67.14
DEC21164	16.5	69.39	33	22.89
AMD K5	88	47.47	176	83.55
PA8000	22	81.16	44	35.71

4. *Compute the normalized effective latency* (NEL) *and normalized die area* (NArea), after removing the feature size dependence (Table 10.1).

5. *Compute,* FUPA = (NEL)(NArea)/100 (Section 10.3.8).

Lower FUPA represents a more efficient FPU design, with the lowest FUPA setting a PAR for the designer to achieve. Table 10.2 lists the FUPAs of some recent microprocessors. From it we observe a wide range of values. The R10000 exhibits the lowest FUPA with both the lowest NArea and the lowest NEL, an unexpected result contrary to the general assumption that decreased latency is achieved by adding parallelism and die area.

10.2 BACKGROUND

Measuring the effectiveness of VLSI implementations and providing area–time bounds for solving computational problems with VLSI are both often investigated issues. In the mid-1960s, Winograd [197] proposed minimum delay bounds in gate delays for arithmetic operations, based on the operand size, the number of inputs per gate, and the logic values. These bounds lack consideration for fanout and wire delay.

In the early 1980s, Ullman [184] and others derived bounds based on a 3D structure of die area (A) and time (T). Three of these bounds are:

- AT bounds, where the volume of the 3D structure limits both the number of I/O signals and the maximum heat dissipation
- AT^2 bounds, where a slice of the 3D structure limits the communications between the two halves ($\sqrt{A}\,T$) of the structure
- A bounds, where the die area limits the number of storage bits

While theoretically interesting, these computational bounds were limited in that they were directed at specific algorithms. It is also difficult to translate these bounds to functions of latency and die area.

The SPEC benchmark [169] has gained popularity by measuring performance based on the execution time of benchmarks. However, SPECmark ratings include performance effects of instruction set, memory hierarchy, compiler optimizations, operating system, and I/O bandwidth. From the SPECmark alone, it is difficult to identify the cost–performance tradeoffs of FPU implementations.

We design FUPA using the AT model, since I/O and heat dissipation limit current microprocessor designs. In addition, FUPA addresses the limitations of previous work by incorporating both latency and area of FPUs.

10.3 COMPONENTS OF FUPA

This section discusses the components of FUPA and the method used to integrate them. For brevity, we merely summarize the models. For more information, a companion report [58] details the delay and area modeling, the device models, and the derivation of FUPA's scale factors.

10.3.1 Technology Scaling

FPU comparisons often ignore another important element—minimum feature size—that affects the die area, power, and latency. Advancing process technology means increased circuit, power, and wiring densities, and lower intrinsic gate switching times. Despite this, comparisons are made between implementations of different process technologies. These comparisons are obviously flawed, since there is no way to distinguish between technology improvements and algorithmic and implementation improvements. By studying how minimum-feature-size scaling affects area, delay, and power, we derive both delay and area scale factors that normalize delay and area and permit feature-size-independent comparisons of FPU implementations.

To derive the delay scale factor, FUPA incorporates BSIM3, a physical SPICE model developed by Huang et al. [68], as the device model for delay scaling with respect to technology scaling. BSIM3 has been shown to conform to experimental device data down to the 0.1-μm range. For latency, the transistor saturation current I_{dsat} determines the time to charge and discharge the capacitive loads that a transistor drives. Instead of the classical MOSFET model,

$$I_{dsat} = \mu C_{ox} W (V_g - V_t)^2 / L, \qquad (10.1)$$

BSIM3 allows for the fact that an inversion-layer charge carrier moves with the saturation velocity v_{sat} at the pinchoff point in the channel, so that

$$I_{dsat} = v_{sat} W C_{ox} (V_g - V_{dsat} - V_t), \qquad (10.2)$$

where V_{dsat} is defined as

$$\frac{1}{V_{dsat}} = \frac{1}{V_g - V_t} + \frac{\mu_n}{2 v_{sat} L_{eff}}, \qquad (10.3)$$

where μ_n is defined as

$$\mu_n = 240 \left(\frac{0.06 T_{ox}}{V_g + V_t} \right)^{1/2}. \qquad (10.4)$$

Equation (10.2) models the current drive of transistors where V_{dsat} is the potential at the pinchoff point in the channel. Equation (10.3) models the relationship between V_{dsat} and the effective channel length (L_{eff}). Equation (10.4) models the reduction in surface mobility because of increasing vertical field. We use the I_{dsat} of each implementation to derive the transistor resistance used for estimating the delay [Equation (10.5) in Section 10.3.3].

10.3.2 Latency Component of FUPA

Of the five aspects of FUPA—latency, die area, power, technology, and profile of applications—FPU designers have paid the most attention to latency. Latency is the delay incurred from the time data is applied to the input of FPU until the time the result is available at the output of the FPU. It is usually expressed as either delay (ns) or number of CPU cycles. FP operations can be pipelined into suboperations with latencies less than the cycle time of the CPU, leading to faster throughput, but pipelining also adds delay as well as die area for storage. FPU designs are often iterative, where each cycle generates additional result bits.

10.3.3 Derivation of Delay Scale Factor

Based on the requirement of feature-size independence, FUPA normalizes the differences in gate delay caused by the different minimum feature sizes of fabrication processes. A delay model was developed [58] unifying the intrinsic gate delay, interconnect delay, and fanout delay, as well as the effects of technology scaling on both devices and interconnects. This delay model consists of an inverter driving four identical loads through local interconnects as shown in Figure 10.1, and it uses a switch-level model where the output resistance (R_{tr}) is $V_{dsat} I_{dsat}$. The formula for $T_{50\%}$ [12] is

$$T_{50\%} = 0.4_{int} C_{int} + 0.7(R_{tr} C_{int} + R_{tr} C_L + R_{int} C_L), \qquad (10.5)$$

where $T_{50\%}$ is the time elapsed between the time when the input reaches 50% of logic$_{one}$ and the time when the output reaches 50% of logic$_{one}$, R_{int} is the interconnect resistance, C_{int} is the interconnect capacitance, R_{tr} is the transistor resistance, and C_L is the fanout capacitance. Since most companies do not announce metal thickness data, we use the local interconnection scaling model from the SIA roadmap [163] in conjunction with equation (10.5) to estimate the effect of interconnect scaling on C_{int} and R_{int}. In addition, we use a bimodal wire-length model to predict both local and global interconnect lengths.

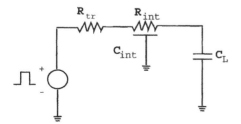

Figure 10.1 Delay model.

We summarize the steps in deriving the delay scale factor as:

- Derive R_{tr} of each process family, using BSIM3.
- Derive R_{int} and C_{int}, using both the interconnect scaling model and the wire-length model for each process family.
- Derive C_L from the self-loading of the inverter and the gate capacitance of the four identical loads for each process family.
- Calculate $T_{50\%}$ for each process family.
- The delay scale factor (Delay$_{sf}$) is the ratio of $T_{50\%}$ for each process family and the $T_{50\%}$ of a baseline 1.0-μm process.

10.3.4   Area Component of FUPA

In published implementation comparisons, die area has received substantially less attention. Its optimization is difficult because die area is a function of transistor size, placement, and routing. In fact, Sahni [147] and Szymanski [178] have shown 2D placement of transistors in the smallest rectangle and 3D routing of transistors with the smallest routing area are both NP-complete problems. Decisions at the algorithmic level directly affect the layout size and regularity of the routing. An example is the design of the multiply PP reduction, where one must choose between Wallace-tree reduction [20] and reduction arrays. At first glance, the Wallace-tree implementation with $O(\log_x n)$ stages[1] of reduction delay seems superior to an array structure with $O(n)$ stages of reduction, where n is the number of operand bits. However, an investigation of the routing requirements of the Wallace tree in terms of wire length and additional tracks suggests otherwise. Circuit design decisions also affect the layout area. Partovi [134] describes a dual-rail circuit design technique that reduces the switching delay, but also doubles the number of wiring tracks at each bit slice; the larger routing requirement may be unacceptable for the given technology's routing density and the design's bit-slice pitch limitations.

FUPA uses the measured FPU area excluding the register file. The measured area is then normalized using the area scale factor for feature-size independence.

10.3.5   Derivation of Area Scale Factor

We study how die area has scaled with respect to scaling the minimum feature size. If die area is related only to transistor packing, one would expect quadratic scaling of die area with the scaling of minimum feature size.

---

[1]Here $x = \text{CSA}_{IN}/\text{CSA}_{OUT}$ where CSA_{IN} and CSA_{OUT} are the numbers of inputs and outputs of the carry-save adders in the reduction array.

However, interconnect area[2] determines most logic elements' area, resulting in less than quadratic scaling[3].

For determining the area scaling factor, FUPA incorporates an area model which uses the larger of either the transistor layout area (Area_{tr}) or the interconnect area (Area_{int}). Area_{tr} is the area of an inverter with W/L ratio of 4. Area_{int} is defined as

$$\text{Area}_{int} = \frac{2 L_{int} P_w}{\sum_{i=1}^{n} E_{wi} N_{wi}}, \tag{10.6}$$

where 2 is number of inputs and outputs for an inverter, P_w is the average wiring pitch, L_{int} is the average interconnect length, E_{wi} is the wiring efficiency, and N_{wi} is the number of wiring levels. In our analysis, we consider only layers used for local interconnect routing.

We summarize the steps in deriving the area scale factor as follows:

- Derive the layout area (Area_{tr}) of an inverter according to MOSIS scalable design rules, using the minimum feature size for each process family and the baseline 1.0-μm process.
- Derive the interconnect area (Area_{int}) of an inverter using both the interconnect scaling model and the wire-length model for each process family and the baseline 1.0-μm process.
- Set $\text{Area}_{inverter}$ to the greater of Area_{tr} and Area_{int} for each process family.
- Derive the area scale factor (Area_{sf}) as the ratio of $\text{Area}_{inverter}$ for each process family to the $\text{Area}_{inverter}$ of a baseline 1.0-μm process.

We use results from this model and area scaling data from microprocessors to produce the area scaling factor (Area_{sf}) used by FUPA to normalize the circuit and interconnect density gains from technology scaling.

10.3.6 Relationship between Area, Operating Frequency, and Power

With added integration through technology scaling, the ability of VLSI systems to both supply power and dissipate heat has become an issue. The intended platform sets the power limits which microprocessor designers must adhere to.

We collect power consumption, die area, and operating frequencies of 62 low-power and high-speed contemporary microprocessors [111]. Figure 10.2 shows the plot of die area $\times$ operating frequency vs power consumption. We perform a linear regression on the data obtaining the following best-fit relationship between area $\times$ frequency and power:

$$\text{Area} \times \text{Frequency} = 4.23 + 16.19 \times \text{Power}. \tag{10.7}$$

---

[2]Neither interconnect pitch nor length scales linearly with respect to feature size.
[3]This is contrary to memory elements, where memory cells scale at close to the quadratic rate.

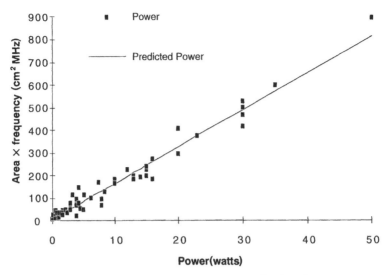

Figure 10.2 Area–speed product vs power consumption for microprocessors.

Using the above linear model, the average difference between the actual and the predicted result is 25%.

In accordance with our goal of keeping FUPA simple, we use the linear relationship between die area × operating frequency and power consumption to remove the need for a power component in FUPA. Since FUPA includes area and delay components, it also implicitly includes power in view of the above relationship.

10.3.7 Application Profiling

FUPA incorporates another key aspect—application profiles. Software applications are constantly evolving, and in turn, microprocessor designers are constantly attempting to optimize their microprocessors to execute applications faster. FUPA uses application profiles to measure the marginal utility of die area and design effort for FPUs, a method often used in instruction-set design. For example, if an instruction executes 1% of the time and takes three cycles to execute, it is usually inappropriate to dedicate 20% of the die area to reduce the latency of executing that instruction. The same idea applies to FPUs, where applications use adds and multiplies more than divides and square roots. We profile the SPECfp92 [169, 168] suite to obtain the dynamic FP operation distribution used in FUPA.

From the SPECfp92 suite, FUPA incorporates the distribution of FP instructions reported in [127] within the *effective latency* (EL). We compiled SPECfp92, an industry standard for comparing workstation systems, on a DECstation 5000 using the MIPS C and Fortran compilers. We then instrumented the binaries using *pixie*, which partitions a program into its basic blocks, and adds extra code to track the execution of each basic block.

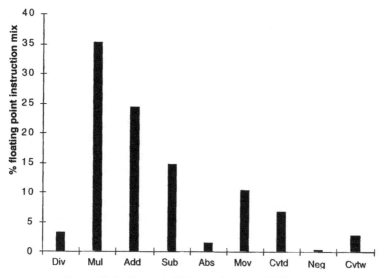

Figure 10.3   Dynamic FP instruction mix of SPECfp92.

Finally, we used *pixstats* to gather the dynamic distribution of FP instructions shown in Figure 10.3.

FUPA uses the cycle time of the processor, the number of cycles to execute each operation, and the dynamic distribution from the profiling to formulate the effective latency (EL) as follows:

$$EL = \sum_{i=1}^{n} \text{CycleTime } OP_{i\text{-latency}} \, OP_{i\text{-distribution}} \cdot \quad (10.8)$$

where $OP_{i\text{-latency}}$ is the number of cycles taken to perform FP add/subtract, multiply, and divide, and $OP_{i\text{-distribution}}$ is the dynamic distribution of FP add/subtract, multiply, and divide among all FP instructions. $OP_{i\text{-distribution}}$ (Figure 10.3) is used as a weighting factor to emphasize operations that occur more frequently.

10.3.8 Computation of FUPA

Now that we have discussed the components of FUPA, we summarize its computation:

$$NArea = Area/Area_{sf}, \quad (10.9)$$

$$EL = \sum_{i=1}^{n} \text{CycleTime } OP_{i\text{-latency}} \, OP_{i\text{-frequency}}, \quad (10.10)$$

$$NEL = \frac{EL}{Delay_{sf}}, \quad (10.11)$$

$$FUPA = \frac{(NEL)(NArea)}{100}. \quad (10.12)$$

Here NArea is the normalized die area utilized by the FPU, scaled according to the minimum drawn channel length (L_{drawn}) of the technology. EL is the latency in nanoseconds of different FPU operations weighted by the frequency of their occurrence. NEL is EL normalized with respect to the delay scale factor of the technology.

The interpretation of FUPA is simple—the smaller the rating, the more efficient the implementation. FUPA is the unweighted product of NEL and NArea based on the concept of AT bounds introduced in Section 10.2. Since latency is related to distance (interconnect) and area (loading), increasing area beyond an optimal point increases the overall latency of an operation; this is seen in the next section, where data shows that the lowest-latency implementation is not the largest implementation.

With the above components in place, we apply FUPA to recent microprocessor designs and present a survey and comparison of microprocessor FPUs. We expect the comparison results can (1) provide insights into the evolution of FPU within both the industry as a whole and within each processor family, (2) allow FPU designers to gauge their FPUs, and (3) bridge the gap between research and industrial FPU designs by focusing on aspects of cost, technology, and application profiles.

10.4 MICROPROCESSOR FPU COMPARISONS

This section provides a comparison of microprocessor FPUs using FUPA. In applying FUPA, we collect both latency and area data from the *Microprocessor Report* [111]. We address the accuracy of the data and the limitations of FUPA in Section 10.5.

10.4.1 Effective and Normalized Effective Latency of Microprocessor FPUs

This section presents the effective latency (EL) and normalized effective latency (NEL) of industrial microprocessors' FPUs. To support feature-size-independent comparisons, we normalize EL with the latency scaling factor ($Delay_{sf}$) to produce NEL.

Figure 10.4 shows both the NEL and the EL of microprocessors' FPUs. Note the general trend of reducing EL within each processor family. Also note that EL is highly dependent upon the intended application of the processor; for example, low-end and embedded processors (e.g., R4200 and MicroSparc) exhibit worse EL. Processors such as SuperSPARC that have lower frequencies exhibit worse EL because the cycle time restricts the per-cycle latency of FPUs more than in other processors. Because of its longer cycle time, SuperSPARC with 3-cycle-latency FP adds and FP multiplies has a worse EL than DEC21164 with 4-cycle FP adds and FP multiplies.

Besides across-the-industry comparisons, EL also measures improvements in FPU performance within processor families. An example of FPU perfor-

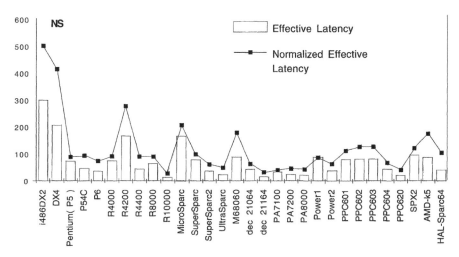

Figure 10.4   FPU effective latencies (EL) vs normalized effective latencies (NEL).

mance improvement within a processor family is the x86 family where, the P5 processor's EL shows a 4 times improvement over the i486DX2 processor.

Whereas EL includes both process and implementation advances, NEL allows-feature-size independent comparisons of FPU latencies. We normalize the EL of processors with more advanced processes such as the the 0.5-μm-L_{drawn} DX4 and DEC 21164 to remove the technology advantage. NEL is effective in showing the true improvement or regression in FPU latencies within the same processor family. Within the x86 family, NEL improves across processor generations from 486 to P5; however, within each generation, process upgrades have not resulted in similar improvements. The processor pair [P5, P54C] shows this lack of NEL improvement and confirms that a good match must exist between the available integration and the implementation/algorithmic complexity. For the MIPS processor family, NEL shows improvement between R4000 and R4400 and slight degradation between R4400 and R8000. We attribute the degradation to the relatively long-cycle time (13.5 ns) of the R8000. Following R8000, R10000 shows 3–4 times improvement in both EL and NEL.

NEL also reflects the performance effects of implementation decisions We attribute the relatively high NEL of R4200 to its merged integer–fp datapath as well as its intended application in low-power and embedded environments. For the SPARC family, SuperSPARC2 shows an improvement over Super-SPARC because of the removal of several critical paths in SuperSPARC2. In contrast, within the HP-PA family, PA7200's NEL deteriorates from PA7100 because of the modest improvement in cycle time despite the more advanced process. The deteriorating NEL is consistent with the fact that in the P5 processor the FPU remains unchanged from P5 to P54C. Unlike the Pentium

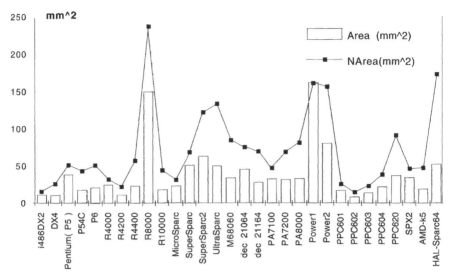

Figure 10.5 Die area (Area) vs normalized die area (NArea) of microprocessor FPUs.

and the HP-PA family, both the IBM Power family and the PPC family show improvement in NEL over previous processor generations.

Overall, depending on technology scaling alone to reduce latency results in degraded or equal NEL between generations. In general, redesigning FPUs between generations of processors usually results in NEL improvements, with the notable exception of R8000, where the degradation is because of its long cycle time.

10.4.2 Die-Area and Normalized-Die-Area Usage of Microprocessor FPUs

As discussed in Section 10.2, decisions at the algorithmic, implementation, and circuit level all affect the final die-area usage. What is implicit in area allocation, however, is the cost-vs-performance optimization that we specifically design FUPA to model. Since die area is related to die yield and area × speed is related to power consumption (Figure 10.2), the floorplanning of a microprocessor is critical to the manufacturing cost of the die, its performance, and its power consumption.

Figure 10.5 shows both the NArea and Area of industrial microprocessor FPUs. Figure 10.6 shows the relationship between NArea and NEL.[4] From these two graphs, we draw four general observations:

1. There is an upward trend in NArea within a processor family where the initial area allocation was low (e.g., PPC family, x86 family, PA7x00 family, SPARC).

---

[4] The areas for the Power2 and R8000 FPU are half their actual areas, since there are two independent FPU units in each.

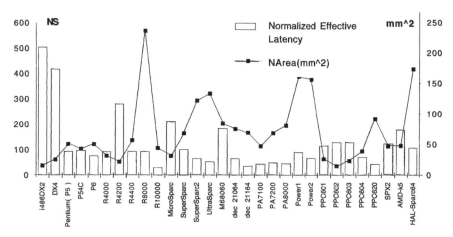

Figure 10.6   FPU normalized die area (NArea) and normalized effective latency (NEL).

2. There is a downward trend in NArea within a processor family where the initial area allocation was high (e.g., Power family).

3. The largest-NArea FPU does not possess the best NEL.

4. The largest NEL FPU possesses a small NArea (i486DX2).

The above observations suggest an optimal area exists for each technology–architecture pair, above or below which the latency increases.

We make more specific observations by investigating the causes of the NArea variations within each processor family. Single-chip FPU implementations such as R8000, Power1, and Power2 have the highest NArea since their NArea includes peripheral circuitry such as the I/O pads. The P54C FPU, a process shrink of the P5, benefits from the shrink, since its NArea decreased. On the other hand, SuperSPARC2, a shrink from SuperSPARC, demonstrates an NArea almost double that of the SuperSPARC because of the addition of a separate unit for divides and square roots to remove a critical timing path in the SuperSPARC. Compared to the DEC21064, the DEC21164 managed to reduce both its NArea and NEL with a split multiply–add data path. For the PA-RISC family, the increases in NArea fail to produce similar decreases in NEL. We attribute this trend to similar FPU designs between PA7100, PA7200, and PA8000. In comparison, the PPC620 doubles the NArea of the PPC604 in return for reduced latencies and a hardware square-root functional unit that increases the performance of applications like SPICE.

10.4.3   FUPA of Microprocessor FPUs

FUPA incorporates area in the NArea component, incorporates latency and the application profile in the NEL formulation, incorporates technology in

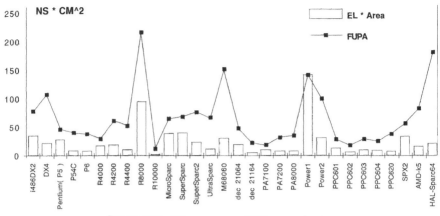

Figure 10.7 Microprocessor FPU comparisons.

the latency and area scale factors, and incorporates power implicitly in the product of NArea and NEL, a result of the relationship between area, speed, and power (Figure 10.2).

Figure 10.7 shows both the product of EL and Area and the FUPA of microprocessor FPUs. In most cases, the data sets track each other. However, the advantage of FUPA lies in allowing designers to evaluate whether the FPU design has made efficient use of current technology in terms of area, delay, and density. For example, comparing the i486DX2 with the DX4 processor shows an improvement in EL × Area; however, FUPA shows otherwise, with DX4's FUPA 30% higher than DX2's. The DX4 FUPA suggests the DX4 FPU should make more efficient use of the available integration. Similar circumstances apply to the processor sets [R4000, R4400], [SuperSPARC, SuperSPARC2], [PA7100, PA7200, PA8000], and [PPC604, PPC620]. Examples where designs have improved within a processor family are [P5, P54C, P6], [DEC21064, DEC21164], and [R8000, R10000].

FUPA can do more than simply allow comparisons within processor families. It permits designers to specify future FPU designs by comparing their FUPA with others in the industry. Figure 10.7 shows R10000 as possessing the best FUPA, with DEC21164 a close second. On the other end of the spectrum, R8000 receives the worst FUPA. We attribute R8000's high FUPA to:

- *Low Use of Integration:* One million transistors occupy 298 mm^2.
- *Off-Chip FPUs:* The Area data includes peripheral circuitry.
- *Long Cycle Time:* The superscalar architecture results in a slower cycle time.

10.5 LIMITATIONS OF FUPA

We have defined FUPA in terms of area, latency, and technology—public information announced during microprocessor introductions—to encourage widespread use of FUPA. To that end, since FUPA uses area measured from die photos, we introduce errors in measurement; however, the error introduced should not prevent FUPA from serving its purpose of providing high-level comparisons and cost–performance tradeoffs of FPU design.

As with any metric, the desire for simplicity and ease of use imposes limitations on FUPA. Specifically, FUPA does not take account of:

- Different circuit design styles
- Throughput of FPUs

Circuit design styles affect latency, area, and power, as well as noise margins and reliability of operation. Processor designs have typically used static CMOS for its ease of design, although dual-rail and dynamic design styles are attractive for switching speed. To first order, latency is a tradeoff between area and power across various circuit design styles. Of course, FUPA is more accurate when used for comparisons within a particular design style.

Throughput of FPUs is the number of FP operations per cycle performed, or the number of FPU operations initiated every cycle. Faster throughput enhances performance during consecutive FP operations and multiple issue of FP operations. However, most recent microprocessor FPUs are fully pipelined and have a throughput of one. Other design choices that affect throughput are: (1) fused operations such as multiply-and-add, (2) shared datapaths for different FP ops, and (3) limited number of FP register ports. We deem these design choices to be second-order effects, and as a result, we choose not to include them in FUPA.

10.6 CONCLUSION

In this chapter, we have introduce the concept of FUPA and applied it to contemporary microprocessor FPUs. FUPA accomplishes our stated goal of incorporating latency, die area, power, technology, and application behavior, the five key elements of VLSI system design.

Besides FUPA's applicability to FPU designs, the ideas and techniques behind FUPA are of general relevance to computer architecture. An equitable comparison of VLSI implementations requires cost analysis in terms of area, latency, and power consumption. In addition to cost analysis, FUPA promotes the notion that only a good match between technology and design complexity results in an efficient design.

FUPA facilitates technology-independent comparisons—a powerful concept that separates advancements in technology from improvements in algorithms and implementation efficiency. The technology projections permits more realistic comparison between implementations using different technologies. We have shown that designs with better FUPAs exhibit more optimized use of current technology in terms of circuit and interconnect densities.

11

HIGH-SPEED CLOCKING USING WAVE PIPELINING

Based upon work by Kevin Nowka

High-performance pipeline clocking techniques are central to the realization of high-throughput arithmetic processors. In addition to the use of aggressive device and circuit technologies, wave pipelining techniques have been explored as a means of approaching the theoretical switching limit of arithmetic processor implementations.

Wave pipelining is a synchronous-circuit pipelining technique which can achieve greater throughput than that possible with conventional techniques by relying on the predictable bounded delay through combinational logic for data storage. Wave pipelining has been demonstrated to achieve clock rates 2 to 6 times those of nonpipelined arithmetic circuits.

SNAP research on wave pipelining has developed theory on the correct operation of wave-pipelined circuits, has evaluated device technologies for their applicability to wave pipelining and quantified the wave-pipeline performance limits for key technologies, has developed performance optimization techniques for wave-pipelines, and has validated the theory, techniques, and tools through the development of demonstration VLSI chips.

11.1 BACKGROUND

In an effort to improve the throughput of digital systems, designers have frequently used pipelining. In a pipelined system, a logic network is partitioned into pipeline stages, each of which operates upon data computed in the previous cycle by the previous pipeline stage. When a logic network is pipelined, synchronizing elements, either latches or registers, are inserted to partition the network into stages. Pipelining of a circuit into N stages can result in a speedup in throughput up to a factor of N. The inserted synchronizing elements increase the area and power consumption of the logic and add to the latency and cycle time overhead.

Wave pipelining is an alternative synchronous circuit clocking technique which allows overlapped execution of multiple operations without using synchronizing elements within the logic. Rather, knowledge of the signal propagation delay characteristics of the logic network is used at design time to manage the signal delays to ensure that operations do not interfere with their predecessor or successor computations.

11.1.1 Pipelining and Wave Pipelining

While improving the throughput of a logic circuit, traditional pipelining of VLSI systems results in additional latency, cycle time, area, and power consumption. Cycle-time overhead results from the time delay required for signals to propagate out of the the synchronizing elements, from the time delay required for signals to set up to the synchronizing elements prior to their being stored in the synchronizing elements, and from the unintentional clock skew in the arrival of the synchronizer clock signal. The latency through the traditional pipeline is defined as the total elapsed time from the introduction of data at the input to the first stage of the pipeline to the arrival of the results of computations performed on that data at the output of the final stage of the pipeline. Latency overhead from pipelining results from the synchronizer overhead of each stage of the pipeline. In addition, it results from pipeline partitioning overhead. In traditional pipelines with a common reference clock for all synchronizers, partitioning overhead occurs if the combinational logic cannot be divided into stages of equal maximum propagation delay. Area and power overhead results from the additional transistors and wires used to implement the synchronizing latches or registers, and from the increased clock buffer area and power necessary to drive the clock inputs to the synchronizers.

Wave pipelining relies on the finite propagation delay of signals through a combinational digital circuit to store data. Rather than allowing data to propagate from a synchronizing element, through the combinational network, to another synchronizing element prior to initiating the subsequent data transfer, wave-pipelined designs apply subsequent data to the network as soon as it can be guaranteed that it will not interfere with the current data wave. In this manner, multiple waves of data are simultaneously propagating through distinct regions of the logic network. Because waves of data are applied to the logic as fast as they can be guaranteed not to interfere, the throughput of wave-pipelined synchronous systems can be greater than can be achieved with conventional pipelining techniques. Wave pipelining can approach the physical switching limit of the devices [35].

Wave pipelining can improve the throughput of a logic circuit while avoiding some of the overheads of traditional pipelining. Wave pipelines avoid the cycle-time overhead of traditional pipelines because there are no internal synchronizers. Instead, the cycle time is determined by the variation in the propagation delay of the signals through the logic and the input and output register delays. Latency through the wave pipeline avoids the traditional pipeline overhead because the signals do not propagate through internal synchronizers. Partitioning overhead is avoided, since the pipeline is not partitioned into stages separated by synchronizers. The area and power overheads of a traditional pipeline are avoided in the wave pipe, since there are no internal synchronizers. Manipulation of the circuitry to maximize performance of wave pipelines can, however, introduce additional area and power overhead.

11.1.2 Wave-Pipeline Research

Significant research in wave pipelining has been conducted over the past thirty years. Latchless pipelining techniques were first used in the development of the IBM System 360/91 FPU in 1967 [5]. With wave pipelining, this design was able to achieve a cycle time which was one-half the latency through the combinational logic. Cotten [35] in 1969 formalized the theory of wave pipelining or maximum-rate pipelining. Ekroot [40] presented constraints for correct wave-pipeline operation and developed a method of optimizing the performance of wave pipelines by the insertion of delays in the logic network.

The wave-pipelining research conducted as part of the SNAP project encompasses theory, tools, and VLSI designs. Wong [198] details the timing constraints for the operation of wave-pipelined circuits and contrasts them to traditional clocking methods. Klass and Flynn [81] compare the performance of wave pipelining and traditional pipelining with the *latency clock period* as a metric. Nowka and Flynn [120] establish the limits of CMOS wave-pipeline performance under varying circuit, environmental, and process conditions and compare the performance of wave pipelining with traditional pipelining.

Wave-pipelining algorithms and tools developed for the SNAP effort optimize the performance of wave-pipelined circuits: Wong [198] presents methods of balancing delays in CML wave-pipelined circuits to optimize the cycle time. Nowka [119] extends these methods to the optimization of wave-pipelined CMOS circuits.

Wave pipelining has been successfully applied in several VLSI designs as part of the SNAP effort. Wong et al. [199] developed a wave-pipelined bipolar population counter with a latency of 10 ns and a cycle time of 4 ns, thus supporting 2.5 concurrent waves. Klass [80] developed a CMOS multiplier which operated at 350 MHz and supported four waves. We have demonstrated the use of wave pipelining in a system design through the development of a wave-pipelined vector processor [119]. This processor integrates wave-pipelined memory and multiple wave-pipelined functional units and operates above 300 MHz.

Other researchers have produced significant demonstration VLSI devices. Chappell et al. [33] applied wave-pipelining techniques in the design of an SRAM which consisted of self-resetting logic blocks which were operated in a wave pipelined fashion. This SRAM had a latency of 3.9 ns and a cycle time of 2 ns, thus supporting 1.9 concurrent waves. Fan et al. [48] developed a CMOS adder using wave pipelining. Simulated operation of this adder achieved 250 MHz and supported more than five waves. Lien and Burleson [93] applied wave pipelining to CMOS domino logic circuits and designed a 100-MHz, two-wave CMOS wave domino multiplier. Additional wave-pipelined VLSI designs include CMOS multipliers [117, 59, 204], CMOS static RAMs [115, 179], and several simple CMOS circuits.

In general, VLSI implementations of wave pipelining have demonstrated two waves of data for a memory device and two to six waves of data for arithmetic circuits.

11.2 THEORY

This section presents the constraints on the correct operation of wave pipelines. Definitions are presented in Table 11.1.

11.2.1 Minimum Clock Period for Traditional Pipelines

The clock period of traditional pipelined synchronous circuits must meet race-through and long-path timing constraints.

The long-path constraint requires that the results from the current cycle's inputs be valid at the next synchronizing element prior to being latched. Thus the propagation from the synchronizing element, through the data network, to the next synchronizing element must be less than the time from the initiating edge of the current clock cycle to the latching edge of the next clock cycle. Figure 11.1 defines the initiating and latching edges for both flow latches and edge-triggered flip-flops.

The race-through constraint requires that in the same clock cycle data cannot propagate out of a synchronizing element, through the combinational network, and into the next synchronizing element prior to the occurrence of the storage transition. Thus the minimum propagation time though the synchronizing element, through the network, to the next synchronizing element must be less that the time from the output-initiating edge to the latching edge of the same cycle. Thus the data resulting from the current input data cannot interfere with the previous results in the next synchronizing element.

For a traditional pipelined system which uses edge-triggered synchronizers and single-phase clocking, the worst-case maximum propagation delay deter-

TABLE 11.1   Definitions of symbols used in wave-pipelined clock theory

cs	The constructive clock skew at the input of a pipeline stage
N	The number of concurrent waves in the wave pipeline
N_{max}	The maximum number of waves in the wave pipeline, also, the maximum speedup of a wave pipeline over the same circuit operated as a traditional pipeline stage
P_{max}	The worst-case maximum propagation delay through the combinational network
P_{max}	The best-case minimum propagation delay through the combinational network
RF_{max}	The maximum rise/fall time of the inputs to the output synchronizer
RF_{min}	The minimum rise/fall time of the inputs to the output synchronizer
T_{clk}	The clock period
T_{ms}	The minimum amount of time a node voltage must be stable to ensure the subsequent level of logic operates correctly
T_{pd}	The propagation delay of combinational logic
T_h	The minimum hold time of the output synchronizer
T_{synch}	The maximum time from the data-initiating edge of the clock to valid output of the input synchronizer
T_s	The maximum setup time of the output synchronizer
T_{trans}	The time over which the latch is open and transparent
α	The ratio of the largest propagation delay through a logic network to the smallest propagation delay through the network
β	The propagation-delay degradation factor due to process and environmental variations
ΔC	The unintentional clock skew between input and output clocks

mines the clock rate:

$$P_{max} + T_{synch} + RF_{max}/2 + T_s + \Delta C \le T_{clk} + cs. \qquad (11.1)$$

The race-through constraint for this clocking is

$$P_{min} + T_{synch} - RF_{min}/2 - T_h - \Delta C - cs \ge 0. \qquad (11.2)$$

For flow latches and single-phase clocking, the following inequalities must hold:

$$P_{max} + T_{synch} + RF_{max}/2 + T_s + \Delta C - cs \le T_{clk}. \qquad (11.3)$$

$$P_{min} + T_{synch} - RF_{min}/2 - T_h - \Delta C - T_{trans} - cs \ge 0 \qquad (11.4)$$

Constraints for other clocking schemes can be found in [198].

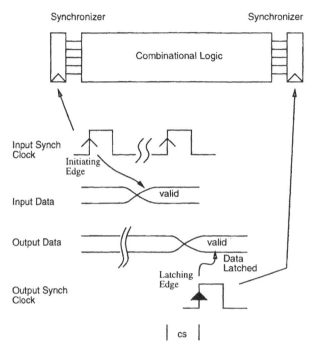

Figure 11.1 Synchronizer edge definitions.

11.2.2 Minimum Clock Period for Wave Pipelines

Wave pipelining relies on the finite signal propagation delay through a combinational digital circuit to store data. Rather than allowing data to propagate from a register through the combinational network to another register prior to initiating the subsequent data transfer, wave-pipelined designs apply subsequent data to the network as soon as it can be guaranteed that it will not interfere with the current data wave. Figure 11.2 shows that wave 2 is launched from the input register as soon as it is guaranteed that at no point in the logic network will it interfere with wave 1.

The primary differences between the constraints for a wave pipeline and a traditional pipeline result from the fact that the data-initiating edge and data-storage edge may be separated by several clock cycles in a wave pipeline. The long-path constraint for wave pipelines requires that the propagation out of the synchronizer, through the combinational logic, and into the output synchronizer be less than the time from the initiating edge to the latching edge which occurs N cycles later. This constraint is [198, 92, 63]

$$N \times T_{\text{clk}} + \text{cs} \geq P_{\text{max}} + \Delta C + T_{\text{s}} + \frac{\text{RF}_{\text{max}}}{2} + T_{\text{synch}}. \qquad (11.5)$$

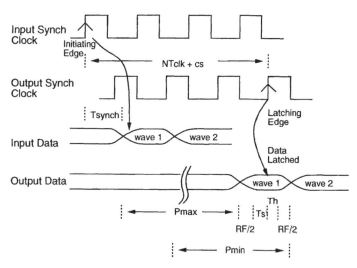

Figure 11.2 Wave-pipeline timing definitions.

In Figure 11.2 this constraint is shown for the wave 1 data. N is the number of clock periods between the application of the input data and the subsequent latching of the results at the output. It is also the number of concurrent waves in the wave pipeline. cs is the constructive skew between the clock at the input synchronizer and the one at the output synchronizer. P_{max} is the worst-case maximum propagation delay through the combinational network. It is measured from the time at which the slowest input of the logic reaches the midpoint of its switching voltage to the time at which the slowest output reaches the midpoint of its switching voltage. ΔC is the unintentional clock skew between input and output clocks. T_s is the maximum setup time of the output synchronizer. RF_{max} is the maximum rise/fall time of the inputs to the output synchronizer. T_{synch} is the maximum time from the data-initiating edge of the clock to valid output of the input synchronizer. The inequality (11.5) ensures that the result of the slowest computation has sufficient time to propagate to the output, all outputs rise or fall to their terminal values, and all outputs meet the minimum setup time of the synchronizer prior to being latched.

In addition, the subsequent wave must not reach the synchronizer prior to the synchronizing-clock edge. Thus the race-through constraint for wave pipelines using edge-triggered registers as synchronizing elements is

$$(N - 1)T_{clk} + cs \leq P_{min} - \Delta C - T_h - \frac{RF_{min}}{2} + T_{synch}. \quad (11.6)$$

In Figure 11.2 this constraint is shown for the wave 2 data. This inequality ensures that the result of the fastest computation is not able to propagate through the logic fast enough to change the voltage of any output in the cycle before the results will be latched. It is for the edge-triggered registers as synchronizing elements. For transparent latches as synchronizing elements, one has instead

$$(N - 1)T_{clk} + T_{trans} + cs \leq P_{min} - \Delta C - \frac{RF_{min}}{2} + T_{synch} - T_h, \quad (11.7)$$

where T_{trans} is the time over which the latch is open and transparent.

In addition to meeting the race-through and long-path constraints, wave-pipelined circuits require that waves of data do not interfere with each other at the output synchronizing element. This constraint results in the following inequality:

$$T_{clk} \geq P_{max} - P_{min} + 2\Delta C + T_s + T_h + \frac{RF_{min} + RF_{max}}{2}. \quad (11.8)$$

In addition to the output constraint, wave-pipelined circuits cannot allow wave interference at any point in the network. This can be represented by the following:

$$T_{clk} \geq P_{max} - P_{min} + \Delta C + T_{ms} + \frac{RF_{min} + RF_{max}}{2} \quad (11.9)$$

where T_{ms} is the minimum amount of time a node voltage must be stable to ensure that the subsequent level of logic operates correctly.

Details of the timing constraints for pipelined and wave-pipelined circuits are found in [198].

A significant difficulty with wave-pipelined designs results from the non-continuous nature of operating cycle times. In wave-pipelined circuits, a wave must be set up at the output register and the subsequent wave must not be less than a hold time away from the register when the register is clocked. These constraints lead to a two-sided clock constraint:

$$\frac{P_{min}}{N - 1} \geq T_{clk} \geq \frac{P_{max}}{N}. \quad (11.10)$$

Thus, a VLSI device designed to operate at 100 MHz may not function properly when operated at 75 MHz. The two-sided clock constraint makes valid clock determination and control difficult when propagation delays vary widely or are difficult to predict.

11.3 DEVICE TECHNOLOGIES: APPLICABILITY AND PERFORMANCE

The characteristics of technologies ideally suited to wave-pipeline design are [198]:

- Numerous points of finely controllable, predictable delay adjustment
- Comparable delay for output-rising and output-falling transitions
- Low variation in delay between input patterns
- Low dependence of delay on previous input patterns
- Low delay variation due to environmental variations
- High noise immunity, low power, high density, and high speed

Wong [198] has shown that the bipolar emitter-coupled logic (ECL), current-mode logic (CML), and superbuffered ECL logic families generally satisfy these criteria: Through the adjustment of the tail current of ECL and CML logic gates, the speed of each gate can be predictably and finely controlled. Rising and falling delays of the logic gates in CML and ECL can be matched to within 5–10%. The emitter followers in ECL, however, can introduce significant rising- and falling-delay imbalance. For the bipolar implementations in SNAP, CML, which avoids stacked structures, was chosen for its high density and balanced delays.

The delay of CMOS logic is controllable, although not as controllable as that of CML. It can have comparable rise and fall times and has excellent immunity, power, density, and speed characteristics. The greatest challenges to the use of CMOS for wave-pipelined circuits are its high degree of data-dependent gate delay and its delay variation due to environmental delay. Klass [80] has shown that despite the high degree of data-dependent delay variation of an individual static-CMOS gate (up to 50%), CMOS implementations of arithmetic logic using two-input static CMOS gates can achieve variations of 15–20%, which is sufficiently small for practical wave pipelining. Methods of decreasing delay variation in CMOS examined in this research include introducing additional transistors in gates with parallel conduction paths [80] and minimizing the capacitive load on gates with parallel conduction paths [119]. Other researchers have proposed using dynamic CMOS logic circuits [93], using biased pseudo-NMOS logic [48], and restructuring logic functions [78] to minimize variation.

Nowka and Flynn [120] have shown that uncompensated delay variations in static CMOS due to environmental conditions and fabrication variations limit the performance of wave-pipelined implementations to a fraction of their potential. The performance limitations of CMOS will be detailed in the following section.

Kissigami et al. [79] have shown that CMOS pass-transistor logic families have balancing characteristics which are practical for wave-pipelining use. Pass mux gates are fast, have tunable delay, and are comparable to static CMOS in data-dependent variation.

11.4 PERFORMANCE LIMITS OF WAVE PIPELINING

This section derives the performance limits for the use of wave pipelining. A more thorough analysis is found in [120] and [119].

To ascertain the performance limits of wave pipelining, the propagation delays and the causes of variations in the propagation delays must be quantified.

Delay in a combinational logic network is modeled as the sum of the individual gate delays. With this model of the gate delay, the maximum delay through a combinational logic network is

$$P_{max} = \sum_{\text{long path}} T_{pd}, \qquad (11.11)$$

and the minimum path delay through the combinational logic network is

$$P_{min} = \sum_{\text{short path}} T_{pd}. \qquad (11.12)$$

As shown in equation (11.8), the clock period of a wave pipeline is constrained by relative differences in propagation delay rather than by the maximum propagation delay. The maximum number of waves, N_{max}, is the maximum speedup which a wave pipeline can achieve compared with an unpipelined circuit; we have

$$N_{max} \approx \frac{P_{max}/P_{min}}{P_{max}/P_{min} - 1}. \qquad (11.13)$$

Thus, the ratio of maximum to minimum propagation delays is needed to ascertain the performance potential of wave-pipelining. The clock rate of wave-pipelined circuits is constrained by the worst-case variation of propagation delay through the network. The sources of variation in the network are:

1. Variations due to differences in propagation of signals along different paths
2. Variations due to differences in the state of network node voltages and gate side inputs (data dependences)
3. Variations due to changes in operating temperature

4. Variations due to supply-voltage drift and noise

5. Variations due to fabrication process variations

6. Variations due to signal noise

11.4.1 Path-Length Imbalance

Each path through a circuit may have a different propagation delay. For highly regular logic structures like memories, the variation in delay between these paths may be relatively small. In more random logic structures the propagation delay along the longest path through the logic network may be many times the delay along the shortest path. Without optimization, wave pipelines of random logic are thus only capable of achieving fractional improvements in the throughput of the pipeline.

Following the theory developed by Ekroot [40], techniques have been developed to balance the path delays of bipolar circuits [198] and CMOS circuits [82, 122] through insertion of delay elements and through the manipulation of the delay characteristics of individual gates. This balancing procedure has been demonstrated to limit delay variation to less than 20% of the maximum propagation delay for static CMOS circuits.

11.4.2 Data Dependences

Data-dependent delay variation results from two effects. First, signal propagation does not generally occur from a single input to a given output along one path. Instead, transitions occur along multiple, interacting paths from any number of inputs to the given output. Thus the delay along a given input-to-output path depends upon the occurrence of transitions on side inputs and their time relation to the transitions occurring along the given path. Secondly, the rate of signal propagation of individual gates may depend upon the state of internal node voltages. For instance, the propagation delay through a two-input static CMOS NAND gate when both inputs are rising depends upon the voltage at the common node in the NMOS transistor stack. This form of data dependence results from previous input transitions.

Klass and Mulder [82] have found that by implementing functions in input-pattern-insensitive logic such as NAND2/INV static CMOS, delay variation can be limited to less than 10% for a 4-bit carry lookahead adder. The balancing procedure for static CMOS circuits presented in Section 11.5.2 has been found to limit the delay variation due to path imbalance and data dependences to less than 20%.

Figure 11.3 presents the limit on the performance of a wave pipeline due to path-length imbalance and data dependences. The ratio of delay along the longest path to delay along the shortest path due simply to the circuit topology determines a limit on the number of waves which can be supported, and thus the speedup possible with wave pipelining.

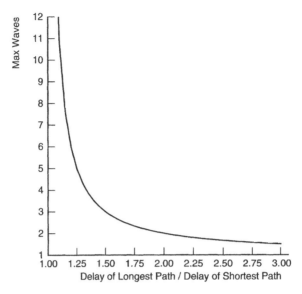

Figure 11.3 Performance limit due to path-length imbalance.

Because the variation in propagation delay due to differences in path length and data dependences are determined primarily by the implementation of the logic function, the performance potential of wave pipelining is presented as a function of the degree of imbalance in the network implementation.

11.4.3 Fabrication Process

In addition to the effects of path-length variation and data dependences, which depend primarily upon the implementation of the logic function, variation in the manufacture of the VLSI integrated circuit and in its operating environment influence the delay of CMOS wave-pipelined circuits. Fabrication process variation strongly influences the propagation delay of a circuit.

Process parameters are characterized as *nominal* and *corner*. The nominal process is the expected process. Corner processes are the limits of acceptable process parameters.

Table 11.2 shows the simulated propagation delay of a chain of 50 inverters for the fabrication corners of a 2-μm MOSIS process [113]. Over these limits, fabrication process variation affects propagation delay by +16% to −19%. Thus, the ratio of maximum delay to minimum delay due to process is 1.43.

Figure 11.4 is a diagram of the propagation delay of a chain of 50 inverters, simulated using SPICE model parameters derived from measure-

TABLE 11.2   Simulated process corner propagation delays

Process	Propagation Delay (ns)
Fast	14.6
Slow	21.0
Typical	18.1

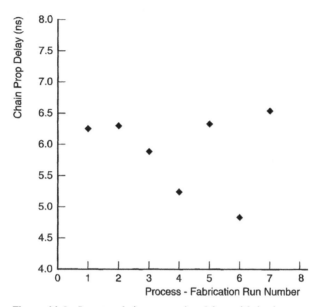

Figure 11.4   Inverter-chain propagation delay vs fabrication run.

ments of seven MOSIS 0.8-μm fabrication runs. For these runs, the maximum propagation delay is longer than the minimum by a factor of 1.35. Compared to the arithmetic average, the variation is $+11\%$ to -18%.

11.4.4   Environmental Variation

In addition to the implementation-dependent variation and the manufacturing process variations, the environmental operating conditions have a significant effect on the delay of CMOS logic circuits.

Spatial and temporal temperature variation can have drastic effects on signal propagation delay. In CMOS, the variation in propagation delay due to temperature is primarily the result of the variation of the channel current of the conducting MOS device. Nowka [120] shows analytically and through simulations that propagation along a given path for a CMOS network can be as much as 50% slower at 125°C than at room temperature.

Supply voltage variation affects propagation delay by altering the channel current and signal voltage swing. Nowka and Flynn [120] demonstrate that propagation along a given path for a CMOS network can vary by 5–10% of the nominal over an operating supply voltage range of 4.5 to 5.5 V. The ratio of maximum delay to minimum delay due to supply changes is thus 1.2.

Coupled noise in CMOS can cause additional delay variation.

11.4.5   CMOS Process and Environmental Performance Limits

The longest path in a circuit is some factor greater than the shortest path for a given temperature, voltage, and process. This factor, represented by α, is due to path-length differences and data-dependent delay variations in the network. Because the relative variation in propagation delay due to temperature and voltage variation is to first order independent of absolute propagation delay, α is a good approximation of the relative path-length difference in the network for any temperature and voltage.

The propagation delay of any path at worst case operating temperature, supply voltage, and process will be some factor larger than the best case propagation delay This factor is represented by β.

Equation (11.13) can be restated as

$$N_{max} \leq \frac{\alpha\beta}{\alpha\beta - 1}. \qquad (11.14)$$

Figure 11.5 gives the maximum number of waves through a wave-pipelined

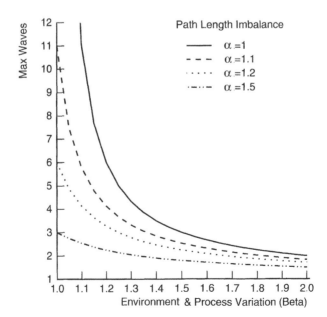

Figure 11.5   Maximum waves vs β.

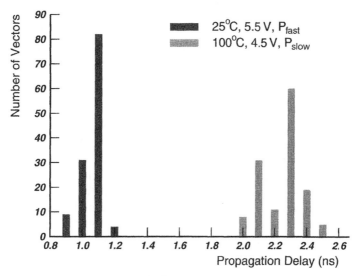

Figure 11.6 $(4, 2)$ counter delay histogram.

network vs the process and environmental delay variation factor, β, for several practical values of the path-length variation factor, α.

For temperatures of 25–125°C and voltages of 4.5–5.5 V for CMOS circuits, β will be 1.4 to 1.7. Therefore, the number of waves in a static CMOS wave-pipelined logic network, independent of its absolute propagation delay, is three or less. Process variation further reduces the number of waves which can be supported. Aggregating the above environmental variation with a process variation of $\beta_{proc} = 1.35$, the number of waves is limited to 1.6.

Figure 11.6 is a histogram of the propagation delays of all paths through a $(4, 2)$ counter circuit for the best- and worst-case operating conditions and fabrication processes. For this circuit, $\alpha = 1.27$ and $\beta = 2.13$. Thus, for this circuit under these conditions, the maximum speedup is 1.58.

11.5 DESIGN OPTIMIZATIONS

To maximize the performance of wave-pipelined implementations, we have developed wave-pipeline optimization techniques, algorithms, and tools in this research effort. To minimize the variation due to differences in delay along different paths through the logic, algorithms for balancing delays have been developed. To minimize the effects of environmental and process variations, delay compensation techniques have been developed.

Delay balancing techniques, algorithms, and tools attempt to equalize the propagation delay of all paths from a wave-pipeline input to output, thereby minimizing the variation in delay and maximizing the throughput. The approach taken for this balancing generally follows two steps [198]: *Rough tuning* inserts a minimal number of delay elements into the logic to correct gross delay imbalance. *Fine tuning* adjusts the drive, and therefore delay, of individual gates in the logic to minimize the circuit delay imbalance.

11.5.1 Rough Tuning

The rough tuning algorithm uses a directed acyclic graph (DAG) representation of the delay of a combinational logic network. Nodes represent the inputs and outputs of gates. Arcs are of two classes: internal and external. Internal arcs represent the delay from a gate input to the gate output and are weighted with the propagation delay of the gate from input to output. External arcs represent the interconnection of outputs of gates to the inputs to which they are connected in the logic. External arcs are weighted with the nominal delay to be added to the interconnections. The goal of the rough tuning algorithm is to find a set of weights for the external arcs which balances the delay along all paths through the logic. Since, however, the delay elements used to implement the weights attached to the external arcs may be limited in the range of delay which they can achieve, the problem solved by the Wong method of rough tuning is to find a set of weights for the external arcs which causes no path to exceed a user-specified maximum path delay while maximizing the length of the shortest path through the logic.

Because the number of paths in a DAG may be exponential in the problem size, Wong transforms the rough-tuning problem into an equivalent one where the weights along the paths of each loop in the undirected graph are balanced. An algorithm to minimize the number of delay elements added to the logic has been developed [198].

11.5.2 Fine Tuning

Wong et al. [199] developed a method of optimizing CML circuits for wave pipelining by providing an algorithm to provide fine delay balance through the setting of the CML gate tail current. Nowka [119] modified this fine tuning algorithm to optimize static CMOS circuits through the setting of the transistor transconductances.

Modeling Circuit Delay Behavior

Circuit delay is represented by a weighted directed acyclic graph. Each node of the graph corresponds to a gate output in the logic network. A directed arc from node i to node j exists when the gate whose output is j has node i as an input. Each arc is labeled with a tuple (rising delay, falling delay, unateness). The unateness field indicates which of rising delay or falling delay will be used for the gate delay from input i to output j for a rising or falling transition at the input i. A source node is introduced into the DAG which

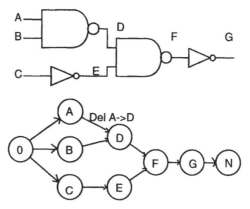

Figure 11.7 Example circuit and graph.

connects to all primary inputs with zero delay, and a sink node is introduced which is connected to all circuit output nodes with zero delay. An example circuit and graph are shown in Figure 11.7.

The delay of any path from the source node to the sink node is represented by a pair of delays (rising sink delay, falling sink delay). Each of these delays is computed by summing the contributions of the individual gates along the path. The contribution from each gate is the tuple entry which results in the appropriate transition at the sink node. For positively unate gates, the input nodes inherit the output node transition direction. Negatively unate gates inherit the opposite transition direction.

DAGs with nonunate gates cannot be represented with unique (rising sink delay, falling sink delay) pairs, but instead are represented by (minimum rising sink delay, maximum rising sink delay, minimum falling sink delay, maximum falling sink delay).

CML Gate and Network Delay

The CML gate propagation delay can be adjusted by controlling the tail current. This process does not effect the delay of the gates connected to the inputs of the gate.

Path delays are computed by adding the propagation delays of the gates.

CMOS Gate and Network Delay

The propagation delay behavior of a static CMOS gate is a function of the capacitive load on the gate, the interconnection of the individual transistors in the gate, the voltage at the other inputs of the gate, the voltages at nodes internal to the gate, and the rate of transition at the input, as well as the temperature, supply voltage, and signal noise at the gate.

A simple model for the propagation delay of a gate as the time required to charge or discharge a capacitance through a MOS transistor results in the following expression for gate delay:

$$T_{pd} = \frac{\text{const} \times V_{dd} C_1 L}{K (V_{dd} - V_t)^2 W},$$ (11.15)

where C_1 is the total load capacitance, V_{dd} is the supply voltage, K is the transconductance per unit channel width-to-length ratio, V_t is the device threshold, W is the effective transistor width, and L is the effective transistor length.

The load capacitance is the sum of the wiring capacitance C_{int} and the gate capacitances of all the transistors driven by the output:

$$C_1 = C_{int} + \sum_i C_{gate\,i}.$$ (11.16)

The first-order gate capacitance of each transistor is related to the oxide capacitance per unit area and the transistor geometry length and width:

$$C_{gate\,i} = C_{ox} W_i L_i.$$ (11.17)

Equation (11.15) can be rewritten so as to represent the driving device as an equivalent resistor:

$$T_{pd} \approx C_1 R_{eq}$$ (11.18)

Circuit path delays are sums of the propagation delays of the gates along the path.

Manipulating CMOS Delay

In equation (11.15), the transistor width and length and the load capacitance can be used to manipulate the delay of CMOS gates. In addition, the effective resistance of the gate can be increased by introducing an additional resistor or transistor in series with the conducting device. The supply voltage and device threshold are generally constant for all devices.

To efficiently balance CMOS wave-pipelined circuits, it is desirable to have the manipulation of the delay of a given gate affect only that gate, not its successors or predecessors. One method of increasing the delay of short-path gates while isolating their predecessors is by increasing the load capacitance of the output nodes by adding discrete capacitors or source–drain-shorted transistors [48]. This requires significant additional area to accomplish the balancing. The effective resistance of the gate can also be increased by the series addition of a poly resistor [74]. Like the added capacitance, this may result in a significant area increase if long poly wires must be introduced.

Manipulation of the length or width of the transistors independently does not have the desired effect. Increasing the length of a slow-path transistor also increases the load capacitance of the gate which drives it. Decreasing the width of the device generally is not acceptable, since as the width is decreased, the capacitive load on the previous stage is decreased. Thus, by increasing the delay of a given stage, the delay of its predecessor stage is decreased.

By manipulating the width and length of the devices together so as to maintain a constant gate capacitance, the delay of the gate can be adjusted without affecting the previous stage. From equation (11.17), the load capacitance is constant when

$$WL = WM_w LM_1, \quad \text{or} \quad M_w = 1/M_1. \tag{11.19}$$

where M_w is the width factor and M_1 is the length factor. Thus, manipulation results in a change in the gate delay of

$$T_{pd}(M_w) = \frac{T_{pd}(M_w = 1)}{M_w^2} \tag{11.20}$$

The delay of a gate then becomes a monotonically decreasing, convex function of the factor M_w.

Fine-Tuning Linear Program Solver

The balancing environment uses HSPICE simulations of each gate type, rather than the simple analytic models of gate delay, to accurately determine the constant-capacitance relationship of transistor length to transistor width for CMOS gates. HSPICE simulations are used to ascertain the gate propagation delay vs the capacitive load vs the transistor width factor for CMOS circuits, and the gate propagation delay vs the tail current for CML gates. These simulations are used to build macromodels used by the balancing linear program solver.

The wave-pipeline balancing process consists in the development of a circuit netlist and parameterizable gate library. It is assumed that the critical paths of the unbalanced netlist have been minimized. Therefore, delay balancing increases the delay along the short paths through the logic network. The unbalanced netlist is first rough-balanced by the Wong rough-balancing algorithm, which inserts buffers into paths which have local delay imbalances greater than a buffer delay [199].

The rough-balanced netlist is converted to a linear program representation, which is solved using the simplex method [110]. The solution to the linear program is used to make the fine adjustments to the circuits. Details of the linear program representations for CML are found in [198], and for CMOS in [119].

11.5.3 CMOS Delay Compensation

Run-to-run process variation can result in a ratio of maximum to minimum delay which exceeds 1.35, temperature variation can result in a ratio equal to 1.3, and supply variation in one equal to 1.2. Coupled noise can result in a ratio as high as 1.13 [119]. Unless these variations are controlled or their effects compensated, the maximum number of waves, or speedup, for a perfectly balanced wave pipeline is 1.7. This section describes methods by which the delay variations can be controlled or their effects compensated.

Sorting

One method of compensating for the variation in delay due to process variation is sorting. Unlike traditional synchronous-circuit sorting, where a bin-sorted IC will run at any clock frequency below the bin upper limit (subject to the limits of any dynamic logic in the design), wave-pipeline sorting is range sorting. Due to the two-sided limit on the valid clock period of a wave pipeline, sorting for wave pipelines involves determination of the valid range of clock periods given the particular device fabrication process of each VLSI device. By range sorting, the effects of process variation between dice can be minimized. Due to the relatively narrow range of valid clock periods for aggressive wave pipelines, range sorting is not a desirable method of compensating for delay variation due to manufacturing processes [119].

Tunable Constructive Clock Skew

A second method of compensating for static delay variation in wave pipelined circuits is through the use of tunable clock skew between the input and output synchronizer clocks of the wave pipeline. Fan et al. [48] used a laboratory-tunable skew between the input and output clocks of their wave-pipelined adder to counteract static process-induced variation. This method, while appropriate for laboratory experiments, is not practical for systems with several wave pipelines, as the clock skew mechanism for each wave pipeline must be externally accessible and controllable. In addition, wave pipelines with feedback present additional problems due to the interrelation of clocks.

Biased Logic

A method for compensation of static delay variation employed by Fan et al. [48] is biased logic. In this compensation method, pseudo-NMOS gates are used for all logic in the wave pipeline. The gate of the PMOS load transistor is driven by a bias voltage, which is set so as to balance gate output rise and fall times under different process characteristics. As a result of the biased PMOS transistor, this method has the circuit problems associated with NMOS circuits: the need to ratio the sizes of the NMOS and PMOS transistors so as to be able to drive the output of the gate sufficiently low, a reduction in noise margins, and static power consumption. In addition, the routing of the bias voltage may increase VLSI area.

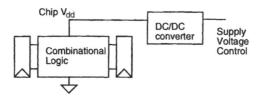

Figure 11.8   Supply-voltage delay compensation.

Other Compensation Techniques

Other methods of compensating delay, such as driver current starving, voltage-controlled driver load, and thermal control, have been analyzed for use in wave pipelining [119]. These generally lack the range of compensation necessary for wave-pipelined VLSI systems.

Supply-Voltage Control

An attractive alternative to counteract the effects of process variation and temporal temperature variation is the adaptive-supply-voltage method. Figure 11.8 illustrates the use of power-supply voltage control for delay compensation.

To compensate for the propagation delay variation, the supply voltage is adjusted to a level which maintains the target delays. The power supply is set to

$$V \approx \frac{V_0}{\beta}. \tag{11.21}$$

Since the ratio of the delay of a circuit path under slowest conditions to the delay of the same path under fastest conditions, β, can be at least two [119], the voltage supply may need to be set as low as half of the nominal supply level.

This method can be used to compensate for dynamic changes in delay, by adaptively adjusting the voltage supply of the wave-pipelined logic so as to maintain circuit delays at their design targets. This adaptive method is capable of compensating for delay-affecting changes for which the variation occurs with time constants greater than the closed-loop bandwidth of the adaptive circuit.

The adaptive circuit consists of a delay error detector and a supply-voltage bucking converter. Delay error detection is performed by phase-comparing a signal with a voltage-controlled delayed version of the same signal. A fixed-frequency source is applied to the input of an inverter chain whose delay, under expected worst case conditions, is half the period of the fixed source. The chain input and output are phase-compared. In the open-loop control, if the phase difference exceeds a threshold, an external indication is toggled to indicate the device is running too fast, and the power-supply voltage is

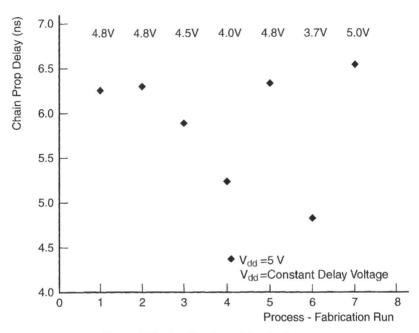

Figure 11.9 Supply-voltage delay simulation.

lowered. Because the error is relative to the expected worst-case delay, the chip supply will not be raised above the nominal supply level.

In a closed-loop adaptive supply circuit, the phase error can be used to charge or discharge a charge pump capacitor. In each adaptation cycle, a fixed amount of charge is added to or removed from the charge pump, depending on whether the delay chain is longer or shorter than the design target.

The supply voltage converter consists of two parts: the delay-chain supply, and the chip supply. A unit-gain amplifier drives the charge pump voltage to the V_{dd} supply rail of the inverter chain. The supply rail thus is modified until the delay matches the design target. For small wave-pipelined circuits, all circuitry can be driven by an on-chip converter. For larger circuits the output of the error detector circuit is used to drive an off-chip dc-to-dc converter.

Figure 11.9 details the effectiveness of the power-supply control method for compensation of process variation. For each process run the simulated delays are shown with the supply at $V_{dd} = 5$ V and at the voltage determined by the constant delay circuit. Without compensation the maximum to minimum delay ratio is 1.35. With the compensation it is 1.04.

Because of its area and power efficiency and its range of delay variation compensation, this method was employed in the wave-pipelined vector unit system developed in this research.

Several difficulties exist in the use of an adaptive supply. Logic which is designed to switch at set voltages or which relies on voltage references and logic in which transistor threshold drops are allowed may not operate properly with a lowered power-supply voltage. In addition, adaptive modification of power-supply voltages may increase the probability of CMOS latch-up and may result in static power consumption at interfaces with circuitry driven with nominal-voltage power supplies.

11.6 SNAP WAVE-PIPELINE DEMONSTRATION VLSI

The theory, techniques, algorithms, and tools developed for SNAP have been used in the design of several VLSI demonstration devices including a bipolar population counter, a CMOS multiplier, and a CMOS vector unit.

11.6.1 Bipolar Population Counter

To demonstrate the applicability of wave pipelining for bipolar circuits, Wong et al. developed a population-counter VLSI chip [199]. The circuit computes the number of 1's in a 63-bit input word. This circuit is used in high-speed multipliers. The number of levels of logic is only slightly smaller than that required for a 64×64 multiply.

The design is split into two major sections. The first is a carry-save adder tree that takes 63 input lines and converts them into two 6-bit numbers. The adder tree is implemented using $(3, 2)$ counters. The second section is a 6-bit carry-propagate adder that adds the two 6-bit numbers and produces the population count as a 6-bit number. The adder is implemented using a basic carry lookahead scheme.

The circuit is a combinational logic circuit with 21 levels of logic and a nominal longest path delay of 8.5 ns for the core logic plus 1 ns for the output pin drivers. After tuning, the path-length difference due to design is about 1.1 ns, excluding the effects of differences in rising vs falling delays and data-dependent delays.

Including registers, Wong estimates that the delay variation should be between 1.8 and 3.5 ns, allowing a 3.3- to 5-ns clock period. Thus, the circuit should support two to three waves of data at a pipeline frequency between 200 and 300 MHz. In contrast, the estimated minimum clock period using ordinary pipelining is 10.25 ns.

The population-counter circuit was designed using the fine- and rough-tuning algorithms. Layout was performed using an automatic placement and routing methodology. The ICs were fabricated using a commercial BiCMOS process and fully tested with cycle times of 3.8 ns.

11.6.2 CMOS Multipler Circuit

To demonstrate the suitability of static CMOS to wave pipelining, Klass [80] developed a wave-pipelined multiplier circuit.

The parallel multiplier circuit operates on 16-bit unsigned operands and produces a truncated 16-bit unsigned product. The parallel multiplier consists of three logic blocks: the PP generators, the PP reduction logic, and a final parallel adder. Booth recoding of the PPs was not employed in this multiplier. The PP reduction logic used [4, 2] compressors.

All circuits were implemented using static CMOS two-input NAND gates and inverters. All delay balancing was done manually through the insertion of inverter pairs and permanently enabled pass gates and by manually sizing transistor widths to manipulate the gate delay.

The simulated maximum delay of the multiplier circuit was 9.5 ns. The multiplier circuit was fabricated in a 1-μm CMOS process. Correct wave-pipelined operation of fabricated ICs was verified between 330 and 350 MHz. This was 3.7 times faster than the maximum clock speed which could be achieved without any wave pipelining.

11.6.3 CMOS VLSI Vector Unit

To demonstrate the applicability of wave pipelining to system design, a CMOS wave-pipelined VLSI integrated circuit was designed. The system implemented is a vector processor unit. This device demonstrates that wave-pipelined CMOS VLSI systems can be designed to perform within the performance speedup limits of 2 to 4 described in [120, 119]. This system integrates and synchronizes multiple heterogeneous wave pipelines. It includes both wave-pipelined functional units and memories. It was designed with the assistance of automated CAD balancing tools. It contains adaptive-power-supply support for the maintenance of wave-pipelined operation over a range of operating conditions and fabrication tolerances.

Vector Unit Architecture

The VLSI vector unit consists of a wave pipelined 8-bit × 8-bit unsigned multiplier, a wave-pipelined 16-bit parallel adder, a wave-pipelined vector register file, a scoreboard to ensure proper operation, a store buffer to interface with an external memory bus, instruction and input data buffers, and decode and issue logic. Test and power-supply-control support logic are also included. Figure 11.10 shows the organization of the VLSI vector unit. Wave-pipelined logic is shaded in this figure.

Parallel Adder. The adder is a modified version of a Brent–Kung parallel adder [24, 48]. It operates on 16-bit unsigned operands and produces a 16-bit unsigned result.

Module selection and balancing for the adder were done using the wave-pipelining design tools. Wave pipelining of the adder resulted in a 15% increase in its area. The delay padding gates added an additional 12%. Delay

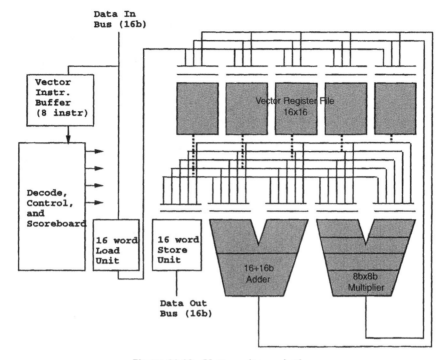

Figure 11.10   Vector-unit organization.

balancing through CMOS transistor sizing resulted in an additional 3% area penalty.

The maximum propagation delay through the adder is 5.5 ns. The path-length variation is 0.6 ns.

Parallel Multiplier. The parallel multiplier circuit operates on 8-bit unsigned operands and produces a 16-bit unsigned product. The parallel multiplier consists of three logic blocks: the PP generators, the PP reduction logic, and a final parallel adder.

Each PP is formed through the logical ANDing of a multiplier bit and a multiplicand bit. Booth recoding of the PPs is not employed in this multiplier.

The PP reduction logic transforms the array of PP bits into a redundant binary form of the product. The redundant binary form is converted to the simple binary result by the final parallel adder. The PP reduction logic consists of two levels of [4, 2] compressors.

Figure 11.11 is a schematic of the [4, 2] compressors used in this design. This circuit counts the number of the inputs A, B, C, D, and Ci which are asserted. This count is output in a redundant binary form in the sum output, which gives the count in the same precedence column as the input bits, and

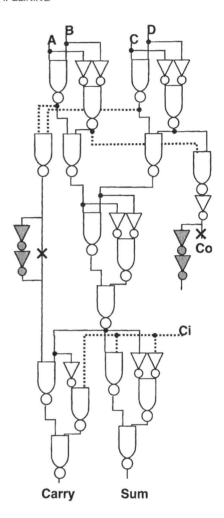

Figure 11.11 $(4, 2)$ counter implementation.   **Carry**   **Sum**

two carry outputs, which represent the portion of the count in the next higher precedence column.

The shaded inverters in Figure 11.11 are delay elements inserted by the rough-tuning pass of the delay balancing tool.

Delay balancing of the multiplier for wave pipelining resulted in a 10% increase in the area of the multiplier. The delay buffers within the counter circuits and the final carry-out delay accounted for an 8% increase in area. The fine-balancing transistor sizing accounted for 2% of the additional area. The maximum propagation delay through the multiplier is 10.8 ns and the path-length variation is 1.37 ns.

Vector-Register File. The vector-register file contains five vector registers. Each register consists of sixteen 16-bit elements. Registers have one read port and one write port. Element address generation is done locally. Delayed clock signals are used for bitline equalization, bitline pullup, and sense enabling. Only stride-one addressing is supported. The register cells are cross-coupled inverters with pairs of read–write NMOS pass transistors. Clocked bitline equalization and pullup are employed. A cross-coupled NMOS sense-amp design was used.

Because the registers are not static CMOS structures, balancing of the registers was performed manually. A method for minimizing delay variation across the memory array was developed [121] and employed in the design of the register file. Within each register, the wordline buffers were sized so as to counteract delay variation due to the wordline proximity to the sense amplifiers. The read data buffers were also sized so as to counteract the variation due to the bitline proximity of the wordline driver. The balancing of the vector registers increased their area by less than 2%. The maximum read access time of the vector registers is 3.7 ns. The minimum simulated cycle time of the vector registers is 2.0 ns.

Load Unit, Store Unit, Instruction Buffer

The *load unit* consists of a 16-element-deep FIFO and FIFO control logic. Each element is 16 bits wide. Entries are loaded into the FIFO from the input data bus under external control at a reduced rate. The FIFO is emptied through the execution of a vector load instruction.

The *store unit* contains a 16-element-deep FIFO and FIFO control logic. Each FIFO entry is 16 bits wide. Entries are loaded into the FIFO through the execution of a vector store instruction. The FIFO is emptied under external control at a reduced rate. The store FIFO output data is placed on the output data bus.

The *instruction buffer* consists of an eight-deep queue of vector instructions. Instructions are loaded in to the buffer via the input data bus under external control at low speed. Instructions are removed from the queue by the fetch–decode logic and executed at chip core frequency.

Scoreboard

The vector-unit scoreboard consists of timers for each functional unit, timers for each vector register for vector reads, timers for each vector register for vector writes, and a scoreboard update state machine.

Constant-Delay Power-Control Logic

The constant-delay adaptive-power logic provides indications of external power-supply modifications which are used to compensate for process and temporal thermal variation. The constant-delay logic consists of a delay chain of inverters, which were balanced at design time to 16.6 ns at the expected slowest process operating under worst-case environmental conditions. This

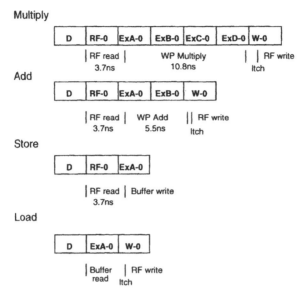

Figure 11.12 Vector-instruction pipeline stages.

delay chain is driven from a chip input. The input and output of the delay chain are phase-compared. The phase comparator output drives a D latch, whose outputs are used to drive the power bump indications. The D latch was designed so as to have an intentional race, which acts as a threshold of phase error, which results in external-power bump indications.

Vector-Unit Operations

The instruction set of the vector unit consists of vector load, vector store, vector add, and vector multiply. The arithmetic operations occur between vector registers exclusively. The load and store operations transfer vectors from the load-unit FIFO to a vector register and from a vector register to the store-unit FIFO, respectively. The pipeline stages for each instruction and the time spent in each functional block are shown in Figure 11.12.

For the vector add and vector multiply, arbitrary source and destination registers are allowed; both sources may be the same register. The destination register can be a source register. Separate read and write ports on the registers and full connectivity between the register file and the ports on the functional units allow this flexibility.

Vector instructions are issued as soon as the *element* in the vector register is valid and the *port* in the register file is free. This allows the vector unit to chain operations between functional units with a single cycle between generation of a vector element and its subsequent use. This flexibility increases the complexity in the scoreboard, but provides better performance.

TABLE 11.3   Vector-unit balancing results

	Value	
Quantity	Multiplier	Adder
Maximum delay (ns)	10.84	5.5
Delay variation (ns)	1.37	0.58
Unbalanced transistors	5526	1322
Balanced transistors	6466	1730
Unbalanced area (mm^2)	1.95	0.40
Balanced area (mm^2)	2.17	0.45
Balancing exec. time[1] (h)	10.94	0.62

[1]Sun SPARCstation 10.

Balancing

This sub-subsection summarizes the balancing results of the wave-pipelined logic used in the vector unit. Table 11.3 details the wave-pipelined overhead in number of transistors and functional unit area for the adder and multiplier circuits. The execution times of the balancing procedure on a Sun SPARC-station 10 are also given.

Vector-Unit Fabrication

The vector unit was fabricated using the Hewlett-Packard CMOS26b 0.8-μm CMOS process through the MOSIS service. This process provides three levels of metal and a single poly layer. Two metal levels were used for signal distribution, and M3 was used for power and ground distribution bars. The feature resolution of this process is 0.1 μm, which allows fine delay resolution for the transistor-sizing delay-balancing procedure. The VLSI vector-unit design contains approximately 47,000 transistors and occupies an area of 43 mm^2. It is packaged in a 132-pin PGA.

A die photograph of the VLSI vector unit is shown in Figure 11.13. Figure 11.14 details the vector register-to-register wave pipelined multiply operation at 300 MHz. In Figure 11.14 the re0 and we2 lines show a single data wave leaving register r0 and a result being written into register r2. The mula line shows multiple data waves entering the vector multiplier, while the mulr line shows the result data waves.

Test Results

Testing of the vector-unit IC consisted of several low-speed functional tests and several high-speed tests. Low-speed functional testing consisted of tests of the on-chip ring oscillator, the vector register, and a low-speed multiplier test.

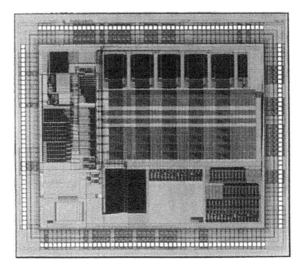

Figure 11.13 Vector-unit die photograph.

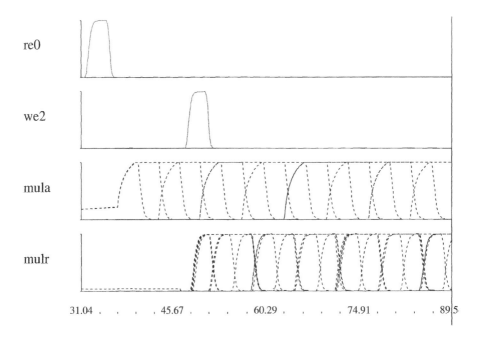

Figure 11.14 Wave-pipelined vector unit multiply.

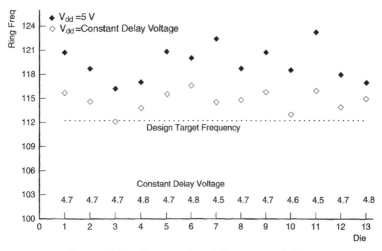

Figure 11.15 Compensation of die-process variation.

To enable proper high-speed wave-pipelined operation of each die, the constant-delay power supply was adjusted so as to track the design target operating frequency. When a power bump indication was received from the die being tested, the power supply was adjusted by 0.1 V. To indicate the effectiveness of the constant-delay power method, the design target frequency of the ring oscillator was compared with the measured oscillator frequency of each die with the power-supply voltage set to the value determined by the constant-delay circuit. At design time, simulations were used to determine the target ring oscillation frequency of 112 MHz.

Figure 11.15 shows the supply voltages specified by the constant-delay indications for each die. For each die, the oscillator frequency at $V_{dd} = 5$ V is indicated with a solid diamond. These points show the delay variation of the ring oscillator circuit across the dice. The frequencies at a 5-V supply were as much as 18% higher than the target frequency. When the supply voltage for each die was set to the value indicated by the constant delay circuit, the frequencies specified by the open diamonds were measured. With the adaptive power method the frequencies were measured at 0% to +5% higher than the target frequency.

Once the lock voltage was determined, wave-pipelined speed testing was performed by loading data and instructions into the instruction-buffer and load-unit FIFOs at low speed, performing the vector instructions at high speed, and finally emptying store-unit FIFOs at low speed and verifying the results. Using this procedure, the eleven functional ICs were tested. Three of the eleven correctly performed a 16,000-vector add test and a 16,000-vector

TABLE 11.4   Comparison of vector-unit results

Quantity	Value	
	Wave Pipe	Latch Pipe
Die area (mm^2)	43.19	44.09
Minimum clock period (ns)	2.8	3.8
Multiply-unit latency (ns)	10.84	11.7
Add-unit latency (ns)	5.5	6.1

multiply test at 303 MHz. Eight of the eleven performed them correctly at 222MHz.

Comparison with Traditional Design

With the performance detailed in the previous section, the wave pipelines demonstrated approximately 1.1 waves of data in the vector-register file, 1.9 waves of data in the adder, and 3.7 waves of data in the multiplier.

To quantitatively determine the performance benefits of wave pipelining in this design, a vector unit was designed using traditional pipelining and the simulated performance was compared.

The traditional pipeline used two-phase clocking and dynamic-flow latches to achieve high performance. The adder and multiplier were redesigned using the latches. The multiplier and adder were implemented using the same cell library as the wave-pipelined implementation, but delay padding elements and delay-balancing transistor sizing were not used. The vector-register file was operated as a single stage in the pipeline and thus was not partitioned into multiple pipeline stages.

Table 11.4 details simulated results for the wave-pipelined vector unit and for a complete layout using latch-based pipelined units and a single-cycle register access.

The traditional pipeline, because of its longer cycle time, had a three-cycle multiply execution rather than the four-cycle execution in the wave-pipelined design. The clocks to the output latches of both the adder and the multiplier were skewed in the traditional pipeline design. Without the use of this clock skew, the latencies would be 7.6 and 15.2 ns, respectively.

Because of the ability of the wave-pipelined design to have more than a single register read operation occurring concurrently, the wave pipeline had a 35% faster cycle time. Because of the lack of intermediate latch delay and partitioning overhead, the wave pipeline had operation latencies up to 10% less than for the traditional pipeline design.

Compared to traditional pipelines designed with less aggressive clocking technologies, such as static latch or register-based pipelines, the wave pipeline's, performance would be even better.

11.7 CONCLUSION

To improve the performance of arithmetic circuits, SNAP researchers have developed the theory, algorithms, design techniques, and tools necessary for the development of high-performance wave-pipelined VLSI. SNAP research has developed theory on the correct operation of wave-pipelined circuits, has evaluated device technologies for their applicability to wave-pipelining and quantified the wave-pipeline performance limits for key technologies, has developed performance optimization techniques for wave pipelines, and has validated the theory, techniques, and tools through the development of demonstration VLSI chips. Using standard device fabrication technology, these VLSI designs achieve operating frequencies of 250 to 350 MHz.

12

RATIONAL ARITHMETIC

Based upon work by Oskar Mencer

12.1 INTRODUCTION

Many applications in signal processing, image processing, graphics, scientific computations, and so on require the evaluation of specific elementary functions or combinations of functions such as trigonometric functions, the Gamma function $\Gamma(x)$, $(\arcsin x)/\sqrt{1 - x^2}$, etc. Rational approximations offer efficient approximation and evaluation of analytic functions represented by the ratio of two polynomials:

$$f(x) \sim \frac{[(a_n x + a_{n-1})x + \cdots + a_1]x + a_0}{[(b_m x + b_{m-1})x + \cdots + b_1]x + b_0}$$

$$= \frac{c_n x^n + c_{n-1} x^{n-1} \cdots c_1 x + c_0}{d_m x^m + d_{m-1} x^{m-1} \cdots d_1 x + d_0}. \qquad (12.1)$$

Koren and Zinaty [86] evaluate rational approximations with a latency of $\max(m, n)$ multiply–add (MA) operations and a final division. Typically, division is implemented either with multiplicative [57] or with digit-serial (iterative) methods, also called digit-recurrence methods [42].

Rational-arithmetic units proposed in this chapter are ideal for speeding up the evaluation of rational approximations. At the core of rational

TABLE 12.1 Symbols and definitions

$\triangleq$	Definition
$\equiv$	Equivalence
$\bar{p}_i$	$1/p_i$
$\bar{s}_i$	$1/s_i$
$\overline{M_i}$	$\sum_{j=1}^{i} M_j$
$0.\bar{3}$	$0.3333\dots$
$\underline{A}$	Matrix
$|\underline{A}|$	Determinant
$\{a, b, c, \dots\}$	A set of values
$\mathcal{N}$	Set of natural numbers $\{1, 2, 3, \dots\}$
$\mathcal{R}$	Set of rational numbers $r = x/y$ where $x, y \in \mathcal{N}$
$[a_0; a_1, \dots a_n]$	$a_0 + \cfrac{1}{\lvert a_1} + \cfrac{1}{\lvert a_2} + \cdots + \cfrac{1}{a_n} = a_0 + \cfrac{1}{a_1 + \cfrac{1}{a_2 + \cdots \cfrac{1}{a_n}}}$
$\langle M_1, M_2, M_3$ $M_4, M_5, \dots, M_n \rangle$	$[0; 2^{M_1}, -(2^{-M_1} + 2^{M_2}), (2^{-M_2} + 2^{M_3}), -(2^{-M_3} + 2^{M_4}),$ $(2^{-M_4} + 2^{M_5})\dots \pm (2^{-M_{n-1}} + 2^{M_n})]$

arithmetic are simple continued fractions (CFs), which are structures such as

$$f(x) = x_0 + \cfrac{1}{x_1 + \cfrac{1}{x_2 + \cfrac{1}{x_3 + \cdots}}}. \qquad (12.2)$$

CFs enable the development of divide–add structures for digits of rational numbers. CF arithmetic deals with computing rational functions where input and output values are represented as simple CFs.

Table 12.1 summarizes the notation that will be used throughout this chapter.

The main focus of this chapter is on efficient general-purpose hardware (VLSI) implementation of rational arithmetic for computer systems, that is, *rational-arithmetic units*. Rational-arithmetic units compute functions that include division. An example for a rational-arithmetic unit is the bilinear function $y = (ax + b)/(cx + d)$. Just as the MA unit is a natural extension of multiplication units, rational-arithmetic units are candidate extensions of current FP divide units.

12.2 CONTINUED FRACTIONS

CFs can be used to represent rational numbers. This section provides the basic definitions and terminology that will be used throughout the chapter.

Let us start by defining some CF forms:

1. *Finite continued fractions* represent rational numbers that are constructed as follows: for $A_i, B_i, a_i, b_i \in \mathcal{R}$

$$\frac{A_n}{B_n} = a_0 + \cfrac{b_1}{a_1 + \cfrac{b_2}{a_2 + \cdots \cfrac{b_n}{a_n}}} = a_0 + \frac{b_1}{\left| a_1 \right.} + \frac{b_2}{\left| a_2 \right.} + \cdots + \frac{b_n}{\left| a_n \right.}. \quad (12.3)$$

2. *Simple continued fractions* form a special case of finite CFs where all partial quotients $b_i = 1$. The following vector notation is used:

$$[a_0; a_1, \ldots, a_n] \triangleq a_0 + \frac{1}{\left| a_1 \right.} + \frac{1}{\left| a_2 \right.} + \cdots + \frac{1}{a_n} = a_0 + \cfrac{1}{a_1 + \cfrac{1}{a_2 + \cdots \cfrac{1}{a_n}}}.$$

$$(12.4)$$

3. *Regular continued fractions* are simple CFs with all $a_i \in \mathcal{N}^+$, except $a_0 \in \mathcal{N}$.

Regular CFs are alternative representations of rational numbers [75]. In addition, CFs are at the basis of rational-approximation theory. Therefore, the representation of rational numbers by CFs connects number representation to the rational approximation of transcendental functions. Peter Henrici has mentioned that "we are still missing a general theory explaining the connection between transcendental functions and continued fractions" (the introduction in [73]). In other words, there currently is no theory explaining the simple CF approximations below. Still, the already known CF expansions cover most useful functions [76]. Examples are:

$$\frac{e}{e-1} = [0; 1, 1, 2, 1, 1, 4, 1, 1, 6, 1, 1, 8, \ldots], \quad (12.5)$$

$$\tan x = \left[0; \frac{1}{x}, -\frac{3}{x}, \frac{5}{x}, -\frac{7}{x}, \frac{9}{x}, -\frac{11}{x}, \ldots \right], \quad (12.6)$$

$$\arctan x = \left[0; \frac{1}{x}, \frac{3}{x}, \frac{5}{x} \left(\frac{1}{2} \right)^2, \frac{7}{x} \left(\frac{2}{3} \right)^2, \frac{9}{x} \left(\frac{3}{4} \right)^2, \ldots \right], \quad (12.7)$$

$$\frac{\arcsin x}{\sqrt{1-x^2}} = \left[0; \frac{1}{x}, -\frac{3}{1 \times 2} \times \frac{1}{x}, \frac{5}{1 \times 2} \times \frac{1}{x}, \frac{7}{3 \times 4} \times \frac{1}{x}, \ldots \right], \quad (12.8)$$

and the incomplete Γ function

$$\Gamma(0.5, x) = e^{-x}x^{0.5}\left[0; x, (0.5)^{-1}, x, (1.5)^{-1}, x, (2.5)^{-1}, x, (3.5)^{-1}, \cdots\right].$$

$$(12.9)$$

Given the above CF approximations, let us take a closer look at a more general way of transforming CFs to rational numbers. The following two inobvious equations are at the heart of CF theory, showing the link between rational numbers and CFs. The step from rational numbers to CFs is one step of the journey from rational binary numbers to CFs, which is required to build the rational-arithmetic units presented in this chapter.

A finite CF with n partial quotients can always be transformed into a ratio A_n/B_n using the iterative equations

$$A_n = a_n A_{n-1} + b_n A_{n-2},$$

$$(12.10)$$

$$B_n = a_n B_{n-1} + b_n B_{n-2},$$

$$(12.11)$$

where A_{n-1}/B_{n-1} corresponds to the value of the same CF without the nth partial quotient. Initial conditions are $A_0 = a_0$, $B_0 = 1$, $A_{-1} = 1$, and $B_{-1} = 0$ (see for example [135, 189]). The iterative equations can be used to convert between CFs and rational values. Evaluating CFs reduces to MA operations with a final division A/B.

Another way of expressing the connection between rational approximations and CFs is given by Wall.

Equivalence 1 ((*Wall* [189]) *Given the rational function $H(z)$ written as the ratio of two polynomials, it is possible to find r_i's and s_i's such that*

$$H(z) = \frac{a_{00}z^n + a_{01}z^{n-1} + \cdots + a_{0n}}{a_{11}z^{n-1} + a_{12}z^{n-2} + \cdots + a_{1n}} \equiv [r_1 z + s_1, r_2 z + s_2, \ldots, r_n z + s_n]$$

$$(12.12)$$

with all $a_{ij} \neq 0$ and $r_i \neq 0$.

Equivalence 1 shows the main advantage of CFs. The powers of z in the polynomial representation are reduced to linear terms for each CF digit. It seems that if we could store and manipulate CFs within a computer system, we could more efficiently compute rational approximations. Ideally, the evaluation of the rational approximation on the left is transformed to a set of linear approximations which can be evaluated in parallel. This suggests that for rational approximations it is possible to make use of symmetries in the CF space. In general, CF algorithms take a CF input and compute a function, storing the result again as a CF. Before we take a look at CF algorithms it is necessary to investigate how to represent CFs in computer systems.

Converting between binary numbers and CFs is nontrivial. In the worst case, conversion requires $O(N)$ divisions, where N is the number of CF digits. Using the above iteration equations (12.10) and (12.11), it is possible to reduce the conversion to $O(N)$ multiply–adds followed by one division. Clearly, this overhead for converting in and out of a number representation is too large.

In order to make CFs attractive for practical arithmetic units, three fundamental problems need to be solved:

1. *What is the Optimal Digit Representation for Simple Continued Fractions?*
   In other words, what is a digit of a CF? What does it look like, and how many bits should we use to represent it? Is there an upper bound on the value of a digit? Mathematical literature focuses on regular CFs with integer digits. However, the value of a regular CF digit has no upper bound, that is, the value of the digit ranges from one to infinity. Clearly we need to restrict the value of a digit. In fact, we need to restrict the range of a digit to a small set of values compared to the number of values of the number that we want to represent with the digits. An upper bound on a regular CF digit has the side effect that we cannot represent *all* rational numbers, even if we use an infinite number of digits. However, all we want to do in computer arithmetic is to represent a finite number of values within one stored number. The problem is to choose the optimal set of values for the CF digits in order to represent the finite number of values of the stored binary number.

2. *How to Convert between Continued Fractions and Binary Numbers?* This problem is related to the first one. Once we choose a digit representation, how do we convert binary digits to CF digits and vice versa without unreasonable effort?

3. *How to Control the Errors during the Computation with Continued Fractions?* Specifically, given a CF with n digits, can we give a bound on the error of the stored number compared to the actual value? For example, $0.\bar{3} = [0; 3]$ is exact; $0.\bar{6} = [0; 1, 2]$ is also exact. But how close is the substring $[0; 1, 2]$ to 0.7, that is, what is the error of the CF after the first two digits? What happens if the digits are not integers?

The remainder of this chapter shows the solution of the three problems of CF arithmetic and shows how to build practical and efficient rational-arithmetic units for extending FP division to rational approximation. For more information on continued fractions see the CF literature, such as [135, 73, 189, 95].

12.3 THE *M*-LOG-FRACTION TRANSFORMATION

Practical arithmetic units based on continued fractions rest on the resolution of three fundamental questions:

1. What is the optimal digit representation for simple CFs?
2. How to convert between CFs and binary numbers?
3. How to control the error during the computation with CFs?

Ideally we are looking for the following three features of the digit representation: First, we need a reasonably compact digit representation with a small number of bits per digit compared to the number of bits for the binary number. In addition, a few such CF digits should suffice to represent the binary number. Second, conversion between binary numbers and CFs has to be very simple and efficient. Third, the values represented by the CFs have to be distributed uniformly to enable us to bound and thus control the error during computation.

The following provides the theoretical treatment of the *M-log-fraction-transformation* (MFT) for rational-arithmetic units, and shows how the MFT implicitly combines all three necessary features outlined above.

Theorem (MFT Theorem) *A binary number B with p binary digits, containing n 1's, is equivalent to a simple continued fraction with n partial quotients: the M-log fraction* $\langle M_1, M_2, M_3, \ldots \rangle$ *where if*

$$B = b_1 b_2 b_3 \ldots b_p = 2^{\beta_1} + 2^{\beta_2} + 2^{\beta_3} + 2^{\beta_4} + 2^{\beta_5} + \cdots + 2^{\beta_n}$$

then

$$B \equiv \left[0; 2^{M_1}, -\left(2^{-M_1} + 2^{M_2}\right), \left(2^{-M_2} + 2^{M_3}\right), -\left(2^{-M_3} + 2^{M_4}\right), \left(2^{-M_4} + 2^{M_5}\right)\right.$$
$$\left. \cdots \pm \left(2^{-M_{n-1}} + 2^{M_n}\right)\right]$$
$$\equiv \langle M_1, M_2, M_3, M_4, M_5, \ldots, M_n \rangle, \tag{12.13}$$

where M_i are related to α_i, the distances between the 1's of the binary number B, by the recursion

$$M_1 = \alpha_1 = -\beta_1, \qquad M_2 = \alpha_2 - M_1, \qquad M_i = \alpha_i - M_{i-1} \tag{12.14}$$

The α's, β's, and M's are maximally *N*-bit integers, where *N* is the number of bits in the binary number *B*. As shown, α_i is the sum of M_i and M_{i-1}. The α's, which are the distances between the 1's, can also be seen as a 0-runlength encoding of the binary number *B*; that is, α_i is the number of 0's

The *M*-log Fraction

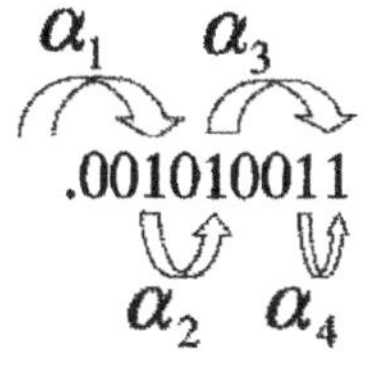

$$\underbrace{.001010011}_{} = 2^{-\alpha_1} + 2^{-\alpha_1-\alpha_2} + 2^{-\alpha_1-\alpha_2-\alpha_3} + 2^{-\alpha_1-\alpha_2-\alpha_3-\alpha_4}$$

$$\alpha_1 \quad \alpha_3$$
$$\alpha_2 \quad \alpha_4$$

$$\boxed{M_i = \alpha_i - M_{i-1}}$$

is equivalent to

$$\equiv \cfrac{1}{2^{M_1} + \cfrac{1}{-(2^{-M_1} + 2^{M_2}) + \cfrac{1}{(2^{-M_2} + 2^{M_3})^{\cdot \cdot}}}} =$$

$$= \left[0; 2^{M_1}, -(2^{-M_1} + 2^{M_2}), (2^{-M_2} + 2^{M_3}), -(2^{-M_3} + 2^{M_4}), (2^{-M_4} + 2^{M_5}) \ldots \right]$$

Figure 12.1 The connection between the distances between the 1's (α's) and the *M*-log Fraction. Here $M_1 = \alpha_1$.

between the ith and $(i + 1)$th 1. Theorem 1 in one sentence is: "An *M*-log fraction of length n is equivalent to n powers of 2 for any $n \in \mathcal{N}$.

Figure 12.1 shows the connection between binary numbers and the *M*-log fraction. Let us look at some implications of the MFT. First, given an *N*-bit binary number, the MFT representation requires at most N digits with log N bits per CF digit. Thus, N log N bits are used to store the binary number in CF (MFT) form. Second, the MFT enables instant conversion between simple CFs and binary numbers. All that is required to convert between binary numbers and an *M*-log fraction is a modified leading one detect circuit similar to the one used in FP units to normalize the mantissa to the required format: 1.*xxxx* . . . . The conversion takes one to two clock cycles. Since *M*-log functions are the equivalent of binary numbers, error bounds for them are equal to those for binary numbers. An 8-bit fractional binary number has an error bound of 2^{-8}. Similarly, an N = digit *M*-log fraction has the same error bound as a fractional binary number with N 1's. In both cases the number of digits determines the error bound.

Figure 12.1 shows the correspondence of the distances between 1's (0-runlength encoding), called α's, and the digits of the *M*-log fraction. 0-runlength encoding refers to counting the number of zeros between ones of a binary numbers, that is, the runlength of a string of zeros. Each α of the binary number is the sum of two consecutive M_i's of the *M*-log fraction.

The full proof of Theorem 1 (the MFT theorem) can be found in [108]. Another way of understanding the principles behind the MFT is to look at the following equivalence of series and CFs.

Equivalence 2   (*Euler's Equivalence for Series and Continued Fractions*) *For* $c_i \neq 0$ [46],

$$c_0 + c_1 + c_2 + \cdots \equiv c_0 + \frac{c_1}{\mid 1} - \frac{c_2/c_1}{\mid 1 + c_2/c_1} - \frac{c_3/c_2}{\mid 1 + c_3/c_2} - \cdots . \quad (12.15)$$

Each partial quotient of the CF on the right depends on two neighboring terms of the series on the left. Thus, the precision of an n-element CF is equivalent to the precision of a finite series of length n. Looking at a binary number as a sum of weighted digits, we obtain the equivalence of binary numbers and CFs.

The basic MFT enables the encoding of binary numbers with a sequence of M_i's as shown above. In fact, the first digit M_1 corresponds to the integer part of the logarithmic representation of B, that is, $M_1 = \lfloor \log B \rfloor$. Thus, theoretically the MFT is a variant of the logarithmic number system [153] with the advantage that conversion just requires counting distances between the 1's.

Although the M-log fraction shown above solves the three problems associated with CFs, there is a small drawback left. A CF digit corresponds roughly to one 1 in the binary number. Given a target precision of 16 bits, it is not clear *a priori* how many iteration are required to compute a satisfactory result. In the worst case with all 1's, 16 iterations are required. In order to enable a regular hardware structure for the rational-arithmetic unit, we introduce the *signed-digit M-log fraction*.

12.4   THE SIGNED-DIGIT *M*-LOG FRACTION

This section shows a modified version of the MFT, using signed-digit binary numbers. Our objective is to use the digits of a binary number $B = s_1 2^{-1} + s_2 2^{-2} + s_3 2^{-3} + s_4 2^{-4} + \cdots + s_n 2^{-n}$ directly to convert B to the M-log fraction. In the binary case $s_i = \{0, 1\}$. The main problem in direct conversion stems from the restriction on Euler's equivalence (12.15), in our case $s_i \neq 0$. In order to circumvent this restriction, we use *signed-digit binary numbers*. In the case of radix 2, the signed digits are in $\{+1, -1\}$.

A drawback of the general M-log fraction is that a CF digit corresponds to a 1 in the binary number. Therefore the result does not converge uniformly and requires a variable number of iterations per result. In fact, in the worst case (all 1's) the algorithm is limited to retiring one bit at a time. Signed-digit binary numbers eliminate the nonuniform convergence and enable us to improve the rate of convergence in the worst case. Applying the signed digits to the MFT leads to the signed-digit MFT.

The signed-digit binary M-log fraction shown below connects signed-digit binary numbers with the MFT. In the weighted positional number system with numbers $B = s_1 2^{\beta_1} + s_2 2^{\beta_2} + s_3 2^{\beta_3} + \cdots + s_n 2^{\beta_n}$, β's are fixed to

$\beta_i = -i$:

$$\{\beta_1, \beta_2, \beta_3, \ldots, \beta_p\} = \{-1, -2, -3, \ldots, -p\}. \qquad (12.16)$$

Fixing the β's enables us to fix the shifts M_i according to Theorem 1. From the β's above we know that $\alpha_i = \beta_{i-1} - \beta_i = 1 = M_i + M_{i-1}$. The most efficient (yielding the smallest hardware implementation) set of M_i's with this restriction is $M_i = i \bmod 2$:

$$\{M_1, M_2, M_3, \ldots, M_n\} = \{1, 0, 1, 0, 1, \ldots, n \bmod 2\}. \qquad (12.17)$$

The resulting equation below is a corollary of Theorem 1:

Corollary 3 (*Signed-Digit Binary M-log Fraction*) *A signed-digit binary number B_R with n 1's (n even) and $s_i \in \{+1, -1\}$ is equivalent to a simple continued fraction with n partial quotients as follows*:

$$\begin{aligned}
B_R &= s_1 2^{-1} + s_2 2^{-2} + s_3 2^{-3} + s_4 2^{-4} + \cdots + s_n 2^{-n} \\
&\equiv \left[0; s_1 2^1, -\left(s_1 2^{-1} + s_2 2^0\right), \left(s_2 2^0 + s_3 2^1\right), \right. \\
&\quad \left. -\left(s_3 2^{-1} + s_4 2^0\right), \ldots, -\left(s_{n-1} 2^{-1} + s_n 2^0\right)\right]
\end{aligned}$$

To convert binary numbers to signed-digit binary M-log fractions requires two steps. The first step is to convert the binary number to a signed-digit binary number. This can be done in about the time required for an addition. For details on converting between signed digits and binary digits see [131]. Second, the signed-digit numbers are converted to the signed-digit M-log fraction as shown in Corollary 3 above. Converting between signed binary digits and CF digits consists in combining two neighboring digits as shown in Corollary 3. The choice of $M_i = i \bmod 2$ keeps the powers of two in the set $\{2^{-1}, 2^0, 2^1\}$—basically a left shift, a right shift, or no shift. The actual implementation of rational-arithmetic units shown in the next section absorbs this conversion operation into the iteration equations of the algebraic algorithm, thus eliminating conversion (MFT) overhead.

12.5 A RATIONAL-ARITHMETIC UNIT

The previous sections describe how to represent the digits of a CF in a computer system, while eliminating the conversion overhead between binary numbers and CFs and keeping the same level of error control as for binary numbers. Why do we want to use CFs in the first place? One of the main reasons is the availability of the CF algorithms shown below. CFs are a natural representation for rational functions. However, until now their use was impractical due to the large overhead of converting in and out of the representation and the nonuniform distribution of representable values. The MFT introduced in the previous section opens up all CF algorithms for practical implementations in computer systems based on binary numbers.

The conventional method to compute rational approximations uses MA structures to evaluate the numerator and denominator, followed by a final division. Each MA step introduces roundoff error, accumulating error for the final result. The following rational-arithmetic units compute entire rational functions in one arithmetic unit. (Such arithmetic units are also called compound arithmetic units.) For example, instead of computing $(ax + b)/(cx + d)$ with two multiplies, two adds, and a final divide, the algorithm proposed below starts with loading a, b, c, d into internal state registers. Then it takes the first input digit of x, and produces the first output digit of the final result after the first iteration. An application example for such extended division units is signal processing, where the bilinear function could be used to compute rational approximations, replacing the MA units that are currently used to evaluate polynomial approximations in digital signal processors (DSPs).

The previous section shows how to convert between binary numbers and CFs. The goal of this section is to show the details of a rational-arithmetic unit. The following CF algorithms use the CF representation, resulting in rational-arithmetic units.

CF algorithms take simple CFs and compute a function returning a result in the form of a CF. Assume we have a simple CF $[x_0, x_1, x_2, \dots]$ representing a number in our computer system and we want to compute a function $f(x)$. A CF algorithm for $f(x)$ takes the digits x_i of the input fraction and produces the output digits o_i of the result:

$$[o_0, o_1, o_2 \dots] = f([x_0, x_1, x_2, \dots]). \tag{12.18}$$

The trivial rational function is the reciprocal. While for conventional number systems computing the reciprocal $f(x) = 1/x$ is a complicated operation, CFs are a natural representation for the reciprocal. Computing the reciprocal of a simple CF consists of a single digit shift:

$$\frac{1}{[a_0; a_1, a_2, \dots]} = \begin{cases} [0; a_0, a_1, a_2, \dots] & \text{if} \quad a_0 \neq 0, \\ [a_1; a_2, \dots] & \text{if} \quad a_0 = 0, \end{cases} \tag{12.19}$$

A simple CF multiplied by a constant c becomes

$$\left[ca_0; \frac{a_1}{c}, ca_2, \frac{a_3}{c}, ca_4, \frac{a_5}{c}, ca_6, \dots \right] \tag{12.20}$$

Next, let's examine the bilinear function $f(x) = (ax + b)/(cx + d)$ which is the simplest nontrivial rational function. In order to compute the bilinear function we use the algebraic algorithm proposed by Gosper et al. [62]. At each iteration the algorithm consumes an input digit or produces an output digit. The amount of state kept by the algorithm stays constant and corresponds to the number of coefficients of the computed rational function. In

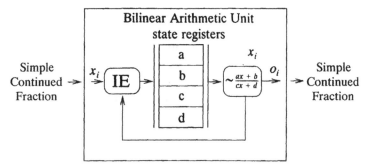

Figure 12.2 The state machine for the iteration equations (IE) of the positional algebraic CF algorithm. The state registers a, b, c, d hold at each iteration the values a_i, b_i, c_i, d_i. The algorithm selects the output digit o_i close to the current state $(a_i x_i + b_i) (c_i x_i + d_i)$, shown without the indices.

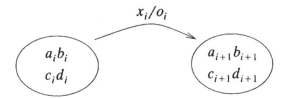

Figure 12.3 A slice of the transition diagram for the positional algebraic CF algorithm. The iteration values a_i, b_i, c_i, d_i go over into the next state $a_{i+1}, b_{i+1}, c_{i+1}, d_{i+1}$, absorbing an input digit x_i, and producing an output digit o_i.

the case of the bilinear function there are four state registers corresponding to the four coefficients a, b, c, and d.

The objective is to compute $[o_0, o_1, o_2 \dots] = f([x_0, x_1, x_2, \dots])$, where the x_i's are the partial quotients of the simple input CF, and $o_i = f(x_i, \text{state})$ are the partial quotients of the output. $T(x)$ is the function that is stored in the state variables. The general structure of the algebraic algorithm is shown in Figure 12.2. The iteration equations (IE) transform the state from i to $i + 1$, consuming an input digit and producing an output digit (Figure 12.3).

How do we obtain the iteration equations? At any given iteration the state of the entire computation is given by the state registers, the remaining input digits, and the produced output digits. The internal state changes on two events: consuming one input digit and producing one output digit. CFs are add–divide structures. Thus, consuming an input digit amounts to an add–divide operation on the argument of the function that we want to compute. Producing an output digit amounts to an add–divide operation on the output of the function that we want to compute. The internal state represents the function that we want to compute. As a consequence, the transformation of the internal state can be described mathematically with the following transformations:

- To *consume* an input quotient x_i apply

$$T'(x) = T\left(x_i + \frac{1}{x}\right).$$

- To *produce* an output quotient o_i apply

$$T''(x) = \frac{1}{T(x) - o_i}.$$

We will use T' and T'' to derive the iteration equations below. $T(x)$ stands for the function that we want to compute—represented by the internal state registers. In the bilinear case $T(x) = (ax + b)/(cx + d)$ with state registers a, b, c, d. The number of coefficients and form of $T(x)$ stay constant across all iterations, thus leading to very efficient hardware structures. Why does the number of coefficients stay constant? The algorithm uses the fact that the homographic function is invariant over the basic CF transformations $T'(x)$ and $T''(x)$. In fact, there are also rational functions of higher degree that satisfy this requirement. This means that we can build arithmetic units for a larger family of functions. In this chapter we focus on rational functions

In general, the algorithm can independently consume an input quotient and/or produce an output quotient at each iteration. However, ensuring that quotients are consumed and produced optimally requires the computation of a large error term, which increases the overall computation time of the algebraic algorithm by an order of magnitude [188].

In order to avoid computing the error term in each iteration to determine if the algorithm should consume or produce a digit, Vuillemin [188] shows that in most common cases we can consume one input and produces one output at each iteration, using the *positional algebraic algorithm*. Consuming and producing a digit at each iteration makes the computation more regular and eliminates the need to compute the error term at each iteration. All arithmetic units discussed in this chapter use the positional algebraic algorithm.

The following section presents three examples of rational functions, their iteration equations, and corresponding output selection functions. These iteration equations can then be combined with the MFT digits, resulting in the design of regular and efficient hardware arithmetic units for computing the rational functions. The following subsections show the derivation of the iteration equations from Figure 12.2.

12.5.1 Linear Fractional Transformation

Linear fractional transformations are also called homographic, or bilinear functions: $T_1(x) = (ax + b)/(cx + d)$. Given an input CF digit x_i and the current state a, b, c, and d, the algorithm chooses[1] an output digit at each iteration, $o_i \sim (ax_i + b)/(cx_i + d)$. In fact, it suffices to choose the next output digit o_i "close" to the real remainder $T(x) = (ax_i + b)/(cx_i + d)$ based on the current state a,b,c, and d. In the original algorithm with integer CF digits, choosing o_i "close" to the real remainder becomes a rounding operation.

Now let us derive the iteration equations for the bilinear transformation. The variable x consists of digits $[x_0; x_1, x_2, \ldots]$. The four coefficients determine the initial values of the four state registers a, b, c, d. The iteration equations for consuming one input digit x_i and producing one output digit o_i follow from applying $T'(x)$ and $T''(x)$ to the bilinear transform. $a_{i+1}, b_{i+1}, c_{i+1}, d_{i+1}$ denote the next state as a function of the previous state. The digit x_i is the current input digit, and $o_i \sim (a_i x_i + b_i)/(c_i x_i + d_i)$ is the chosen output digit. Thus the next state is given by

$$T_{i+1}(x) = \frac{a_{i+1}x + b_{i+1}}{c_{i+1}x + d_{i+1}} = \frac{1}{\dfrac{a_i(x_i + 1/x) + b_i}{c_i(x_i + 1/x) + d_i} - o_i}. \qquad (12.21)$$

After simplifying equation (12.21) to a bilinear form in x, the state iteration equations are obtained as the new coefficients:

$$\begin{aligned}
a_{i+1} &= c_i x_i + d_i, & b_{i+1} &= c_i, \\
c_{i+1} &= a_i x_i + b_i - o_i(c_i x_i + d_i), & d_{i+1} &= a_i - o_i c_i.
\end{aligned} \qquad (12.22)$$

The output digit is chosen in order to force c to zero. In the bilinear case, the state can be represented by the matrix

$$\underline{A} = \begin{pmatrix} a & b \\ c & d \end{pmatrix}.$$

The iteration equations above have the property that $|\underline{A}| = $ constant [188]. As a nontrivial consequence, for increasing i, c_i converges to zero, b_i converges to zero, d_i converges to one, and a_i converges to $|\underline{A}|$.

---

[1] "Choose" refers to the fact that the algorithm can choose any output digit. The iteration equations adapt the state according to the chosen output quotient.

12.5.2   Quadratic Transformations

In the quadratic case the algorithm computes the transformation $T_2(x) = ax^2 + (bx + c)/(dx^2 + ex + f)$, with x as the current input digit and o as the current output digit (indices i are omitted for simplicity). The algorithm first chooses $o \sim (ax^2 + bx + c)/(dx^2 + ex + f)$, and afterwards updates the state registers as follows:

$$
\begin{aligned}
a_{i+1} &= dx^2 + ex + f, & d_{i+1} &= ax^2 + bx + c - oa_{i+1}, \\
b_{i+1} &= 2dx + e, & e_{i+1} &= b + 2ax - ob_{i+1}, & (12.23) \\
c_{i+1} &= d, & f_{i+1} &= a - oc_{i+1}.
\end{aligned}
$$

In the quadratic case with two input variables x, y, the algorithm computes the transformation $T_3(x, y) = (axy + bx + cy + d)/(exy + fx + gy + h)$, where x, y are inputs to the following iteration equations for the state registers. For input digits x, y, and corresponding output digit $o \sim (axy + bx + cy + d)/(exy + fx + gy + h)$ the iteration equations are:

$$
\begin{aligned}
a_{i+1} &= exy + fx + gy + h, & e_{i+1} &= axy + bx + cy + d_o a_{i+1}, \\
b_{i+1} &= ex + g, & f_{i+1} &= ax + c - ob_{i+1}, \\
c_{i+1} &= ey + f, & g_{i+1} &= ay + b - oc_{i+1}, & . \; (12.24) \\
d_{i+1} &= e, & h_{i+1} &= a - od_{i+1}
\end{aligned}
$$

Quadratic units have more state variables than the bilinear unit. In addition, the iterations per variable require more operations. However, due to the available parallelism in the equations, the minimal latency per iteration does not increase significantly.

12.6   A SHIFT-AND-ADD-BASED RATIONAL-ARITHMETIC UNIT

Rational-arithmetic units are candidate extensions for FP division units. The following implementation focuses on the mantissa part of the FP divider and shows the rational-arithmetic unit for FP rational numbers. This section describes the implementation of rational-arithmetic units based on combining the iteration equations for the algebraic algorithms from above with the MFT.

The signed-digit binary M-log fraction (Corollary 3) combined with the positional algebraic algorithm results in the implementation specified below. Figure 12.4 shows the structure of the proposed arithmetic unit. We use the MFT to convert a binary number to the M-log fraction. The M-log fraction is fed into the positional algorithm. Finally, the inverse MFT converts the M-log fraction back to a binary number. More specifically, the input digit x_i and the output digit o_i are chosen according to the MFT. Rewriting the

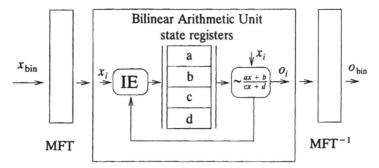

Figure 12.4 The state machine for the iteration equations (IE) of a bilinear arithmetic unit using the positional algorithm. The input digits enter the algorithm in the form of MFT digits. The algorithm selects the output digit o_i to fit the MFT digit value closest to the current state $(ax + b)/(cx + d)$.

iteration equations with the particular x_i and o_i leads to rational-arithmetic units without any overhead for the MFT and inverse MFT.

Next let us take a look at a detailed implementation of a bilinear arithmetic unit.

12.6.1 Implementing the Bilinear Function $(ax + b)/(cx + d)$

The bilinear (linear fractional) arithmetic unit (Figure 12.4) computes output $o_{bin} = T(x_{bin}) = (ax_{bin} + b)/(cx_{bin} + d)$. The following steps detail the operations to compute $(ax + b)/(x + d)$ given four binary coefficients a, b, c, d, and a *binary* input x_{bin}, producing a binary output o_{bin}:

1. Load state registers a, b, c, d with coefficient values. The coefficients are used as starting values a_0, b_0, c_0, d_0 for the state registers
2. The input value x_{bin} is converted to a signed-digit representation with digits $t_i \in \{-1, 1\}$.
3. Combine neighboring digits t_i, t_{i-1} to form MFT digits according to the signed-digit MFT: for even digits, $x_{i \text{ even}} = -(t_i + (t_{i-1})/2)$, and for odd digits; $x_{i \text{ odd}} = (2t_i + t_{i-1})$; $t_0 = 0$.
4. For all CF digits x_i:
   (a) Compute the output CF digit $o_i \sim (a_i x_i + b_i)/(c_i x_i + d_i)$. Output digits o_i are restricted by the CF digit form required by the MFT. In fact, all we have to do is choose the proper signed digit s_i: for even digits, $o_{i \text{ even}} = -(s_i + (s_{i-1})/2)$, and for odd digits, $o_{i \text{ odd}} = 2s_i + s_{i-1}$; $s_0 = 0$. Using these identities, we choose $s_i = \text{sign}(f(a, b, c, d, s_{i-1}))$ with $f(x)$ depending on the position i of the digit.

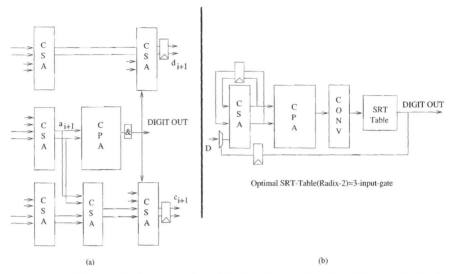

Figure 12.5 (a) A possible implementation of the iteration equations for a bilinear radix-2 unit based on the MFT, and (b) a general SRT-table divider based on results from [126]. The sizes of the boxes indicate the approximate relative VLSI–area relations. Note that $b_{i+1} = c_i$ and is therefore missing in the figure.

(b) Update state variables with the iteration equations (IE) from equations (12.22):

$$a_{i+1} = c_i x_i + d_i, \qquad\qquad b_{i+1} = c_i,$$
$$c_{i+1} = a_i x_i + b_i - o_i(c_i x_i + d_i), \quad d_{i+1} = a_i - o_i c_i. \qquad (12.25)$$

5. Convert signed digits s_i to the actual output value $o_{\text{bin}} = s_1 s_2 s_3 \dots s_n = (a x_{\text{bin}} + b)/(c x_{\text{bin}} + d)$.

In the actual implementation the conversion between signed digits and MFT digits can be absorbed into the iteration equations. To get a sense of the complexity of designing a rational-arithmetic unit, Figure 12.5 shows the microarchitecture of an iterative rational-arithmetic unit. Carry-save adders (CSA) and carry-propagate adders (CPA) are the building blocks of our design. For detailed explanation of adder technology refer to standard textbooks such as [195] or more advanced texts on computer arithmetic [192, 71, 87, 131]. CSA units mostly contribute to the area of a circuit and have very short delays: latency $O(1)$. CPAs have significant delays due to the full propagation of the carry signal with latencies between $O(\log N)$ and $O(N)$ depending on the microarchitecture (N is the number of bits).

Figure 12.5 shows that the rational arithmetic unit for $T(x) = (ax + b)/(cx + d)$ has a delay, or cycle time, of $O(\text{CPA delay} + \epsilon)$, just like a regular divide unit. The additional functionality is bought with additional area for CSAs for a and d. Similar structures for quadratic rational functions follow from iteration equations (12.23) and (12.24).

12.7 VLSI IMPLEMENTATION OF RATIONAL ARITHMETIC UNITS

The algebraic algorithm enables the computation of rational functions such as $T(x) = (ax + b)/(cx + d)$ *and* $T(x) = (ax^2 + bx + c)/(dx^2 + ex + f)$, but also functions of multiple variables such as $T(x, y) = (axy + bx + cy + d)/(exy + fx + gy + h)$. The microarchitecture of these arithmetic units can be constructed from the iteration equations (12.22), (12.23) and (12.24).

In this section we implement division, linear, and quadratic rational-arithmetic units at the RTL level using Verilog. The purpose is to get an understanding of the area–time tradeoff between the different degrees of the polynomials of rational functions. More specifically, Synopsys RTL Analyzer [176] is used to obtain timing and area estimates for the rational-arithmetic units.

Figure 12.6 shows the VLSI area and latency results for MFT-based division, linear, and quadratic fractional transformations. The arithmetic

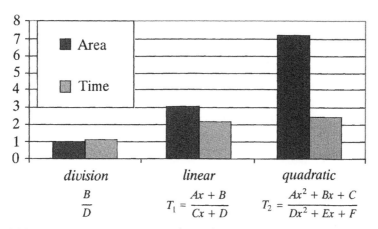

Figure 12.6 The tradeoff of area and time (latency) for shift-and-add-based (class 1) rational-arithmetic units implemented in Verilog and synthesized with a commercial synthesis tool. The results are shown relative to division. B/D requires about 1 unit of area and 1 unit of time.

units are implemented in Verilog and synthesized with Synopsys Design Compiler [177]. With increasing degree N of the polynomials, the area grows with at least $O(N^2)$, making implementations of higher-degree polynomials less attractive. Given enough area, the latency growth of the proposed rational-arithmetic units is less than $O(N)$.

All the arithmetic units above use radix-2 digits, and thus, for results with X bits of precision, X iterations are required. In order to speed up computation, we investigate higher-radix rational arithmetic algorithms next.

12.8 HIGHER-RADIX RATIONAL ARITHMETIC

For conventional iterative division units, increasing the radix reduces the number of iterations per result. This section considers using an arbitrary radix r. The radix-r algorithms use redundant digit sets such as $s_i = \{-(r-1), \dots, r-1\}$.

In general, high $-$ radix algorithms (e.g., for division) reduce the number of iterations at the cost of additional area and, possibly, a longer delay per iteration. As a consequence, the current state of the art in SRT division does not scale well to efficient dividers much beyond radix 8. The MFT enables us to design efficient higher-radix algorithms with an algebraic formulation of the selection functions, as shown for radix 2 in the previous sections.

The M-log fraction for the desired radix, shown below, leads to the design of the iterative algorithm for radix-r numbers (rrn). Let us compute the linear fractional transformation $y = (ax + b)/(cx + d)$ with $x_{\mathrm{rrn}} = t_1 t_2 t_3 \dots = [x_1, x_2, x_3, \dots]$ and $y_{\mathrm{rrn}} = s_1 s_2 s_3 \dots = [y_1, y_2, y_3, \dots]$. Here t_i, s_i are radix-r digits, and x_i, y_i are the equivalent CF digits:

$$y_{\mathrm{rrn}} = s_1 r^{-1} + s_2 r^{-2} + s_3 r^{-3} + s_4 r^{-4} + \cdots$$

$$= [0; y_1, y_2, y_3, \dots], \tag{12.26}$$

$$y_1 = \frac{r}{s_1}, \qquad p_1 = s_1^{-1}, \qquad \overline{p_1} \triangleq \frac{1}{p_1} = s_1, \tag{12.27}$$

$$y_i = (-1)^{i-1} \left(p_i + r^{-1} \overline{p_{i-1}} \right) q_i \tag{12.28}$$

with temporary variables

$$p_i = \overline{p_{i-1}} \frac{s_{i-2}}{s_{i-1}}, \qquad \overline{p_i} \triangleq \frac{1}{p_i} = p_{i-1} \frac{s_{i-1}}{s_{i-2}}, \tag{12.29}$$

$$q_i = \begin{cases} r, & i \text{ odd}, \\ 1, & i \text{ even}. \end{cases} \tag{12.30}$$

The next digit selection function for radix-r arithmetic is similar to the selection function in the radix-2 case:

$$y_i \sim \frac{a_i x_i + b_i}{c_i x_i + d_i}. \tag{12.31}$$

Equations (12.28) and (12.31) lead to the next output digit s_i (radix r) as a function

$$s_i = f(a_i, b_i, c_i, d_i, y_i). \tag{12.32}$$

The above equations are valid for all bilinear units. A special case of the bilinear unit is division. High-radix division is important for decreasing the number of iterations for the division operation. Below we show the next-digit selection function for high-radix division.

Figure 12.7 shows the microarchitecture of the above algorithm simplified to radix-r division. Tables T1 and T2 use the most significant bits of X and Y

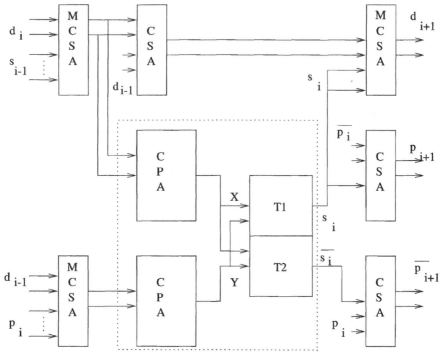

Figure 12.7 A radix-r base implementation of the proposed division unit. $\overline{s_i} \triangleq 1/(s_i)$, $\overline{p_i} \triangleq 1/(p_i)$; MCSA denotes ($\log r$)-level CSA structures. Consequently, the variables d, p, and $\bar{p}$ hold full-precision values. T1, T2 are small ($\log r$)-by-($\log r$) tables. However, as in the case of radix 2, a redundant digit representation might enable us to reduce the complexity of choosing the next digit s_i to a few gates. The broken line encapsules the area that could be simplified.

to choose the next output digit $s_i \sim X/Y$. In general, increasing the radix r increases the number of levels of CSAs and increases the required precision in tables T1 and T2.

Formally, the next digit selection function from equation (12.23) becomes

$$s_i \sim \frac{X}{Y} = \begin{cases} \dfrac{d_i s_{i-1} r}{-p_i d_{i-1} r - d_i}, & i \text{ even,} \\ \dfrac{d_i s_{i-1} r}{p_i d_{i-1} d_i}, & i \text{ odd,} \end{cases} \qquad (12.33)$$

with p_i computed by equation (12.29).

In summary, arbitrary radix-r-rational arithmetic units quickly increase in complexity. Even in the simplest case (division), retiring higher-radix digits requires substantial computational effort as shown in Figure 12.7. The approach presented in this section can be used to derive high-radix rational-arithmetic units for bilinear functions and quadratic rational functions, leading to high-speed implementations of the rational-arithmetic units introduced in this chapter.

12.9 RELATED WORK

Early investigations found a very high potential [22, 145, 146] (very optimistic [161]) for CF arithmetic. Vuillemin [188] and Kornerup and Matula [88] formalize Gosper's ideas and investigate software and hardware implementations. Additional CF algorithms such as sorting CFs are summarized in [54].

The conventional way of computing rational functions is based on MAs and a final division [86]. The advantage of the MFT method is that the most significant digit is produced immediately (with the delay of one iteration), given the first input digit. Figure 12.8 shows a direct comparison of the two options. The overall delays of the operations are similar, but depend on the particular implementation. An advantage of the MFT-based design is a *fast first digit out*, that is, the first result digit is produced immediately after the first input digit is consumed. In addition, a single iteration step can be used in a loop to compute an entire function that would require multipliers, adders, and a divider.

There are many shift-and-add-based algorithms approximating elementary functions. One of the most popular is CORDIC [187, 191]. CORDIC algorithms were formally introduced by Volder in [187] and unified to compute elementary functions by Walther in [191]. CORDIC functional units compute up to two elementary functions at the same time. Given three arguments x, y, z, minor modifications to the CORDIC architecture compute function

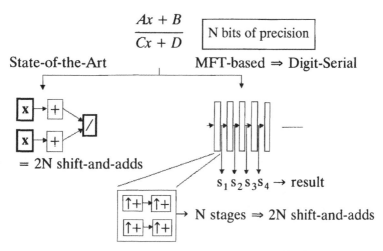

Figure 12.8 A conceptual comparison of the structures of computation for class 1 MFT-based arithmetic units computing a bilinear function, and the conventional approach of computing two MAs followed by a final division. A box with an arrow and a plus stands for a shift-and-add-step. Outputs s_i are the digits of the result in most-significant-digit first order.

pairs such as:

$$x \cos z - y \sin z, \, y \cos z - x \sin z,$$
$$\{x, y - xz\},$$
$$\{x \cosh z - y \sinh z, \, y \cosh z - x \sinh z\},$$
$$\left\{ \sqrt{x^2 + y^2}, \, z - \tan^{-1}(y/x) \right\},$$
$$\{x, z - (y/x)\},$$
$$\left\{ \sqrt{x^2 - y^2}, \, z - \tanh^{-1}(y/x) \right\}.$$

The fundamental mathematical principles behind CORDIC algorithms can be found in their scalar form in the work of T. C. Chen [34] as pointed out by Ahmed in [1]. Ahmed showed that if Chen's convergence computation technique is applied, instead of real numbers (as assumed by Chen), to complex numbers, one obtains the class of CORDIC algorithms. The real power of CORDICs lies in the ability to compute two functions simultaneously, where a conventional functional unit only computes one scalar function.

Although the set of functions that can be computed appears to be limited, CORDICs are very popular, especially in signal processing, due to their simplicity of implementation in hardware [109].

Ercegovac [43, 44] generalizes digit-recurrence algorithms such as SRT division to matrices and vectors, creating the *E method*. Ercegovac uses linear algebra to derive linear matrix equations that represent polynomial and rational expressions. The E method is a shift-and-add method solving the resulting linear system that represents the approximation. The required computation is done in linear time, that is, it produces one output digit per iteration, like the MFT method proposed in this work. The E method is a more general method capable of computing various expressions such as polynomial and rational approximations, given a specific set of restrictions. In the case of rational approximation, however, the E method has very tight restrictions on the values of the coefficients.

Low-latency, parallel arithmetic algorithms use substantially more VLSI area than the previous methods to obtain an approximation. Examples are table-based methods such as bipartite tables [39, 152] or multiplier–CSA-tree-based methods [154, 171].

12.10   CONCLUSIONS

We provide an effective algorithm to convert between binary numbers and CFs. The resulting transformation is called the M log fraction transformation (MFT). The MFT provides a means to determine the optimal representation of binary numbers in the CF space, and allows for error control.

The MFT enables the first practical implementation of CF algorithms for computer systems. It bridges the gap between CFs and the binary number representation, enabling the design of a new class of efficient-rational arithmetic units.

From a distance the M-log fraction and MFT look like a redundant representation of binary numbers utilizing the integer distances between 1's, similar to 0-runlength encoding (counting the 0's between the 1's of a binary number). Runlength encoding is a very fast way of converting between CFs and binary numbers, reducing the conversion overhead by orders of magnitude. This fast conversion allows us to exploit the symmetries in the CF space while computing and storing binary numbers.

12.11   HISTORICAL NOTES ON CONTINUED FRACTIONS IN ARITHMETIC

The fundamental ideas behind CFs can be traced back to Euclid's algorithm for finding the greatest common divider (GCD) of two integers. Cataldi [31] was the first to mention CFs in 1613. The theory of them has its roots in the works of Euler [46], Lagrange [91], Legendre, Lambert, and many other mathematicians over the centuries.

In the 20th century Khinchin [75] studied regular CFs as a number representation, and gave the distribution of values of partial quotients found by Kuzmin in 1928. Wall [189] summarizes the analytic theory of CFs with an emphasis on convergence and function theory. The best discussion of the theory of CFs is given by Perron [135].

Homographic function evaluation with simple CFs, as discussed in this chapter, was first studied by Hurwitz ([70], 1896). Hall [65] follows up on Hurwitz's work, and Raney [142] shows a simplified algorithm based on linear algebra and finite-state machines.

Knuth [84] considers CFs for semi-numerical algorithms. Gosper et al. [62] note how to evaluate homographic functions to CFs, given CF inputs. Vuillemin [188] formalizes and extends Gosper's work to the algebraic and positional algebraic algorithms. Kornerup and Matula [88] investigate a hardware implementation of Gosper's algorithm. A more theoretical use of CFs and the 2D quadratic rational form is suggested by Potts [137] who extends the notion of representing exact real numbers with expression trees of tensors (rational forms).

BIBLIOGRAPHY

[1] H. M. Ahmed, *Signal Processing Algorithms and Architectures*, PhD thesis, Electrical Engineering Dept., Stanford, June 1982.

[2] H. Al-Twaijry and M. J. Flynn, "Multipliers and datapaths," Tech. Rep. CSL-TR94-654, Computer Systems Lab., Stanford Univ., Dec. 1994.

[3] R. Alverson and D. Matula, Private communication between Tera Computer, Seattle, WA and Dept. of Computer Science and Engineering, Southern Methodist Univ., Dallas, TX, 1991.

[4] N. Anderson, "Minimum relative error approximations for $1/t$," *Numerische Mathematik*, pp. 117–124, 1988.

[5] S. F. Anderson, J. G. Earle, R. E. Goldschmidt, and D. M. Powers, "The IBM System/360 model 91: Floating-point execution unit," *IBM Journal of Research and Development*, pp. 34–53, Jan. 1967.

[6] T. Asprey et al., "Performance features of the PA7100 microprocessor," *IEEE Micro*, pp. 22–35, June 1993.

[7] D. Atkins, "Higher-radix division using estimates of the divisor and partial remainders," in *International Conference on Computer Design*, pp. 221–226, 1988.

[8] D. E. Atkins, "Higher-radix division using estimates of the divisor and partial remainders," *IEEE Transactions on Computers*, pp. 925–934, Oct. 1968.

[9] A. Avizienis, "Signed digit number representation for fast parallel arithmetic," *ITE Transactions on Electronic Computers*, vol. EC-10, pp. 340–346, Sept. 1961.

[10] A. Avizienis, *A Study of Redundant Number Representations for Parallel Digital Computers*, PhD thesis, Univ. of Illinois. 1960.

[11] Philip Morrison and Emily Morrison, editors, *Charles Babbage and his Calculating Engines: Selected Writings*, Dover, 1961.

[12] H. B. Bakoglu, *Circuits, Interconnections, and Packaging for VLSI*, Prentice Hall, 1990.

[13] P. Bannon et al., "Internal architecture of alpha 21164 microprocessor," in *Digest of Papers COMPCON 95*, Mar. 1995, pp. 79–87.

[14] A. Barna and D. Porat, *Integrated Circuits in Digital Electronics*, Wiley, 1973.

[15] O. J. Bedrij, "Carry-select adder," *IRE Transactions on Electronic Computers*, vol. EC-11, pp. 340–346,1962.

[16]   B. J. Benschneider, W. J. Bowhill, E. M. Cooper, M. N. Gavrielov, P. E. Gronowski, V. K. Maheshwari, V. Peng, J. D. Pickholtz, and S. Samudrala, "A pipelined 50-Mhz CMOS 64-bit floating-point arithmetic processor," *IEEE Transactions on Computers*, vol. 24, no. 5, pp. 1317–1323, Oct. 1989.

[17]   G. Bewick, *Fast Multiplication: Algorithms and Implementations*, PhD thesis, Stanford Univ., Feb. 1994.

[18]   G. Bewick, P. Song, G. DeMicheli, and M. Flynn, "Approaching a nanosecond: A 32-bit adder," in *Proceedings of the International Conference on Computer Design*, 1988, pp. 221–224.

[19]   G. Bewick, Private communication with Computer Systems Lab., Stanford Univ., 1990.

[20]   G. Bewick and M. J. Flynn, "Binary multiplication using partially redundant multiples,"Tech. Rep. CSL-TR-92-528, Computer Systems Lab, Stanford Univ., June 1992.

[21]   A. D. Booth, "A signed binary multiplication technique," *Quarterly Journal of Mechanics and Applied Mathematics*, pp. 236–240, June 1951.

[22]   A. Bracha-Barack, "Application of continued fractions for fast evaluation of certain functions on a digital computer," *IEEE Transactions on Computers*, March 1974.

[23]   E. L. Braun, *Digital Computer*, Academic Press, 1963.

[24]   R. Brent and H. Kung. "A regular layout for parallel adders," *IEEE Transactions on Computers*, vol. C-31, pp. 260–264, 1982.

[25]   W. Briggs and D. Matula, "Method and apparatus for performing the square root function using a rectangular aspect ratio multiplier," United States Patent No. 5,060,182, Oct. 1991.

[26]   W. Briggs and D. Matula, "Method and apparatus for performing division using a rectangular aspect ratio multiplier," United States Patent No. 5,046,038, Sept. 1991.

[27]   T. Brightman, Presentation at 9th Symposium on Computer Arithmetic, 1989.

[28]   M. Birman, A. Samuels, G. Chu, T. Chuk, L. Hu, J. McLeod, and J. Barns, "Developing the WTL3170/3171 SPARC floating-point coprocessor," *IEEE Micro*, pp. 55–64, Feb. 1990.

[29]   N. Burgess and T. Williams, "Choices of operand truncation in the SR division algorithm," *IEEE Transactions on Computers*, pp. 933–937, July 1995.

[30]   A. W. Burks, H. H. Goldstine, and J. Von Neumann, "Preliminary discussion of the logical design of an electronic computing instrument," Institute for Advanced Study Report, Princeton, reproduced in E. Schwarzlander, Ed., *Computer Design Development: Principal Papers*, Hayden Book, Rochelle Park, NJ, pp. 221–259, 1946.

[31]   P. A. Cataldi, *Trattato del modo brevissimo di trovare la radice quadra delli numeri, et regole di approssimarsi di continuo al vero nelle radici dei numeri non quadrati, con le cause et inventioni loro*, Bologna, Italy, 1613; see [135].

[32]   P. K. Chan, M. D. F. Schlag, C. D. Thomborson, and V. G. Oklobdzija, "Delay optimization of carry-skip adders and block carry-lookahead adders using multidimensional dynamic programming," *IEEE Transactions on Computers*, vol. 41, no. 8, pp. 920–930, 1992.

[33] T. Chappell, B. Chappell, S. Schuster, J. Allan, S. Klepner, R. Joshi, and R. Franch, "A 2-ns cycle, 3.8-ns access 512-kb CMOS ECL SRAM with a fully pipelined architecture," *IEEE Journal of Solid-State Circuits*, Nov. 1991.

[34] T.C. Chen, "Automatic computation of exponentials, logarithms, ratios and square roots," *IBM Journal of Research and Development*, July 1972.

[35] L. Cotten. "Maximum rate pipelined systems," in *Proceedings AFIPS Spring Joint Computer Conference*, pp. 581–586, 1969.

[36] G. Cybenko et al., "Supercomputer performance evaluation and the Perfect Benchmarks," in *International Conference on Supercomputing*, pp. 254–266, June 1990.

[37] L. Dadda, "Some schemes for parallel multipliers," *Alta Frequenza*, pp. 349–356, Mar. 1965.

[38] M. Darley et al., "The TMS390C602A floating-point coprocessor for SPARC systems," *IEEE Micro*, pp. 36–47, June 1990.

[39] D. Das Sarma and D. W. Matula, "Faithful bipartite ROM reciprocal tables," in *12th IEEE Symposium on Computer Arithmetic*, pp. 17–28, July 1995.

[40] B. Ekroot, *Optimization of Pipelined Processors by Insertion of Combinational Logic Delay*, PhD thesis, Dept. of Electrical Engineering, Stanford Univ., Sept. 1987.

[41] M. Ercegovac and T. Lang, "Fast radix-2 division with quotient digit prediction," *Journal of VLSI Signal Processing*, pp. 169–180, Nov. 1989.

[42] M. D. Ercegovac and T. Lang, *Division and Square Root: Digit-Recurrence Algorithms and Implementations*, Kluwer Academic, 1994.

[43] M. D. Ercegovac, *A General Method for Evaluation of Functions and Computation in a Digital Computer*, PhD thesis, Dept. of Computer Science, Univ. of Illinois, Urbana-Champaign, 1975.

[44] M.D. Ercegovac, "A general hardware-oriented method for evaluation of functions and computations in a digital omputer, *IEEE Transactions on Computers*, vol. C-26, no. 7, July 1977.

[45] M. Ercegovac et al., "Very high radix division with selection by rounding and prescaling," in *11th IEEE Symposium on Computer Arithmetic*, pp. 112–119, July 1993.

[46] L. Euler, *Introductio in analysin infinitorum I*, 1748, translated into English, Springer-Verlag, New York, 1980.

[47] J. Fadavi-Ardekani, "$M \times n$ booth encoded multiplier generator using optimized Wallace trees," *IEEE Transactions on Very Large Scale Integration (VLSI) Systems*, pp. 120–125, June 1993.

[48] D. Fan, C. Gray, W. Farlow, T. Hughes, W. Liu, and R. Cavin. "A CMOS parallel adder using wave pipelining," *MIT Advanced Research in VLSI and Parallel Systems*, pp. 147–164, Mar. 1992.

[49] J. Fandrianto, "Algorithm for high speed shared radix 4 division and radix 4 square-root," in *8th IEEE Symposium on Computer Arithmetic*, pp. 73–79, 1987.

[50] J. Fandrianto, "Algorithm for high speed shared radix 8 division and radix 8 square root," in *9th IEEE Symposium on Computer Arithmetic*, pp. 68–75, Sept. 1989.

[51] M. P. Farmwald, *On the Design of High Performance Digital Arithmetic Units*, PhD thesis, Stanford Univ., Aug. 1981.

[52] M. P. Farmwald, "High bandwidth evaluation of elementary functions," in *5th Symposium on Computer Arithmetic*, pp. 139–142, 1981.

[53] C. T. Fike, "Starting approximations for square root calculation on IBM System/360," *Communications of ACM*, pp. 297–299, Apr. 1966.

[54] P. Flajolet and B. Vallee, "Continued fraction algorithms, functional operators, and structure constants," *Theoretical Computer Science*, vol. 194, pp. 1–34, 1998.

[55] M. Flynn et al., "Sub-nanosecond arithmetic," Tech. Rep. CSL-TR-90-428, Computer Systems Lab., Stanford Univ., May 1990.

[56] M. Flynn, "On division by functional iteration," *IEEE Transactions on Computers*, pp. 702–706, Aug. 1970.

[57] M. J. Flynn, *Computer Architecture, Pipelined and Parallel Processor Design*, Jones and Bartlett, 1995.

[58] S. Fu, "Architecture evaluator's work bench and its application to microprocessor floating point units," Tech. Rep. CSL-TR-95-668, Computer Systems Lab., Stanford Univ., June 1995.

[59] D. Ghosh and S. K. Nandy, "A 400 Mhz wave-pipelined 8×8-bit multiplier in CMOS technology," in *Proceedings of the International Conference on Computer Design*, pp. 189–201, 1993. A slightly more detailed presentation is given in D. Ghosh and S. K. Nandy, "Design and realization of high-performance wave-pipelined 8×8 b multiplier in CMOS technology," *IEEE Transactions on Very Large Scale Integration (VLSI) Systems*, pp. 36–48, Mar. 1995.

[60] L. Glasser and D. Dobberpuhl, *The Design and Analysis of VLSI Circuits*, Addison-Wesley, 1985.

[61] R. E. Goldschmidt, *Applications of Division by Convergence*, PhD thesis, Massachusetts Institute of Technology, 1964.

[62] R. W. Gosper, R. Schroeppel, and M. Beeler, "HAKMEM, continued fraction arithmetic," MIT AI Memo 239, Feb. 1972.

[63] C. T. Gray, W. Liu, and R. K. Cavin III. "Timing constraints for wave pipelined systems," Tech. Rep. NCSU-VLSI-92-06, Dept. of Electrical Engineering, North Carolina State Univ., Dec. 1992.

[64] D. Greenley et al., "UltraSPARC: The next generation superscalar 64-bit SPARC," in *Digest of Papers COMPCON 95*, pp.442–451, Mar.1995.

[65] M. Hall, "On the sum and product of continued fractions," *Annals of Mathmathematics*, vol. 48, pp. 966–993, 1947.

[66] R. W. Hamming, *Numerical Methods for Scientists and Engineers*, McGraw-Hill, 1973.

[67] J. L. Hennessy and D. A. Patterson, *Computer Architecture, a Quantitative Approach*, Morgan-Kaufmann, 1990.

[68] J. H. Huang et al., "A robust physical and predictive model for deep-submicrometer MOS circuit simulation," Tech. Rep. M93/75, UCB/ERL, Mar. 1993.

[69] J. C. Huck and M. J. Flynn, *Analyzing Computer Architectures*, IEEE Computer Society Press, 1989.

[70] A. Hurwitz, "Über die Kettenbrüche, deren Teilnenner arithmetische Reihen bilden," *Vierteljahrsschrift der Naturforschunge Gesellschaft*, Zürich, Jahrgang 41, 1896.

[71] K. Hwang, *Computer Arithmetic: Principles, Architecture and Design*, Wiley, 1979.

[72] The Institute of Electrical and Electronics Engineers, Inc., *ANSI/IEEE Std 754-1985: IEEE Standard for Binary Floating-Point Arithmetic*, Aug. 1985.

[73] W.B. Jones and W.J. Thron, *Continued Fractions: Analytic Theory and Applications*, Encyclopedia of Mathematics and its Applications, Vol. 11, Addison-Wesley, Reading, MA, 1980.

[74] D. Joy and M. Ciesielski, "Placement for clock period minimization with multiple wave propagation," in *Proceedings of the 28th Design Automation Conference*, San Francisco, pp. 640–643, 1991.

[75] A. Khinchin, *Continued Fractions*, 1935, translated from Russian, Univ. of Chicago Press, 1964.

[76] A.N. Khovanskii, *The Application of Continued Fractions and Their Generalizations to Problems in Approximation Theory*, 1956; translated by Peter Wynn, P. Noordhoff, Groningen, 1963.

[77] T. Kilburn, D. B. G. Edwards, and D. Aspinall, "Parallel addition in a digital computer—a new fast carry circuit," *Proceedings of the IEE*, vol. 106B, pp. 460–464, 1959.

[78] T. Kim, W. Burleson, and M. Ciesielski, Logic restructuring for wave-pipelined circuits," in *International Workshop on Logic Synthesis*, 1993.

[79] H. Kissigami, K. Nowka, and M. Flynn, "Delay balancing of wave pipelined multiplier counter trees using pass transistor multiplexers," Tech. Rep. CSL-TR-96-693, Computer Systems Lab., Dept. of Electrical Engineering, Stanford Univ., Jan. 1996.

[80] E. F. Klass, *Wave Pipelining: Theoretical and Practical Issues in CMOS*, PhD thesis, Dept. of Electrical Engineering, Delft Univ. of Technology, Sept. 1994.

[81] F. Klass and M. Flynn, "Comparative studies of pipelined circuits," Tech. Rep. CSL-TR-93-579, Computer Systems Lab., Dept. of Electrical Engineering, Stanford Univ., July 1993.

[82] F. Klass and J. Mulder, "CMOS implementation of wave pipelining," Tech. Rep. 1-68340-44(1990)02, Dept. of Electrical Engineering, Delft Univ. of Technology, December 1990.

[83] J. Klir, "A note on Svoboda's algorithm for division," in *9th Symposium on Information Processing Machines*, 1963, pp. 35–39.

[84] D. E. Knuth, *The Art of Computer Programming, Vol. 2, Seminumerical Algorithms*, Addison-Wesley, Reading, MA, 1969.

[85] L. Kohn and S. W. Fu, "A 1,000,000 transistor microprocessor," in *IEEE International Solid-State Circuits Conference*, 1989, pp. 54–55.

[86] I. Koren and O. Zinaty, "Evaluating elementary functions in a numerical coprocessor based on rational approximations," *IEEE Transactions on Computers*, vol. 39, no. 8, Aug. 1990.

[87] I. Koren, *Computer Arithmetic Algorithms*, Prentice Hall, 1993.

[88] P. Kornerup and D. W. Matula, "An algorithm for redundant binary bit-pipelined rational arithmetic," *IEEE Transactions on Computers*, vol. 39, no. 8, Aug. 1990.

[89] E. Krishnamurthy, "On range-transformation techniques for division," *IEEE Transactions on Computers*, pp. 157–160, Feb. 1970.

[90] R. E. Ladner and M. J. Fischer, "Parallel prefix computation," *Journal of the ACM*, vol. 27, no. 4, pp. 831–838, Oct. 1980.

[91] J. L. Lagrange, *Additions aux éléments d'algebre d'Euler*, 1798.

[92] W. Lam, R. Brayton, and A. Sangiovanni-Vincentelli, "Valid clocking in wavepipelined circuits," in *Proceedings of IEEE Conference on Integrated Circuits and Computer Aided Design*, 1992.

[93] W. Lien and W. Burleson, "Wave-domino logic: Timing analysis and applications," in *Proceedings of TAU92*, 1992.

[94] H. Ling, "High speed binary adder," *IBM Journal of Research and Development*, vol. 25, no. 3, pp. in 156–166, 1981.

[95] L. Lorentzen and H. Waadeland, *Continued Fractions with Applications*, Studies in Computational Mathematics 3, North-Holland, 1982.

[96] P. Y. Lu, A. Jain, J. Kung, and P. H. Ang, "A 32-mflop 32b CMOS floating-point processor," *International Solid State Circuits Conference*, pp. 28–29, 1988.

[97] R. Lyu and D. Matula, "Redundant binary booth recoding," *Proceedings of IEEE Symposium on Computer Arithmetic*, pp. 50–57, 1995.

[98] "LSI logic LCB500K standard-cell library," LSI Corp., Milpitas, CA, 1994.

[99] O. L. MacSorley, "High-speed arithmetic in binary computers," *Proceedings of the IRE*, vol. 49, pp. 67–91, Jan. 1961.

[100] D. M. Mandelbaum, "A systematic method for division with high average bit skipping," *IEEE Transactions on Computers*, pp. 127–130, Jan. 1990.

[101] D. M. Mandelbaum, "Some results on a SRT type division scheme," *IEEE Transactions on Computers*, vol. 42, no. 1, pp. 102–106, Jan. 1993.

[102] D. M. Mandelbaum and S. G. Mandelbaum, "A fast, efficient parallel-acting method of generating functions defined by power series, including logarithm, exponential and sine, cosine," *IEEE Transactions on Parallel and Distributed Systems*, vol. 7, no. 1, pp. 33–45 Jan. 1996.

[103] P. Markstein, "Computation of elementary functions on the IBM RISC System/6000 processor," *IBM Journal of Research and Development*, pp. 111–119, Jan. 1990.

[104] M. Matsui et al., "An 8 ns 1Mb ECL BiCMOS SRAM," in *International Solid State Circuits Conference*, pp. 38–39, Feb. 1989.

[105] D. Matula, "Highly parallel divide and square root algorithms for a new generation floating point processor," presentation at SCAN-89 Symposium on Computer Arithmetic and Self-Validating Numerical Methods, Oct. 1989.

[106] D. Matula, "Design of a highly parallel IEEE standard floating point arithmetic unit," presentation at Symposium on Combinational Optimization on Science and Technology, Apr. 1991.

[107] G. McFarland and M. Flynn, "Limits of scaling MOSFETs," Tech. Rep. CSL-TR-95-662 Revised, Computer Systems Lab., Stanford Univ., Nov. 1995.

[108] O. Mencer, *Rational Arithmetic Units in Computer Systems*, PhD Thesis, Electrical Engineering Dept., Stanford Univ., Feb. 2000.

[109] O. Mencer, L. Semeria, M. Morf, and J. M. Delosme, "Application of reconfigurable CORDIC architectures," *The Journal of VLSI Signal Processing*, Special Issue: VLSI on Custom Computing Technology, Kluwer, Mar. 2000.

[110] B. Murtagh and M. Saunders, "Minos 5.1 user's guide," Tech. Rep. SOL 83-20R, Systems Optimization Lab., Dept. of Operations Research, Stanford Univ., Jan. 1987.

[111] *Microprocessor Report*, MicroDesign Resources, Sunnyvale, CA, 1988–1995.

[112] R. Montoye, E. Hokenek, and S. Runyon, "Design of the IBM RISC System/6000 floating-point execution unit," *IBM Journal of Research and Development*, pp. 59–70, Jan. 1990.

[113] The MOSIS Service, "MOSIS parametric test results," 1993.

[114] J. M. Mulder, N. T. Quach, and M. J. Flynn, "An area model for on-chip memories and its application," *IEEE Journal of Solid State Circuits*, pp. 98–105, Feb. 1991.

[115] K. Nakamura, S. Kuhara, T. Kimura, M. Takada, H. Suzuki, H. Yoshida, and T. Yamazaki, "A 220 MHz pipelined 16 Mb biCMOS SRAM with PLL proportional self-timing generator," in *Proceedings of the 1994 IEEE International Solid-State Circuits Conference*, San Francisco, pp. 258–259, Feb. 1994.

[116] "NAS Parallel Benchmarks," NASA Ames Research Center, Moffett Field, CA, Aug. 1991.

[117] V. Nguyen, W. Liu, C. Gray, and R. Cavin, "A CMOS signed multiplier using wave pipelining," in *Proceedings of IEEE 1993 Custom Integrated Circuits Conference*, 1993.

[118] T. Ngai and M. Irwin, "Regular, area–time efficient carry-lookahead adders," *Proceedings of the 7th Symposium on Computer Arithmetic*, pp. 9–15, 1985.

[119] K. Nowka, *High Performance CMOS VLSI System Design Using Wave Pipelining*, PhD thesis, Dept. of Electrical Engineering, Stanford Univ., 1995.

[120] K. Nowka and M. Flynn, "Environmental limits on the performance of CMOS wave-pipelined circuits," Tech. Rep. CSL-TR-94-600, Stanford Univ., Computer Systems Laboratory, Dept. of Electrical Engineering, January 1994.

[121] K. Nowka and M. Flynn, "Wave pipelining of high performance CMOS static RAM," Tech. Rep. CSL-TR-94-615, Computer Systems Lab., Dept. of Electrical Engineering, Stanford Univ., Jan. 1994.

[122] K. Nowka and M. Flynn, "System design using wave-pipelining: A CMOS VLSI vector unit," in *Proceedings of the 1995 IEEE International Conference on Circuits and Systems*, pp. 2301–2304, 1995.

[123] S. F. Oberman and M. J. Flynn, "Minimizing the complexity of SRT tables," *IEEE Transactions on VLSI Systems*, vol. 6, p. 141, 1998.

[124] S. F. Oberman and M. J. Flynn, "Division algorithms and implementations," *IEEE Transactions on Computers*, vol. 46, p. 833, 1997.

[125] S. F. Oberman and M. J. Flynn, "Design issues in high performance floating point arithmetic units," Tech. Rep. CSL-TR-96-711, Computer Systems Lab., Stanford Univ., Dec. 1996.

[126] S. Oberman, *Design Issues in High Performance Floating Point Arithmetic Units*, PhD thesis, Dept. of Electrical Engineering, Stanford Univ., Nov. 1996.

[127] S. Oberman, "Design issues in division and other floating-point operations," *IEEE Transactions on Computers*, vol. 46, p. 154, 1997.

[128] S. F. Oberman and M. J. Flynn, "Reducing the mean latency of floating point addition," *Theoretical Computer Science*, vol. 196:, p. 201, 1998.

[129] N. Ohkubo et al., "A 4.4 ns CMOS 54*54-b multiplier using pass-transistor multiplexor," *IEEE Journal of Solid-State Circuits*, pp. 251–257, Mar. 1995.

[130] V. G. Oklobdzija, D. Villeger, and S. S. Liu, "A method for speed optimized partial product reduction and generation of fast parallel multipliers using an algorithmic approach," *IEEE Transactions on Computers*, vol. 45, no. 3, pp. 294–306, Mar. 1996.

[131] A. Omondi, *Computer Arithmetic Systems*, Prentice-Hall, 1994.

[132] *DEC Fortran Language Reference Manual*, 1992.

[133] Z. Mou and F. Jutand, "A class of close to optimum adder trees allowing regular and compact layout," in *IEEE International Conference on Computer Design: VLSI in Computer Design*, pp. 251–254, 1990.

[134] Hamid Partovi, "A regenerative push–pull differential logic family," in *IEEE International Solid-State Circuits Conference*, 1994, p. 294.

[135] O. Perron, *Die Lehre von den Kettenbrüchen*, Band I, II , Teubner Verlag, Stuttgart, 1957.

[136] S. D. Pezaris, "A 40-ns 17-bit by 17-bit array multiplier," *IEEE Transactions on Computers*, pp. 442–447, Apr. 1971.

[137] P. J. Potts, *Exact Real Arithmetic Using Möbius transformations*, PhD thesis, Imperial College, London, Mar. 1999.

[138] N. T. Quach and M. J. Flynn, "High-speed addition in CMOS," *IEEE Transactions on Computers*, vol. 41, no. 12, pp. 1612–1615, Dec. 1992.

[139] N. T. Quach and M. J. Flynn, "An improved algorithm for high-speed floating-point addition," Tech. Rep. CSL-TR-90-442, Computer Systems Lab., Stanford Univ., Aug. 1990.

[140] N. Quach and M. Flynn, "Design and implementation of the SNAP floating-point adder," Tech. Rep. CSL-TR-91-501, Computer Systems Lab., Stanford Univ., Dec. 1991.

[141] C. V. Ramamoorthy, J. R. Goodman, and K. H. Kim, "Some properties of iterative square-rooting methods using high-speed multiplication," *IEEE Transactions on Computers*, pp. 837–847, Aug. 1972.

[142] G.N. Raney, "On continued fractions and finite automata, Mathematische Annalen, vol. 206, pp. 265–283, 1973.

[143] R. K. Richards, *Arithmetic Operations in Digital Computers*, Van Nostrand, 1955.

[144] J. E. Robertson, "A new class of digital division methods," *IRE Transactions on Electronic Computers*, pp. 88–92, Sept. 1958.

[145] J. E. Robertson and K. S. Trivedi, "The status of investigations into computer hardware design based on the use of continued fractions," *IEEE Transactions on Computers*, vol. C-22, no. 6, June 1973.

[146] J. E. Robertson and K. S. Trivedi, "On the use of continued fractions for digital computer arithmetic," *IEEE Transactions on Computers*, July 1977.

[147] S. Sahni, "The complexity of design automation problems," in *Proceedings of DAC*, pp. 402–411, June 1980,

[148] M. Santoro, *Design and Clocking of VLSI Multipliers*, PhD thesis, Stanford Univ., 1989.

[149] M. Santoro and M. Horowitz, "SPIM: A pipelined 64 × 64b iterative array multiplier," in *IEEE International Solid State Circuits Conference*, pp. 35–36, Feb. 1988.

[150] M. Santoro, *Design and Clocking of VLSI Multipliers*, PhD thesis, Stanford Univ., 1989.

[151] W. G. Schneeweiss, *Boolean Functions with Engineering Applications and Computer Programs*, Springer-Verlag, 1989.

[152] M. Schulte and J. Stine, "Symmetric bipartite tables for accurate function approximation," Presentation at IEEE Symposium on Computer Arithmetic, 1997.

[153] E. E. Schwartzlander and A. G. Alexpoulos "The sign-logarithm number system," *IEEE Transactions on Computers*, Dec. 1975.

[154] E. M. Schwarz, *High-Radix Algorithms for High-Order Arithmetic Operations*, PhD thesis, Electrical Engineering Dept., Stanford Univ., Jan. 1993.

[155] E. M. Schwarz and M. J. Flynn, "Cost-efficient high-radix division," *Journal of VLSI Signal Processing*, pp. 293–305, Oct. 1991.

[156] E. M. Schwarz and M. J. Flynn, "Parallel high-radix non-restoring division," Unpublished, Oct. 1991.

[157] E. M. Schwarz and M. J. Flynn, "Approximating the sine function with combinational logic," in *26th Asilomar Conference on Signals, Systems, and Computers*, 1992.

[158] E. M. Schwarz and M. J. Flynn, "Direct combinatorial methods for approximating trigonometric functions," Tech. Rep. CSL-TR-92-525, Computer Systems Lab., Stanford Univ., Mar. 1992.

[159] E. M. Schwarz and M. J. Flynn, "Using a floating-point multiplier to sum signed boolean elements," Tech. Rep. CSL-TR-92-540, Computer Systems Lab., Stanford Univ., Aug. 1992.

[160] E. M. Schwarz and M. J. Flynn, "Using a floating-point multiplier's internals for high-radix division and square root," Tech. Rep. CSL-TR-93-554, Computer Systems Lab., Stanford Univ., Jan. 1993.

[161] R. B. Seidensticker, "Continued fractions for high-speed and high-accuracy computer arithmetic," *6th IEEE Symposium on Computer Arithmetic*, pp. 184–193, June 1983.

[162] D. T. Shen and A. Weinberger, "4-2 carry-save adder implementation using send circuits," *IBM Technical Disclosure Bulletin*, vol. 20, no. 9, Feb. 1978.

[163] Semiconductor Industry Association, "The national technology roadmap for semiconductors," 1994.

[164] H. P. Sit, M. R. Nofal, and S. Kimn, "An 80 MFLOPS floating-point engine in the Intel i860 processor," in *IEEE International Conference on Computer Design*, pp. 374–379, 1989.

[165] J. Slansky, "Conditional sum addition logic," *IRE Transactions on Electronic Computers*, vol. EC-9, pp. 226–231, 1960.

[166] M. D. Smith, "Tracing with Pixie," Tech. Rep. CSL-TR-91-497, Computer Systems Lab., Stanford Univ., Nov. 1991.

[167] P. Song and G. De Micheli, "Circuit and architecture tradeoffs for high-speed multiplication," *IEEE Journal of Solid-State Circuits*, pp. 1184–1198, Sept. 1991.

[168] B. Case, "Updated SPEC benchmarks released," *Microprocessor Report*, p. 14, Sept. 1992.

[169] "SPEC benchmark suite release," Standard Performance Evaluation Corp., Warrenton, VA, Feb. 1992.

[170] A. Srivastava and A. Eustace, "ATOM: A system for building customized program analysis tools," in *SIGPLAN '94 Conference on Programming Language Design and Implementation*, pp. 196–205, June 1994.

[171] R. Stefanelli, "A suggestion for a high-speed parallel binary divider," *IEEE Transactions on Computers*, pp. 42–55, Jan. 1972.

[172] W. Stenzel, W. Kubitz, and G. Garcia, "A compact high-speed multiplication scheme," *IEEE Trans. Computers*, vol. C-26, no 10, pp. 948–957, Oct. 1977.

[173] D. W. Sweeney, "Analysis of floating-point addition," *IBM Systems Journal*, vol. 4, pp. 31–42, 1965.

[174] M. Suzuki et al., "A 1.5 ns 32b CMOS ALU in double pass-transistor logic," *IEEE Transactions on Computers*, pp. 1145–1151, Nov. 1993.

[175] A. Svoboda, "An algorithm for division," in *9th Symposium on Information Processing Machines*, pp. 25–34, 1963.

[176] SYNOPSYS Products, *RTL Analyzer*, http://www.synopsys.com/products/

[177] "Synopsys design compiler version v3.2b," Synopsys Corp., Mt. View, CA, 1995.

[178] T. G. Szymanski, "Dogleg channel routing is NP-complete," *IEEE Transactions on CAD/ICAS*, pp. 31–41, 1985.

[179] S. Tachibana, H. Higuchi, K. Takasugi, K. Sasaki, T. Yamanaka, and Y. Nakagome, A 2.6-ns wave-pipelined CMOS SRAM with dual-sensing-latch, in *Proceedings of the 1994 Symposium on VLSI Circuits*, Honolulu, pp. 117–118, June 1994.

[180] N. Takagi, H. Yasuura, and S. Yajima, "High-speed VLSI multiplication algorithm with a redundant binary addition tree," *IEEE Transactions on Computers*, pp. 34–39, Sept. 1985.

[181] K. G. Tan, "The theory and implementation of high-radix division," in *4th IEEE Symposium on Computer Arithmetic*, pp. 154–163, June 1978.

[182] G. S. Taylor, "Radix 16 SRT dividers with overlapped quotient selection stages," in *7th IEEE Symposium on Computer Arithmetic*, pp. 64–71, June 1985.

[183] H. Tran et al., "An 8 ns BiCMOS 1Mb ECL SRAM with a configurable memory array size," in *International Solid State Circuits Conference*, pp. 36–37, Feb. 1989.

[184] Jeffery D. Ullman, *Computational Aspects of VLSI*, Computer Science Press, 1984.

[185] S. Vassiliadis, E. M. Schwarz, and D. J. Hanrahan, "A general proof for overlapped multiple-bit scanning multiplications," *IEEE Transactions on Computers*, pp. 172–183, Feb. 1989.

[186] S. Vassiliadis, E. M. Schwarz, and B. M. Sung, "Hard-wired multipliers with encoded partial products," *IEEE Transactions on Computers*, pp. 1181–1197, Nov. 1991.

[187] J. E. Volder, "The CORDIC trigonometric computing technique," *IRE Transactions on Electronic Computers*, vol. EC-8, no. 3, pp. 330–334, Sept. 1959.

[188] J. E. Vuillemin, "Exact Real Computer Arithmetic with Continued Fractions," *IEEE Transactions on Computers,*, vol. 39, no. 8, Aug. 1990.

[189] H. S. Wall, *Analytic Theory of Continued Fractions*, Chelsea, Bronx, NY., 1948.

[190] C. S. Wallace, "A suggestion for a fast multiplier," *IEEE Transactions on Computers*, pp. 14–17, Feb. 1964.

[191] J. S. Walther, "A unified algorithm for elementary functions," in *AFIPS Conference Proceedings*, vol. 38, pp. 379–385, 1971.

[192] S. Waser and M. J. Flynn, *Introduction to Arithmetic for Digital Systems Designers*, Holt, Rinehart and Winston, NY., 1982.

[193] A. Weinberger, "4:2 carry-save adder module," *IBM Technical Disclosure Bulletin*, vol. 23, Jan. 1981.

[194] A. Weinberger and J. L. Smith, "A one-microsecond adder using one-megacycle circuitry," *IRE Transactions on Computers*, vol. EC-5, pp. 65–73, 1956.

[195] N. H. E. Weste and K. Eshraghian, *Principles of CMOS VLSI Design*, Addison-Wesley, 1993.

[196] T. E. Williams and M. A. Horowitz, "A zero-overhead self-timed 160-ns 54-b CMOS divider," *IEEE Journal of Solid State Circuits*, pp. 1651–1661, Nov. 1991.

[197] S. Winograd, "On the time required to perform addition," *Journal of the ACM*, vol. 12, no. 2, pp. 277–285, 1965.

[198] D. Wong. *Techniques for Designing High Performance Digital Circuits Using Wave Pipelining*, PhD thesis, Dept. of Electrical Engineering, Stanford Univ., 1991.

[199] D. Wong, G. De Micheli, and M. Flynn, "A bipolar population counter using wave pipelining to achieve 2.5 × normal clock frequency," in *Proceedings of IEEE International Solid-State Circuits Conference*, San Francisco, Feb. 1992.

[200] D. Wong, G. De Micheli, and M. Flynn, "Designing high-performance digital circuits using wave pipelining," in *VLSI '89 Conference*, pp. 241–252, Aug. 1989.

[201] D. Wong and M. Flynn, "Fast division using accurate quotient approximations to reduce the number of iterations," in *10th IEEE Symposium on Computer Arithmetic*, pp. 191–201, June 1991.

[202] D. Wong and M. Flynn, "Fast division using accurate quotient approximations to reduce the number of iterations," *IEEE Transactions on Computers*, pp. 981–995, Aug. 1992.

[203] K. Yamaguchi, H. Nanbu, K. Kanetani, et al., "An experimental soft-error immune 64-Kb 3 ns ECL bipolar RAM," in *Bipolar Circuits and Technology Meeting*, pp. 26–27, Sept. 1988.

[204] X. Zhang and R. Sridhar, "CMOS wave pipelining using transmission-gate logic," in *Proceedings of Seventh Annual IEEE International ASIC Conference and Exhibit*, Rochester, NY, Sept. 1994.

[205] D. Zuras and W. McAllister, "Balanced delay trees and combinatorial division in VLSI," *IEEE Journal of Solid-State Circuits*, pp. 814–819, Oct. 1986.

INDEX

(3,2) counters, *see* counters
(7,3) counters, *see* counters
[4:2] compressors, *see* compressors
[6:2] compressors, *see* compressors
[9:2] compressors, *see* compressors

Adder
  Babbage's "carriage anticipating," 8
  basic, 8
  Brent–Kung, 274
  canonic, 4, 9
  carry-lookahead, 4, 8
  carry-save, 9
  carry-select, 3, 8
  carry-skip, 2, 8
  conditional sum, 3, 8
  hybrid, 9
  Ling, 6, 9
  Manchester carry chain, 2, 8
  multilevel carry-skip, 2, 9
  prefix, 9
  ripple, 2, 8
Adder parade, 8–9
Addition
  carry-save, 65
  floating-point, *see* FP addition
  integer, 1
  signed digit, 65
Algorithm A1, *see* FP addition
Algorithm A2, *see* FP addition
Array topology, *see* Multiplier topologies

Babbage's "carriage anticipating" adder, 8
Balanced-delay tree topology, *see* Multiplier topologies
Basic adder, 8
Bilinear arithmetic unit, 299
Bilinear function, 294
Binary tree layout of multipliers, 106

Binary tree topologies, *see* Multiplier topologies
Bipartite tables, 306
Bipolar population counter, wave-pipelined, 273
Booth multipliers, for function approximation, 189
Booth's algorithm, 46
  with bias, 53
Booth 2 algorithm, 46
  example, 47
  partial-product selection, 47
Booth 3 algorithm, 47
  example, 47
  fully redundant partial products, 50
  partially redundant partial products, 52
  partial-product selection, 48
  with bias, 53
Booth 4 algorithm, 50

Canonic adder, 4, 9
Carry-lookahead adder, 4, 8
Carry-save adder, 9
Carry-save addition, 65
Carry-select adder, 3, 8
Carry-skip adder, 2, 8
Channels in multipliers, 68
CLOSE path for FP adders, 25, 34
CMOS multiplier, wave-pipelined, 273
CMOS VLSI vector unit, wave-pipelined, 274
Compensating elements for function approximation, 198
Compiler effects on division, 120
Complementary metal–oxide semiconductor (CMOS), 14
  delay compensation, 270

321

.

Printed and bound by CPI Group (UK) Ltd, Croydon, CR0 4YY

27/10/2024

14580344-0001